PENGUIN BOOKS
THE PEOPLE OF THE INDUS

Nikhil Gulati loves stories that evoke wonder and inspire compassion. He has written and illustrated graphic works for Puffin and Pratham Books, in addition to writing and illustrating a mini graphic novel on the history of Golconda and several short comics on various themes. *The People of the Indus* is his first longform work. He is a graduate of the University of Texas, Austin, and the Indian Institute of Management, Ahmedabad. His work can be found at www.oddballcomics.in.

Jonathan Mark Kenoyer is a professor of archaeology and anthropology at the University of Wisconsin, Madison. He has been excavating the site of Harappa intensively for over thirty-five years and has served as field director of the Harappa Archaeological Research Project since 1986. He has worked on excavations in India, Pakistan and Oman, and is considered one of the foremost authorities of Indus archaeology. He has authored several books, journal articles and encyclopedia entries on the Indus civilization and has helped curate major exhibitions at several venues, including the Metropolitan Museum of Art, New York. His work has been featured in the *National Geographic Magazine* and *Scientific American*, and on the website www.harappa.com.

35
INDIA

Celebrating 35 Years of
Penguin Random House India

ADVANCE PRAISE FOR THE BOOK

'One of the tasks of comics is to find new ways of exploring pedagogy. Nikhil Gulati uses great skill and imagination to expand on a dense subject and make it comprehensible without compromising its complexity. His style of direct storytelling and his ability to incorporate various stands of scholarship reveal his understanding and craft. I hope that books like *The People of the Indus* make educational institutions take notice and include them in their future curriculum.'

—**Sarnath Banerjee**, graphic novelist and co-founder of Phantomville

'Whether you're a history buff or not, the engaging visual narrative of *The People of the Indus* will draw you into the story of one of the world's most enigmatic civilizations. This is history at its most fun and accessible!'

—**Devika Cariapa**, author and winner of the
Sahitya Akademi Bal Sahitya Puraskar 2019

'*The People of the Indus* is a marvellous achievement, harnessing the clarity and scope of the comics medium to explore history as a series of questions and stories. Excavating the "truth" of a distant, almost-inscrutable civilization, the book leads us to also examine how we humans live with each other, and what we mean by civilization. People are front and centre in this graphic novel, and the artful blend of imagined stories and scientific rigour creates an intricate—and poignant—gateway into the lives of another time.'

—Angshuman Chakraborty, **For the Love of Comics**, *YouTube*

'Delightful and instructive both, *The People of the Indus* is a beautiful—and often humorous and witty—introduction to the world of the Indus Valley civilization. I learnt a good deal from it, and with pleasure too.'

—**Manu S. Pillai**, author and historian

'A wonderfully fun way to look back at the Harappans. Nikhil's delightful illustrations bring alive the mysteries and debates about one of the world's oldest civilizations.'

—**Sanjeev Sanyal**, bestselling writer and eminent economist

'*The People of the Indus* is a sensitive portrayal of the rise, evolution and fall of the Indus Valley civilization. With intelligent extrapolation and imagination, Nikhil Gulati builds carefully upon all that is known by historians, linguists and archaeologists about the fascinating, rich and mysterious life of these people. His minimalist line drawings prove to be perfect for the task—transporting us back in time to the teeming urban life of cities we know of today only through excavated ruins that had lain forgotten underground for thousands of years.

This book undertakes a challenging task with great aplomb and adds perhaps a whole new genre of "Historical Reconstruction" to the growing corpus of Indian graphic novels on various themes and subjects that we have witnessed in recent times...and it sets the bar very satisfyingly high for future authors and artists who will surely be inspired by it!'

—**Orijit Sen**, graphic novelist, artist and designer

THE PEOPLE OF THE INDUS

and the birth of civilization in South Asia

Written and illustrated by NIKHIL GULATI
with JONATHAN MARK KENOYER

PENGUIN BOOKS

An imprint of Penguin Random House

PENGUIN BOOKS

USA | Canada | UK | Ireland | Australia
New Zealand | India | South Africa | China

Penguin Books is part of the Penguin Random House group of companies
whose addresses can be found at global.penguinrandomhouse.com

Published by Penguin Random House India Pvt. Ltd
4th Floor, Capital Tower 1, MG Road,
Gurugram 122 002, Haryana, India

First published in Penguin Books by Penguin Random House India 2022

Text and illustrations copyright © Nikhil Gulati 2022

ISBN 9780143461814

Typeset in CC Joe Kubert

www.penguin.co.in

'History is one way of telling stories, just like myth, fiction or oral storytelling. But over the last hundred years, history has preempted the other forms of storytelling because of its claim to be absolute, objective truth. Trying to be scientists, historians stood outside of history and told the story of how it was. All that has changed radically over the last twenty years. Historians now laugh at the pretence of objective truth. They agree that every age has its own history, and if there is any objective truth we can't reach it with words. *History is not a science, it's an art.*'

- Ursula Le Guin, 1993

INTRODUCTION

This book came about due to a chance visit to Lothal a few years ago. I was studying in college in Gujarat at that time, when one day a few friends planned a day trip to Lothal. There was an empty seat in the car, and they asked me if I would like to join. I had never heard of Lothal, and even about the Indus civilization I knew very little. Wasn't that where they had had drains or something?

While I was still deciding whether to go, I did a quick Wikipedia search which told me that Lothal had been a city 4500 years ago, at the same time when the Pyramids were being built in Egypt. That really intrigued me. So, I went.

On the way, I kept imagining the temples and tombs of Egypt, which I had seen on TV and read about in books and was expecting to find something similar in Lothal. However, when we got there, I was sorely disappointed. All that was left were a few brick foundations here and there and some pottery fragments. Was this really a city? It looked nothing bigger than a village. I asked the caretaker of the site, who was sitting under a tree, if this was it. He mentioned that only a fraction of the site had been excavated. The rest was still underground. Then, he pointed in a certain direction and asked if I had been over there. I hadn't, so I walked through the bushes to see. Suddenly, the landscape opened up before me and what I saw took my breath away. It looked to me like a giant swimming pool, dug 12 feet deep into the ground, and lined with brick walls. It was in such contrast to the rest of the site that I knew immediately there was a lot more to Lothal than met the eye.

I left Lothal that day still somewhat underwhelmed, expecting as I was to see Egypt-like artefacts, but very intrigued. Who were these people? Why did they not build giant Pyramids? What were they doing instead? I started researching the Indus civilization, and the more I researched the more I was surprised, and fascinated, by what I learnt.

The Indus civilization was absolutely unique amongst all the ancient civilizations. While the Egyptian, Mesopotamian and the Chinese urban societies of the time were heavily centralized (with kings and bureaucracies) and very war-like, the Indus presented a completely different picture. It appeared to have little centralization and no evidence of warfare, and yet its people were materially rich and excelled in crafts, industry and trade. What is more, the people of this civilization were expert sailors.

At this time, I had begun dabbling in the creation of comics and started to appreciate the tremendous power of this medium to communicate stories and information in an intuitive way. I wanted to try telling history through the language of comics. I have always felt history to be very visual. Whenever history books talked about artefacts like coins and weapons, I always wanted to know what they looked like. When they spoke of ancient cities, I wanted to feel what it would have been like to stand on a rooftop or stroll in the streets. This, I felt, comics could do very effectively.

During my research on the Indus civilization, I realized that there were very few popular books that tackled this time period, and almost none that did it in a visual manner. So, I decided to do it myself. Taking on a project of this size was a daunting task. Several times during its creation, I was ready to give up. But many people encouraged me, and I kept going. When I had finally completed a draft of the graphic novel, I sent it to a number of people. One of them was Dr Kenoyer, an archaeologist who has excavated the site of Harappa for decades, and whose work I had used extensively in my research. To my great surprise Dr Kenoyer responded. He praised the narrative and the presentation but felt there were several gaps academically. I asked him if he could recommend someone who could help fix the errors, at which he very generously offered his help. Over the next few months, we reworked a lot of the factual details. Being an artist and having previously visualized the cities and the people himself, Dr Kenoyer gave very important inputs into the depictions of clothes, jewellery, hairstyles, architecture and landscapes of the Indus people.

Thanks to Dr Kenoyer's collaboration on this book, I feel very confident about what is being presented here. However, it is likely many experts will disagree about the specifics. This is to be expected, even encouraged. As my father likes to say, the past is like a collection of colourful fragments and history like a kaleidoscope. The more you turn it in your hands the more patterns emerge. This is what makes history so compelling to me. This book is not meant to be the final word on the Indus people. My only hope is that it will kindle an interest in some of the readers towards exploring the past further.

Nikhil Gulati
Goa, India
15 May 2022

Introduction

The Indus civilization is often touted as one of the least known of the ancient urban societies, but in fact, we know a great deal about this civilization. Excavations of Indus sites began as early as the 1920s, under the direction of the Archaeological Survey of India. After the establishment of independent India and Pakistan in 1947, archaeologists from various universities and government institutions in both countries, as well as international scholars, have continuously carried out regional surveys, small-scale excavations and numerous large-scale multi-year excavation projects. Although the number of excavations carried out on Indus sites is much lower than those being conducted in regions such as Egypt, Europe or East Asia, both the quantity and the quality of the data available is exceptional. This data provides a great deal of information that can be used to better understand the origins, character and regional variations of ancient Indus society.

Excavations and regional surveys, as well as more detailed laboratory analyses of artefacts have created a vast corpus of both published and unpublished information that is often difficult to keep up with. In this book, we have tried to provide an overview of the most important characteristics of the Indus civilization. We have tried to present multiple perspectives, along with important references, so that readers will be able to further investigate specific topics on their own.

Archaeology as a science is often misunderstood due to the manner in which it is presented to the public. There are popular films that glorify the discovery of temples, tombs and incredible buried wealth. In reality, however, archaeology can be very tedious, painstaking and frustrating, since we can only recover small fragments of information, at a time, to help reconstruct the past. But this is also what makes archaeology stimulating and exciting.

When I pick up a broken stone bead, for example, I see a very complex story. Examining the rock using various scientific analyses can tell us its probable source region. Studying its manufacturing technique can indicate the tools used to shape and perforate the bead. Finally, the amount of wear on the interior and edges of the drill hole can be used to understand if it was worn for a long period before it was broken and discarded. Comparing the types of stones, where they came from, how they were made and used, coupled with observations of modern bead crafts in South Asia, can help to reconstruct the ancient bead industry and trade networks as well as the overall value of these ornaments.

The tedious, painstaking nature of archaeological research challenges us to extract as much information as possible from the few remains that we do find. We need to remember that the evidence we obtain is only fragmentary and can never be used to 'prove' any specific interpretation. The more data we collect the more refined our interpretations can be, but nothing is final, and the discovery of new data may change our interpretations in the future. For example, many people want to know what the ancient Indus script says. However, we will never be able to understand the precise meanings of this writing system without the aid of a bilingual text. The same holds true of studying the genetic history of the Indus people. Physical anthropologists have been studying the few human skeletal remains from Indus sites since their discovery in the 1920s and 30s. We can conclude that the few recovered skeletons represent a relatively diverse population that included people from many different communities. More recently, studies of ancient human DNA from archaeological skeletal remains have become an innovative way to study ancient populations. However, due to the preservation factors in the Indus region, it is almost impossible to recover any DNA from the bones found in the few excavated Indus burials. The one fragmentary DNA recently recovered at Rakhigarhi provides some hope that more DNA will eventually be recovered as new techniques for recovery are developed. However, we must remember that only a very small segment of Indus society practised the burial of the dead. Most of the ancient Indus dead would have been treated in other ways, such as cremation, water burial or exposure in the forests. Since we will never be able to recover DNA from most of the people who lived in these cities, we need to understand from the outset that we may never sort out the diversity of people living in these early urban centres from DNA studies alone.

Archaeologists also need to present their interpretations in ways that can be easily understood by general readers. In this graphic novel, the drawings and graphic presentations by Nikhil Gulati represent a unique approach to illustrating the key aspects of Indus archaeological research, combined with narrations and questions posed by an inquisitive student of the past. My contributions include the specific details of archaeological data and an attempt to provide additional context for the finds themselves.

This combination of graphic depictions and various interpretations will hopefully allow the reader to experience Indus archaeology in a totally new way. However, just as archaeologists are often left wondering what the best interpretation is, the reader will also be left with many unanswered questions. Hopefully, these challenges will inspire some readers to take up new investigations into the past.

We also hope that the readers will appreciate the immense value of the ancient remains and help to preserve them so that future generations can continue to learn from them. It is important to emphasize that although these remains are found in South Asia, the legacy of the Indus civilization is something that is important for everyone throughout the world. Future studies of the Indus sites and artefacts will undoubtedly provide even more lessons for our modern society. We hope that this book will help the reader to appreciate the people who lived in these early cities and treasure the remains they have left behind.

Jonathan Mark Kenoyer
University of Wisconsin, Madison, USA
15 May 2022

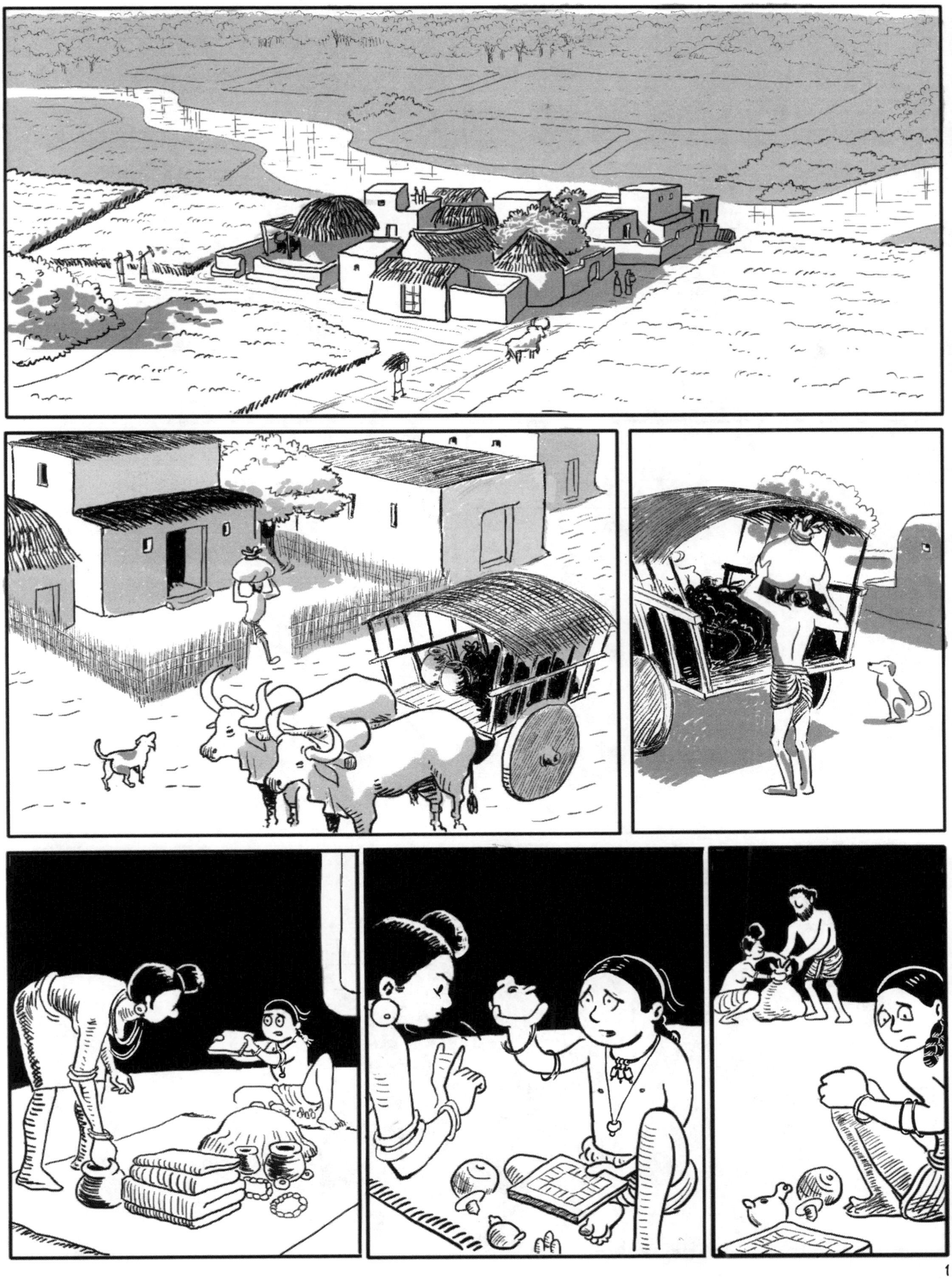

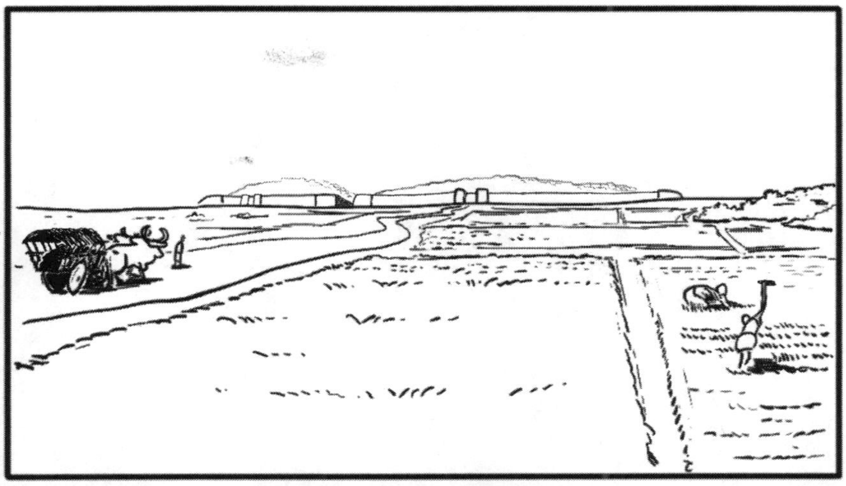

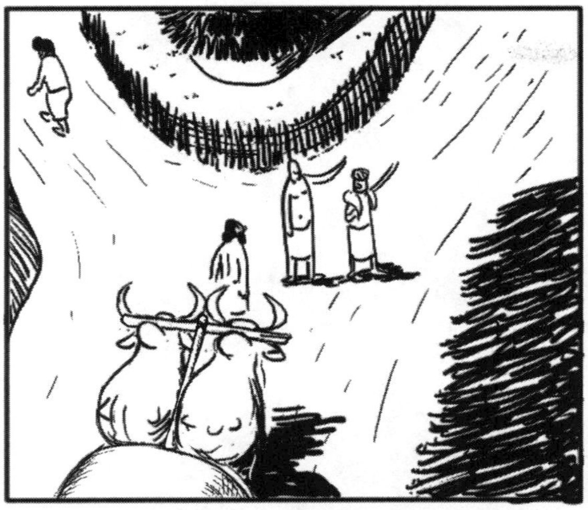

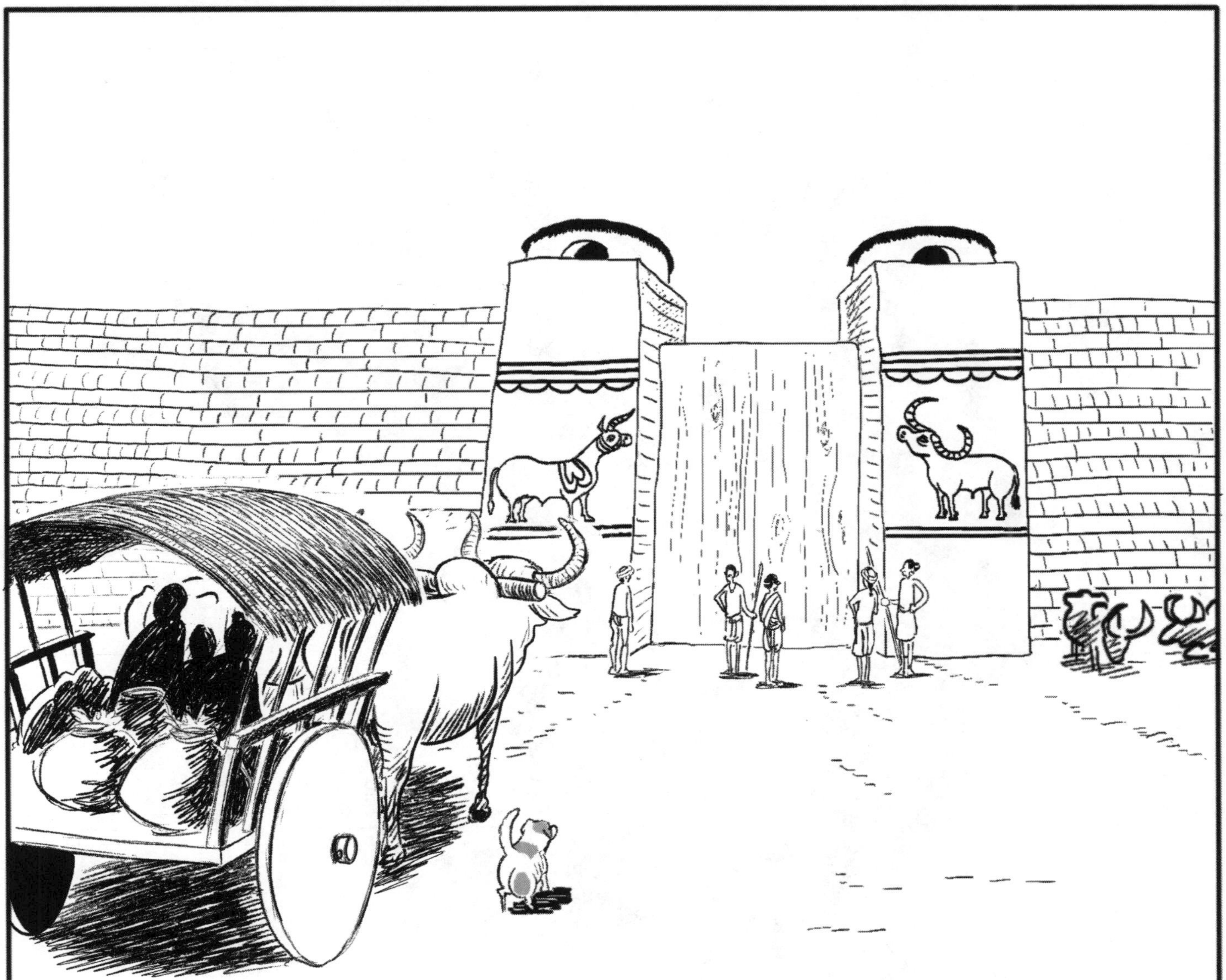

CHAPTER ONE

Mohenjo Daro 2600 BCE

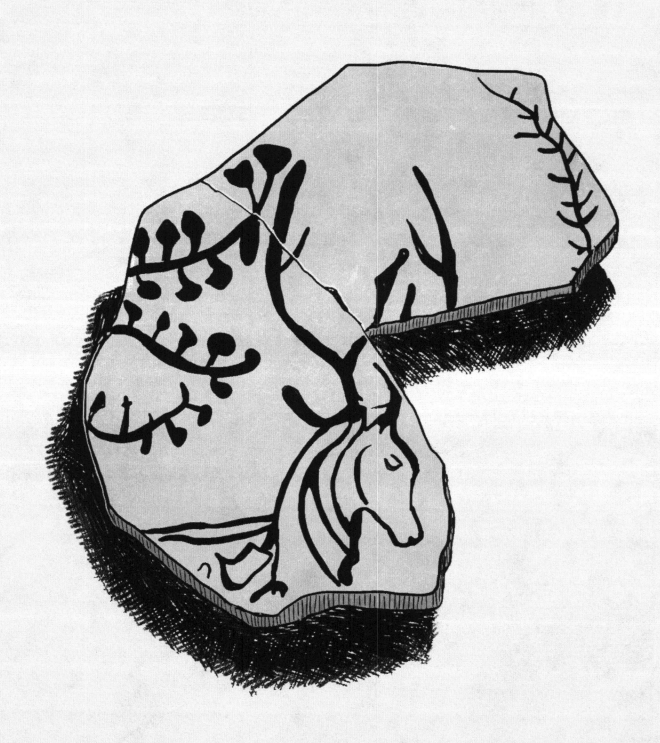

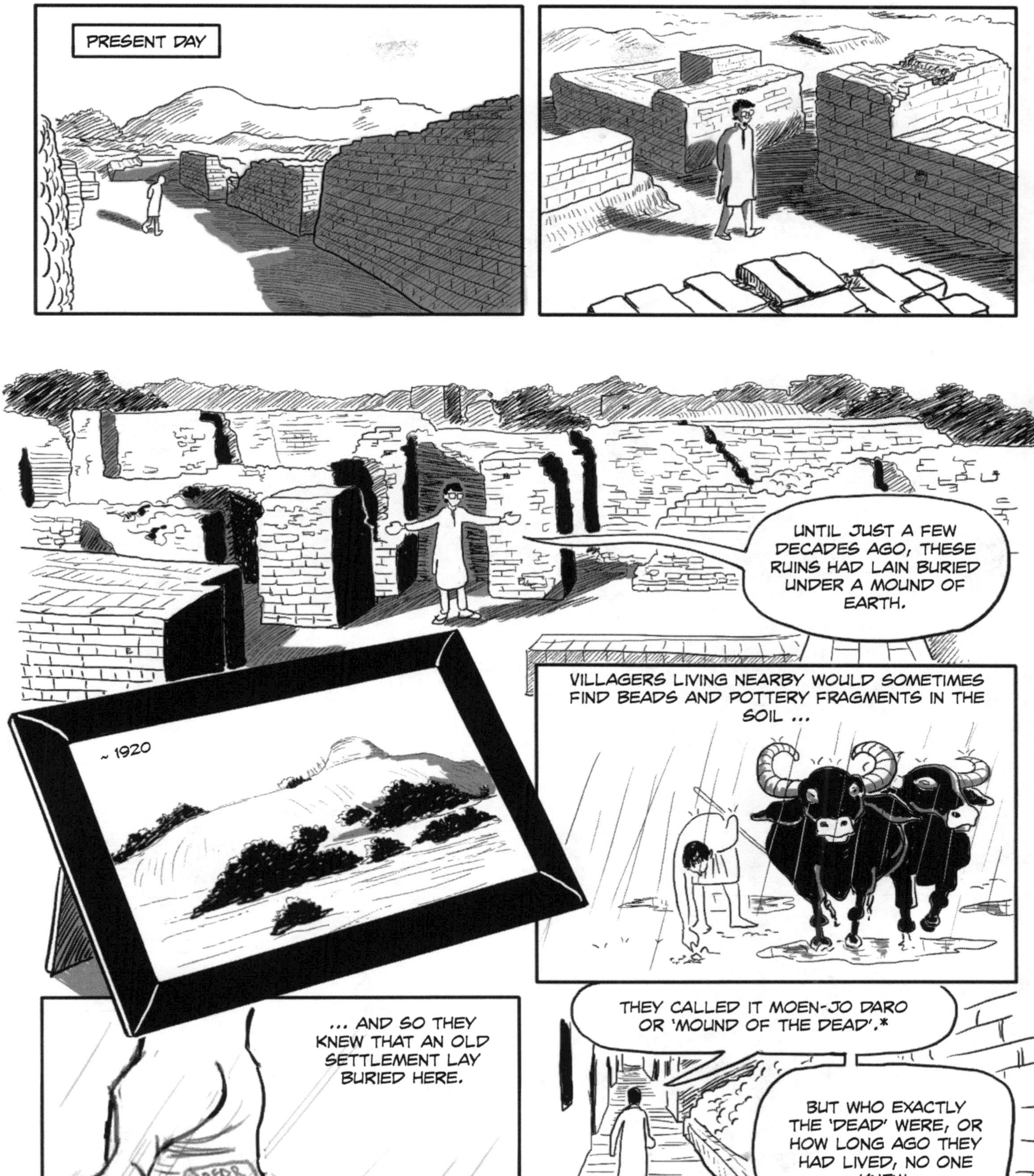
PRESENT DAY
UNTIL JUST A FEW DECADES AGO, THESE RUINS HAD LAIN BURIED UNDER A MOUND OF EARTH.
~ 1920
VILLAGERS LIVING NEARBY WOULD SOMETIMES FIND BEADS AND POTTERY FRAGMENTS IN THE SOIL ...
... AND SO THEY KNEW THAT AN OLD SETTLEMENT LAY BURIED HERE.
THEY CALLED IT MOEN-JO DARO OR 'MOUND OF THE DEAD'.*
BUT WHO EXACTLY THE 'DEAD' WERE, OR HOW LONG AGO THEY HAD LIVED, NO ONE KNEW.
* THE NAME COULD HAVE COME FROM THE SINDHI TERM MOHAN-JO DARO OR THE MOUND OF MOHAN (KRISHNA).

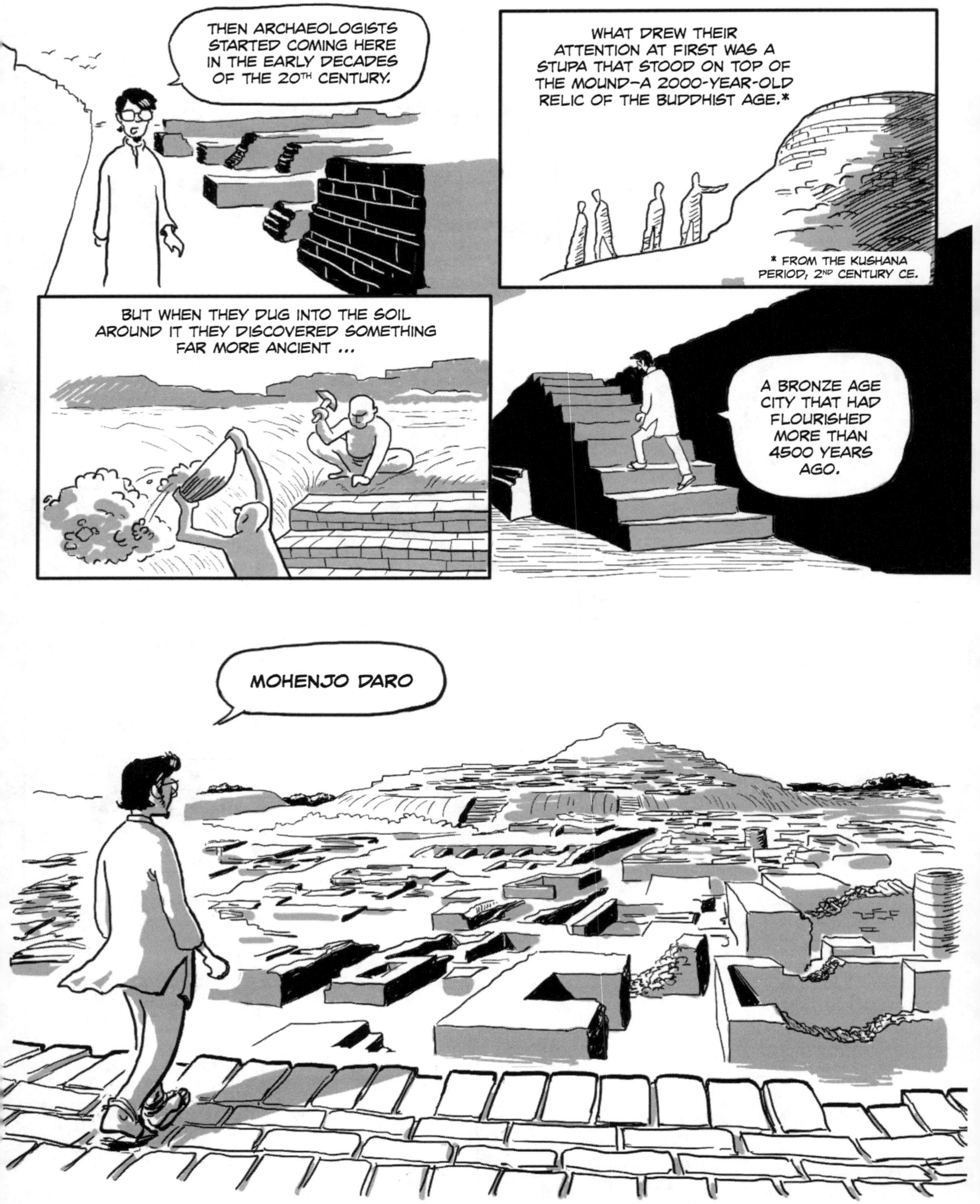
THEN ARCHAEOLOGISTS STARTED COMING HERE IN THE EARLY DECADES OF THE 20TH CENTURY.
WHAT DREW THEIR ATTENTION AT FIRST WAS A STUPA THAT STOOD ON TOP OF THE MOUND—A 2000-YEAR-OLD RELIC OF THE BUDDHIST AGE.*
* FROM THE KUSHANA PERIOD, 2ND CENTURY CE.
BUT WHEN THEY DUG INTO THE SOIL AROUND IT THEY DISCOVERED SOMETHING FAR MORE ANCIENT ...
A BRONZE AGE CITY THAT HAD FLOURISHED MORE THAN 4500 YEARS AGO.
MOHENJO DARO

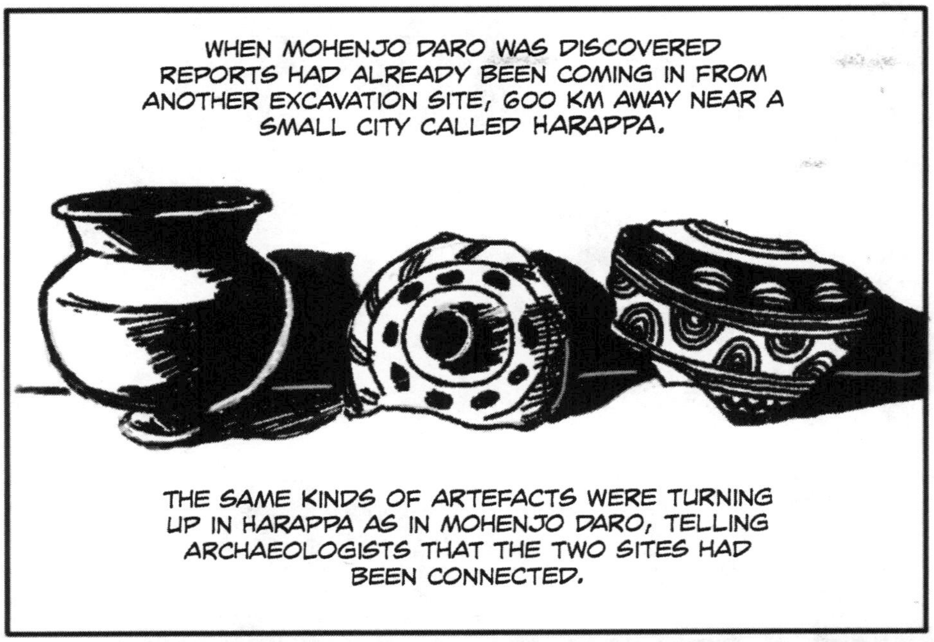
WHEN MOHENJO DARO WAS DISCOVERED REPORTS HAD ALREADY BEEN COMING IN FROM ANOTHER EXCAVATION SITE, 600 KM AWAY NEAR A SMALL CITY CALLED HARAPPA.
THE SAME KINDS OF ARTEFACTS WERE TURNING UP IN HARAPPA AS IN MOHENJO DARO, TELLING ARCHAEOLOGISTS THAT THE TWO SITES HAD BEEN CONNECTED.

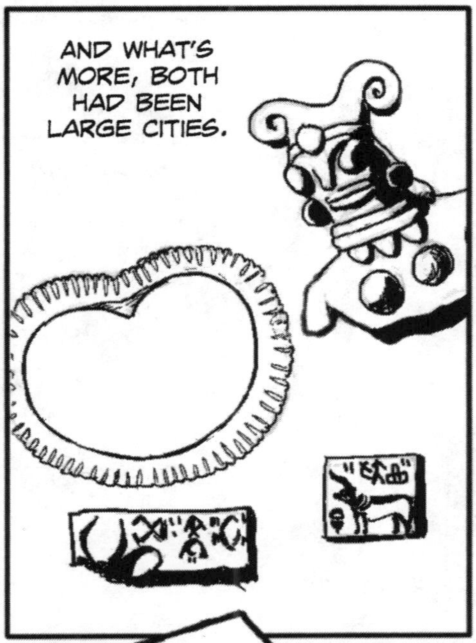
AND WHAT'S MORE, BOTH HAD BEEN LARGE CITIES.

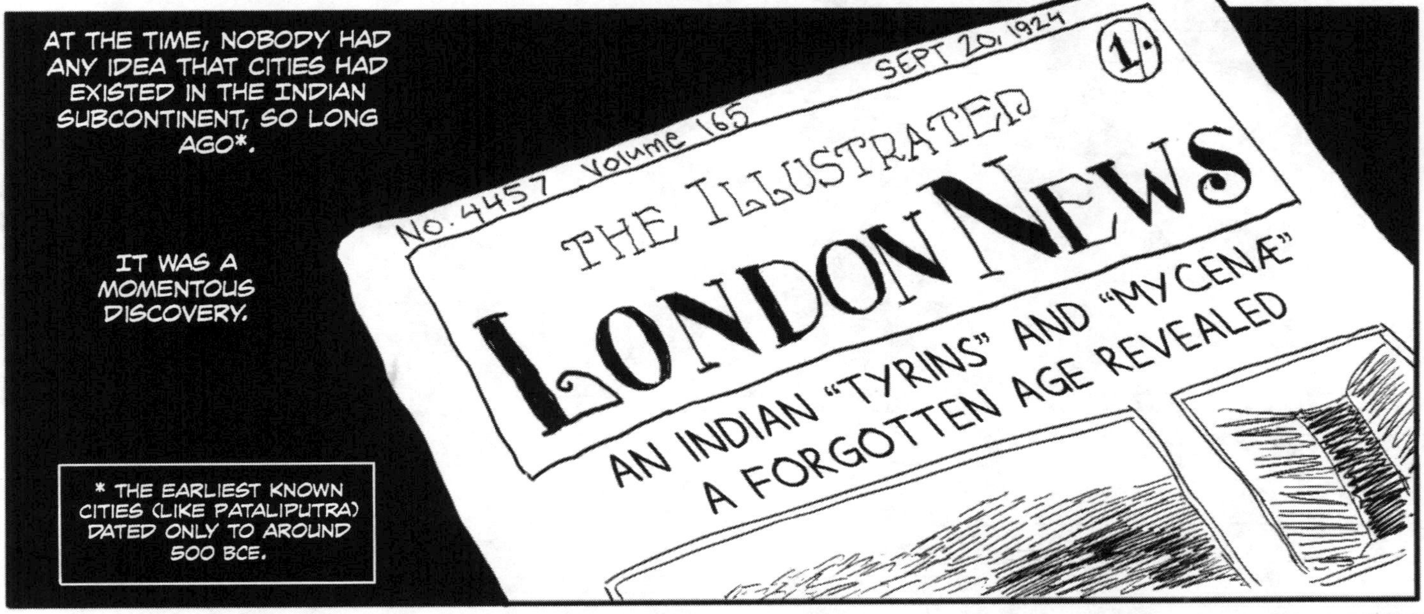
AT THE TIME, NOBODY HAD ANY IDEA THAT CITIES HAD EXISTED IN THE INDIAN SUBCONTINENT, SO LONG AGO*.
IT WAS A MOMENTOUS DISCOVERY.
* THE EARLIEST KNOWN CITIES (LIKE PATALIPUTRA) DATED ONLY TO AROUND 500 BCE.
SEPT 20, 1924
1/-
No. 4457 Volume 165
THE ILLUSTRATED
LONDON NEWS
AN INDIAN "TYRINS" AND "MYCENÆ"
A FORGOTTEN AGE REVEALED

SINCE THEN ARCHAEOLOGISTS HAVE UNEARTHED FOUR LARGE CITIES AND THOUSANDS OF SMALLER TOWNS AND VILLAGES, ALL DATING TO THE SAME TIME PERIOD.

ALL OF THESE SITES HAD BEEN INTEGRATED INTO A SINGLE WEB OF ECONOMIC AND SOCIAL RELATIONS WHICH TODAY WE CALL THE **INDUS CIVILIZATION***.

* ALSO CALLED **HARAPPAN CIVILIZATION** AFTER THE FIRST SITE THAT WAS DISCOVERED.

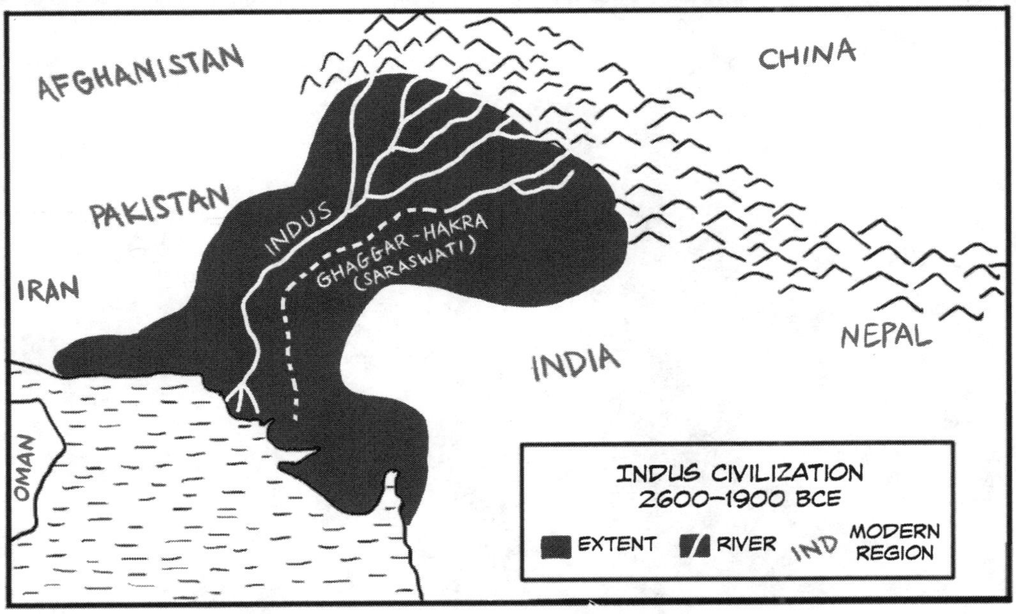
AFGHANISTAN
CHINA
PAKISTAN
INDUS
GHAGGAR-HAKRA (SARASWATI)
IRAN
NEPAL
INDIA
OMAN
INDUS CIVILIZATION
2600–1900 BCE
EXTENT
RIVER
IND MODERN REGION

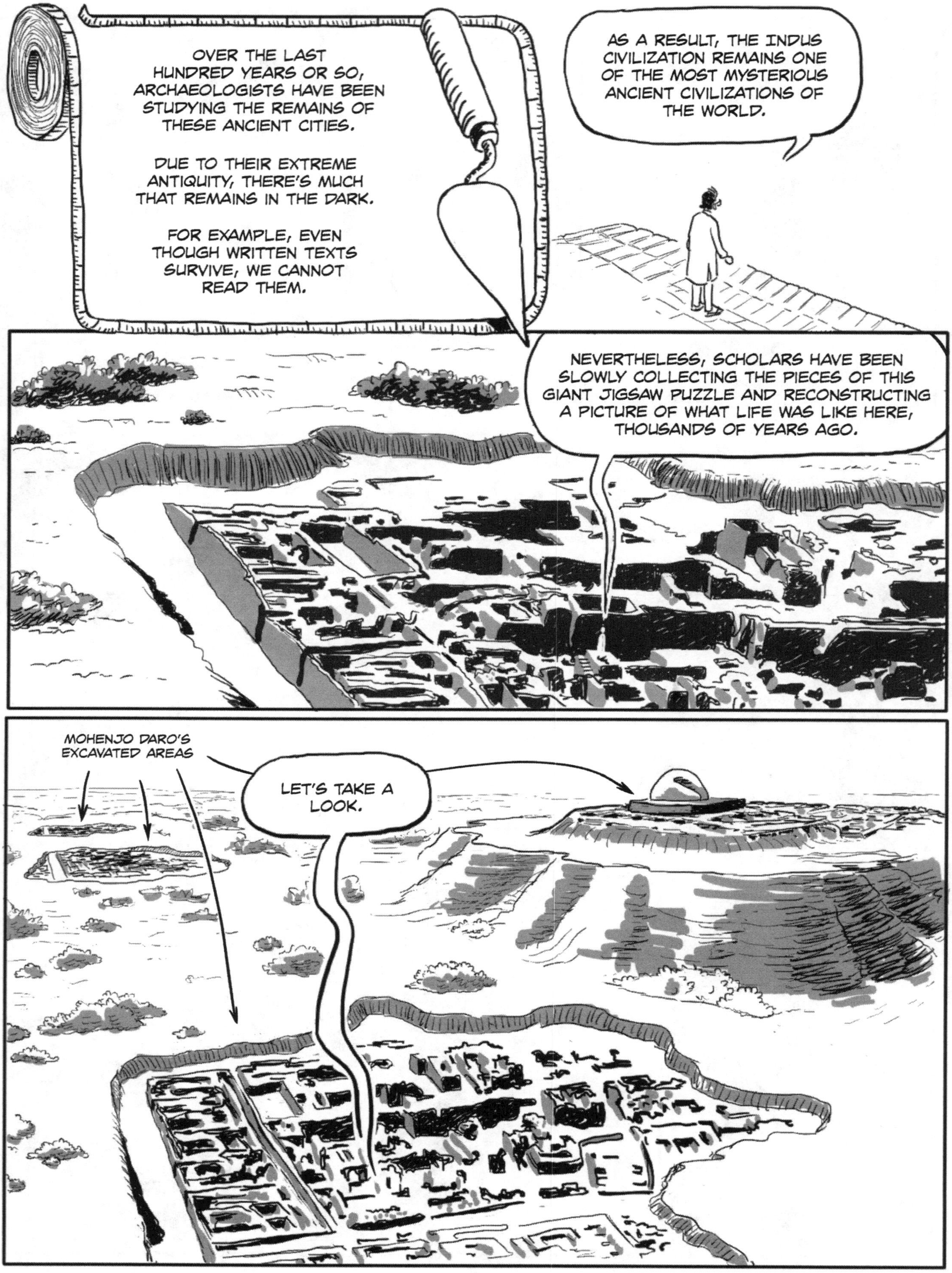
OVER THE LAST HUNDRED YEARS OR SO, ARCHAEOLOGISTS HAVE BEEN STUDYING THE REMAINS OF THESE ANCIENT CITIES.
DUE TO THEIR EXTREME ANTIQUITY, THERE'S MUCH THAT REMAINS IN THE DARK.
FOR EXAMPLE, EVEN THOUGH WRITTEN TEXTS SURVIVE, WE CANNOT READ THEM.
AS A RESULT, THE INDUS CIVILIZATION REMAINS ONE OF THE MOST MYSTERIOUS ANCIENT CIVILIZATIONS OF THE WORLD.
NEVERTHELESS, SCHOLARS HAVE BEEN SLOWLY COLLECTING THE PIECES OF THIS GIANT JIGSAW PUZZLE AND RECONSTRUCTING A PICTURE OF WHAT LIFE WAS LIKE HERE, THOUSANDS OF YEARS AGO.
MOHENJO DARO'S EXCAVATED AREAS
LET'S TAKE A LOOK.

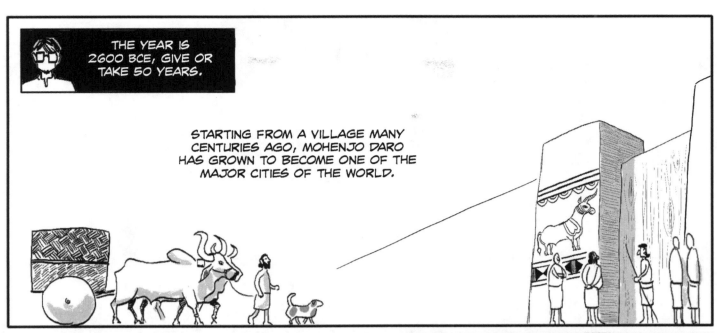

THE YEAR IS 2600 BCE, GIVE OR TAKE 50 YEARS.

STARTING FROM A VILLAGE MANY CENTURIES AGO, MOHENJO DARO HAS GROWN TO BECOME ONE OF THE MAJOR CITIES OF THE WORLD.

IT HAS GROWN NOT ONLY INDIGENOUSLY BUT ALSO FROM THE MIGRATION OF PEOPLE FROM DISTANT PLACES.

THIS IS A FAMILY OF COPPERSMITHS WHO DECIDED TO MOVE TO MOHENJO DARO FROM THEIR VILLAGE AFTER HEARING OF THE GREAT DEMAND FOR COPPER WORKERS IN THE CITY.

CREEAK

9

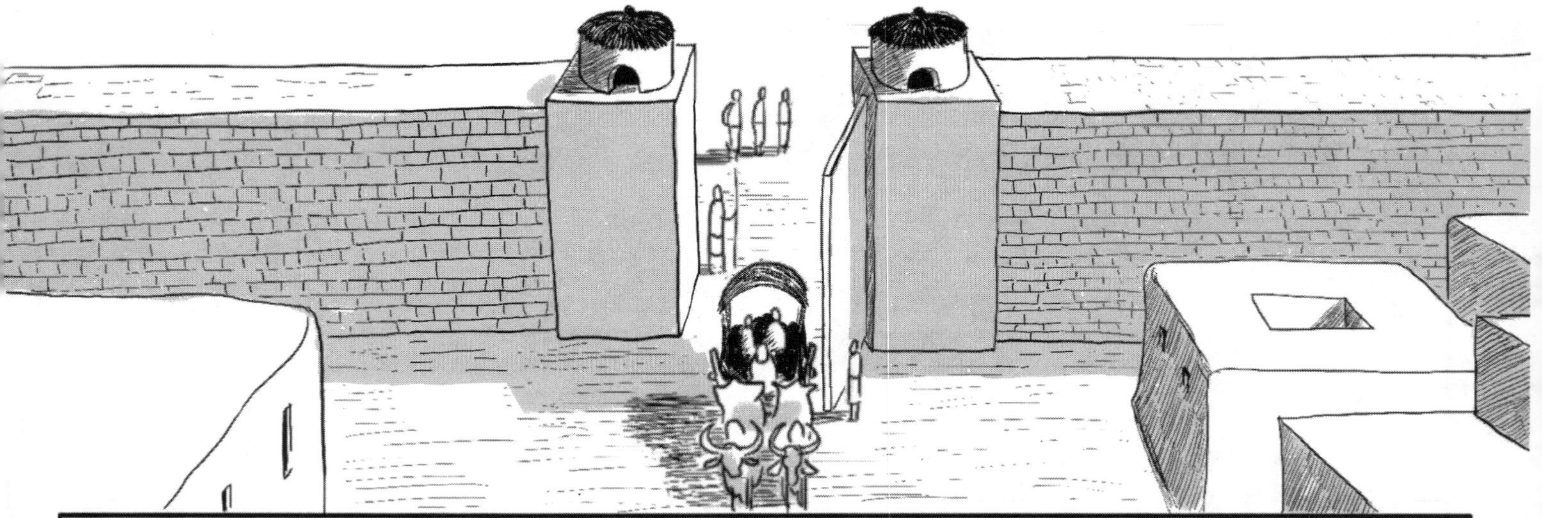
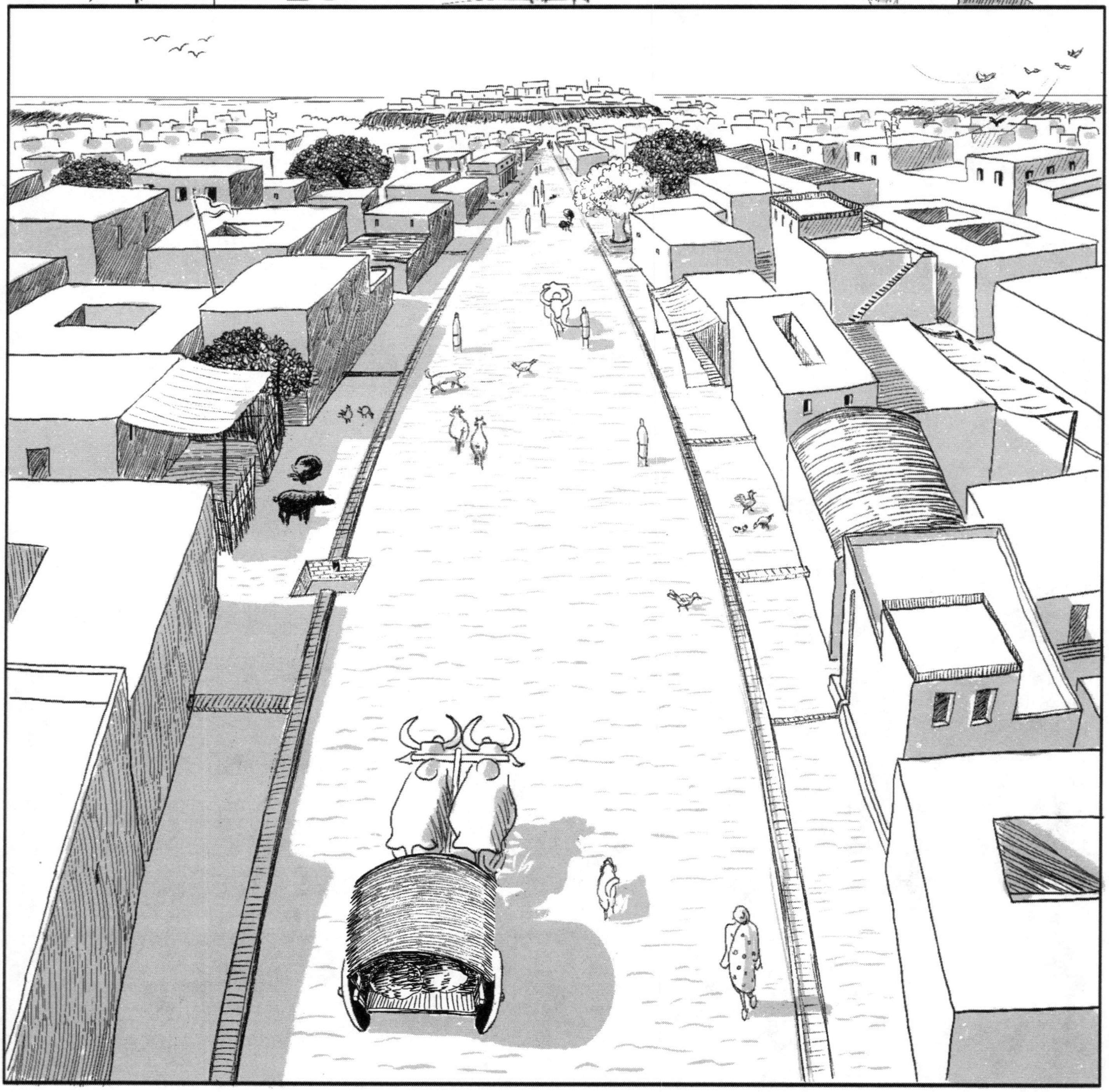

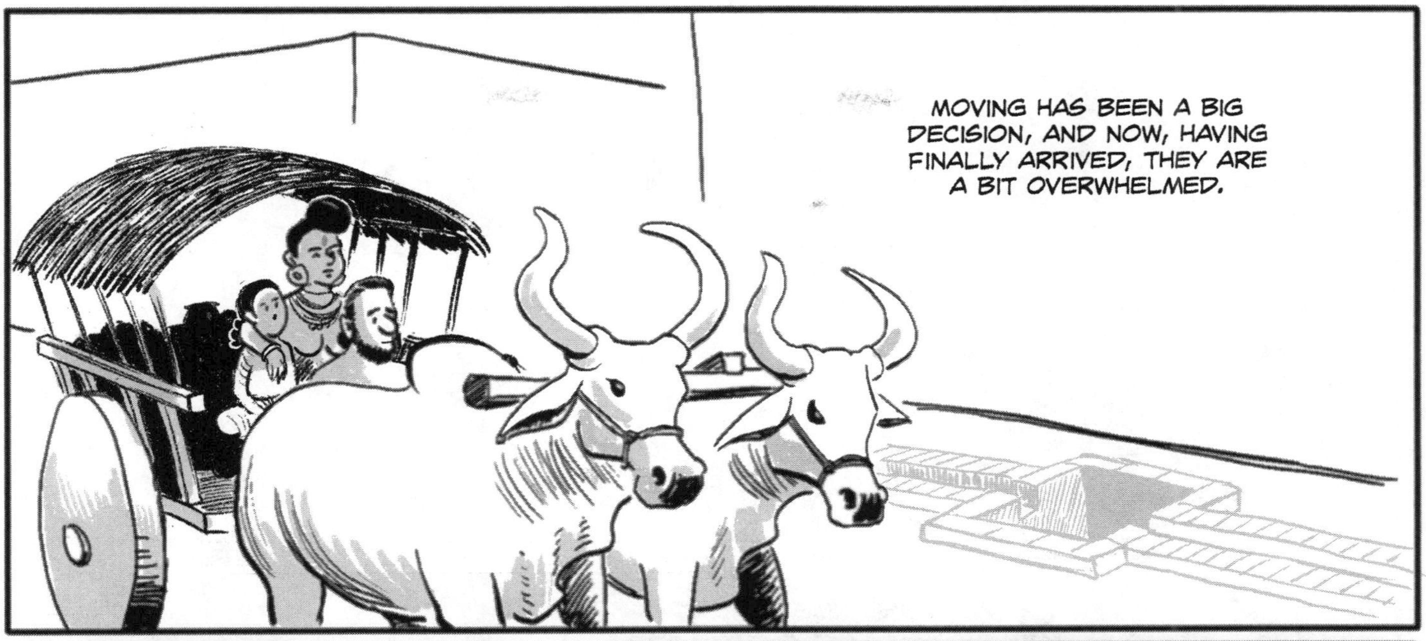
MOVING HAS BEEN A BIG DECISION, AND NOW, HAVING FINALLY ARRIVED, THEY ARE A BIT OVERWHELMED.

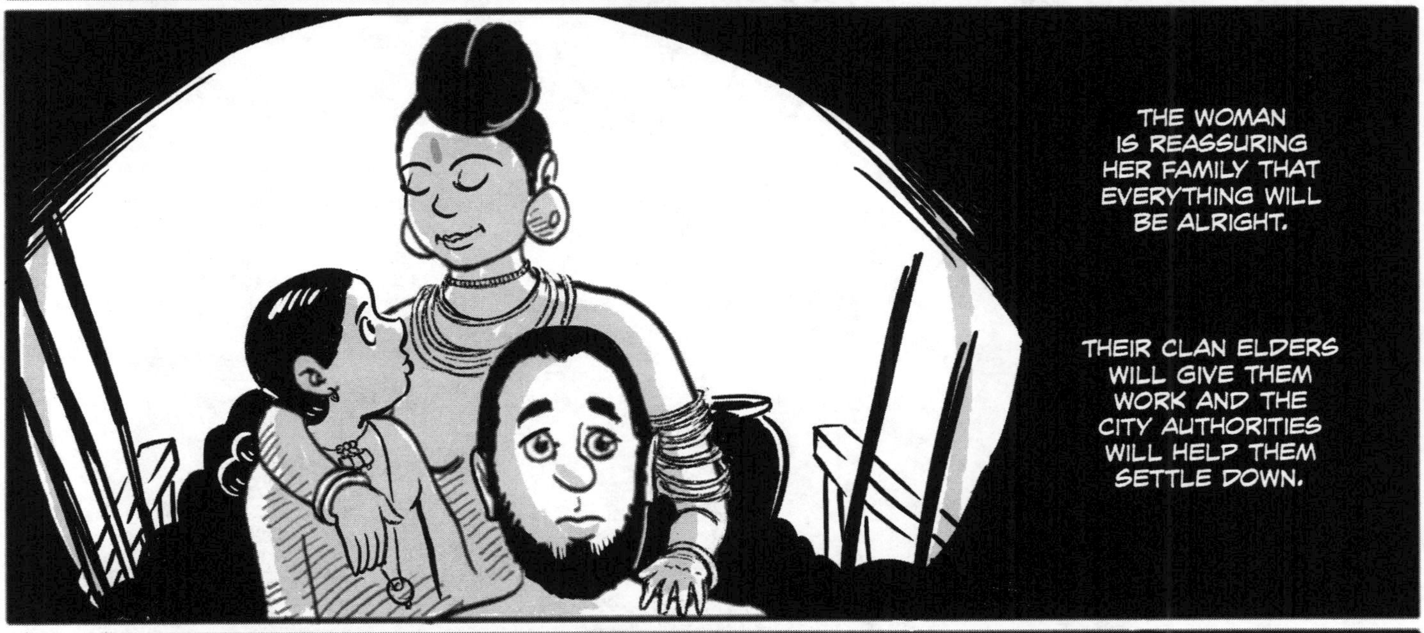
THE WOMAN IS REASSURING HER FAMILY THAT EVERYTHING WILL BE ALRIGHT.
THEIR CLAN ELDERS WILL GIVE THEM WORK AND THE CITY AUTHORITIES WILL HELP THEM SETTLE DOWN.

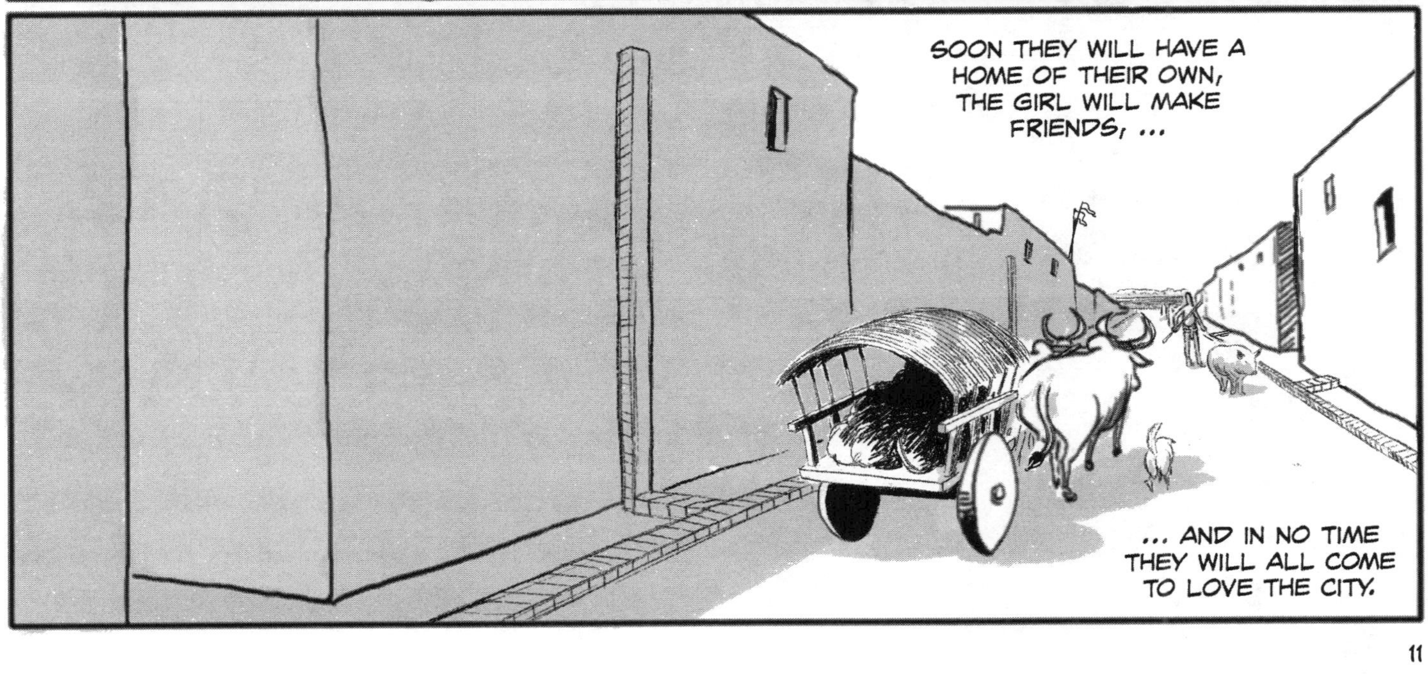
SOON THEY WILL HAVE A HOME OF THEIR OWN, THE GIRL WILL MAKE FRIENDS, ...
... AND IN NO TIME THEY WILL ALL COME TO LOVE THE CITY.

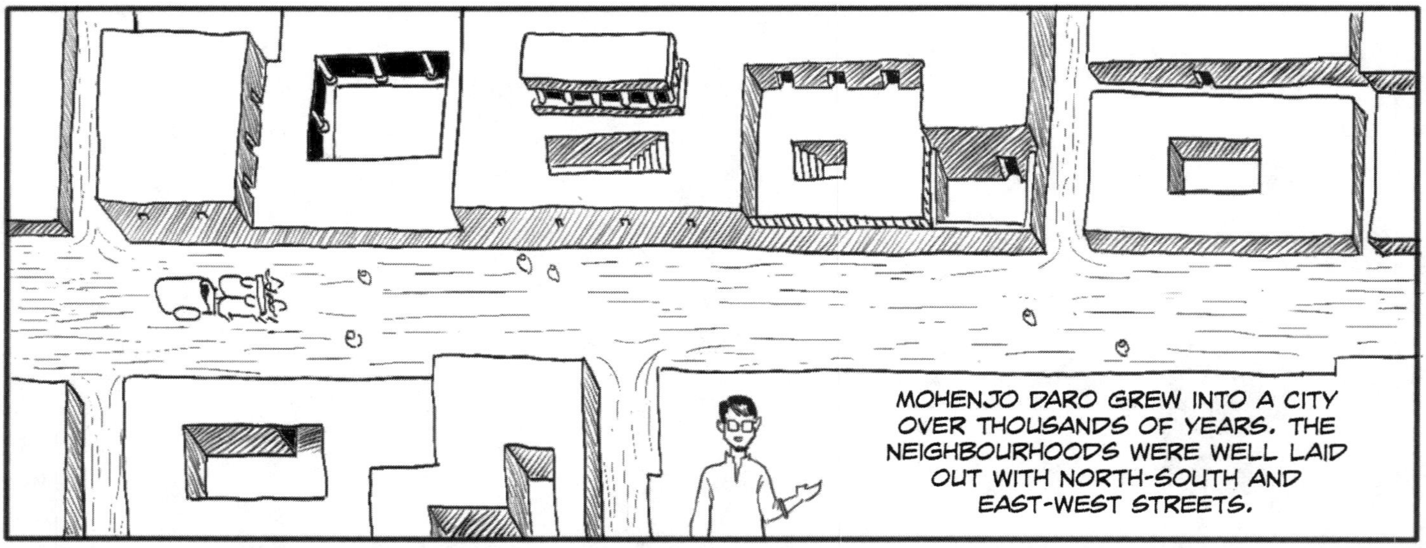
MOHENJO DARO GREW INTO A CITY OVER THOUSANDS OF YEARS. THE NEIGHBOURHOODS WERE WELL LAID OUT WITH NORTH-SOUTH AND EAST-WEST STREETS.

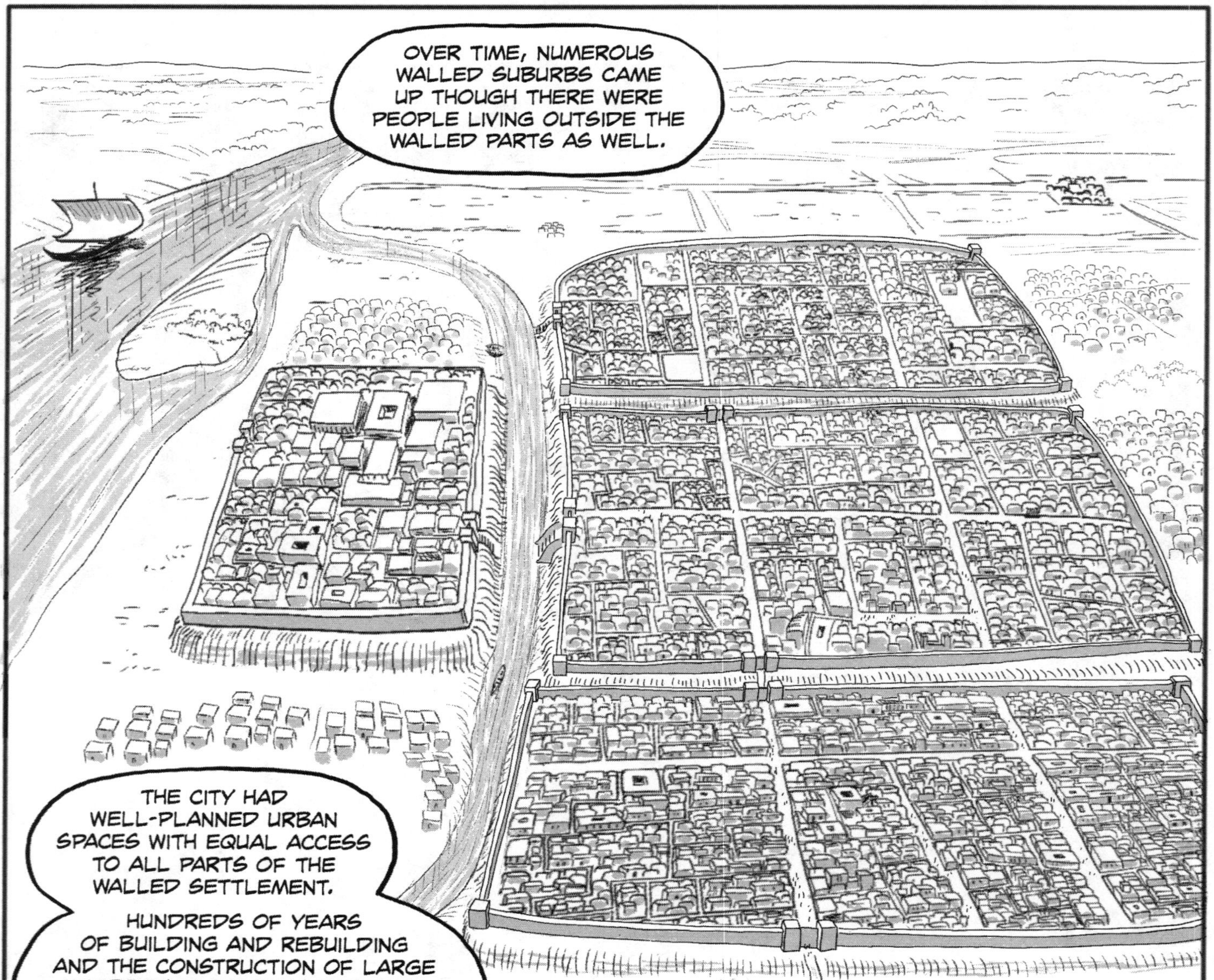
OVER TIME, NUMEROUS WALLED SUBURBS CAME UP THOUGH THERE WERE PEOPLE LIVING OUTSIDE THE WALLED PARTS AS WELL.
THE CITY HAD WELL-PLANNED URBAN SPACES WITH EQUAL ACCESS TO ALL PARTS OF THE WALLED SETTLEMENT.
HUNDREDS OF YEARS OF BUILDING AND REBUILDING AND THE CONSTRUCTION OF LARGE MUDBRICK PLATFORMS RESULTED IN SOME AREAS BEING HIGHER THAN OTHERS AND THUS WELL PROTECTED FROM THE ANNUAL FLOODING.

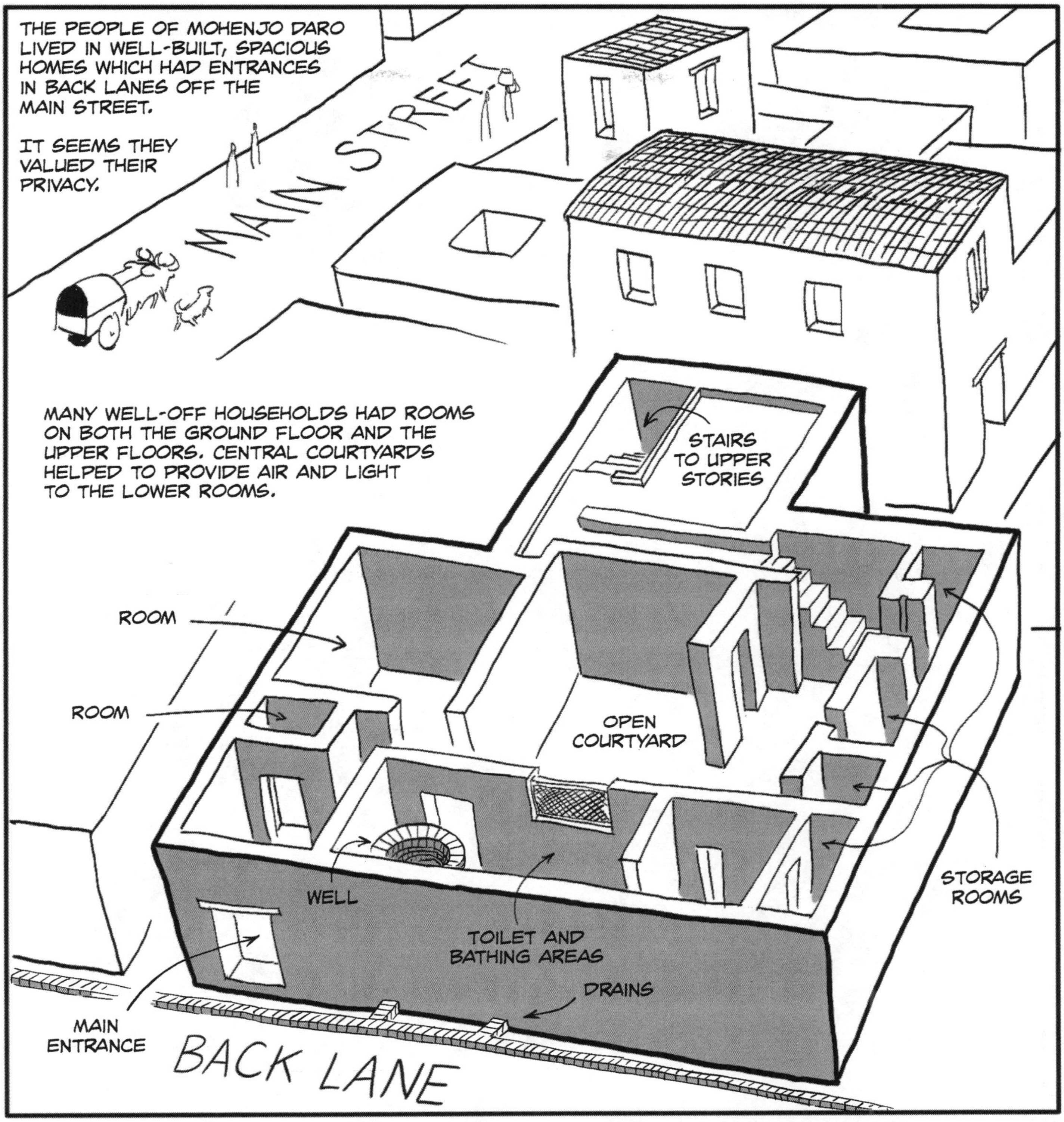
THE PEOPLE OF MOHENJO DARO LIVED IN WELL-BUILT, SPACIOUS HOMES WHICH HAD ENTRANCES IN BACK LANES OFF THE MAIN STREET.
IT SEEMS THEY VALUED THEIR PRIVACY.
MAIN STREET
MANY WELL-OFF HOUSEHOLDS HAD ROOMS ON BOTH THE GROUND FLOOR AND THE UPPER FLOORS. CENTRAL COURTYARDS HELPED TO PROVIDE AIR AND LIGHT TO THE LOWER ROOMS.
STAIRS TO UPPER STORIES
ROOM
ROOM
OPEN COURTYARD
WELL
STORAGE ROOMS
TOILET AND BATHING AREAS
DRAINS
MAIN ENTRANCE
BACK LANE
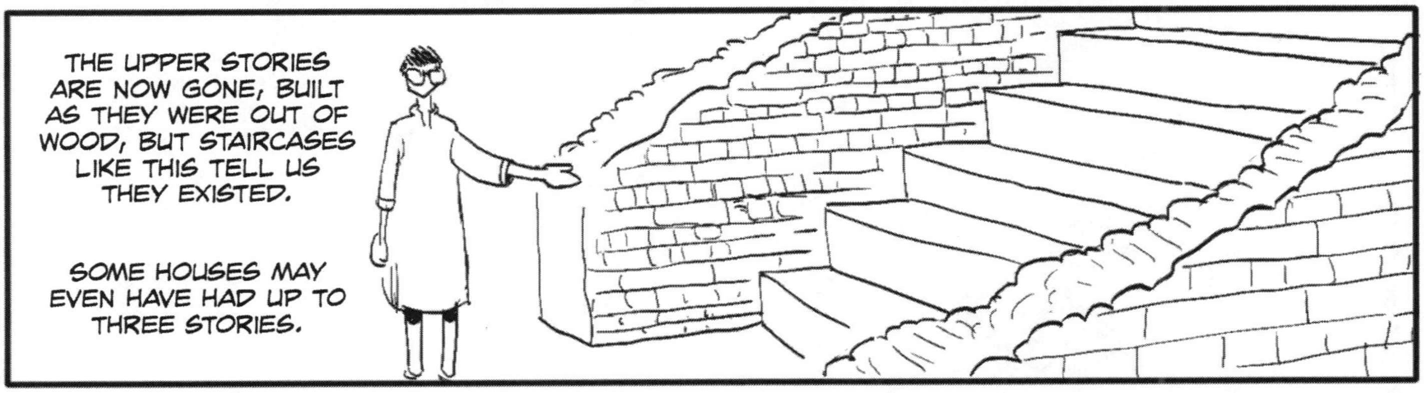
THE UPPER STORIES ARE NOW GONE, BUILT AS THEY WERE OUT OF WOOD, BUT STAIRCASES LIKE THIS TELL US THEY EXISTED.
SOME HOUSES MAY EVEN HAVE HAD UP TO THREE STORIES.

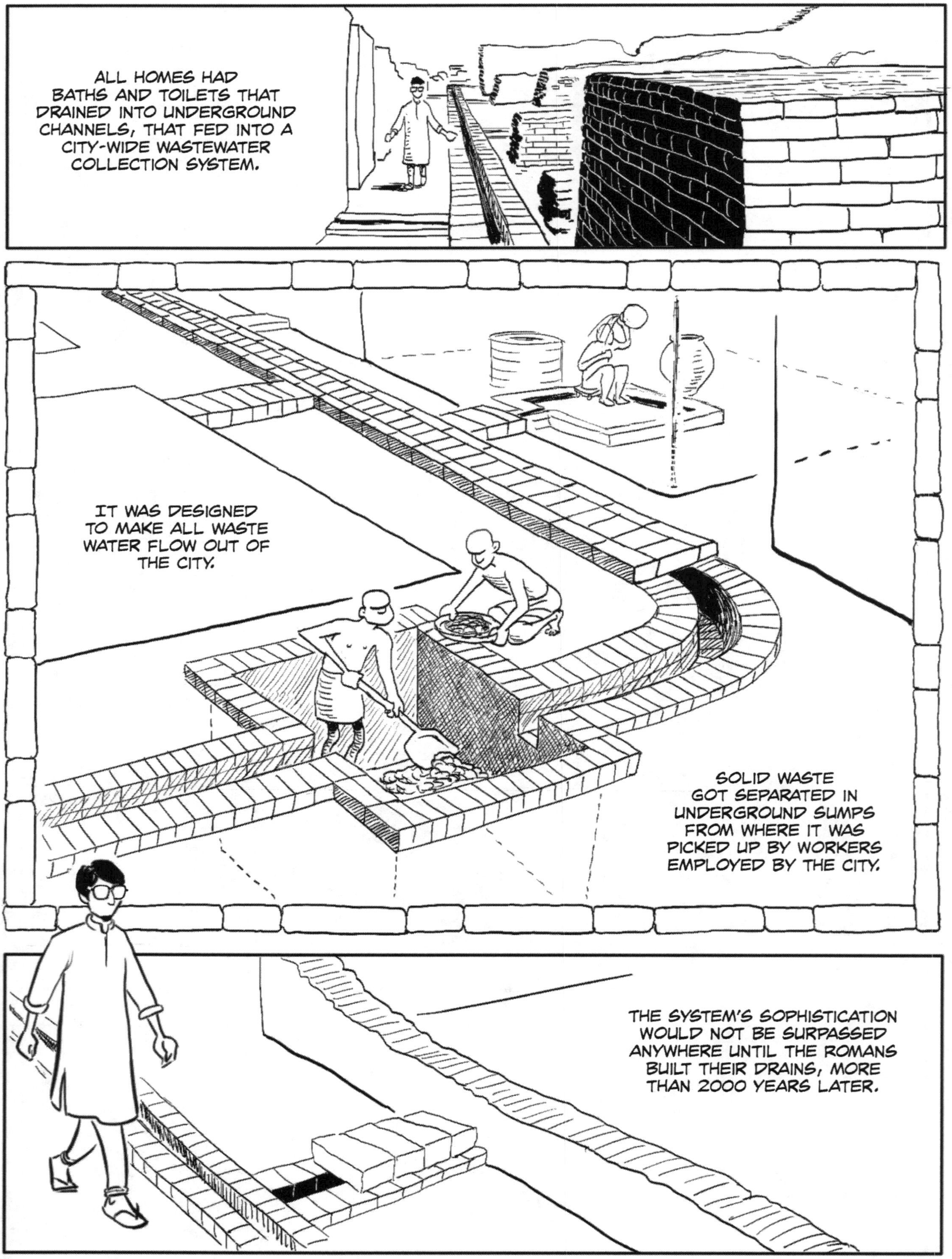
ALL HOMES HAD BATHS AND TOILETS THAT DRAINED INTO UNDERGROUND CHANNELS, THAT FED INTO A CITY-WIDE WASTEWATER COLLECTION SYSTEM.
IT WAS DESIGNED TO MAKE ALL WASTE WATER FLOW OUT OF THE CITY.
SOLID WASTE GOT SEPARATED IN UNDERGROUND SUMPS FROM WHERE IT WAS PICKED UP BY WORKERS EMPLOYED BY THE CITY.
THE SYSTEM'S SOPHISTICATION WOULD NOT BE SURPASSED ANYWHERE UNTIL THE ROMANS BUILT THEIR DRAINS, MORE THAN 2000 YEARS LATER.

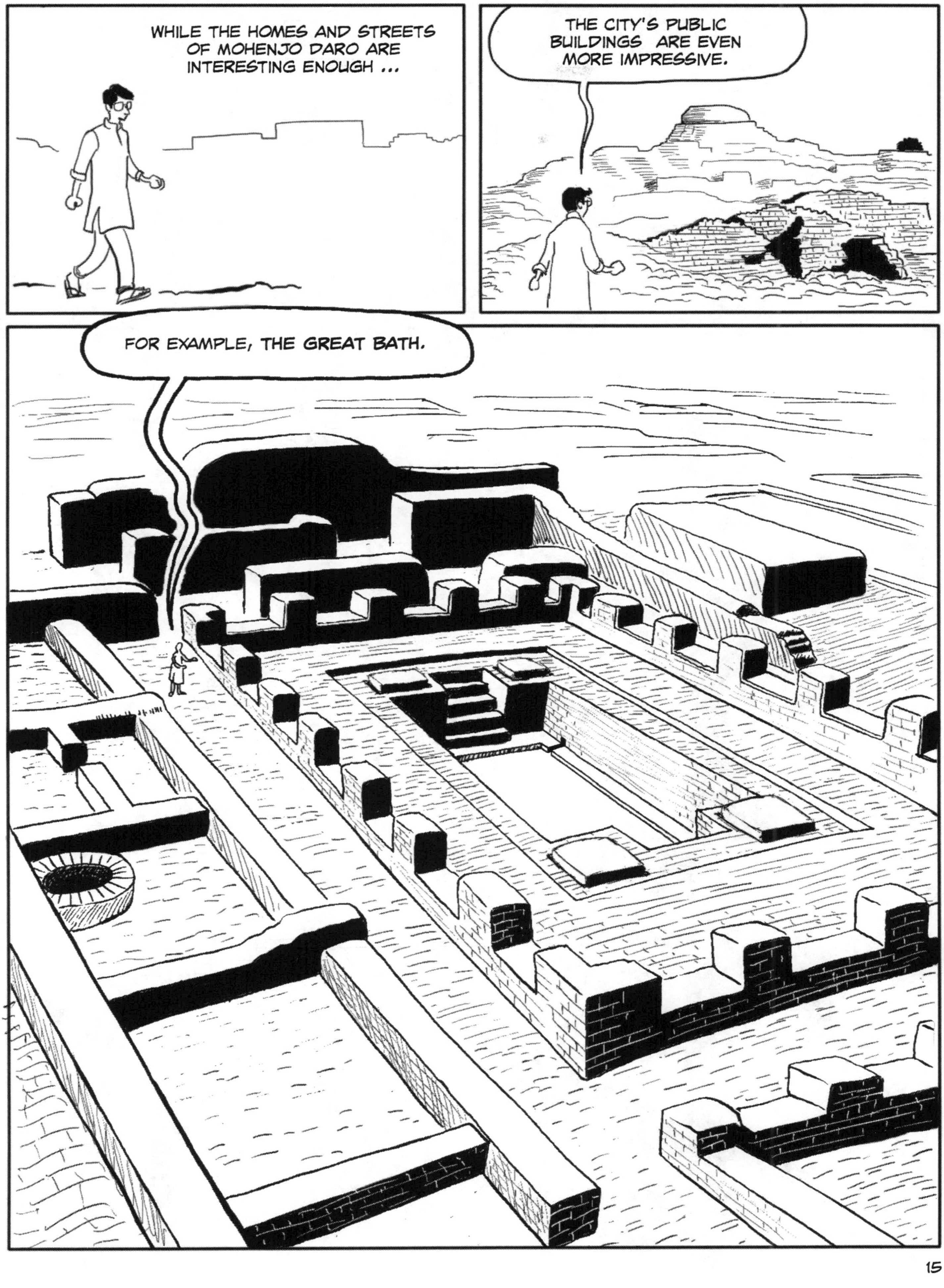
WHILE THE HOMES AND STREETS OF MOHENJO DARO ARE INTERESTING ENOUGH ...
THE CITY'S PUBLIC BUILDINGS ARE EVEN MORE IMPRESSIVE.
FOR EXAMPLE, THE GREAT BATH.

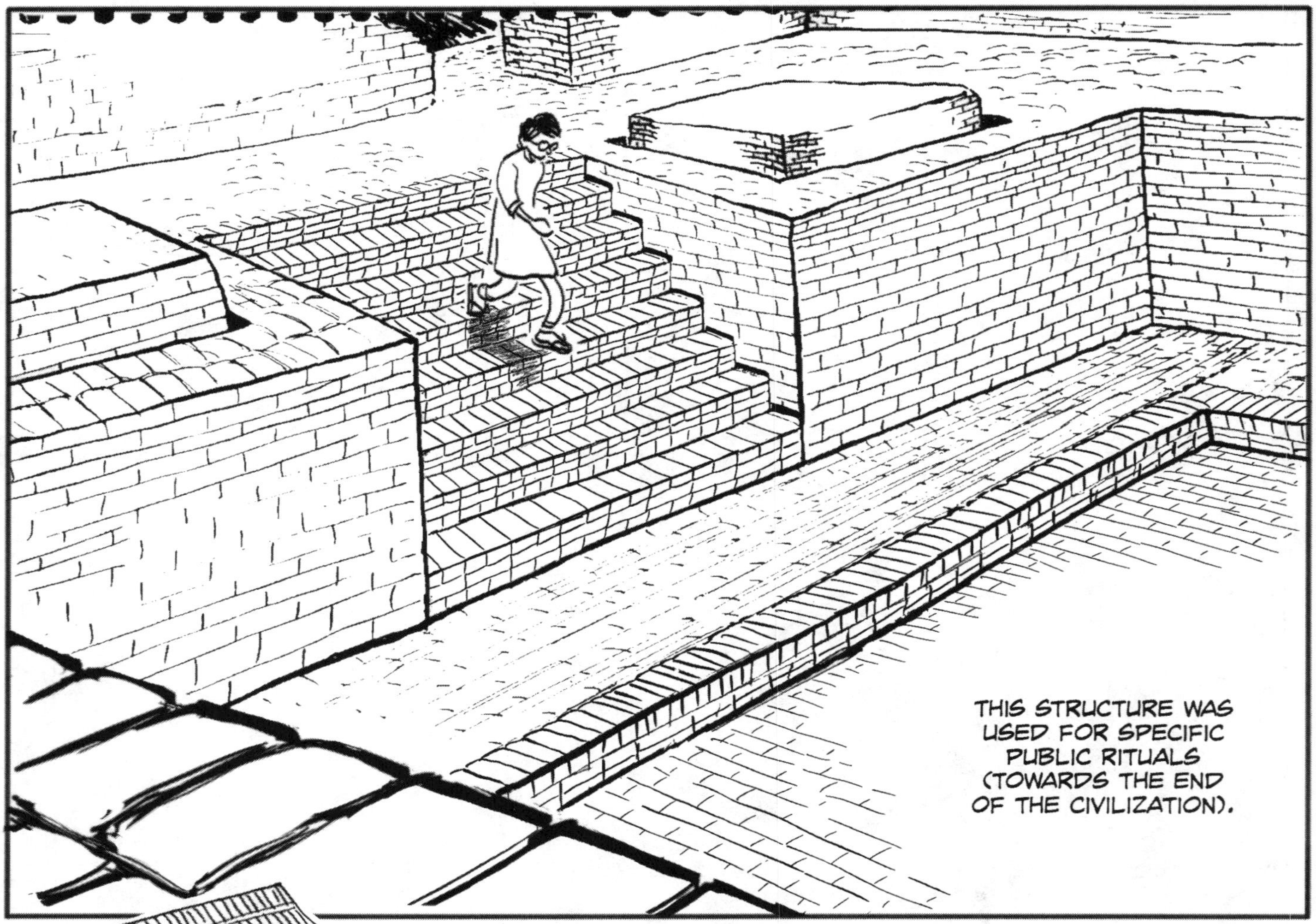
THIS STRUCTURE WAS USED FOR SPECIFIC PUBLIC RITUALS (TOWARDS THE END OF THE CIVILIZATION).

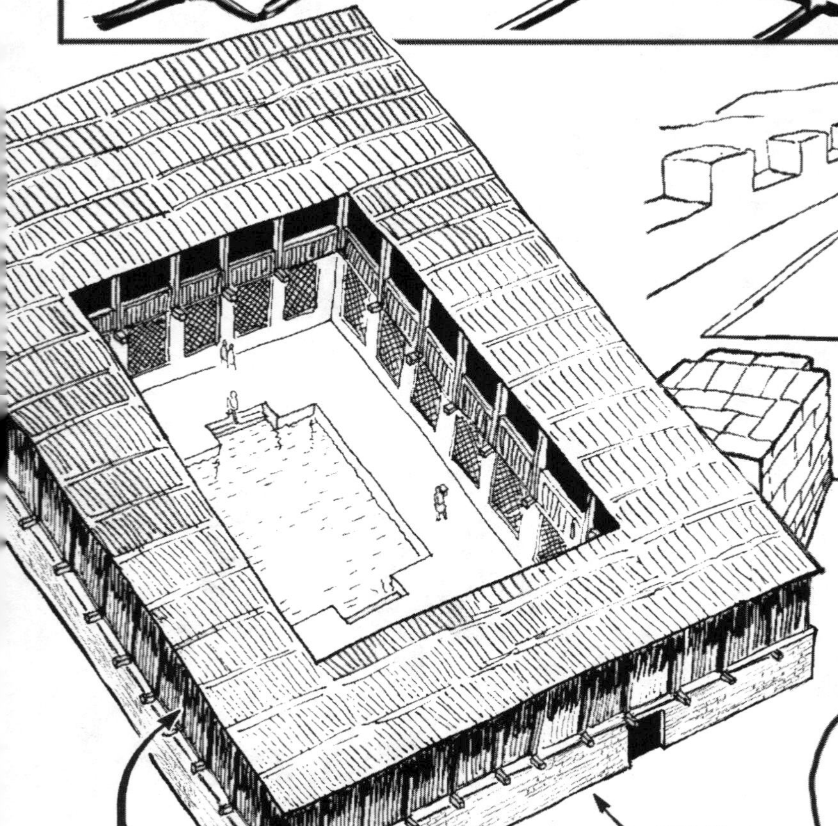
WOODEN SUPER-STRUCTURE
BRICK BASE
RECONSTRUCTION[1]

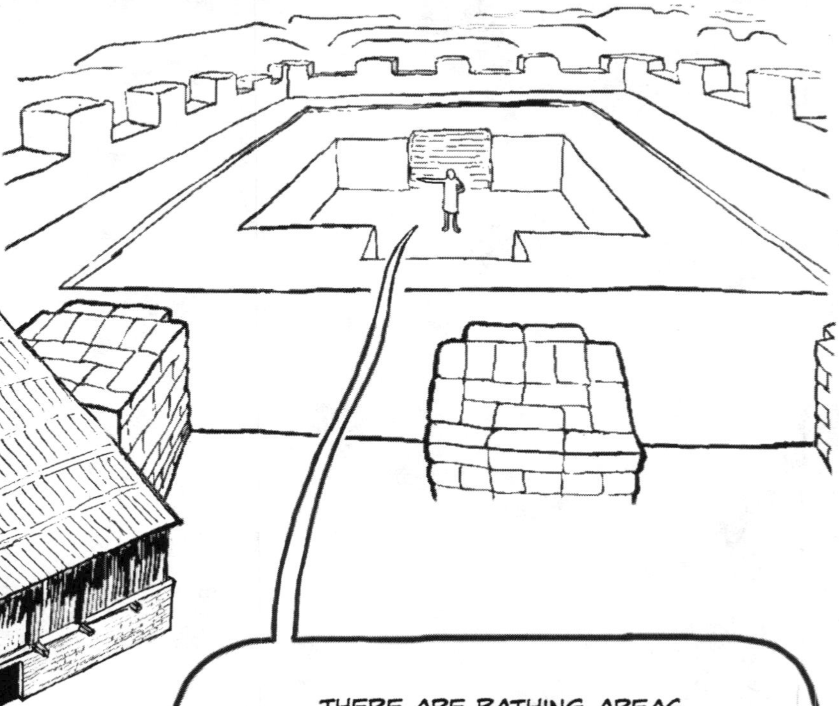
THERE ARE BATHING AREAS WHERE PEOPLE WOULD HAVE BATHED BEFORE ENTERING THE GREAT BATH.

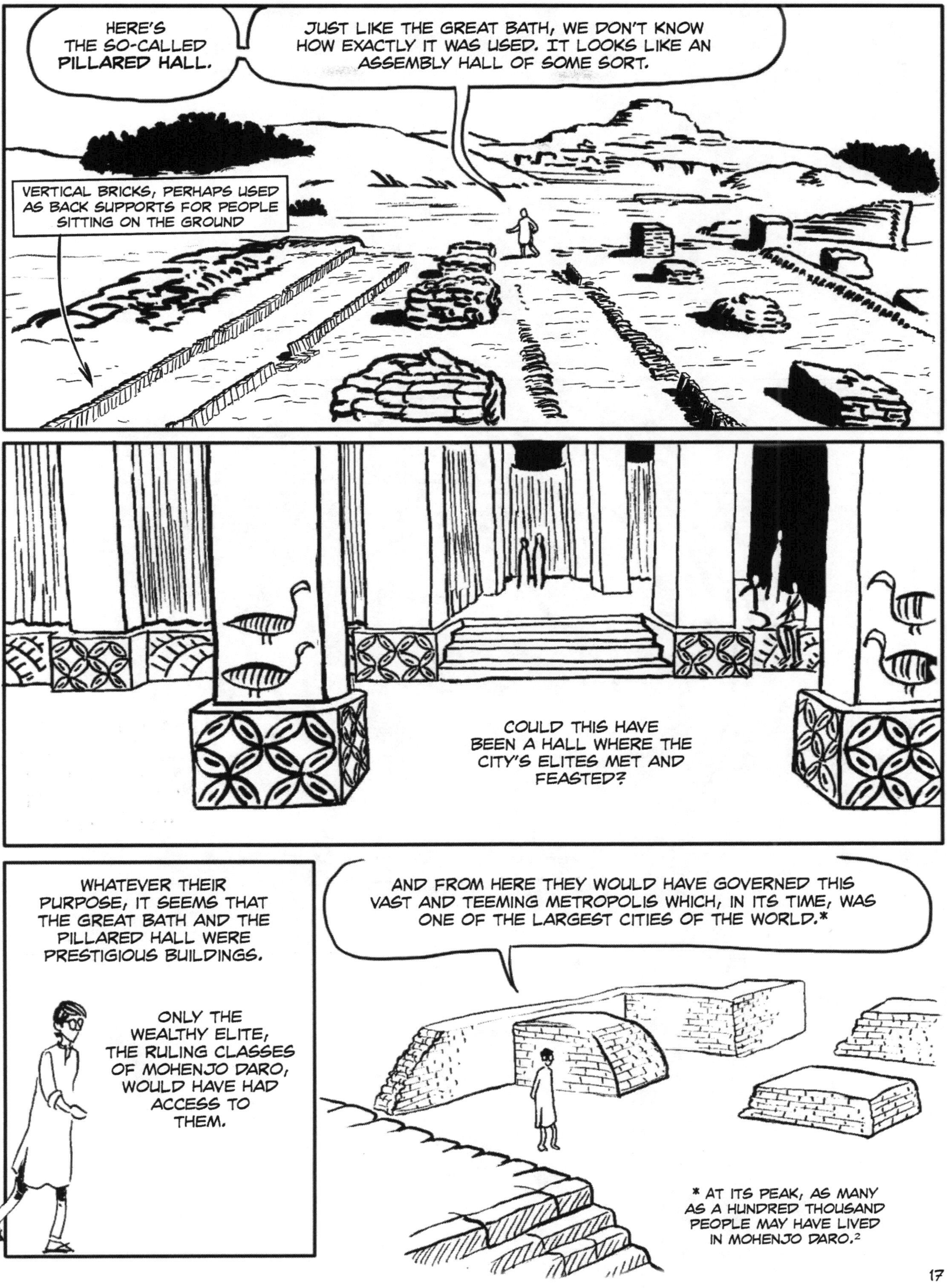
HERE'S THE SO-CALLED PILLARED HALL.
JUST LIKE THE GREAT BATH, WE DON'T KNOW HOW EXACTLY IT WAS USED. IT LOOKS LIKE AN ASSEMBLY HALL OF SOME SORT.
VERTICAL BRICKS, PERHAPS USED AS BACK SUPPORTS FOR PEOPLE SITTING ON THE GROUND
COULD THIS HAVE BEEN A HALL WHERE THE CITY'S ELITES MET AND FEASTED?
WHATEVER THEIR PURPOSE, IT SEEMS THAT THE GREAT BATH AND THE PILLARED HALL WERE PRESTIGIOUS BUILDINGS.
ONLY THE WEALTHY ELITE, THE RULING CLASSES OF MOHENJO DARO, WOULD HAVE HAD ACCESS TO THEM.
AND FROM HERE THEY WOULD HAVE GOVERNED THIS VAST AND TEEMING METROPOLIS WHICH, IN ITS TIME, WAS ONE OF THE LARGEST CITIES OF THE WORLD.*
* AT ITS PEAK, AS MANY AS A HUNDRED THOUSAND PEOPLE MAY HAVE LIVED IN MOHENJO DARO.2

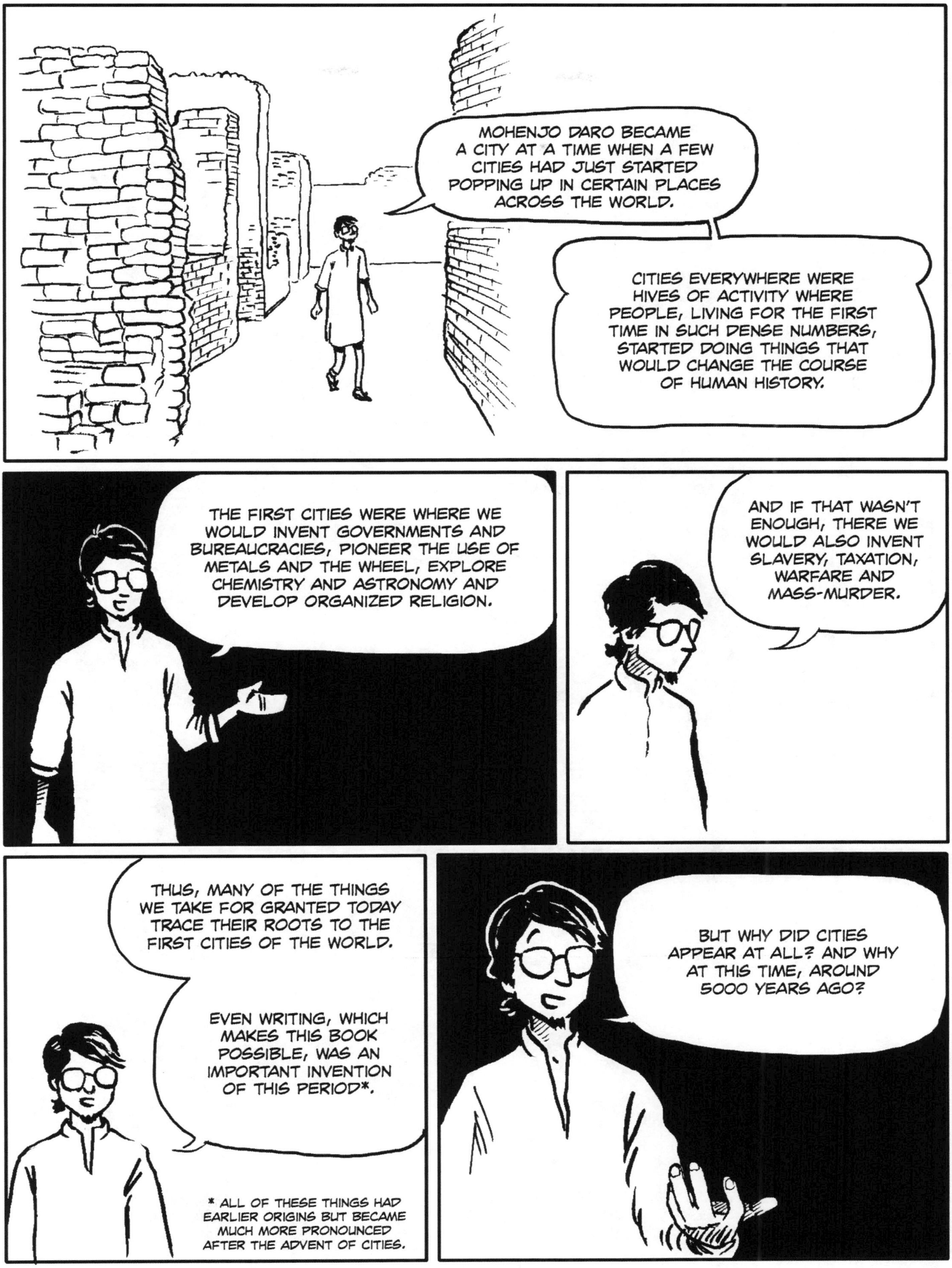
MOHENJO DARO BECAME A CITY AT A TIME WHEN A FEW CITIES HAD JUST STARTED POPPING UP IN CERTAIN PLACES ACROSS THE WORLD.
CITIES EVERYWHERE WERE HIVES OF ACTIVITY WHERE PEOPLE, LIVING FOR THE FIRST TIME IN SUCH DENSE NUMBERS, STARTED DOING THINGS THAT WOULD CHANGE THE COURSE OF HUMAN HISTORY.
THE FIRST CITIES WERE WHERE WE WOULD INVENT GOVERNMENTS AND BUREAUCRACIES, PIONEER THE USE OF METALS AND THE WHEEL, EXPLORE CHEMISTRY AND ASTRONOMY AND DEVELOP ORGANIZED RELIGION.
AND IF THAT WASN'T ENOUGH, THERE WE WOULD ALSO INVENT SLAVERY, TAXATION, WARFARE AND MASS-MURDER.
THUS, MANY OF THE THINGS WE TAKE FOR GRANTED TODAY TRACE THEIR ROOTS TO THE FIRST CITIES OF THE WORLD.
EVEN WRITING, WHICH MAKES THIS BOOK POSSIBLE, WAS AN IMPORTANT INVENTION OF THIS PERIOD*.
* ALL OF THESE THINGS HAD EARLIER ORIGINS BUT BECAME MUCH MORE PRONOUNCED AFTER THE ADVENT OF CITIES.
BUT WHY DID CITIES APPEAR AT ALL? AND WHY AT THIS TIME, AROUND 5000 YEARS AGO?

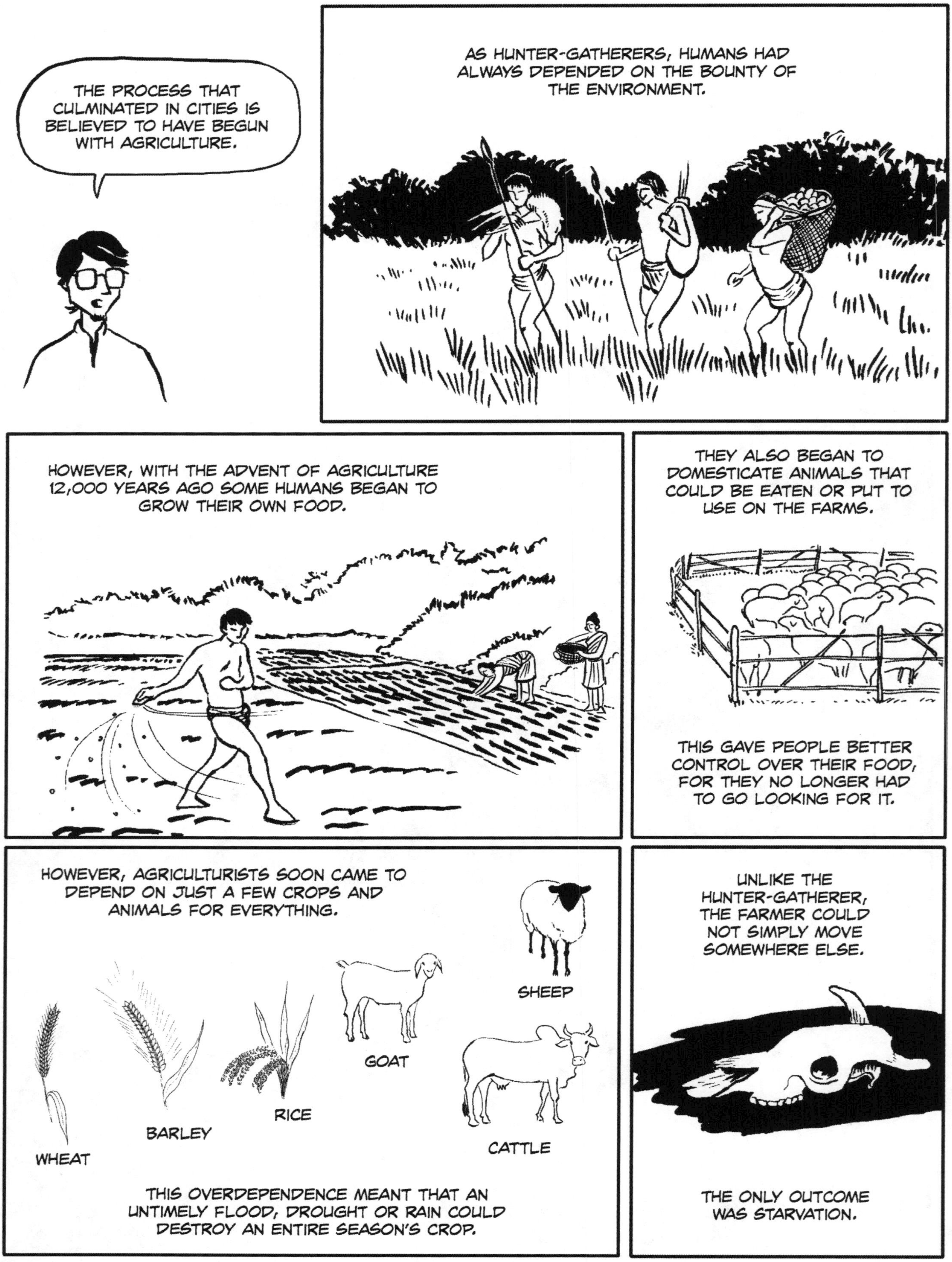
THE PROCESS THAT CULMINATED IN CITIES IS BELIEVED TO HAVE BEGUN WITH AGRICULTURE.
AS HUNTER-GATHERERS, HUMANS HAD ALWAYS DEPENDED ON THE BOUNTY OF THE ENVIRONMENT.
HOWEVER, WITH THE ADVENT OF AGRICULTURE 12,000 YEARS AGO SOME HUMANS BEGAN TO GROW THEIR OWN FOOD.
THEY ALSO BEGAN TO DOMESTICATE ANIMALS THAT COULD BE EATEN OR PUT TO USE ON THE FARMS.
THIS GAVE PEOPLE BETTER CONTROL OVER THEIR FOOD, FOR THEY NO LONGER HAD TO GO LOOKING FOR IT.
HOWEVER, AGRICULTURISTS SOON CAME TO DEPEND ON JUST A FEW CROPS AND ANIMALS FOR EVERYTHING.
SHEEP
GOAT
WHEAT
BARLEY
RICE
CATTLE
THIS OVERDEPENDENCE MEANT THAT AN UNTIMELY FLOOD, DROUGHT OR RAIN COULD DESTROY AN ENTIRE SEASON'S CROP.
UNLIKE THE HUNTER-GATHERER, THE FARMER COULD NOT SIMPLY MOVE SOMEWHERE ELSE.
THE ONLY OUTCOME WAS STARVATION.

SO, IN TIMES OF PLENTY, FARMERS STARTED SAVING UP.
THEY STARTED STORING SURPLUS FOOD GRAIN. NOW PEOPLE'S LIVES WERE ENTIRELY TIED TO A PIECE OF LAND AND SOON PERMANENT VILLAGES CAME UP.
REMAINS OF MEHRGARH, PAKISTAN, 6500-2500 BCE
OVER TIME, FARMING METHODS IMPROVED– THE PLOUGH WAS INVENTED, IRRIGATION WAS DEVELOPED, AND BETTER CROP VARIETIES WERE SELECTED.
WITH EACH IMPROVEMENT THE PRODUCTIVITY OF THE LAND GREW.
EUPHRATES
TIGRIS
NILE
INDUS
SARASWATI
YANGTZE
IN SOME RIVER VALLEYS, WHERE THE SOIL WAS FERTILE AND WATER PLENTIFUL, POPULATIONS EXPLODED.
IN THE NORTHWESTERN PART OF THE INDIAN SUBCONTINENT, HUNDREDS OF FARMING VILLAGES HAD COME UP BY AROUND 5000 BCE.

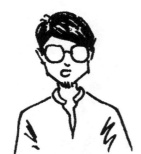

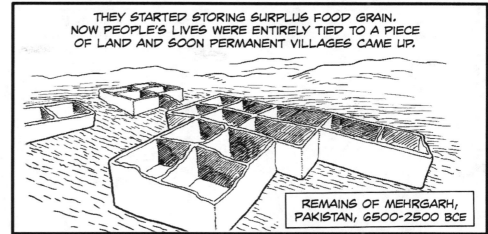

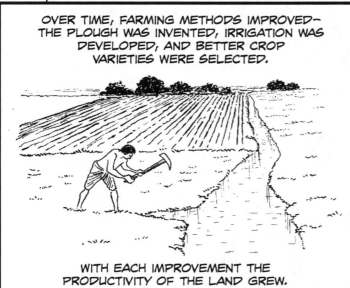

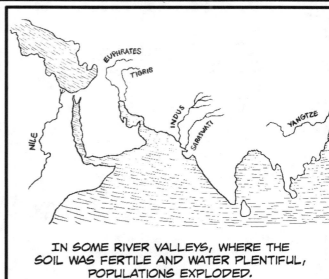

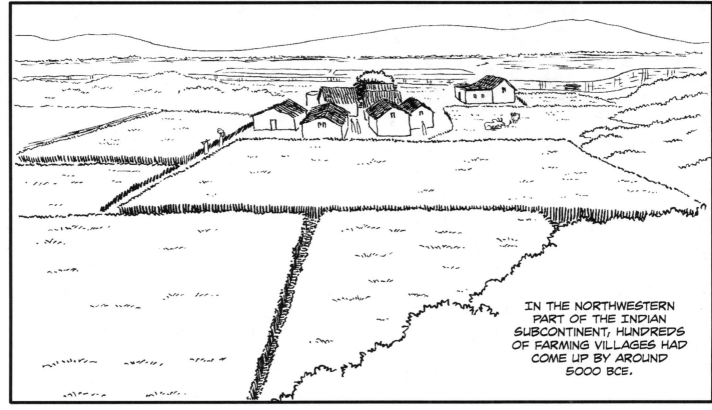

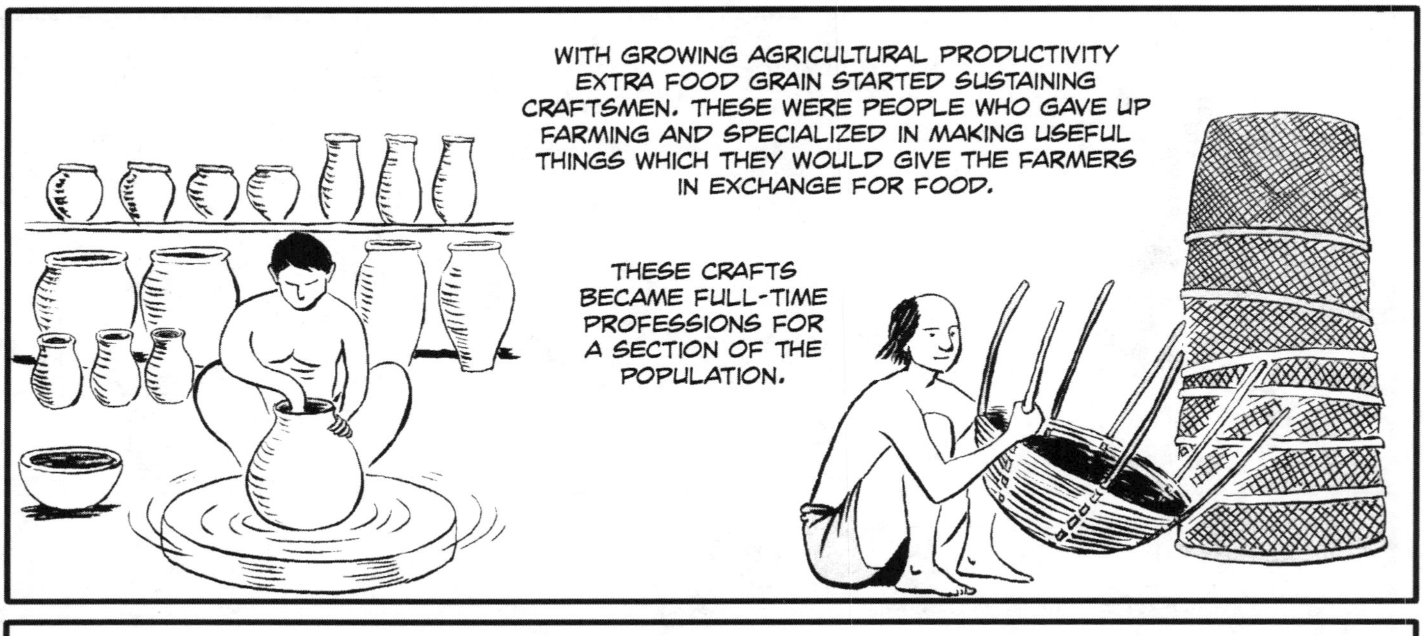
WITH GROWING AGRICULTURAL PRODUCTIVITY EXTRA FOOD GRAIN STARTED SUSTAINING CRAFTSMEN. THESE WERE PEOPLE WHO GAVE UP FARMING AND SPECIALIZED IN MAKING USEFUL THINGS WHICH THEY WOULD GIVE THE FARMERS IN EXCHANGE FOR FOOD.
THESE CRAFTS BECAME FULL-TIME PROFESSIONS FOR A SECTION OF THE POPULATION.

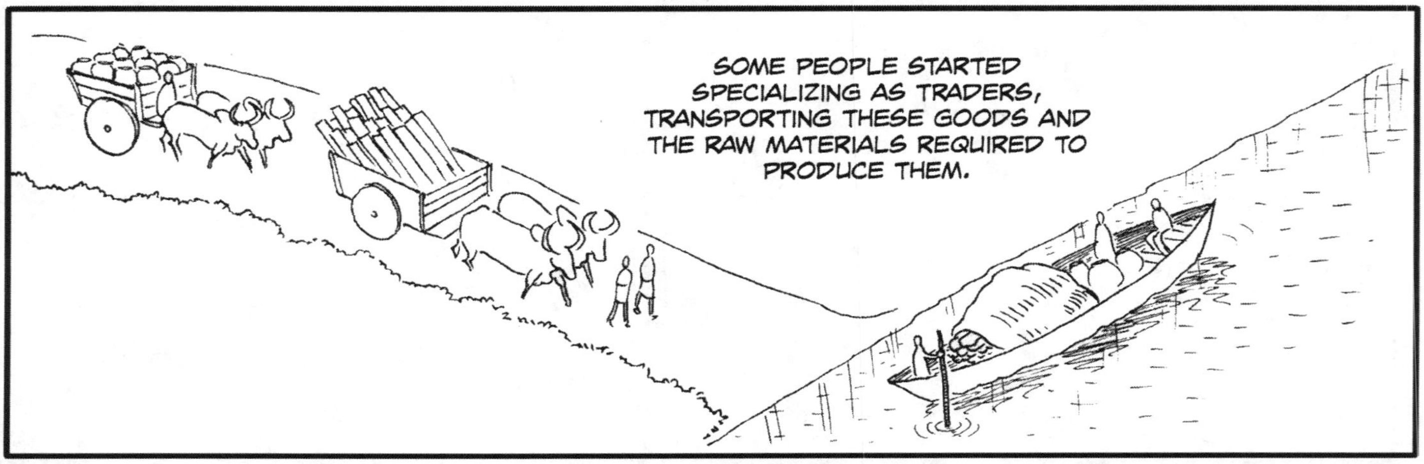
SOME PEOPLE STARTED SPECIALIZING AS TRADERS, TRANSPORTING THESE GOODS AND THE RAW MATERIALS REQUIRED TO PRODUCE THEM.

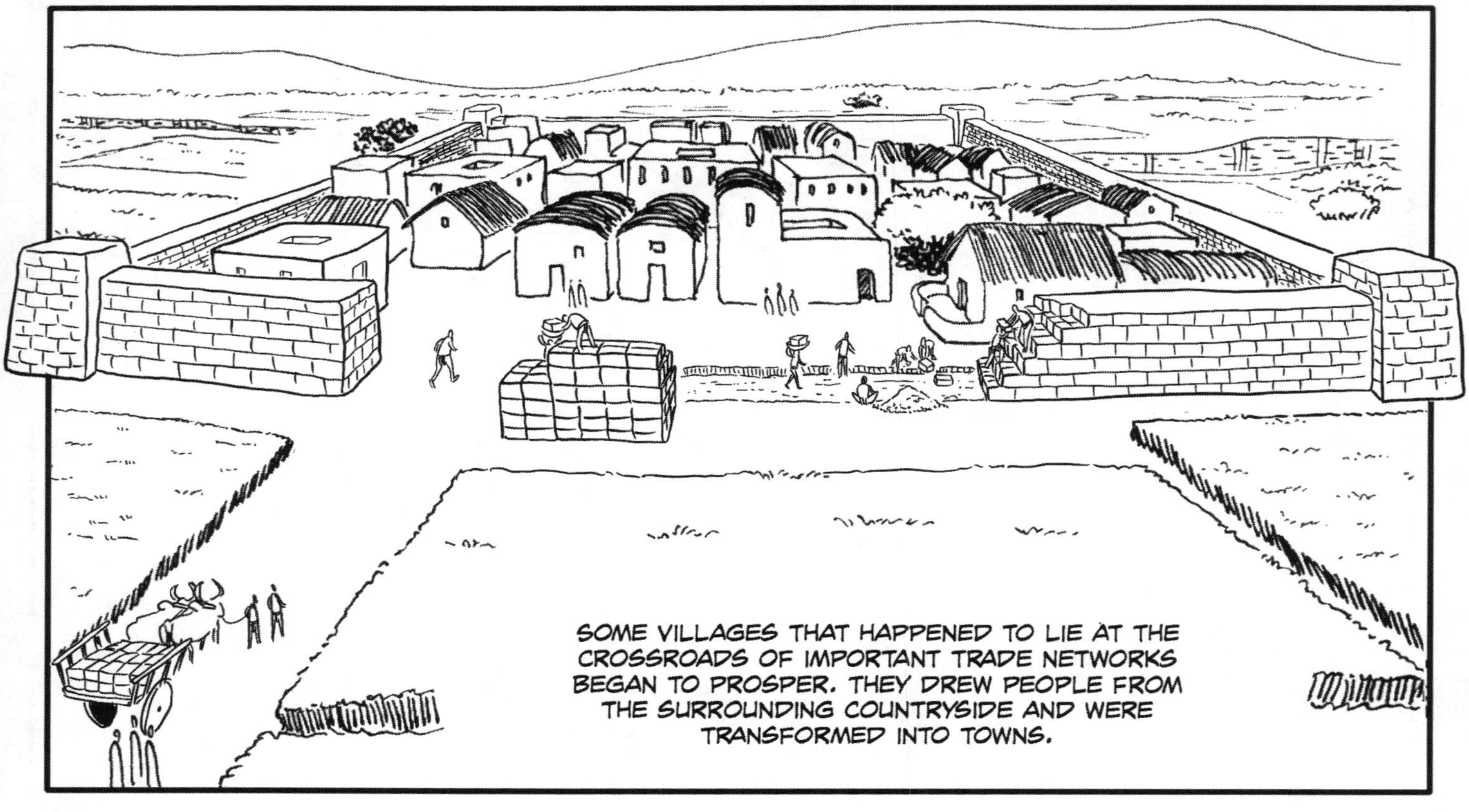
SOME VILLAGES THAT HAPPENED TO LIE AT THE CROSSROADS OF IMPORTANT TRADE NETWORKS BEGAN TO PROSPER. THEY DREW PEOPLE FROM THE SURROUNDING COUNTRYSIDE AND WERE TRANSFORMED INTO TOWNS.

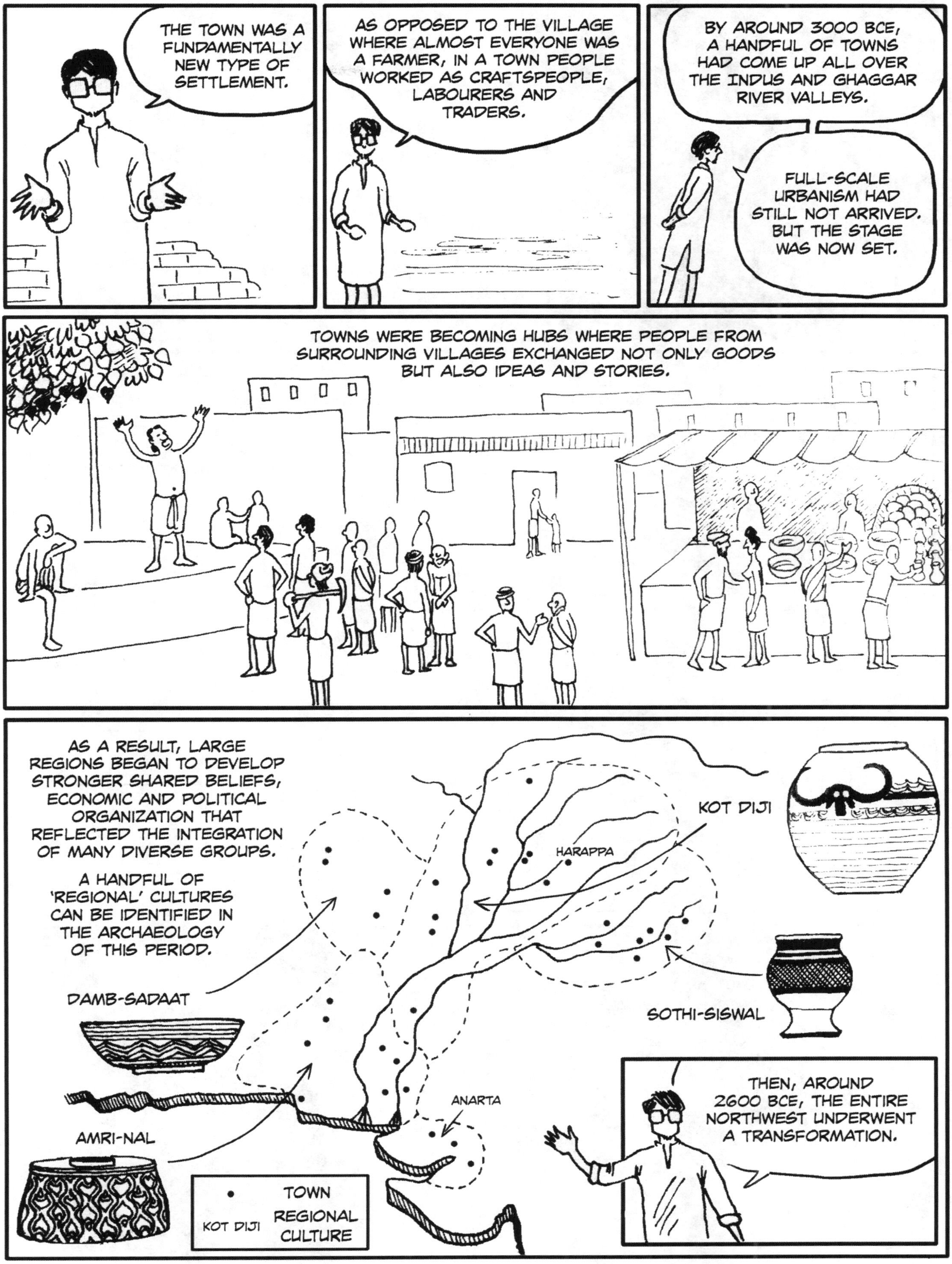
THE TOWN WAS A FUNDAMENTALLY NEW TYPE OF SETTLEMENT.
AS OPPOSED TO THE VILLAGE WHERE ALMOST EVERYONE WAS A FARMER, IN A TOWN PEOPLE WORKED AS CRAFTSPEOPLE, LABOURERS AND TRADERS.
BY AROUND 3000 BCE, A HANDFUL OF TOWNS HAD COME UP ALL OVER THE INDUS AND GHAGGAR RIVER VALLEYS.
FULL-SCALE URBANISM HAD STILL NOT ARRIVED. BUT THE STAGE WAS NOW SET.
TOWNS WERE BECOMING HUBS WHERE PEOPLE FROM SURROUNDING VILLAGES EXCHANGED NOT ONLY GOODS BUT ALSO IDEAS AND STORIES.
AS A RESULT, LARGE REGIONS BEGAN TO DEVELOP STRONGER SHARED BELIEFS, ECONOMIC AND POLITICAL ORGANIZATION THAT REFLECTED THE INTEGRATION OF MANY DIVERSE GROUPS.
A HANDFUL OF 'REGIONAL' CULTURES CAN BE IDENTIFIED IN THE ARCHAEOLOGY OF THIS PERIOD.
HARAPPA
KOT DIJI
DAMB-SADAAT
SOTHI-SISWAL
ANARTA
AMRI-NAL
• TOWN
KOT DIJI REGIONAL CULTURE
THEN, AROUND 2600 BCE, THE ENTIRE NORTHWEST UNDERWENT A TRANSFORMATION.

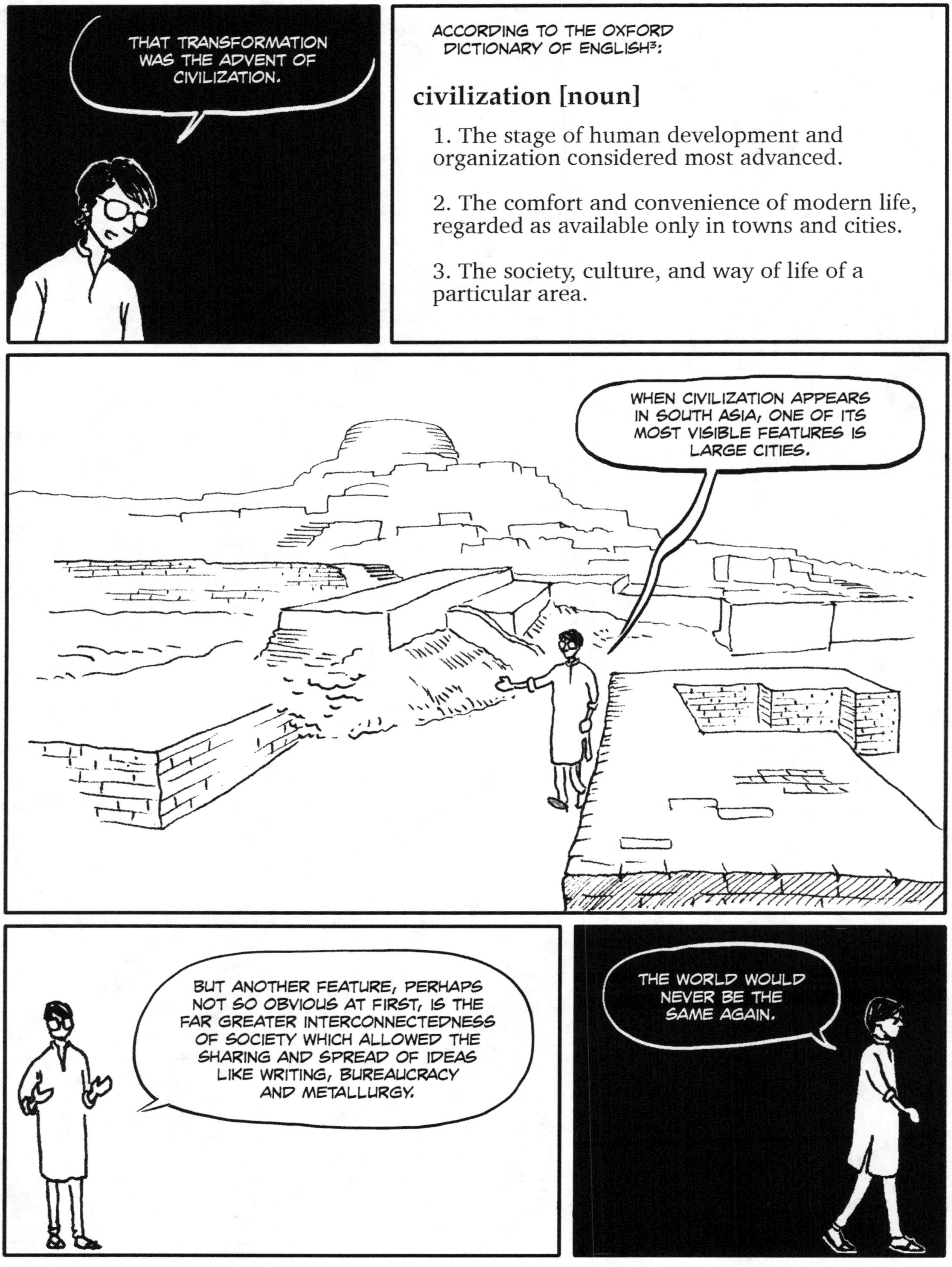
THAT TRANSFORMATION WAS THE ADVENT OF CIVILIZATION.
ACCORDING TO THE OXFORD DICTIONARY OF ENGLISH[3]:
civilization [noun]
1. The stage of human development and organization considered most advanced.
2. The comfort and convenience of modern life, regarded as available only in towns and cities.
3. The society, culture, and way of life of a particular area.
WHEN CIVILIZATION APPEARS IN SOUTH ASIA, ONE OF ITS MOST VISIBLE FEATURES IS LARGE CITIES.
BUT ANOTHER FEATURE, PERHAPS NOT SO OBVIOUS AT FIRST, IS THE FAR GREATER INTERCONNECTEDNESS OF SOCIETY WHICH ALLOWED THE SHARING AND SPREAD OF IDEAS LIKE WRITING, BUREAUCRACY AND METALLURGY.
THE WORLD WOULD NEVER BE THE SAME AGAIN.

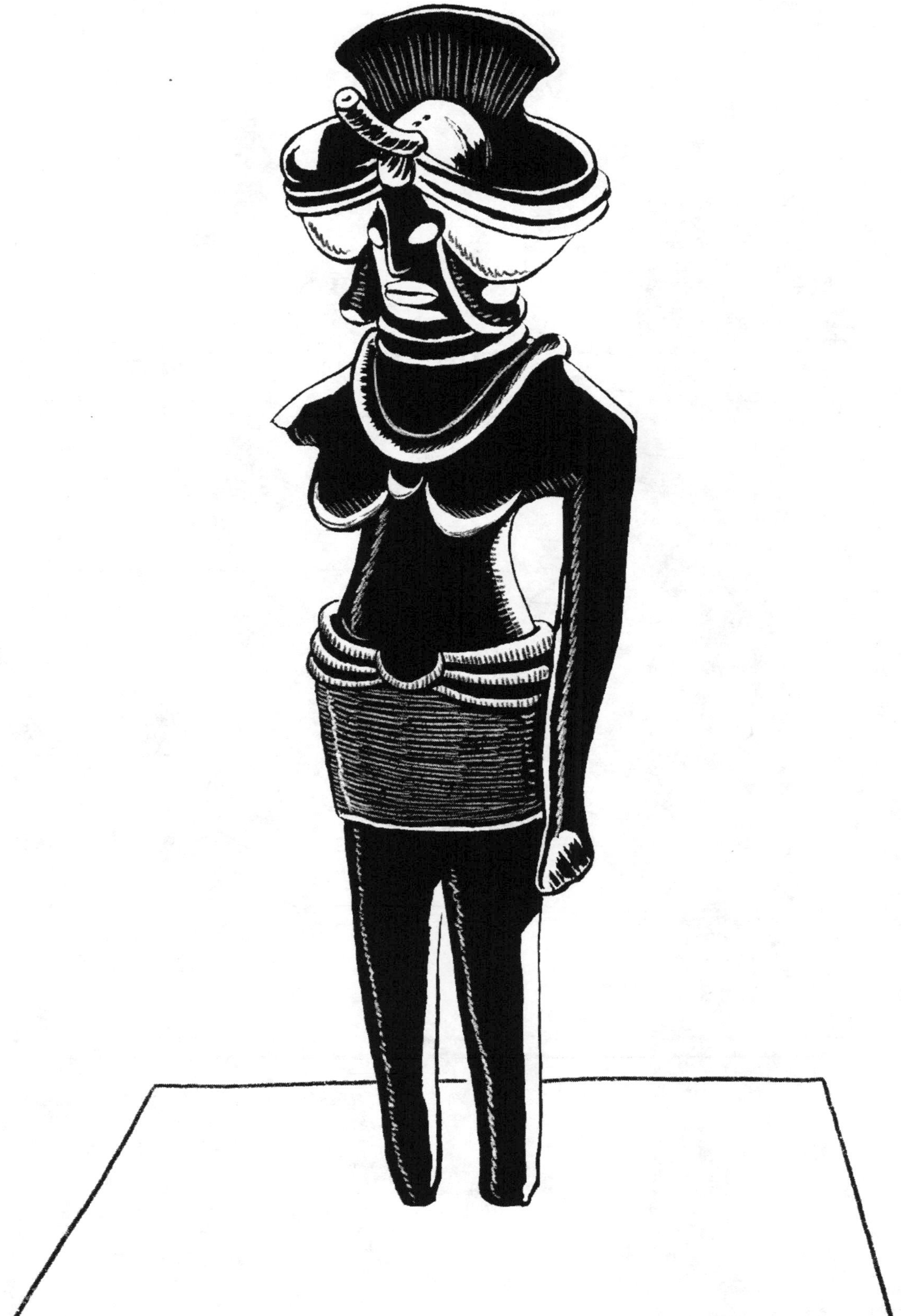

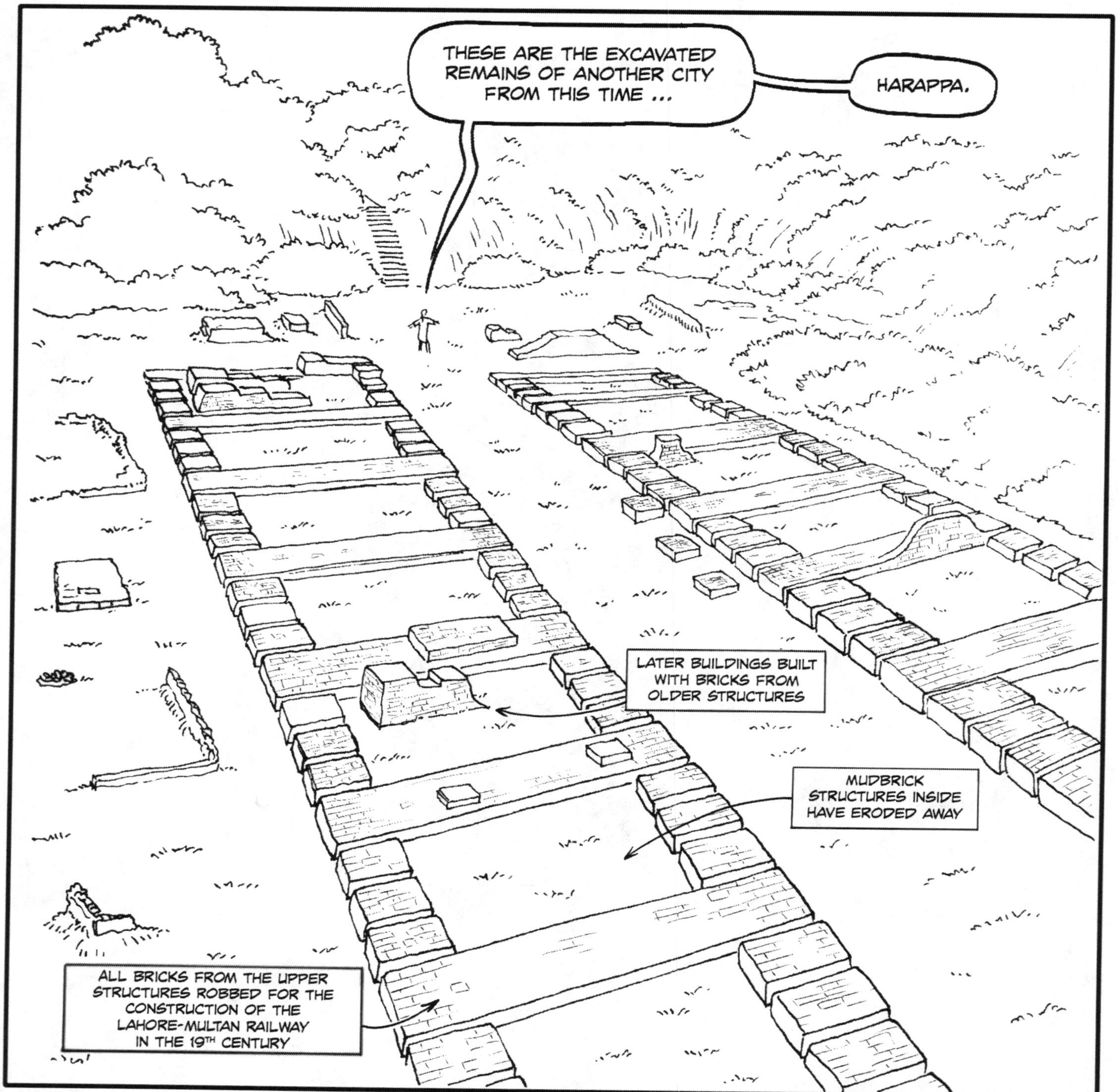
THESE ARE THE EXCAVATED REMAINS OF ANOTHER CITY FROM THIS TIME ...
HARAPPA.
LATER BUILDINGS BUILT WITH BRICKS FROM OLDER STRUCTURES
MUDBRICK STRUCTURES INSIDE HAVE ERODED AWAY
ALL BRICKS FROM THE UPPER STRUCTURES ROBBED FOR THE CONSTRUCTION OF THE LAHORE-MULTAN RAILWAY IN THE 19TH CENTURY

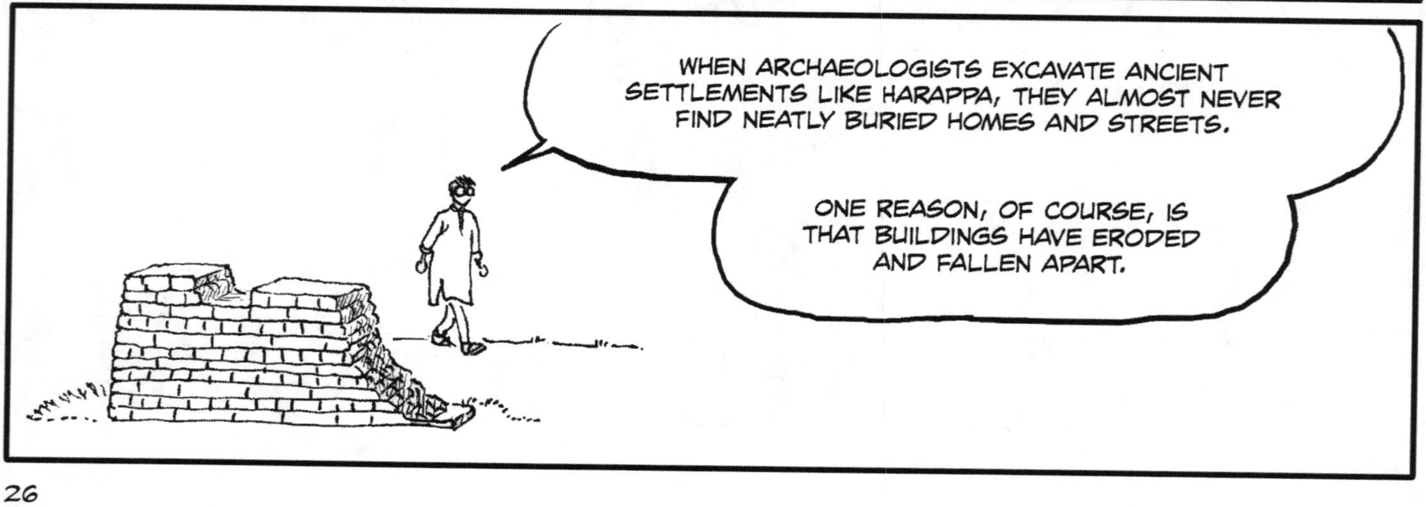
WHEN ARCHAEOLOGISTS EXCAVATE ANCIENT SETTLEMENTS LIKE HARAPPA, THEY ALMOST NEVER FIND NEATLY BURIED HOMES AND STREETS.
ONE REASON, OF COURSE, IS THAT BUILDINGS HAVE ERODED AND FALLEN APART.

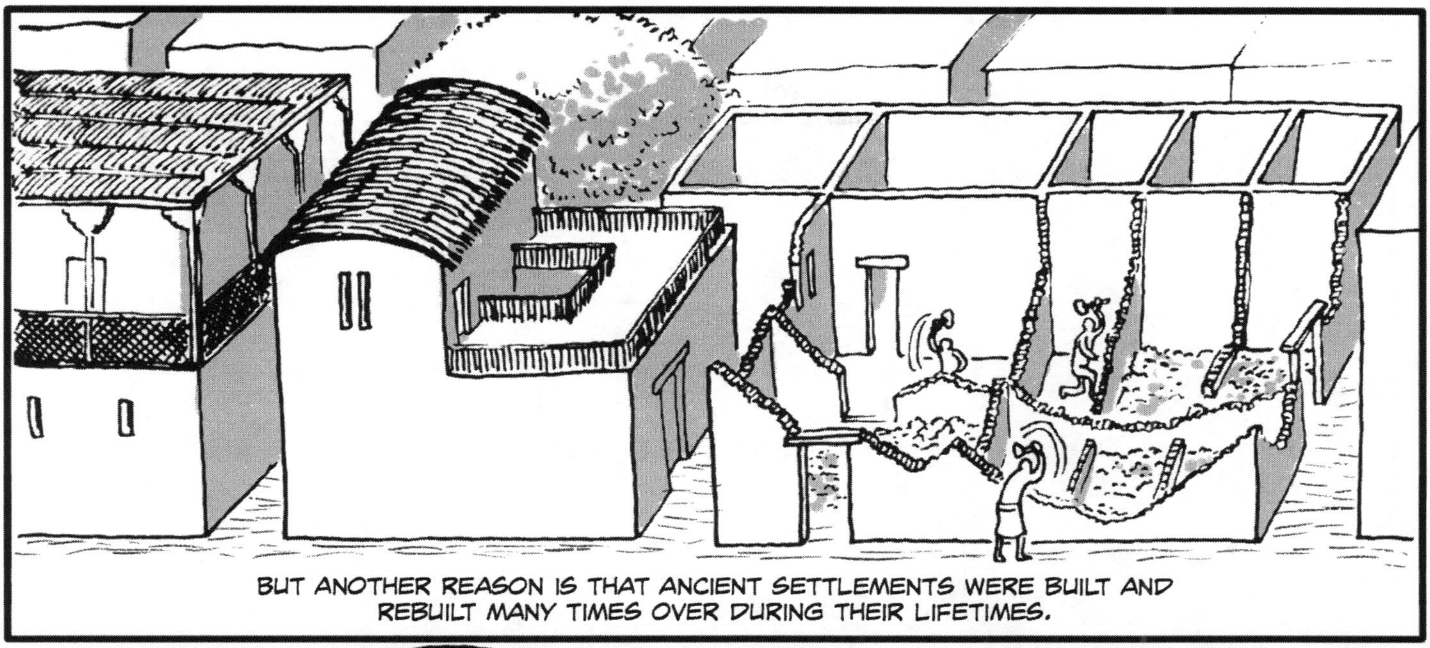
BUT ANOTHER REASON IS THAT ANCIENT SETTLEMENTS WERE BUILT AND REBUILT MANY TIMES OVER DURING THEIR LIFETIMES.

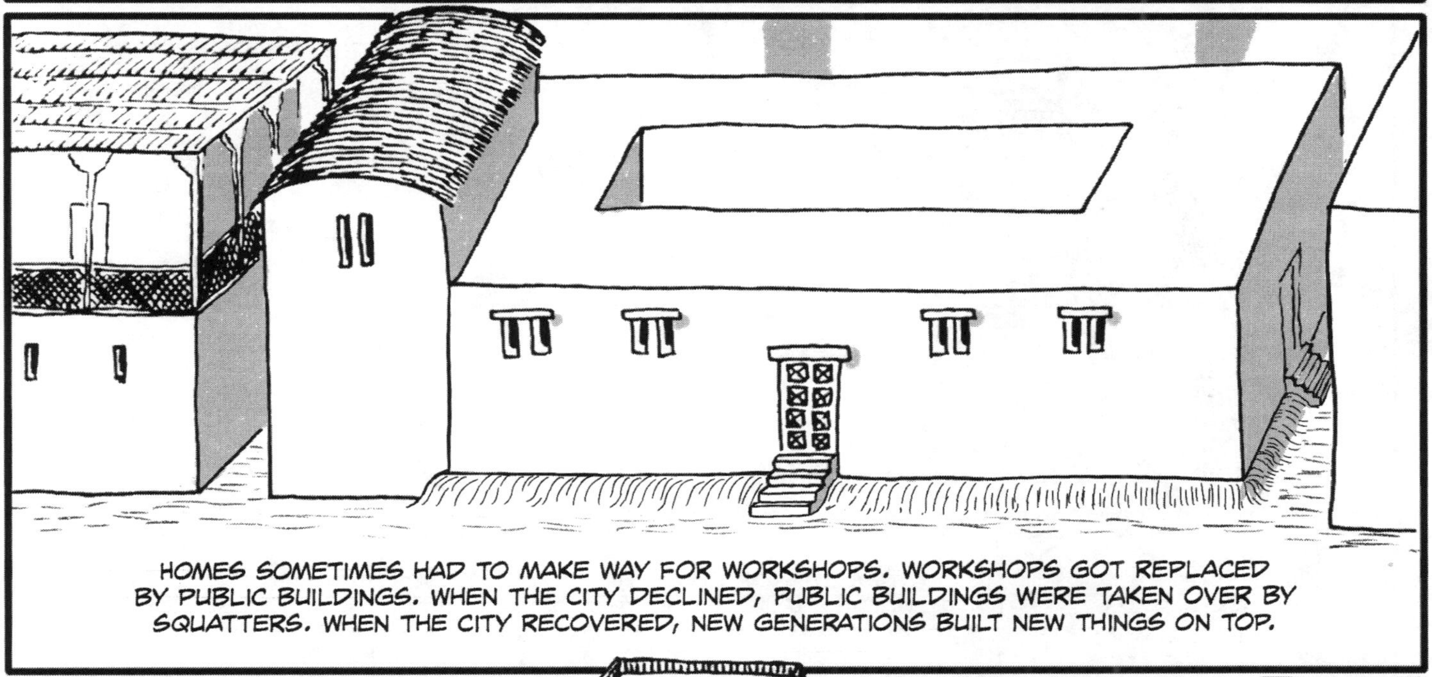
HOMES SOMETIMES HAD TO MAKE WAY FOR WORKSHOPS. WORKSHOPS GOT REPLACED BY PUBLIC BUILDINGS. WHEN THE CITY DECLINED, PUBLIC BUILDINGS WERE TAKEN OVER BY SQUATTERS. WHEN THE CITY RECOVERED, NEW GENERATIONS BUILT NEW THINGS ON TOP.

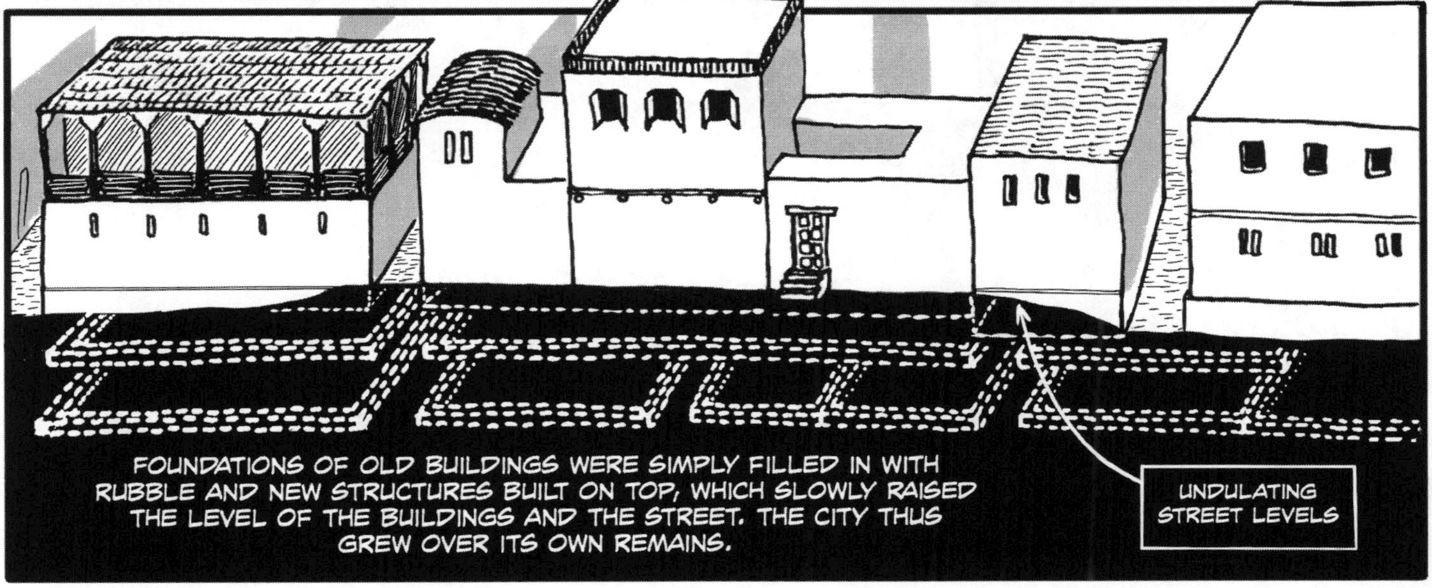
FOUNDATIONS OF OLD BUILDINGS WERE SIMPLY FILLED IN WITH RUBBLE AND NEW STRUCTURES BUILT ON TOP, WHICH SLOWLY RAISED THE LEVEL OF THE BUILDINGS AND THE STREET. THE CITY THUS GREW OVER ITS OWN REMAINS.
UNDULATING STREET LEVELS

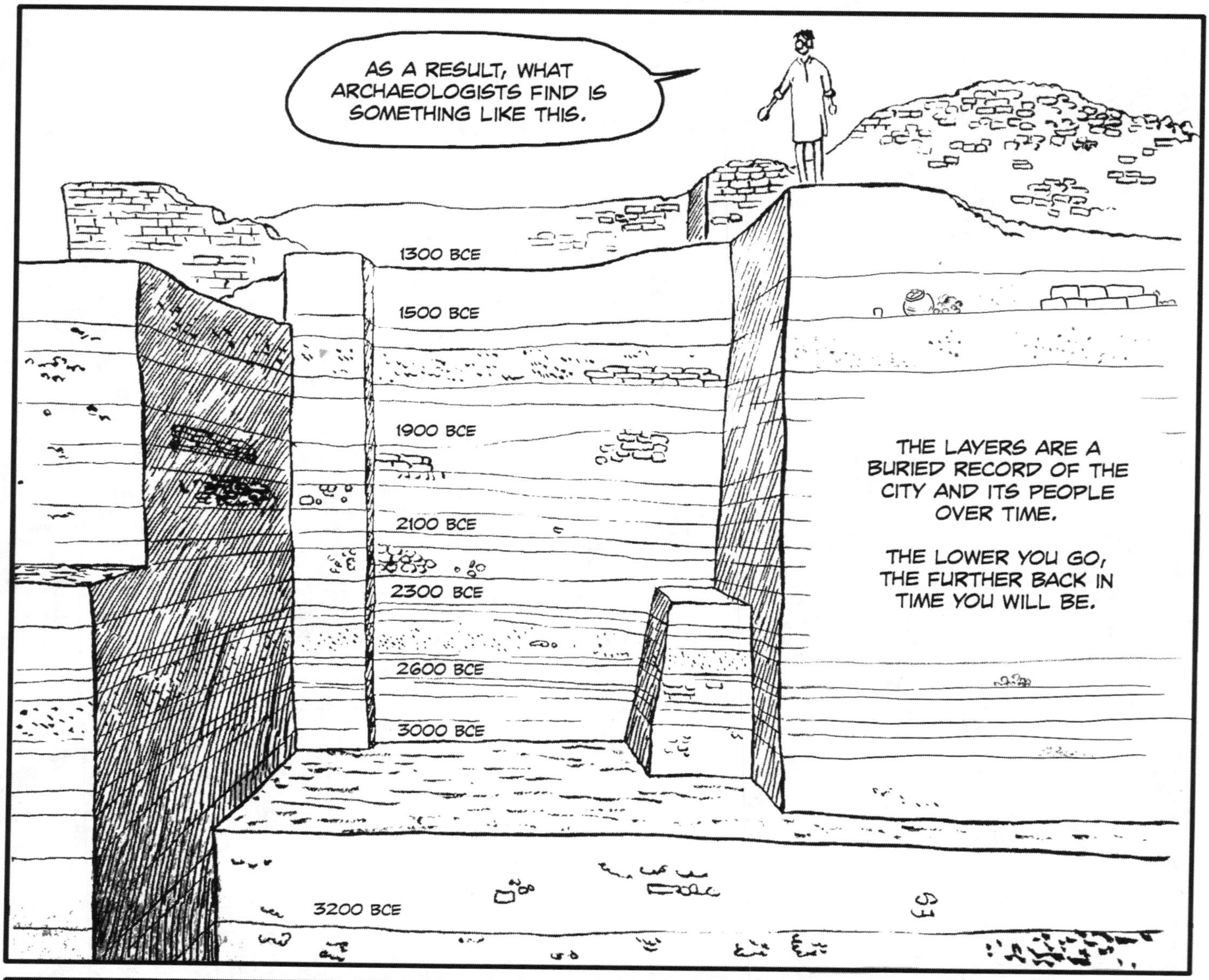
AS A RESULT, WHAT ARCHAEOLOGISTS FIND IS SOMETHING LIKE THIS.
1300 BCE
1500 BCE
1900 BCE
2100 BCE
2300 BCE
2600 BCE
3000 BCE
3200 BCE
THE LAYERS ARE A BURIED RECORD OF THE CITY AND ITS PEOPLE OVER TIME.
THE LOWER YOU GO, THE FURTHER BACK IN TIME YOU WILL BE.

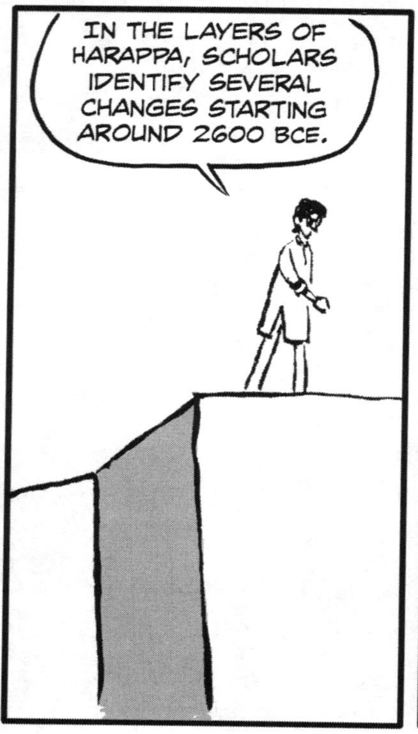
IN THE LAYERS OF HARAPPA, SCHOLARS IDENTIFY SEVERAL CHANGES STARTING AROUND 2600 BCE.

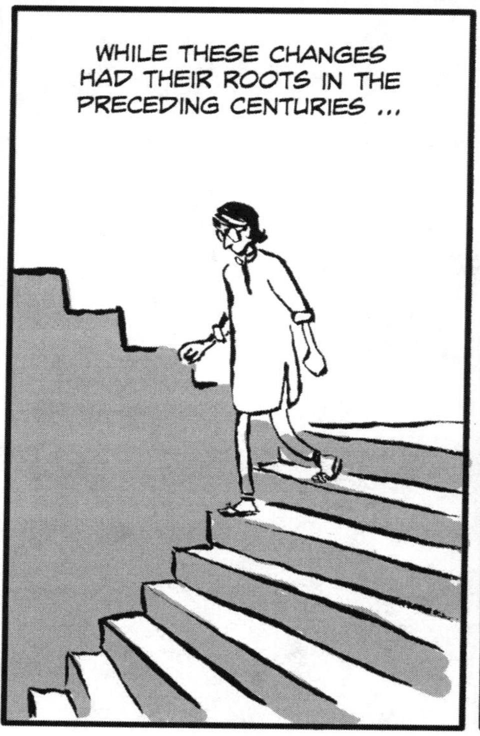
WHILE THESE CHANGES HAD THEIR ROOTS IN THE PRECEDING CENTURIES ...

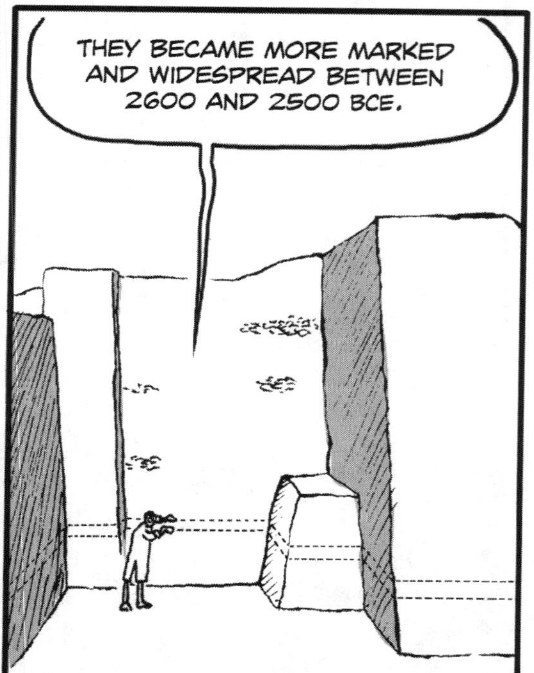
THEY BECAME MORE MARKED AND WIDESPREAD BETWEEN 2600 AND 2500 BCE.

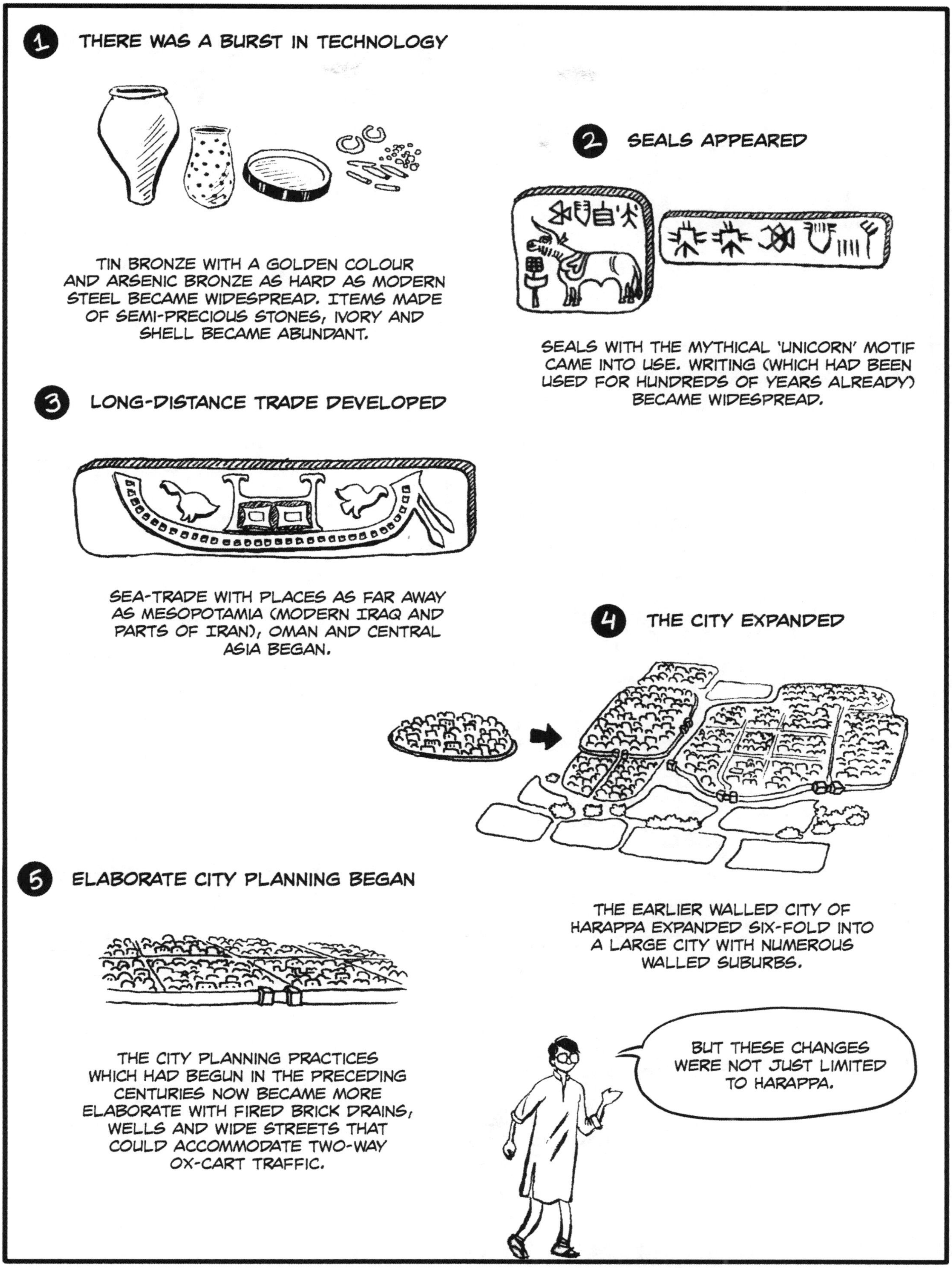

1 THERE WAS A BURST IN TECHNOLOGY

TIN BRONZE WITH A GOLDEN COLOUR AND ARSENIC BRONZE AS HARD AS MODERN STEEL BECAME WIDESPREAD. ITEMS MADE OF SEMI-PRECIOUS STONES, IVORY AND SHELL BECAME ABUNDANT.

2 SEALS APPEARED

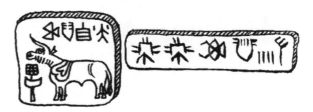

SEALS WITH THE MYTHICAL 'UNICORN' MOTIF CAME INTO USE. WRITING (WHICH HAD BEEN USED FOR HUNDREDS OF YEARS ALREADY) BECAME WIDESPREAD.

3 LONG-DISTANCE TRADE DEVELOPED

SEA-TRADE WITH PLACES AS FAR AWAY AS MESOPOTAMIA (MODERN IRAQ AND PARTS OF IRAN), OMAN AND CENTRAL ASIA BEGAN.

4 THE CITY EXPANDED

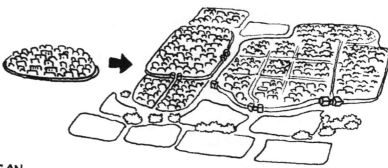

THE EARLIER WALLED CITY OF HARAPPA EXPANDED SIX-FOLD INTO A LARGE CITY WITH NUMEROUS WALLED SUBURBS.

5 ELABORATE CITY PLANNING BEGAN

THE CITY PLANNING PRACTICES WHICH HAD BEGUN IN THE PRECEDING CENTURIES NOW BECAME MORE ELABORATE WITH FIRED BRICK DRAINS, WELLS AND WIDE STREETS THAT COULD ACCOMMODATE TWO-WAY OX-CART TRAFFIC.

BUT THESE CHANGES WERE NOT JUST LIMITED TO HARAPPA.

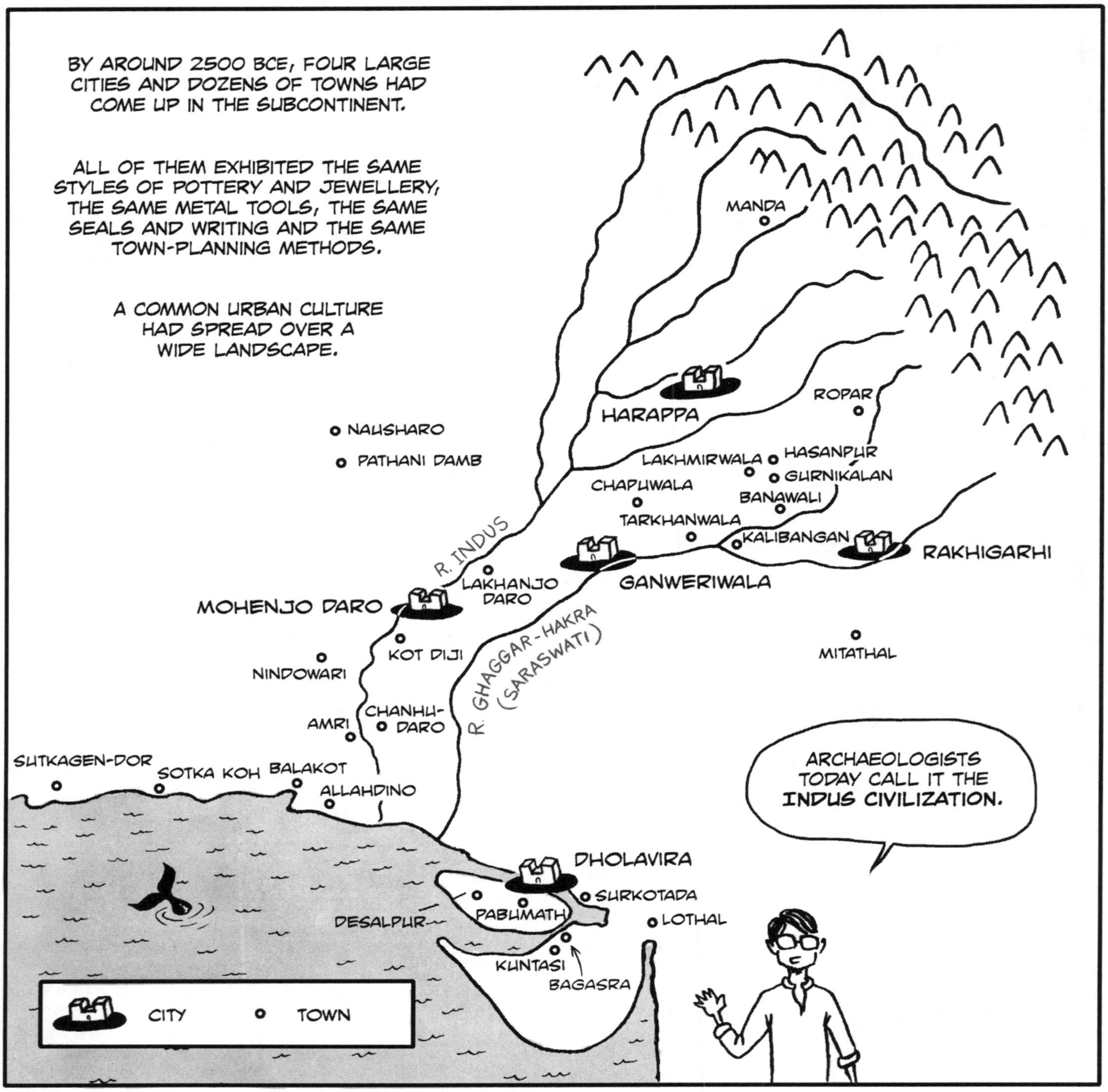
BY AROUND 2500 BCE, FOUR LARGE CITIES AND DOZENS OF TOWNS HAD COME UP IN THE SUBCONTINENT.
ALL OF THEM EXHIBITED THE SAME STYLES OF POTTERY AND JEWELLERY, THE SAME METAL TOOLS, THE SAME SEALS AND WRITING AND THE SAME TOWN-PLANNING METHODS.
A COMMON URBAN CULTURE HAD SPREAD OVER A WIDE LANDSCAPE.
MANDA
HARAPPA
ROPAR
NAUSHARO
PATHANI DAMB
LAKHMIRWALA
HASANPUR
GURNIKALAN
CHAPUWALA
BANAWALI
TARKHANWALA
KALIBANGAN
RAKHIGARHI
R. INDUS
LAKHANJO DARO
GANWERIWALA
MOHENJO DARO
KOT DIJI
R. GHAGGAR-HAKRA (SARASWATI)
MITATHAL
NINDOWARI
CHANHU-DARO
AMRI
SUTKAGEN-DOR
SOTKA KOH
BALAKOT
ALLAHDINO
ARCHAEOLOGISTS TODAY CALL IT THE INDUS CIVILIZATION.
DHOLAVIRA
SURKOTADA
PABUMATH
DESALPUR
LOTHAL
KUNTASI
BAGASRA
CITY
TOWN

THE INITIAL DISCOVERIES WERE ALL MADE ALONG THE INDUS RIVER AND ITS TRIBUTARIES (HENCE THE NAME INDUS CIVILIZATION). SINCE THEN, HUNDREDS OF NEW SITES HAVE BEEN FOUND ALONG ANOTHER MAJOR RIVER KNOWN TODAY AS GHAGGAR (HAKRA IN SOME REGIONS) WHICH DRIED UP IN ANTIQUITY. SOME SCHOLARS IDENTIFY THIS TO BE THE SARASWATI RIVER OF VEDIC TEXTS.

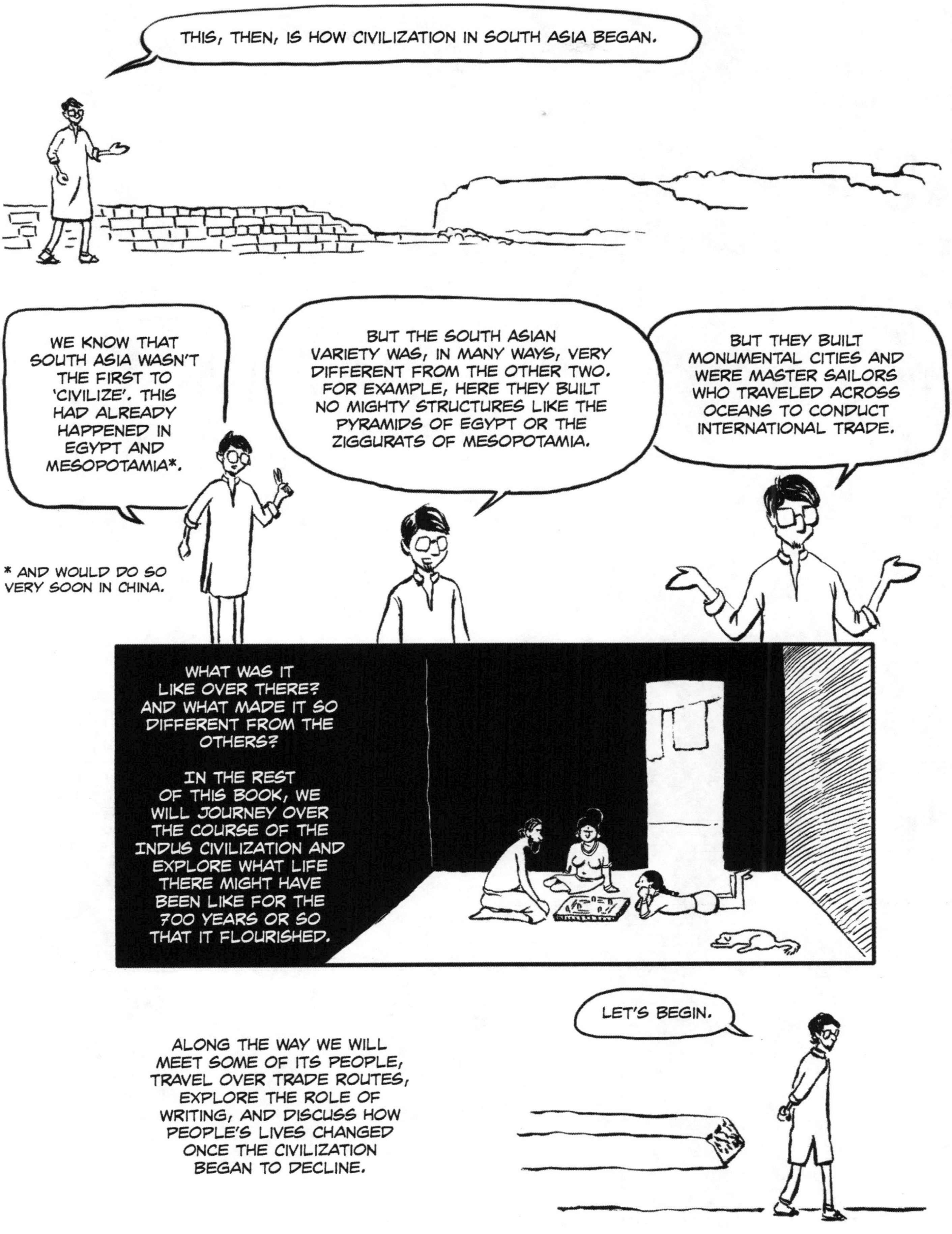
THIS, THEN, IS HOW CIVILIZATION IN SOUTH ASIA BEGAN.
WE KNOW THAT SOUTH ASIA WASN'T THE FIRST TO 'CIVILIZE'. THIS HAD ALREADY HAPPENED IN EGYPT AND MESOPOTAMIA*.
* AND WOULD DO SO VERY SOON IN CHINA.
BUT THE SOUTH ASIAN VARIETY WAS, IN MANY WAYS, VERY DIFFERENT FROM THE OTHER TWO. FOR EXAMPLE, HERE THEY BUILT NO MIGHTY STRUCTURES LIKE THE PYRAMIDS OF EGYPT OR THE ZIGGURATS OF MESOPOTAMIA.
BUT THEY BUILT MONUMENTAL CITIES AND WERE MASTER SAILORS WHO TRAVELED ACROSS OCEANS TO CONDUCT INTERNATIONAL TRADE.
WHAT WAS IT LIKE OVER THERE? AND WHAT MADE IT SO DIFFERENT FROM THE OTHERS?
IN THE REST OF THIS BOOK, WE WILL JOURNEY OVER THE COURSE OF THE INDUS CIVILIZATION AND EXPLORE WHAT LIFE THERE MIGHT HAVE BEEN LIKE FOR THE 700 YEARS OR SO THAT IT FLOURISHED.
ALONG THE WAY WE WILL MEET SOME OF ITS PEOPLE, TRAVEL OVER TRADE ROUTES, EXPLORE THE ROLE OF WRITING, AND DISCUSS HOW PEOPLE'S LIVES CHANGED ONCE THE CIVILIZATION BEGAN TO DECLINE.
LET'S BEGIN.

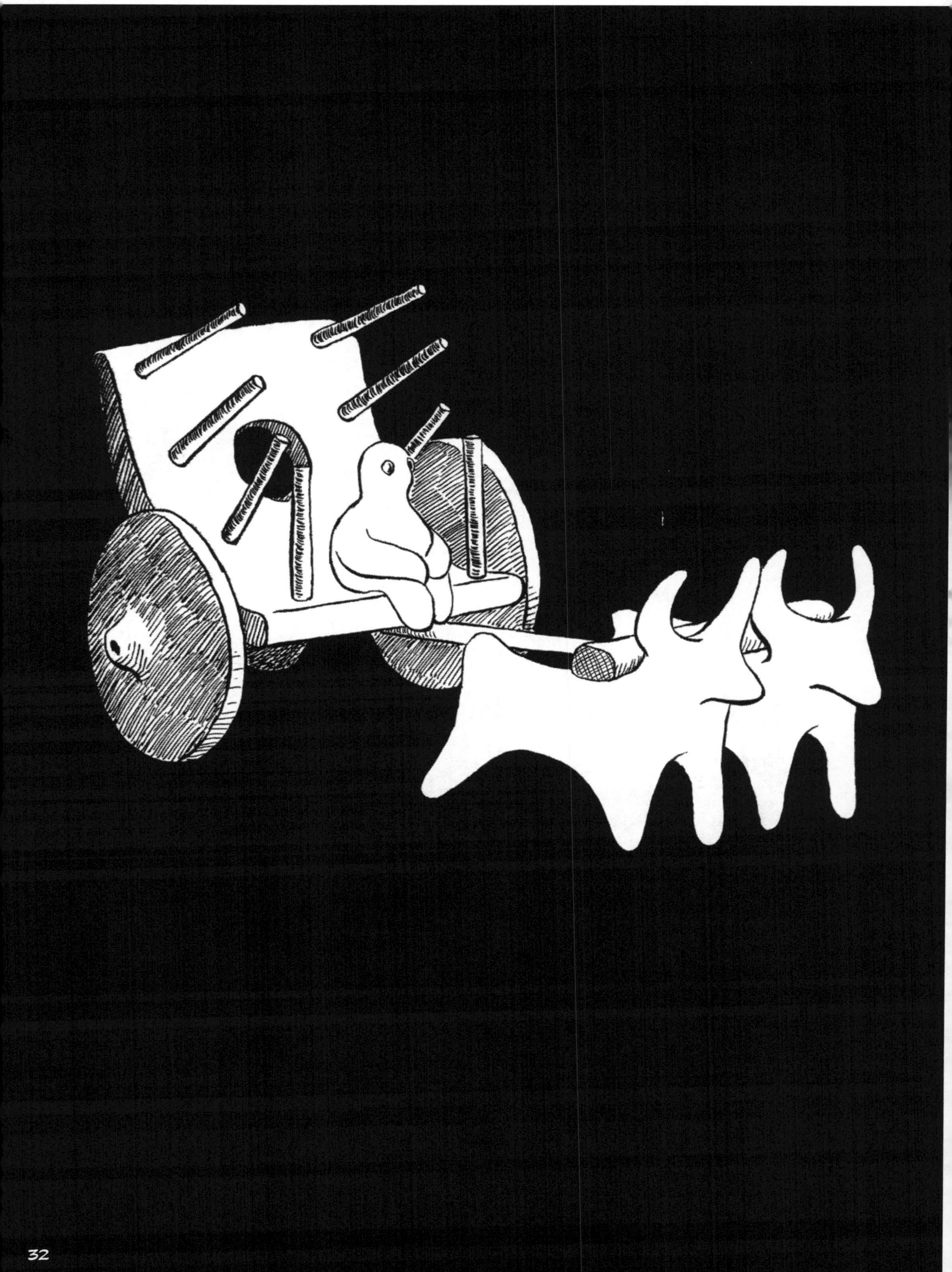

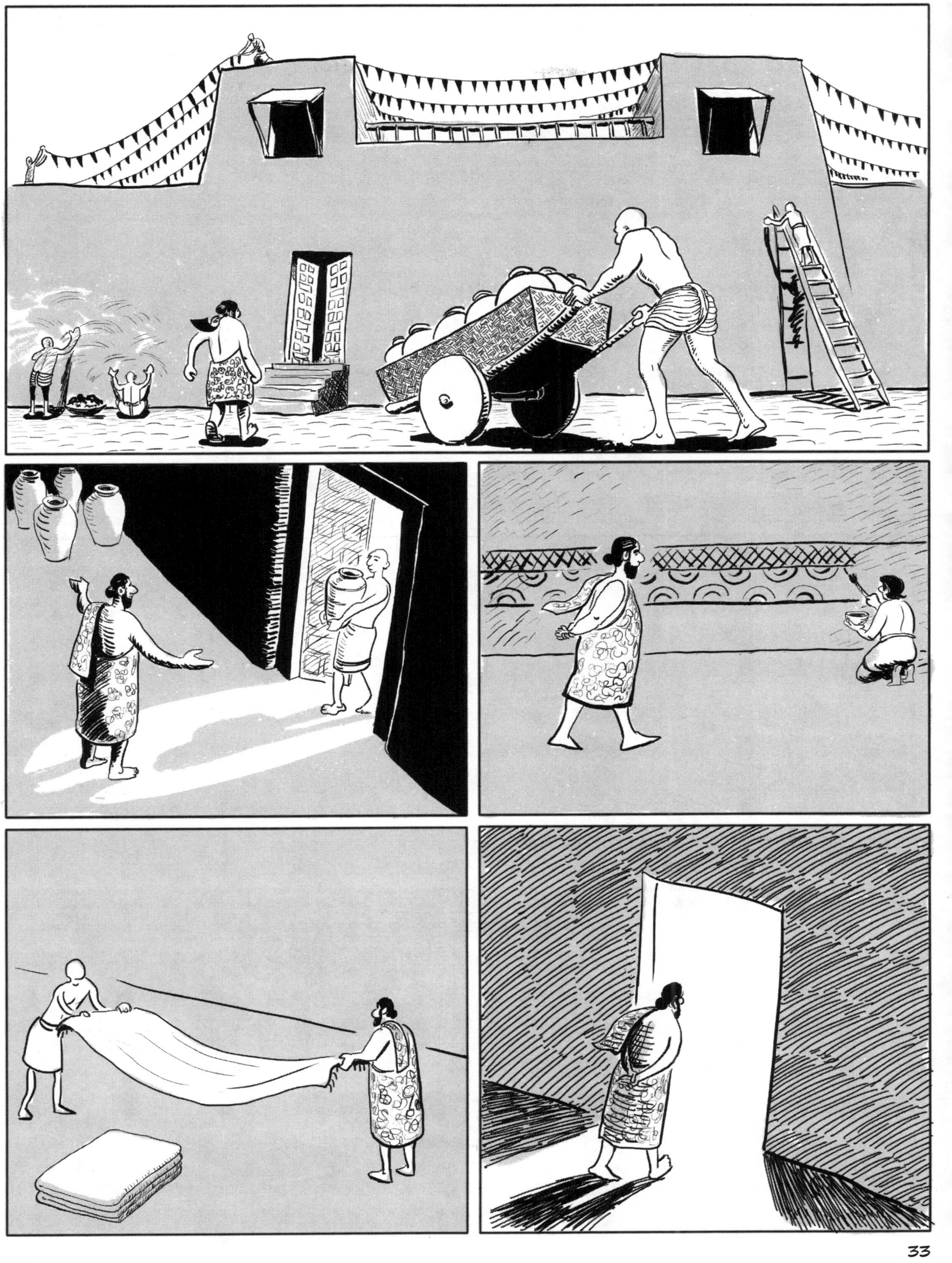

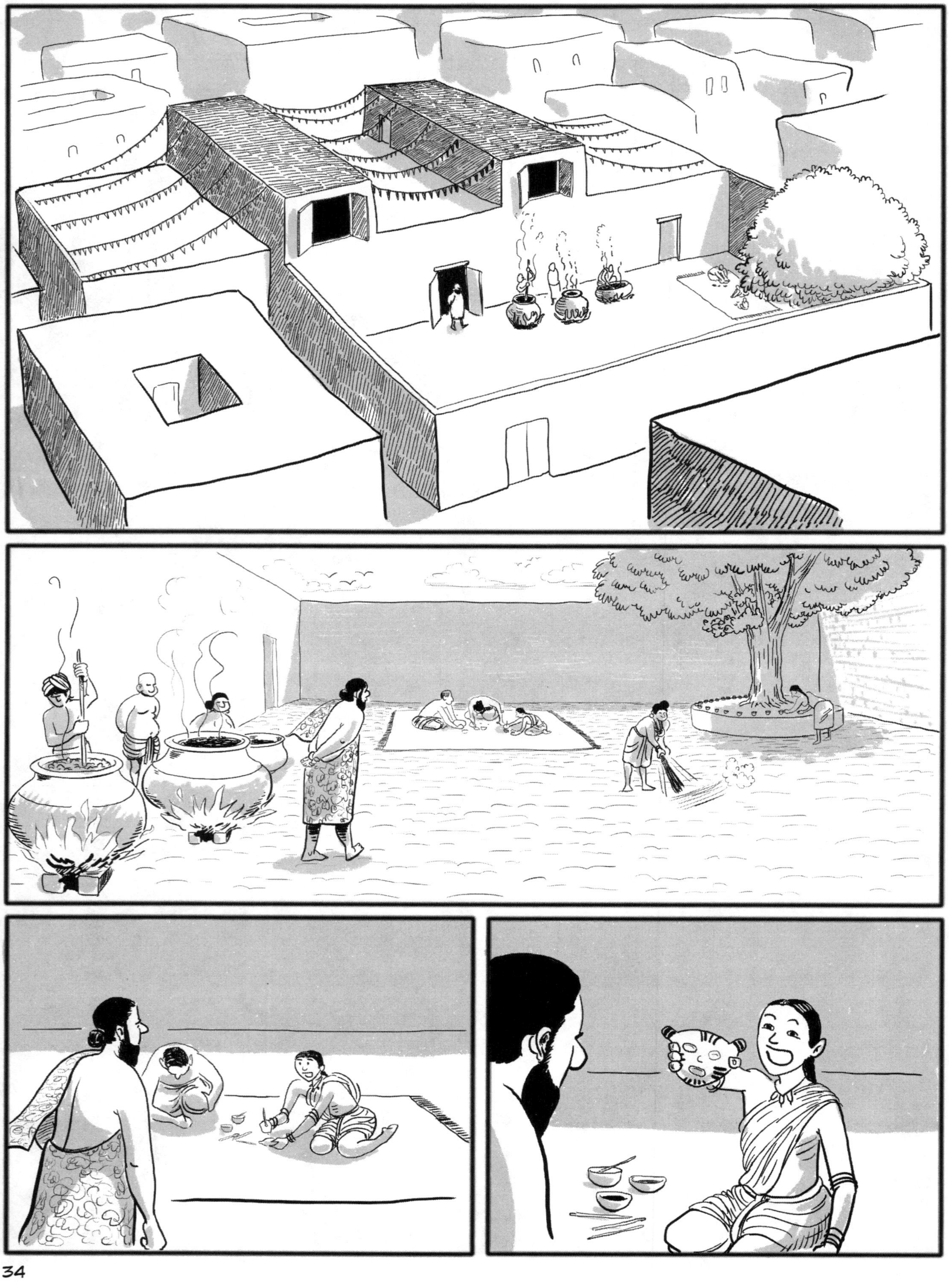

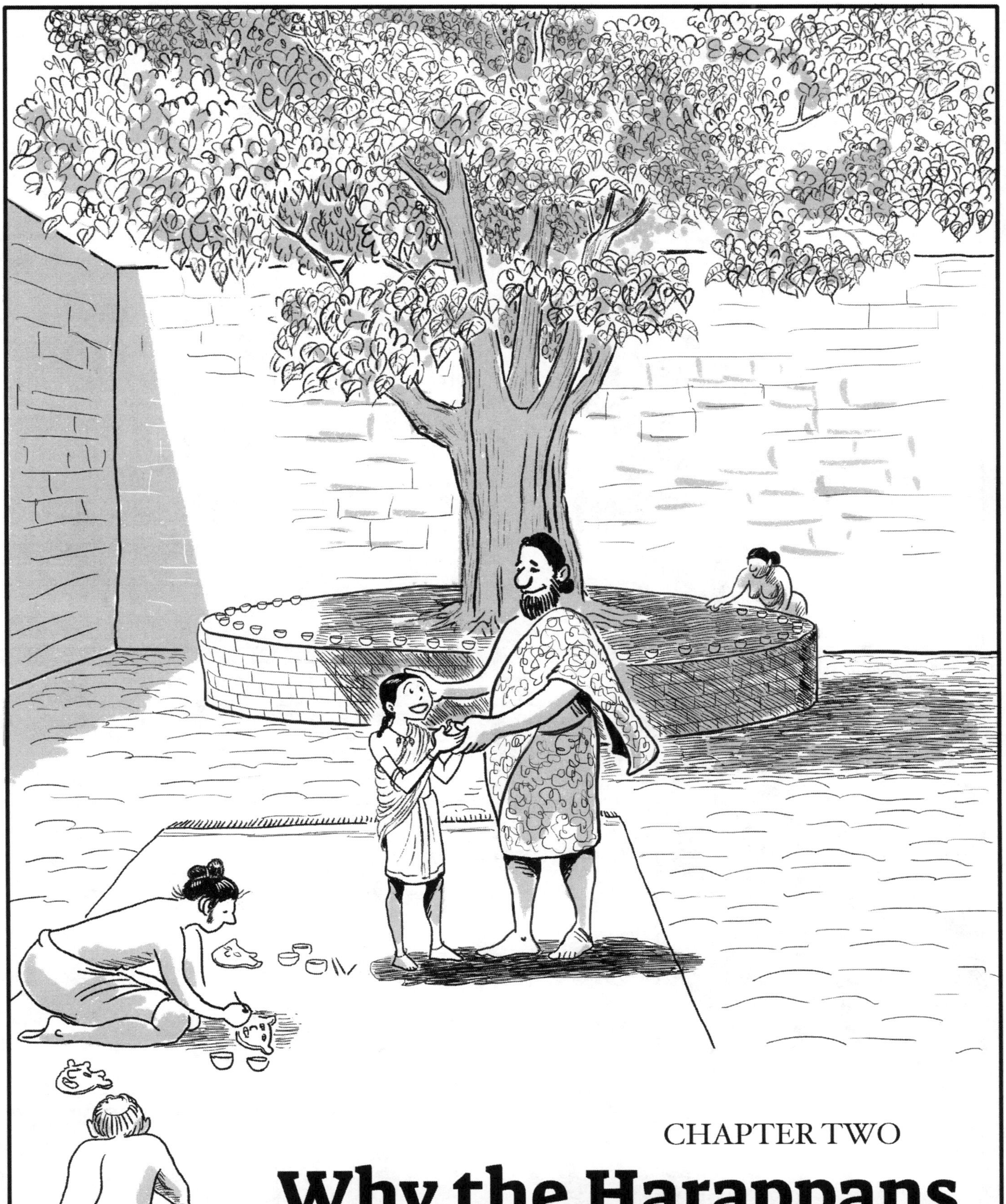

CHAPTER TWO

Why the Harappans Never Built Pyramids

CONSIDER THIS.

WE EVOLVED AS A SPECIES TO SURVIVE THROUGH COOPERATION.

A FEW HUMANS WORKING TOGETHER COULD ACCOMPLISH THINGS NO INDIVIDUAL COULD.

WORKING WITHIN A GROUP REQUIRED THE ABILITY TO KEEP TRACK OF SOCIAL CUES LIKE WHO WAS TRUSTWORTHY AND WHO WASN'T, WHO WAS GOOD AT MAKING ARROWS, WHAT DID SO-AND-SO THINK OF ANOTHER PERSON, AND SO ON.

FOR THIS WE HAD EVOLVED AN INSTINCT.

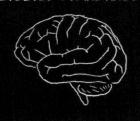

BUT THERE IS A LIMIT TO THIS INSTINCT. THE NUMBER OF PEOPLE WE CAN WORK WITH BASED ON INSTINCT ALONE IS AROUND 150. IN GROUPS BIGGER THAN THAT, THE NUMBER OF INTERRELATIONSHIPS BECOMES TOO LARGE AND THUS COOPERATION BASED ON INSTINCT ALONE GETS BEYOND OUR CAPABILITIES.

AND YET HUMANS SOMEHOW LEAPFROGGED THIS EVOLUTIONARY LIMITATION TO START LIVING IN DENSE CITIES WHERE COOPERATION WAS REQUIRED WITH TENS OF THOUSANDS OF PEOPLE.

HOW DID WE DO THIS?

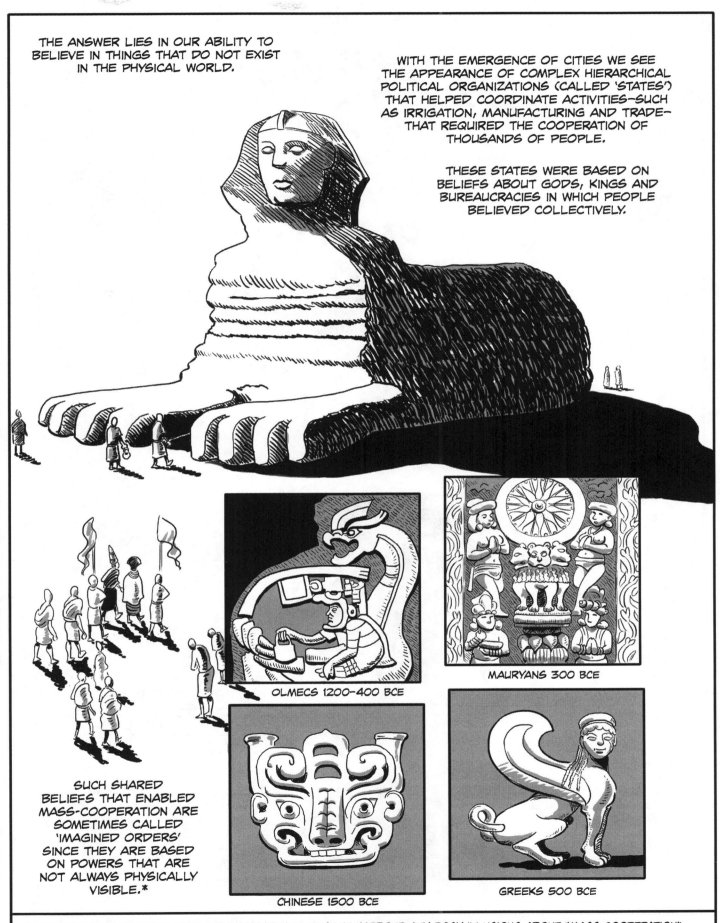

THE ANSWER LIES IN OUR ABILITY TO BELIEVE IN THINGS THAT DO NOT EXIST IN THE PHYSICAL WORLD.

WITH THE EMERGENCE OF CITIES WE SEE THE APPEARANCE OF COMPLEX HIERARCHICAL POLITICAL ORGANIZATIONS (CALLED 'STATES') THAT HELPED COORDINATE ACTIVITIES—SUCH AS IRRIGATION, MANUFACTURING AND TRADE—THAT REQUIRED THE COOPERATION OF THOUSANDS OF PEOPLE.

THESE STATES WERE BASED ON BELIEFS ABOUT GODS, KINGS AND BUREAUCRACIES IN WHICH PEOPLE BELIEVED COLLECTIVELY.

SUCH SHARED BELIEFS THAT ENABLED MASS-COOPERATION ARE SOMETIMES CALLED 'IMAGINED ORDERS' SINCE THEY ARE BASED ON POWERS THAT ARE NOT ALWAYS PHYSICALLY VISIBLE.*

OLMECS 1200–400 BCE

MAURYANS 300 BCE

CHINESE 1500 BCE

GREEKS 500 BCE

* ACCORDING TO HISTORIAN YUVAL NOAH HARARI, 'WE MUSTN'T HARBOUR ANY ROSY ILLUSIONS ABOUT "MASS COOPERATION"... COOPERATION SOUNDS VERY ALTRUISTIC BUT IT IS NOT ALWAYS VOLUNTARY AND SELDOM EGALITARIAN.'¹

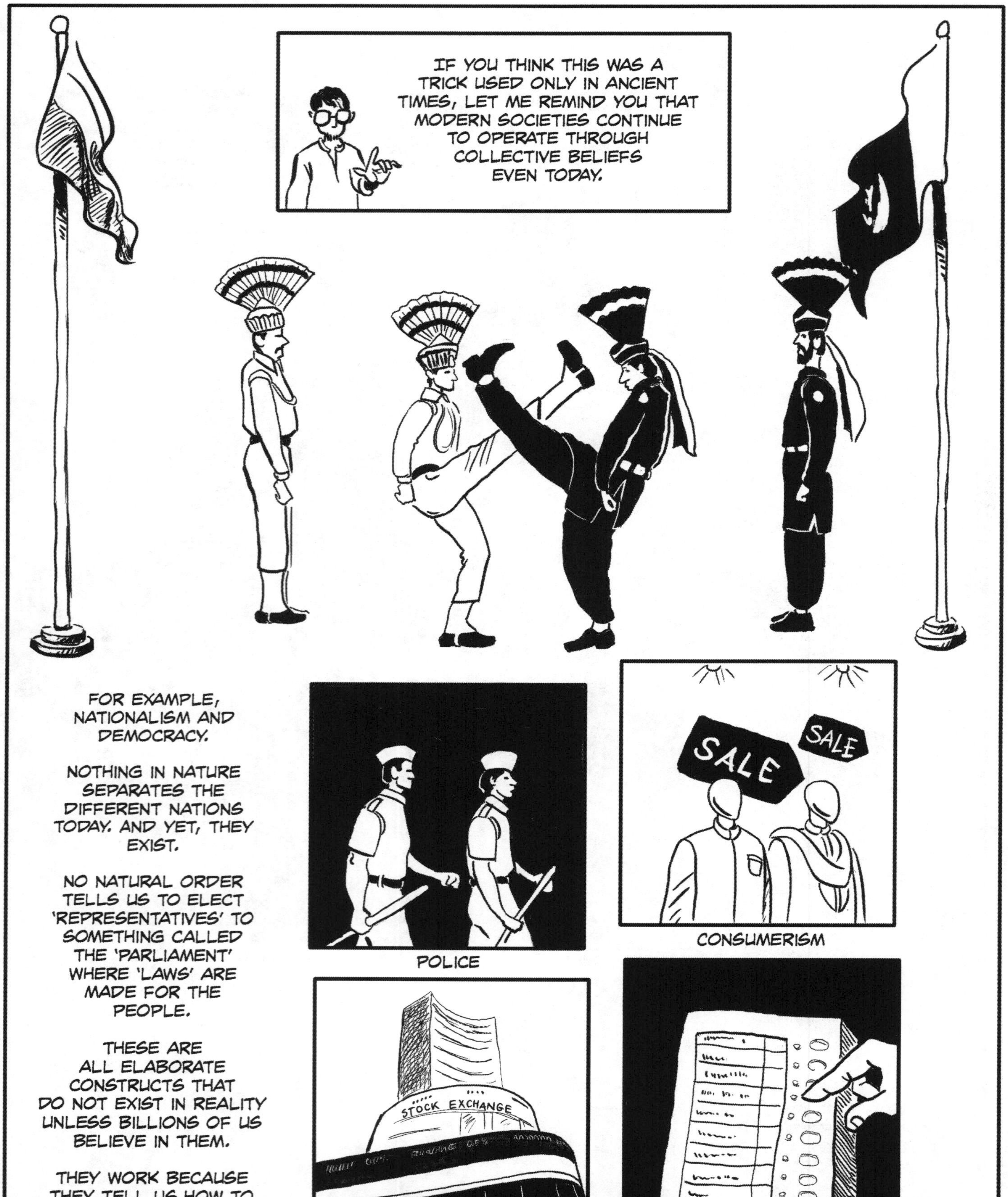
IF YOU THINK THIS WAS A TRICK USED ONLY IN ANCIENT TIMES, LET ME REMIND YOU THAT MODERN SOCIETIES CONTINUE TO OPERATE THROUGH COLLECTIVE BELIEFS EVEN TODAY.
FOR EXAMPLE, NATIONALISM AND DEMOCRACY.
NOTHING IN NATURE SEPARATES THE DIFFERENT NATIONS TODAY. AND YET, THEY EXIST.
NO NATURAL ORDER TELLS US TO ELECT 'REPRESENTATIVES' TO SOMETHING CALLED THE 'PARLIAMENT' WHERE 'LAWS' ARE MADE FOR THE PEOPLE.
THESE ARE ALL ELABORATE CONSTRUCTS THAT DO NOT EXIST IN REALITY UNLESS BILLIONS OF US BELIEVE IN THEM.
THEY WORK BECAUSE THEY TELL US HOW TO COOPERATE.
HERE ARE A FEW MORE OF THEM:
POLICE
SALE
SALE
CONSUMERISM
STOCK EXCHANGE
CAPITALISM
ELECTIONS

SINCE THEY WERE IMAGINED, DIFFERENT
ORDERS EMERGED IN DIFFERENT PLACES.

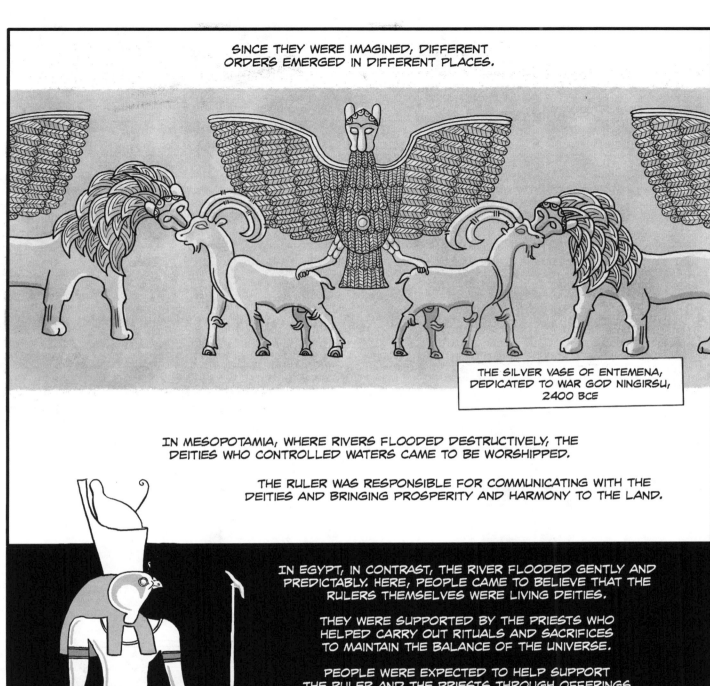

THE SILVER VASE OF ENTEMENA,
DEDICATED TO WAR GOD NINGIRSU,
2400 BCE

IN MESOPOTAMIA, WHERE RIVERS FLOODED DESTRUCTIVELY, THE
DEITIES WHO CONTROLLED WATERS CAME TO BE WORSHIPPED.

THE RULER WAS RESPONSIBLE FOR COMMUNICATING WITH THE
DEITIES AND BRINGING PROSPERITY AND HARMONY TO THE LAND.

IN EGYPT, IN CONTRAST, THE RIVER FLOODED GENTLY AND
PREDICTABLY. HERE, PEOPLE CAME TO BELIEVE THAT THE
RULERS THEMSELVES WERE LIVING DEITIES.

THEY WERE SUPPORTED BY THE PRIESTS WHO
HELPED CARRY OUT RITUALS AND SACRIFICES
TO MAINTAIN THE BALANCE OF THE UNIVERSE.

PEOPLE WERE EXPECTED TO HELP SUPPORT
THE RULER AND THE PRIESTS THROUGH OFFERINGS
OF GOODS AND LABOUR.

HORUS
200 BCE

SAHURE, A PHARAOH
2500 BCE

39

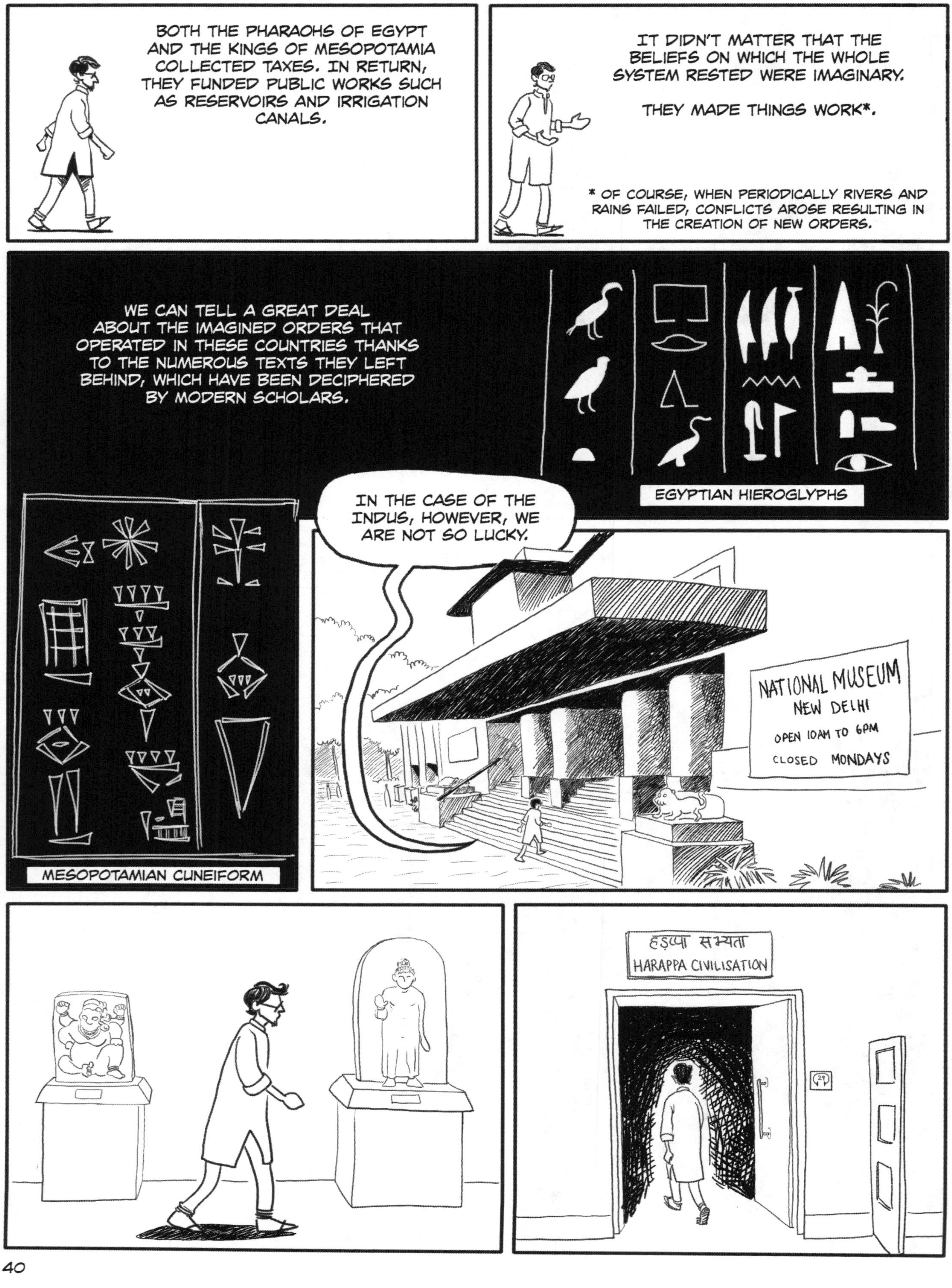
BOTH THE PHARAOHS OF EGYPT AND THE KINGS OF MESOPOTAMIA COLLECTED TAXES. IN RETURN, THEY FUNDED PUBLIC WORKS SUCH AS RESERVOIRS AND IRRIGATION CANALS.
IT DIDN'T MATTER THAT THE BELIEFS ON WHICH THE WHOLE SYSTEM RESTED WERE IMAGINARY.
THEY MADE THINGS WORK*.
* OF COURSE, WHEN PERIODICALLY RIVERS AND RAINS FAILED, CONFLICTS AROSE RESULTING IN THE CREATION OF NEW ORDERS.
WE CAN TELL A GREAT DEAL ABOUT THE IMAGINED ORDERS THAT OPERATED IN THESE COUNTRIES THANKS TO THE NUMEROUS TEXTS THEY LEFT BEHIND, WHICH HAVE BEEN DECIPHERED BY MODERN SCHOLARS.
EGYPTIAN HIEROGLYPHS
MESOPOTAMIAN CUNEIFORM
IN THE CASE OF THE INDUS, HOWEVER, WE ARE NOT SO LUCKY.
NATIONAL MUSEUM
NEW DELHI
OPEN 10AM TO 6PM
CLOSED MONDAYS
हड़प्पा सभ्यता
HARAPPA CIVILISATION

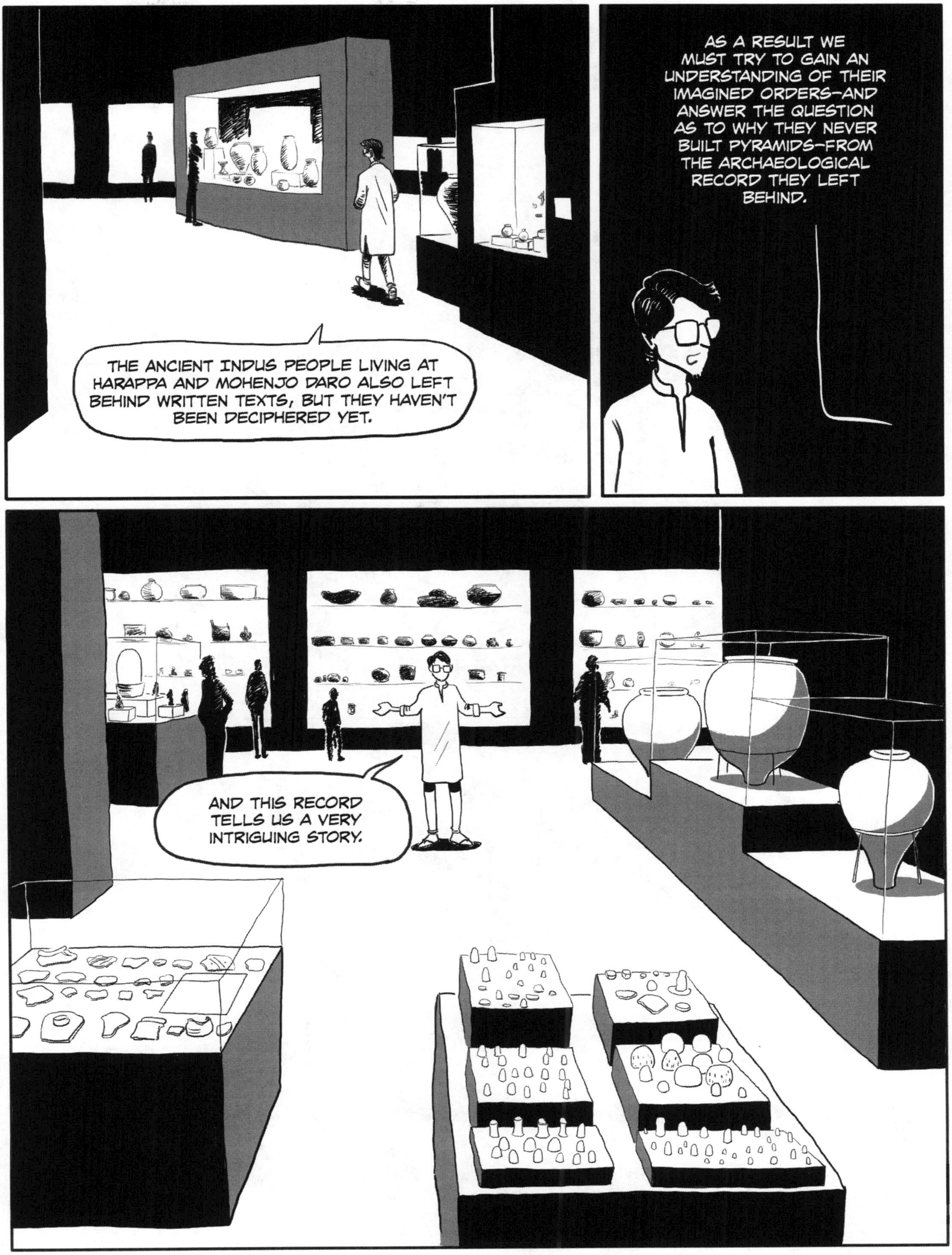
THE ANCIENT INDUS PEOPLE LIVING AT HARAPPA AND MOHENJO DARO ALSO LEFT BEHIND WRITTEN TEXTS, BUT THEY HAVEN'T BEEN DECIPHERED YET.
AS A RESULT WE MUST TRY TO GAIN AN UNDERSTANDING OF THEIR IMAGINED ORDERS—AND ANSWER THE QUESTION AS TO WHY THEY NEVER BUILT PYRAMIDS—FROM THE ARCHAEOLOGICAL RECORD THEY LEFT BEHIND.
AND THIS RECORD TELLS US A VERY INTRIGUING STORY.

IN INDUS ARCHAEOLOGY, THREE
THINGS STAND OUT:

1) DECENTRALIZED POWER

THIS IS THE PLAN OF THE
MESOPOTAMIAN CITY OF **UR.**

NOTE THE WALLED COMPLEX—
THE SEAT OF AUTHORITY—IN THE
MIDDLE OF THE CITY.

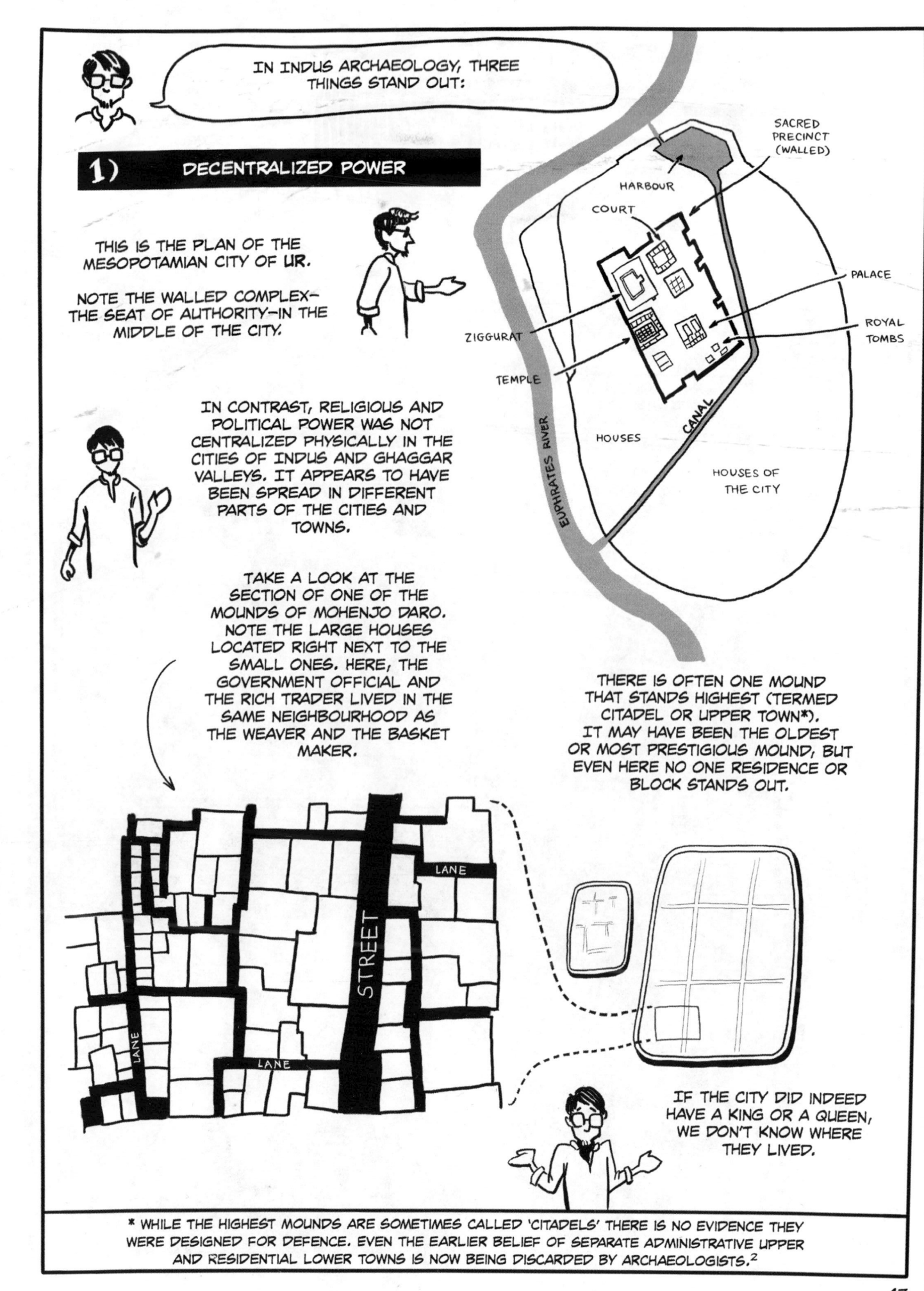

SACRED
PRECINCT
(WALLED)

HARBOUR

COURT

ZIGGURAT

TEMPLE

PALACE

ROYAL
TOMBS

HOUSES

EUPHRATES RIVER

CANAL

HOUSES OF
THE CITY

IN CONTRAST, RELIGIOUS AND
POLITICAL POWER WAS NOT
CENTRALIZED PHYSICALLY IN THE
CITIES OF INDUS AND GHAGGAR
VALLEYS. IT APPEARS TO HAVE
BEEN SPREAD IN DIFFERENT
PARTS OF THE CITIES AND
TOWNS.

TAKE A LOOK AT THE
SECTION OF ONE OF THE
MOUNDS OF MOHENJO DARO.
NOTE THE LARGE HOUSES
LOCATED RIGHT NEXT TO THE
SMALL ONES. HERE, THE
GOVERNMENT OFFICIAL AND
THE RICH TRADER LIVED IN THE
SAME NEIGHBOURHOOD AS
THE WEAVER AND THE BASKET
MAKER.

THERE IS OFTEN ONE MOUND
THAT STANDS HIGHEST (TERMED
CITADEL OR UPPER TOWN*).
IT MAY HAVE BEEN THE OLDEST
OR MOST PRESTIGIOUS MOUND, BUT
EVEN HERE NO ONE RESIDENCE OR
BLOCK STANDS OUT.

LANE

STREET

LANE

LANE

IF THE CITY DID INDEED
HAVE A KING OR A QUEEN,
WE DON'T KNOW WHERE
THEY LIVED.

* WHILE THE HIGHEST MOUNDS ARE SOMETIMES CALLED 'CITADELS' THERE IS NO EVIDENCE THEY
WERE DESIGNED FOR DEFENCE. EVEN THE EARLIER BELIEF OF SEPARATE ADMINISTRATIVE UPPER
AND RESIDENTIAL LOWER TOWNS IS NOW BEING DISCARDED BY ARCHAEOLOGISTS.[2]

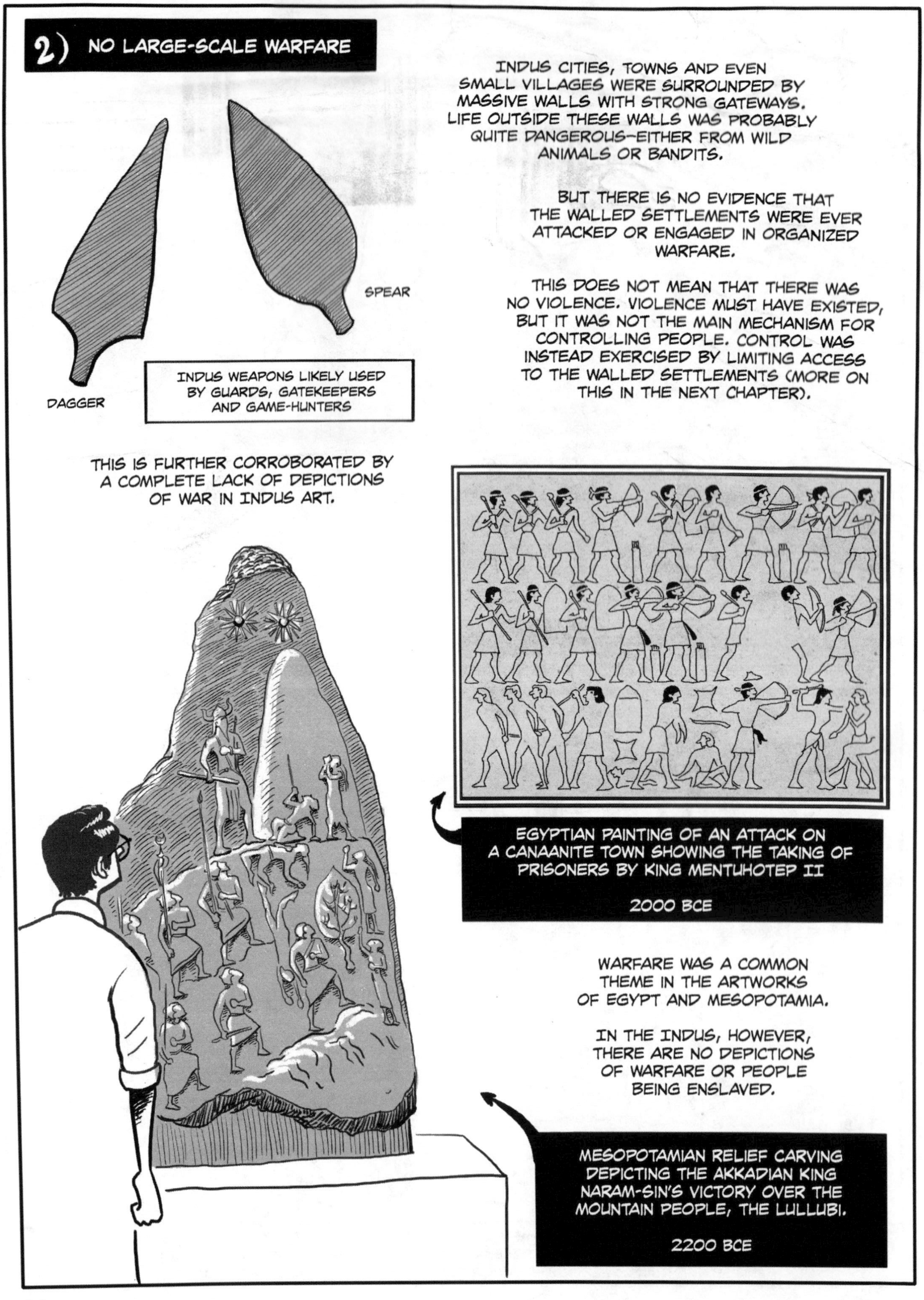
2) NO LARGE-SCALE WARFARE
INDUS CITIES, TOWNS AND EVEN SMALL VILLAGES WERE SURROUNDED BY MASSIVE WALLS WITH STRONG GATEWAYS. LIFE OUTSIDE THESE WALLS WAS PROBABLY QUITE DANGEROUS—EITHER FROM WILD ANIMALS OR BANDITS.
BUT THERE IS NO EVIDENCE THAT THE WALLED SETTLEMENTS WERE EVER ATTACKED OR ENGAGED IN ORGANIZED WARFARE.
THIS DOES NOT MEAN THAT THERE WAS NO VIOLENCE. VIOLENCE MUST HAVE EXISTED, BUT IT WAS NOT THE MAIN MECHANISM FOR CONTROLLING PEOPLE. CONTROL WAS INSTEAD EXERCISED BY LIMITING ACCESS TO THE WALLED SETTLEMENTS (MORE ON THIS IN THE NEXT CHAPTER).
SPEAR
DAGGER
INDUS WEAPONS LIKELY USED BY GUARDS, GATEKEEPERS AND GAME-HUNTERS
THIS IS FURTHER CORROBORATED BY A COMPLETE LACK OF DEPICTIONS OF WAR IN INDUS ART.
EGYPTIAN PAINTING OF AN ATTACK ON A CANAANITE TOWN SHOWING THE TAKING OF PRISONERS BY KING MENTUHOTEP II
2000 BCE
WARFARE WAS A COMMON THEME IN THE ARTWORKS OF EGYPT AND MESOPOTAMIA.
IN THE INDUS, HOWEVER, THERE ARE NO DEPICTIONS OF WARFARE OR PEOPLE BEING ENSLAVED.
MESOPOTAMIAN RELIEF CARVING DEPICTING THE AKKADIAN KING NARAM-SIN'S VICTORY OVER THE MOUNTAIN PEOPLE, THE LULLUBI.
2200 BCE

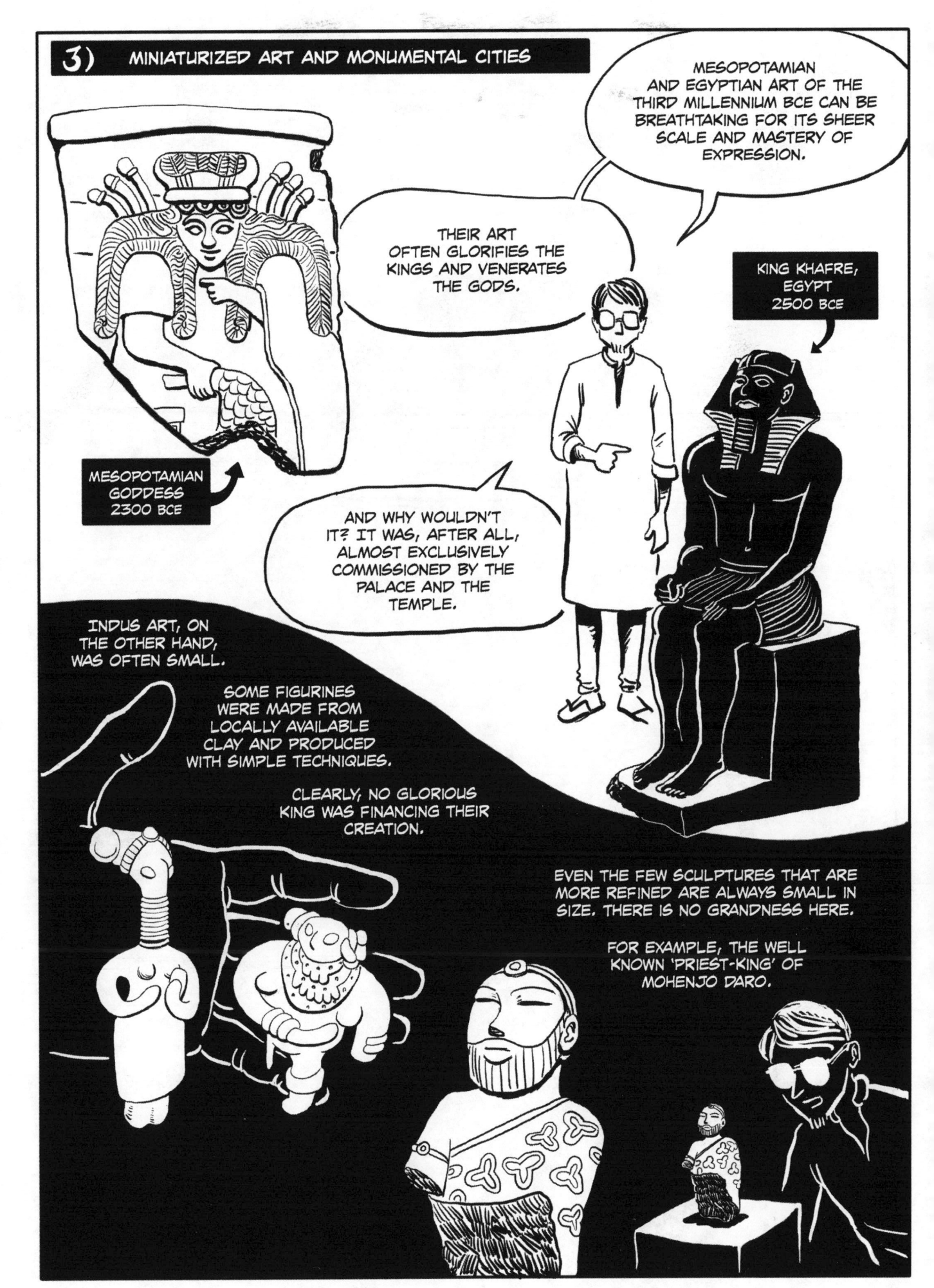

3) MINIATURIZED ART AND MONUMENTAL CITIES

MESOPOTAMIAN AND EGYPTIAN ART OF THE THIRD MILLENNIUM BCE CAN BE BREATHTAKING FOR ITS SHEER SCALE AND MASTERY OF EXPRESSION.

THEIR ART OFTEN GLORIFIES THE KINGS AND VENERATES THE GODS.

KING KHAFRE, EGYPT 2500 BCE

MESOPOTAMIAN GODDESS 2300 BCE

AND WHY WOULDN'T IT? IT WAS, AFTER ALL, ALMOST EXCLUSIVELY COMMISSIONED BY THE PALACE AND THE TEMPLE.

INDUS ART, ON THE OTHER HAND, WAS OFTEN SMALL.

SOME FIGURINES WERE MADE FROM LOCALLY AVAILABLE CLAY AND PRODUCED WITH SIMPLE TECHNIQUES.

CLEARLY, NO GLORIOUS KING WAS FINANCING THEIR CREATION.

EVEN THE FEW SCULPTURES THAT ARE MORE REFINED ARE ALWAYS SMALL IN SIZE. THERE IS NO GRANDNESS HERE.

FOR EXAMPLE, THE WELL KNOWN 'PRIEST-KING' OF MOHENJO DARO.

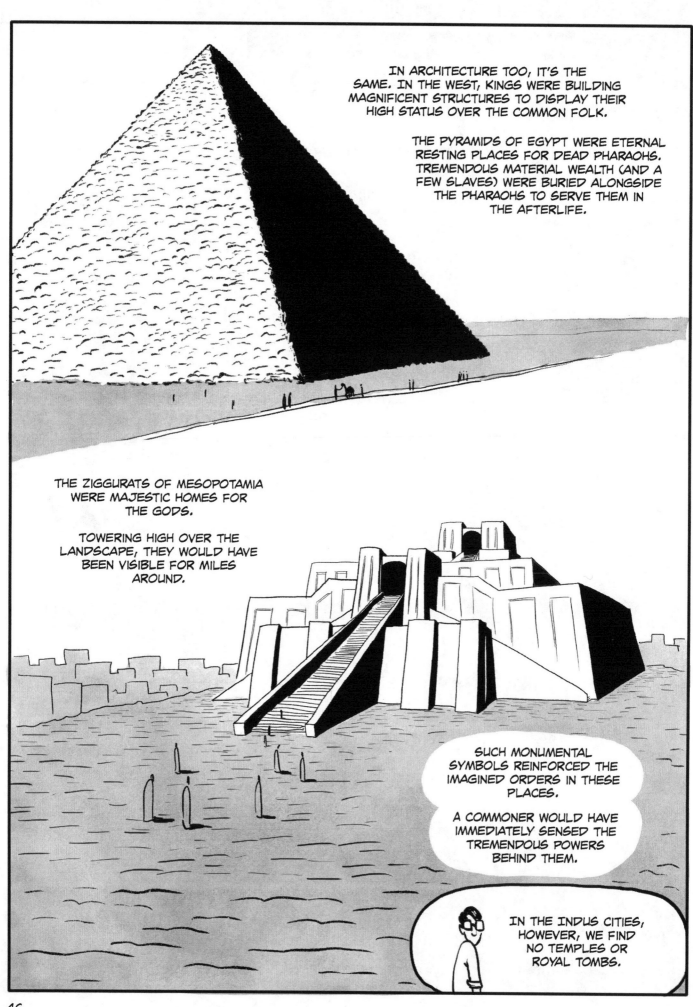

IN ARCHITECTURE TOO, IT'S THE SAME. IN THE WEST, KINGS WERE BUILDING MAGNIFICENT STRUCTURES TO DISPLAY THEIR HIGH STATUS OVER THE COMMON FOLK.

THE PYRAMIDS OF EGYPT WERE ETERNAL RESTING PLACES FOR DEAD PHARAOHS. TREMENDOUS MATERIAL WEALTH (AND A FEW SLAVES) WERE BURIED ALONGSIDE THE PHARAOHS TO SERVE THEM IN THE AFTERLIFE.

THE ZIGGURATS OF MESOPOTAMIA WERE MAJESTIC HOMES FOR THE GODS.

TOWERING HIGH OVER THE LANDSCAPE, THEY WOULD HAVE BEEN VISIBLE FOR MILES AROUND.

SUCH MONUMENTAL SYMBOLS REINFORCED THE IMAGINED ORDERS IN THESE PLACES.

A COMMONER WOULD HAVE IMMEDIATELY SENSED THE TREMENDOUS POWERS BEHIND THEM.

IN THE INDUS CITIES, HOWEVER, WE FIND NO TEMPLES OR ROYAL TOMBS.

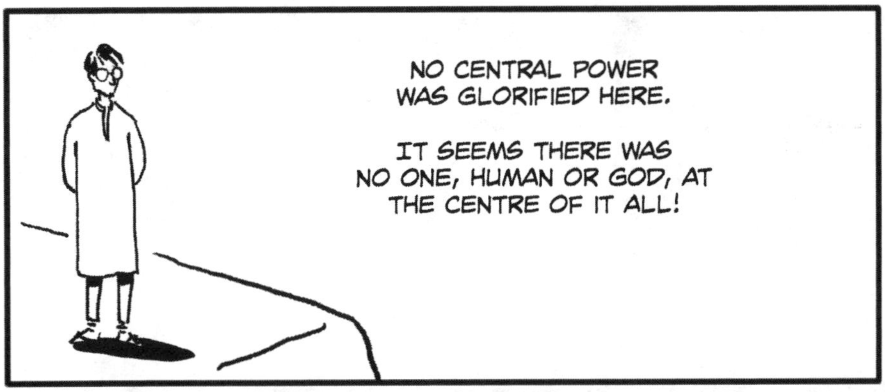
NO CENTRAL POWER WAS GLORIFIED HERE.
IT SEEMS THERE WAS NO ONE, HUMAN OR GOD, AT THE CENTRE OF IT ALL!

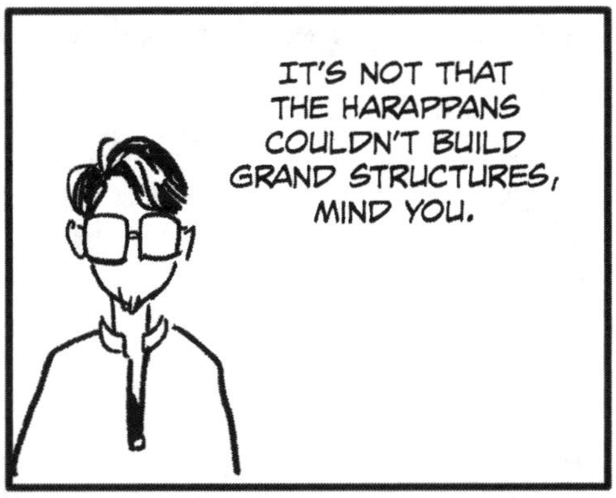
IT'S NOT THAT THE HARAPPANS COULDN'T BUILD GRAND STRUCTURES, MIND YOU.

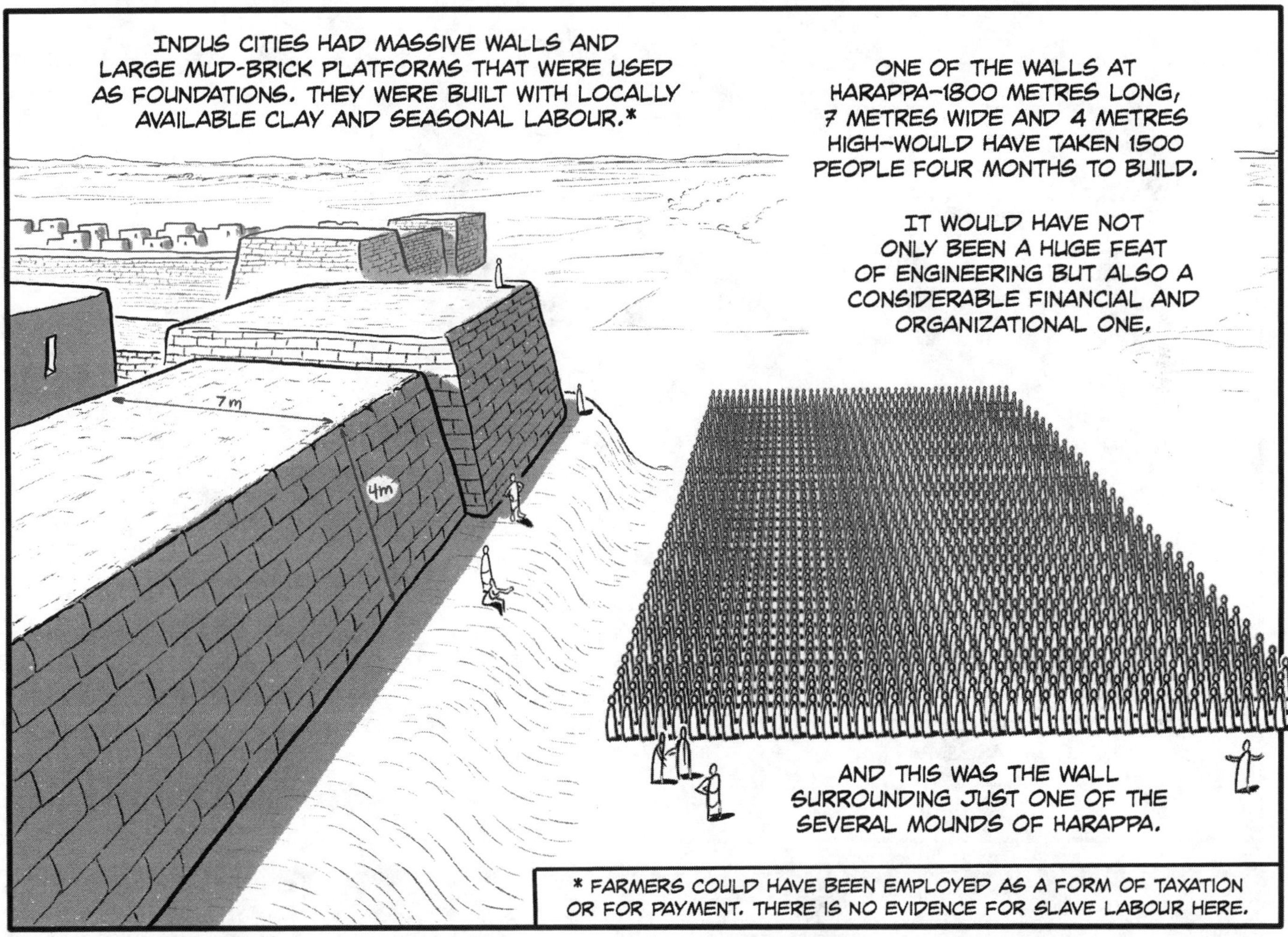
INDUS CITIES HAD MASSIVE WALLS AND LARGE MUD-BRICK PLATFORMS THAT WERE USED AS FOUNDATIONS. THEY WERE BUILT WITH LOCALLY AVAILABLE CLAY AND SEASONAL LABOUR.*
ONE OF THE WALLS AT HARAPPA–1800 METRES LONG, 7 METRES WIDE AND 4 METRES HIGH–WOULD HAVE TAKEN 1500 PEOPLE FOUR MONTHS TO BUILD.
IT WOULD HAVE NOT ONLY BEEN A HUGE FEAT OF ENGINEERING BUT ALSO A CONSIDERABLE FINANCIAL AND ORGANIZATIONAL ONE.
7m
4m
AND THIS WAS THE WALL SURROUNDING JUST ONE OF THE SEVERAL MOUNDS OF HARAPPA.
* FARMERS COULD HAVE BEEN EMPLOYED AS A FORM OF TAXATION OR FOR PAYMENT. THERE IS NO EVIDENCE FOR SLAVE LABOUR HERE.

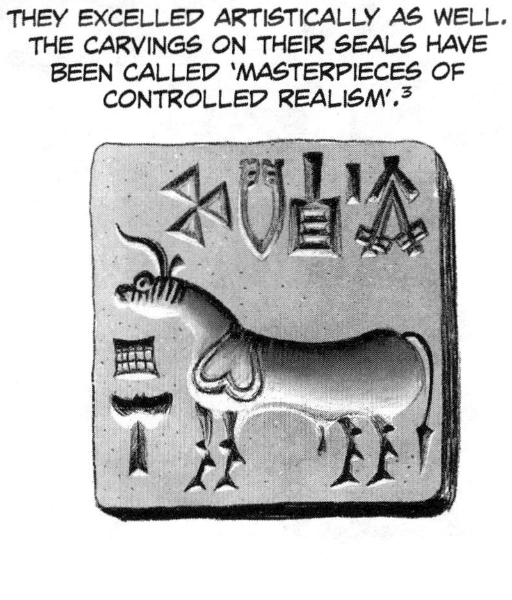
THEY EXCELLED ARTISTICALLY AS WELL. THE CARVINGS ON THEIR SEALS HAVE BEEN CALLED 'MASTERPIECES OF CONTROLLED REALISM'.[3]

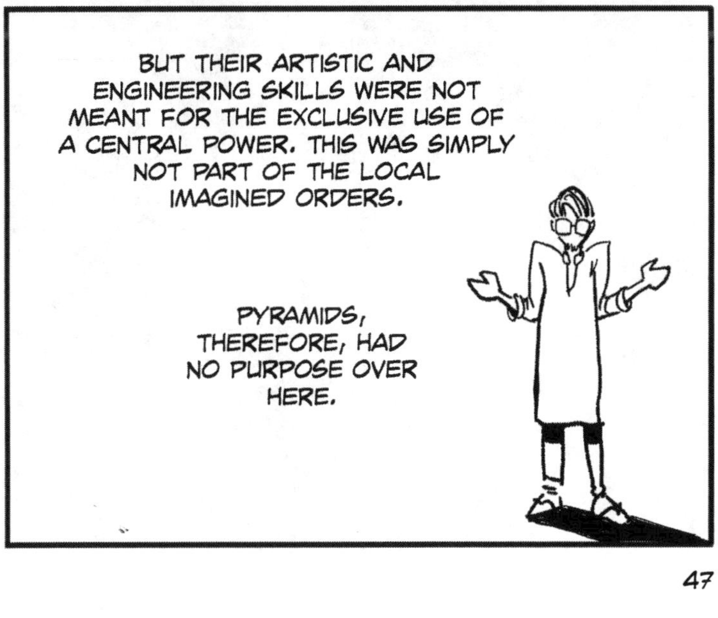
BUT THEIR ARTISTIC AND ENGINEERING SKILLS WERE NOT MEANT FOR THE EXCLUSIVE USE OF A CENTRAL POWER. THIS WAS SIMPLY NOT PART OF THE LOCAL IMAGINED ORDERS.
PYRAMIDS, THEREFORE, HAD NO PURPOSE OVER HERE.

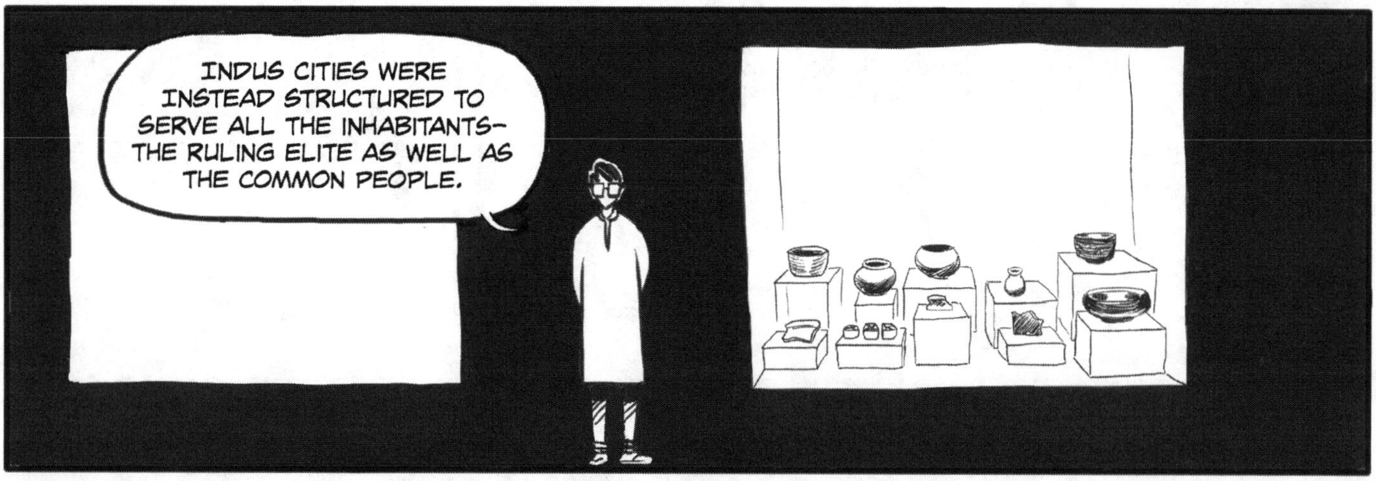
INDUS CITIES WERE INSTEAD STRUCTURED TO SERVE ALL THE INHABITANTS—THE RULING ELITE AS WELL AS THE COMMON PEOPLE.

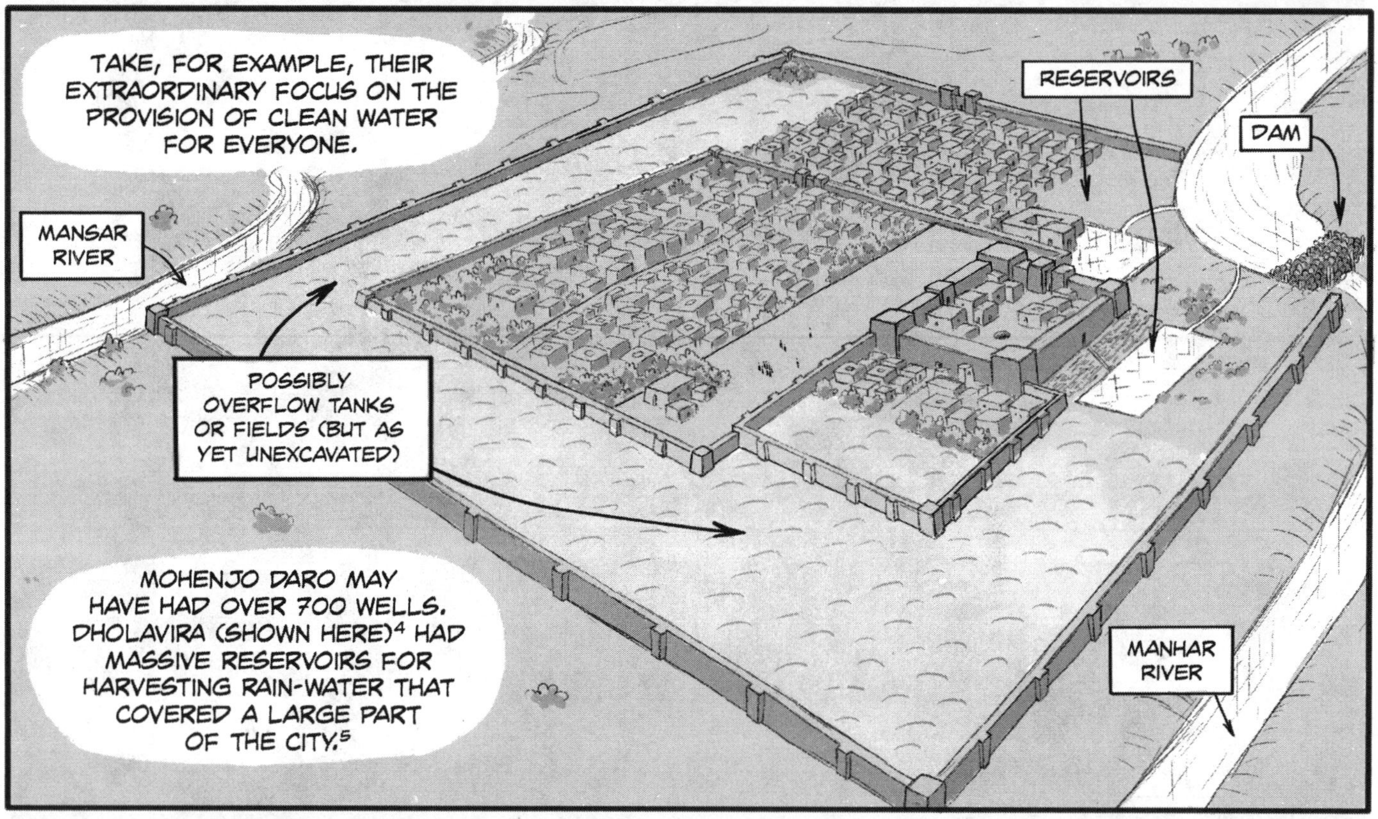
TAKE, FOR EXAMPLE, THEIR EXTRAORDINARY FOCUS ON THE PROVISION OF CLEAN WATER FOR EVERYONE.
RESERVOIRS
DAM
MANSAR RIVER
POSSIBLY OVERFLOW TANKS OR FIELDS (BUT AS YET UNEXCAVATED)
MOHENJO DARO MAY HAVE HAD OVER 700 WELLS. DHOLAVIRA (SHOWN HERE)[4] HAD MASSIVE RESERVOIRS FOR HARVESTING RAIN-WATER THAT COVERED A LARGE PART OF THE CITY.[5]
MANHAR RIVER

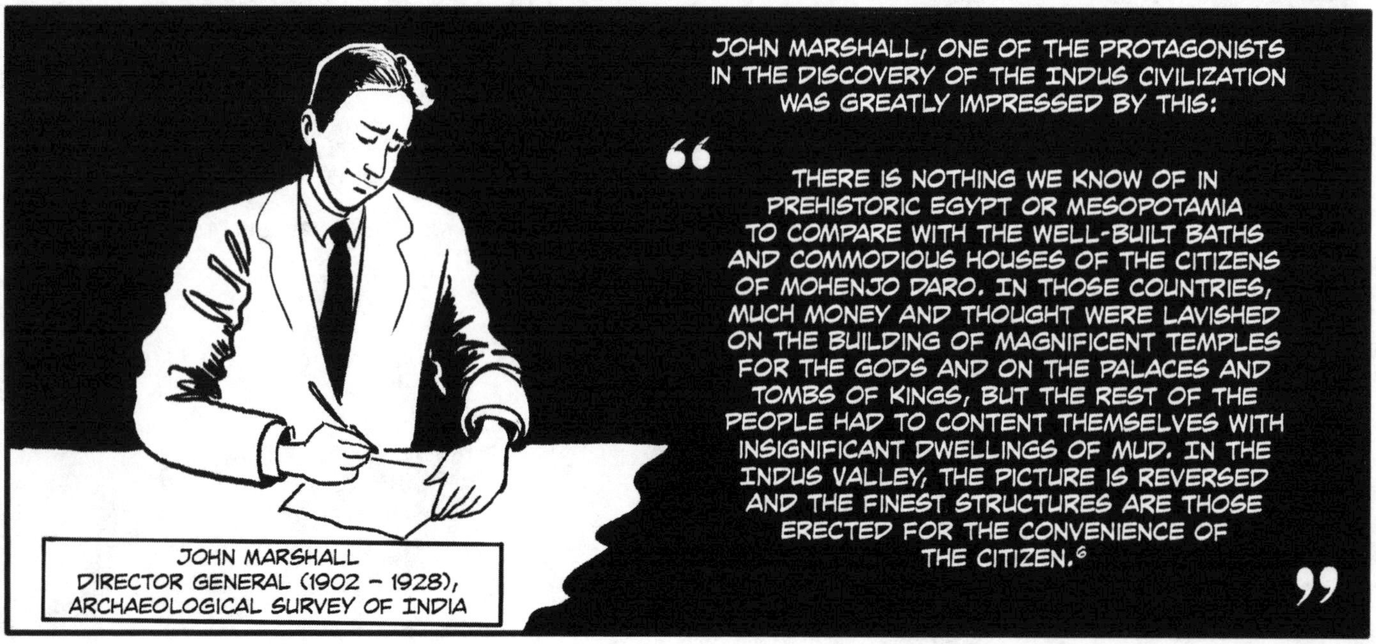
JOHN MARSHALL DIRECTOR GENERAL (1902 – 1928), ARCHAEOLOGICAL SURVEY OF INDIA
JOHN MARSHALL, ONE OF THE PROTAGONISTS IN THE DISCOVERY OF THE INDUS CIVILIZATION WAS GREATLY IMPRESSED BY THIS:
“THERE IS NOTHING WE KNOW OF IN PREHISTORIC EGYPT OR MESOPOTAMIA TO COMPARE WITH THE WELL-BUILT BATHS AND COMMODIOUS HOUSES OF THE CITIZENS OF MOHENJO DARO. IN THOSE COUNTRIES, MUCH MONEY AND THOUGHT WERE LAVISHED ON THE BUILDING OF MAGNIFICENT TEMPLES FOR THE GODS AND ON THE PALACES AND TOMBS OF KINGS, BUT THE REST OF THE PEOPLE HAD TO CONTENT THEMSELVES WITH INSIGNIFICANT DWELLINGS OF MUD. IN THE INDUS VALLEY, THE PICTURE IS REVERSED AND THE FINEST STRUCTURES ARE THOSE ERECTED FOR THE CONVENIENCE OF THE CITIZEN.[6]”

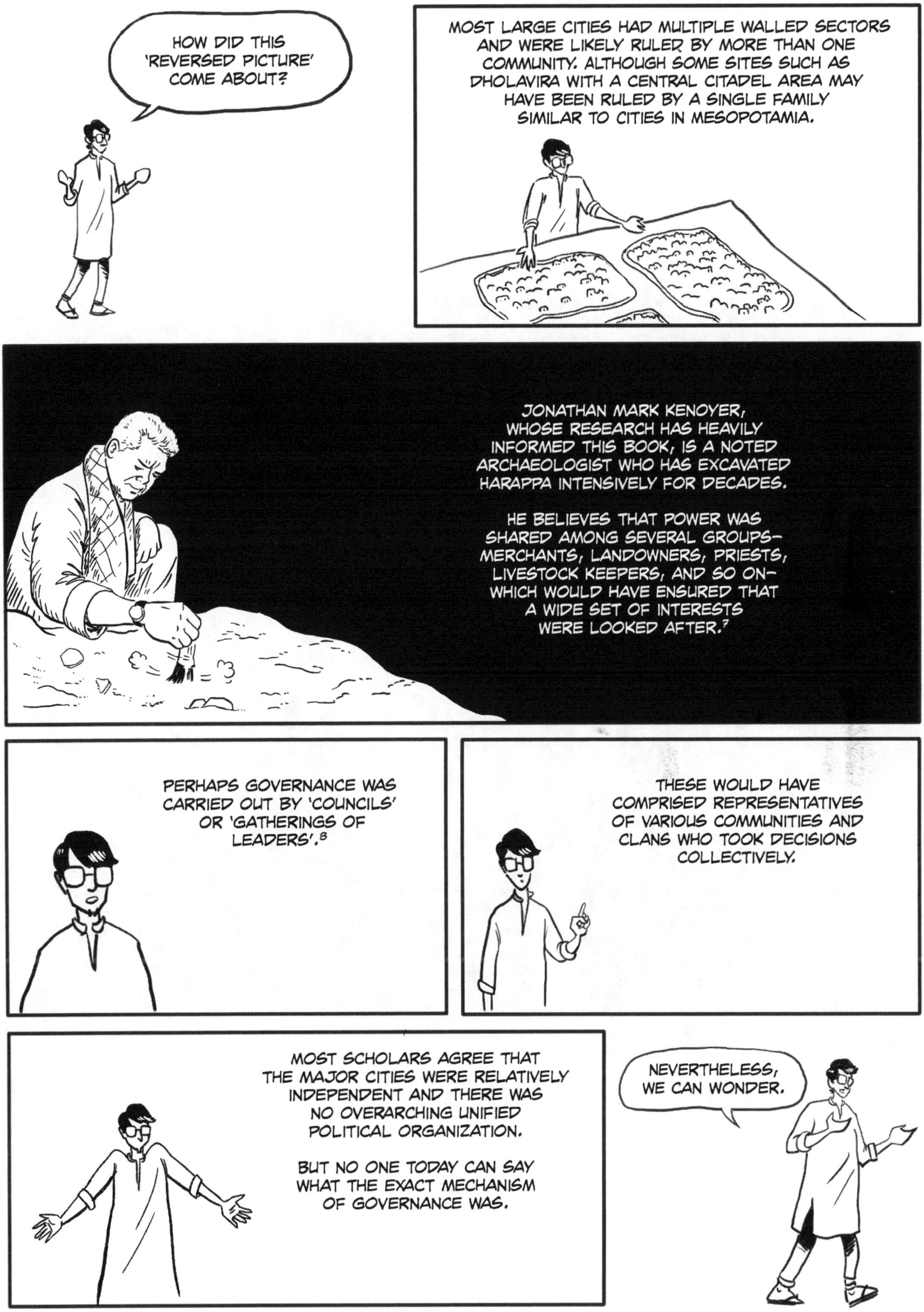
HOW DID THIS 'REVERSED PICTURE' COME ABOUT?
MOST LARGE CITIES HAD MULTIPLE WALLED SECTORS AND WERE LIKELY RULED BY MORE THAN ONE COMMUNITY. ALTHOUGH SOME SITES SUCH AS DHOLAVIRA WITH A CENTRAL CITADEL AREA MAY HAVE BEEN RULED BY A SINGLE FAMILY SIMILAR TO CITIES IN MESOPOTAMIA.
JONATHAN MARK KENOYER, WHOSE RESEARCH HAS HEAVILY INFORMED THIS BOOK, IS A NOTED ARCHAEOLOGIST WHO HAS EXCAVATED HARAPPA INTENSIVELY FOR DECADES.
HE BELIEVES THAT POWER WAS SHARED AMONG SEVERAL GROUPS–MERCHANTS, LANDOWNERS, PRIESTS, LIVESTOCK KEEPERS, AND SO ON–WHICH WOULD HAVE ENSURED THAT A WIDE SET OF INTERESTS WERE LOOKED AFTER.[7]
PERHAPS GOVERNANCE WAS CARRIED OUT BY 'COUNCILS' OR 'GATHERINGS OF LEADERS'.[8]
THESE WOULD HAVE COMPRISED REPRESENTATIVES OF VARIOUS COMMUNITIES AND CLANS WHO TOOK DECISIONS COLLECTIVELY.
MOST SCHOLARS AGREE THAT THE MAJOR CITIES WERE RELATIVELY INDEPENDENT AND THERE WAS NO OVERARCHING UNIFIED POLITICAL ORGANIZATION.
BUT NO ONE TODAY CAN SAY WHAT THE EXACT MECHANISM OF GOVERNANCE WAS.
NEVERTHELESS, WE CAN WONDER.

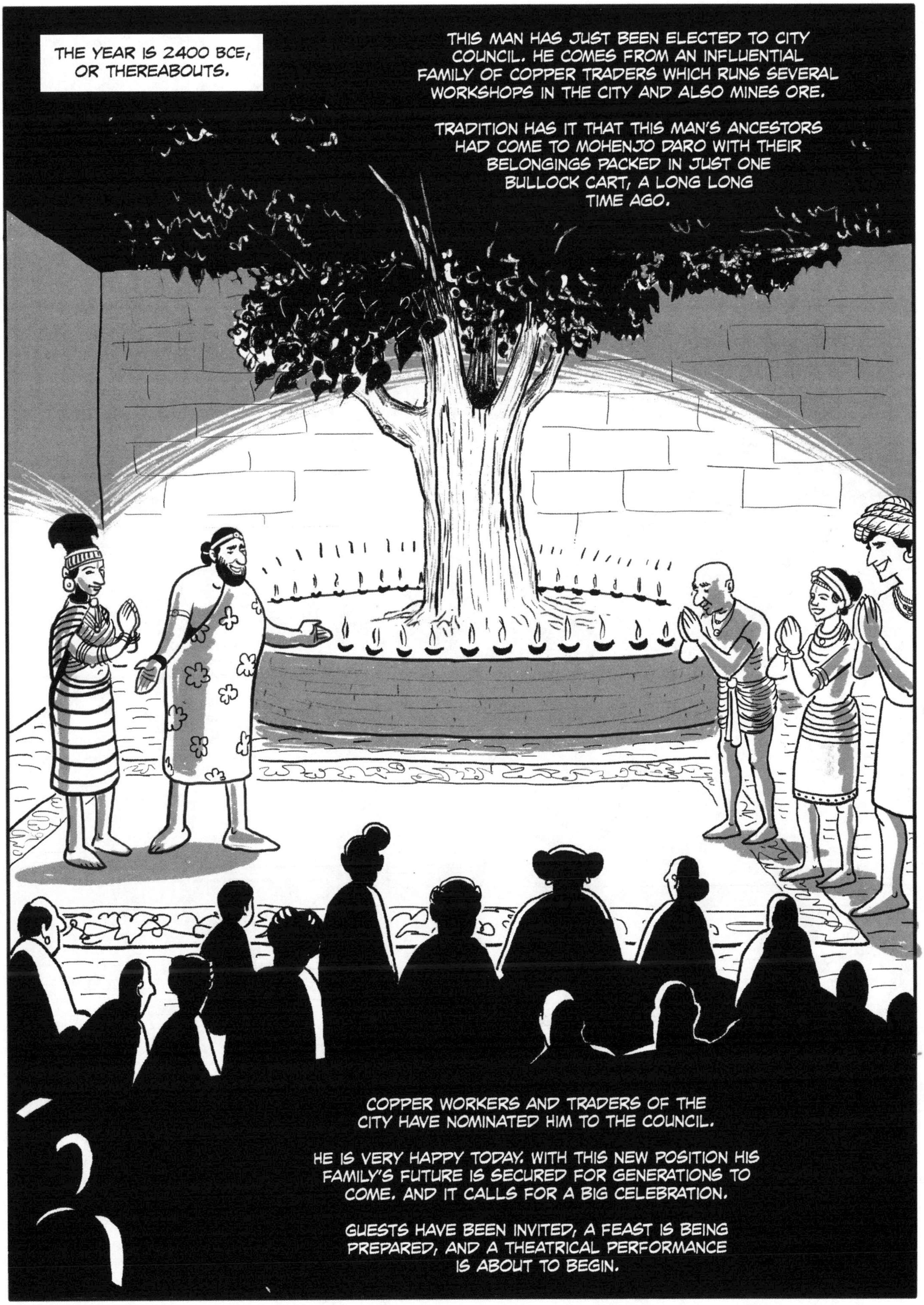
THE YEAR IS 2400 BCE, OR THEREABOUTS.
THIS MAN HAS JUST BEEN ELECTED TO CITY COUNCIL. HE COMES FROM AN INFLUENTIAL FAMILY OF COPPER TRADERS WHICH RUNS SEVERAL WORKSHOPS IN THE CITY AND ALSO MINES ORE.
TRADITION HAS IT THAT THIS MAN'S ANCESTORS HAD COME TO MOHENJO DARO WITH THEIR BELONGINGS PACKED IN JUST ONE BULLOCK CART, A LONG LONG TIME AGO.
COPPER WORKERS AND TRADERS OF THE CITY HAVE NOMINATED HIM TO THE COUNCIL.
HE IS VERY HAPPY TODAY. WITH THIS NEW POSITION HIS FAMILY'S FUTURE IS SECURED FOR GENERATIONS TO COME. AND IT CALLS FOR A BIG CELEBRATION.
GUESTS HAVE BEEN INVITED, A FEAST IS BEING PREPARED, AND A THEATRICAL PERFORMANCE IS ABOUT TO BEGIN.

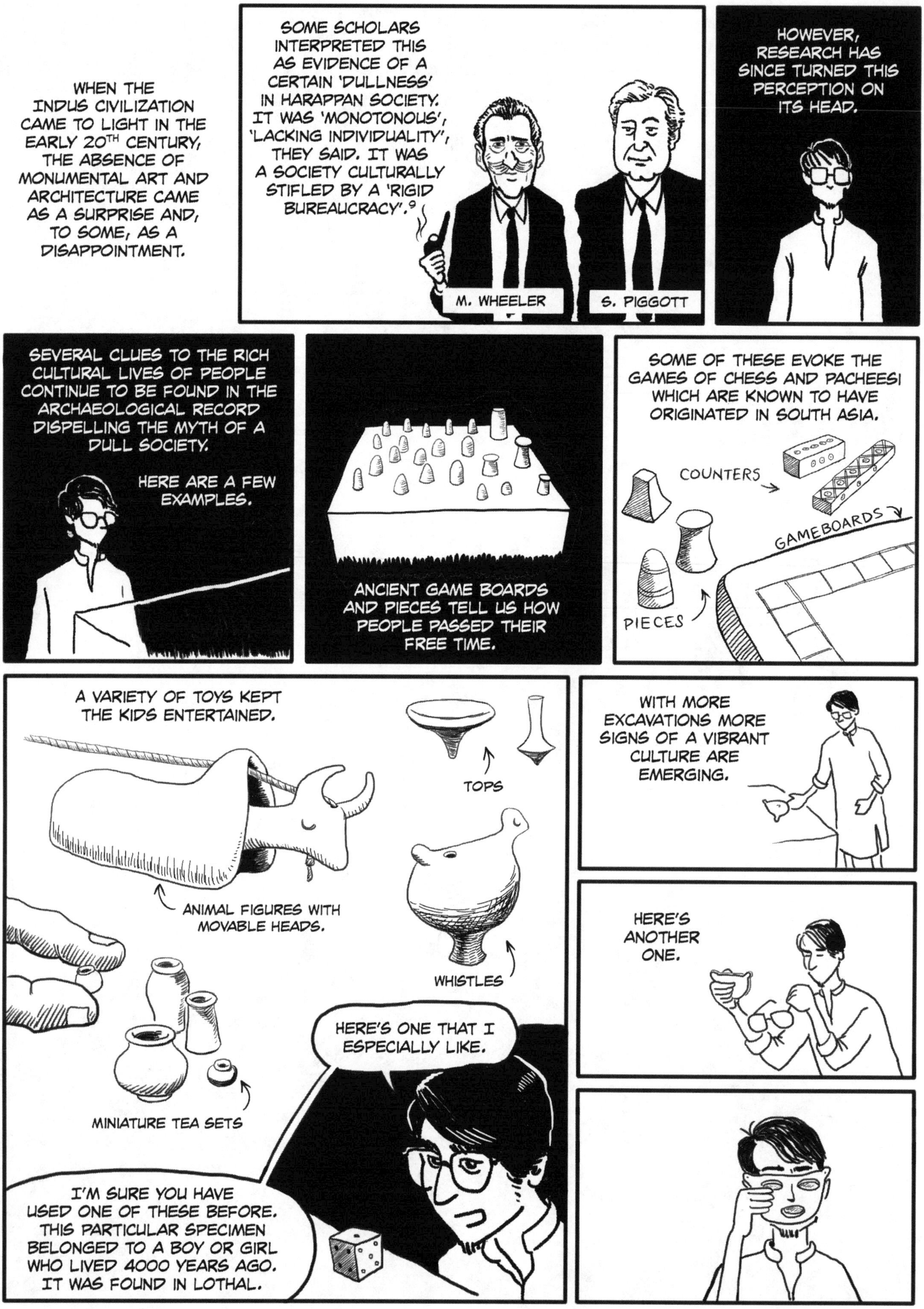
WHEN THE INDUS CIVILIZATION CAME TO LIGHT IN THE EARLY 20TH CENTURY, THE ABSENCE OF MONUMENTAL ART AND ARCHITECTURE CAME AS A SURPRISE AND, TO SOME, AS A DISAPPOINTMENT.
SOME SCHOLARS INTERPRETED THIS AS EVIDENCE OF A CERTAIN 'DULLNESS' IN HARAPPAN SOCIETY. IT WAS 'MONOTONOUS', 'LACKING INDIVIDUALITY', THEY SAID. IT WAS A SOCIETY CULTURALLY STIFLED BY A 'RIGID BUREAUCRACY'.[9]
M. WHEELER
S. PIGGOTT
HOWEVER, RESEARCH HAS SINCE TURNED THIS PERCEPTION ON ITS HEAD.
SEVERAL CLUES TO THE RICH CULTURAL LIVES OF PEOPLE CONTINUE TO BE FOUND IN THE ARCHAEOLOGICAL RECORD DISPELLING THE MYTH OF A DULL SOCIETY.
HERE ARE A FEW EXAMPLES.
ANCIENT GAME BOARDS AND PIECES TELL US HOW PEOPLE PASSED THEIR FREE TIME.
SOME OF THESE EVOKE THE GAMES OF CHESS AND PACHEESI WHICH ARE KNOWN TO HAVE ORIGINATED IN SOUTH ASIA.
COUNTERS
GAMEBOARDS
PIECES
A VARIETY OF TOYS KEPT THE KIDS ENTERTAINED.
TOPS
ANIMAL FIGURES WITH MOVABLE HEADS.
WHISTLES
MINIATURE TEA SETS
HERE'S ONE THAT I ESPECIALLY LIKE.
I'M SURE YOU HAVE USED ONE OF THESE BEFORE. THIS PARTICULAR SPECIMEN BELONGED TO A BOY OR GIRL WHO LIVED 4000 YEARS AGO. IT WAS FOUND IN LOTHAL.
WITH MORE EXCAVATIONS MORE SIGNS OF A VIBRANT CULTURE ARE EMERGING.
HERE'S ANOTHER ONE.

THE CELEBRATIONS ARE UNDERWAY.

THIS IS AN IMPORTANT EVENT AND EVERYONE HAS COME DRESSED TO THE NINES. LET'S TAKE THIS CHANCE TO NOTE THE FASHION TRENDS OF THE DAY.

THE VARIETY AND COMPLEXITY OF HAIRSTYLES DEPICTED IN STATUETTES SUGGEST THE EXISTENCE OF PROFESSIONAL HAIRSTYLISTS.

EVEN MEN WORE ELABORATE HAIRDOS, AS ONE MALE SKELETON BURIED WITH THOUSANDS OF MICROBEADS STRUNG IN HIS HAIR SHOWS.

STEATITE MICROBEADS

SHELL RINGS

STONE BEAD

WE HAVE NO IDEA WHAT STORIES THESE PERFORMANCES DEPICTED. ONLY SOME FAINT CLUES ARE PROVIDED BY ARTWORKS SUCH AS THIS ONE.

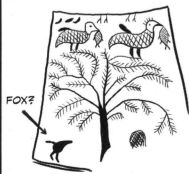

FOX?

IT ECHOES THE STORIES OF THE PANCHATANTRA.

OTHER ARTWORKS SHOW PROCESSIONS WHICH WOULD HAVE MARKED IMPORTANT DATES AND FESTIVALS.

IT IS SUGGESTED THAT STORIES, PERFORMANCES AND PROCESSIONS RATHER THAN PALACES, TOMBS AND TEMPLES, WERE THE MEANS OF LEGITIMIZING THE POLITICAL SYSTEMS OF THIS CIVILIZATION.

APART FROM ENTERTAINING PEOPLE, THEY WOULD HAVE ALSO REINFORCED THE IMAGINED ORDERS OF THE DAY. MUCH LIKE SOME PROCESSIONS DO TODAY.

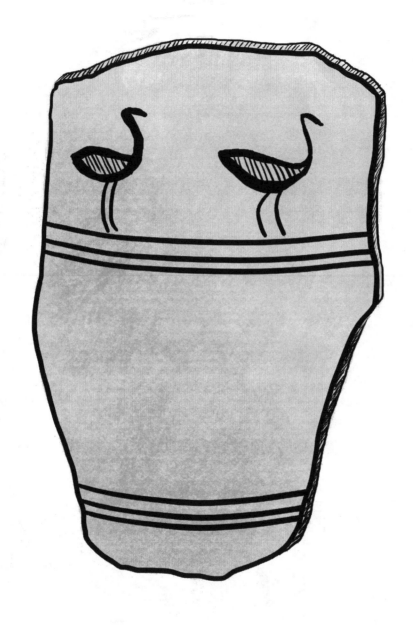

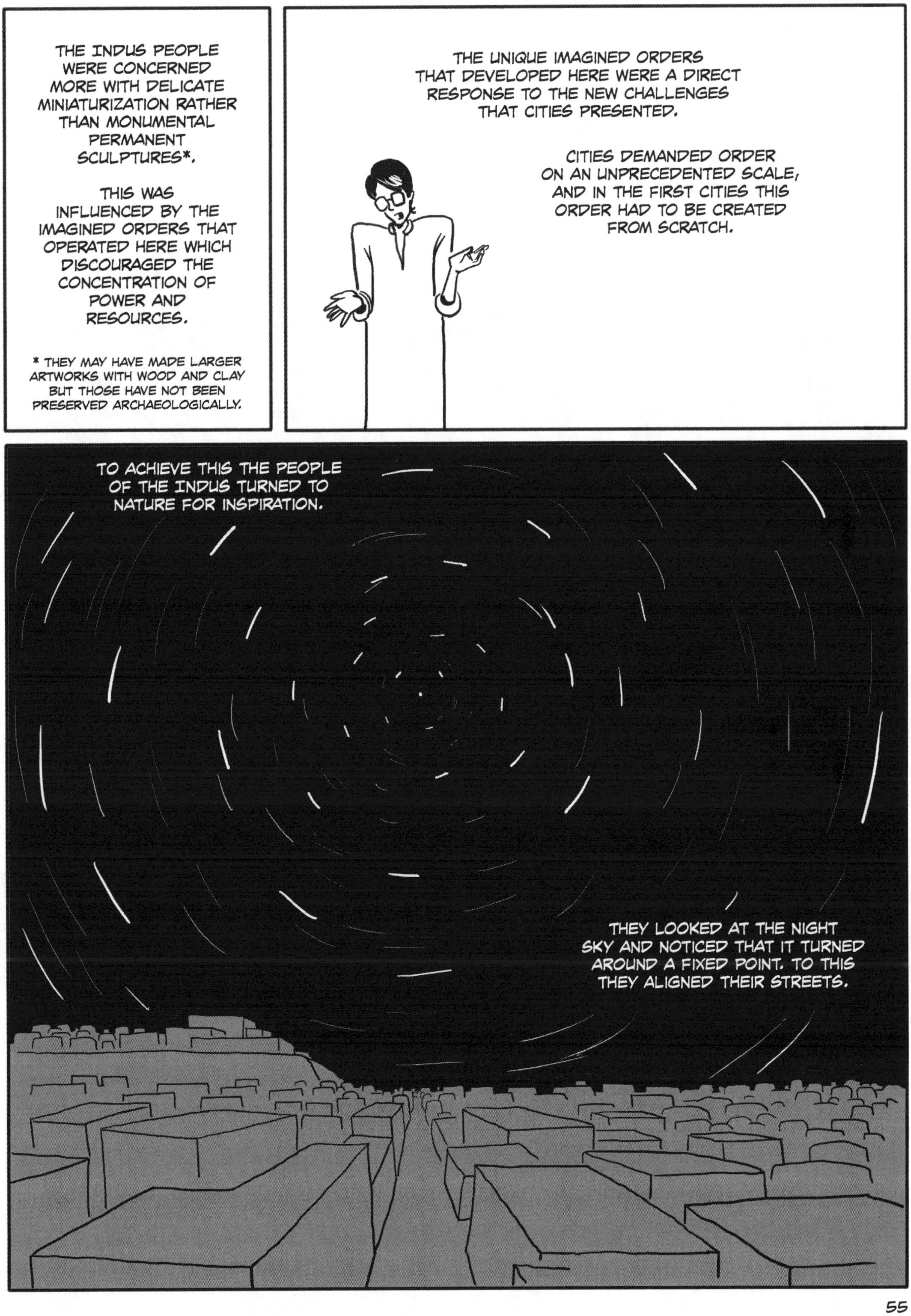
THE INDUS PEOPLE WERE CONCERNED MORE WITH DELICATE MINIATURIZATION RATHER THAN MONUMENTAL PERMANENT SCULPTURES*.
THIS WAS INFLUENCED BY THE IMAGINED ORDERS THAT OPERATED HERE WHICH DISCOURAGED THE CONCENTRATION OF POWER AND RESOURCES.
* THEY MAY HAVE MADE LARGER ARTWORKS WITH WOOD AND CLAY BUT THOSE HAVE NOT BEEN PRESERVED ARCHAEOLOGICALLY.
THE UNIQUE IMAGINED ORDERS THAT DEVELOPED HERE WERE A DIRECT RESPONSE TO THE NEW CHALLENGES THAT CITIES PRESENTED.
CITIES DEMANDED ORDER ON AN UNPRECEDENTED SCALE, AND IN THE FIRST CITIES THIS ORDER HAD TO BE CREATED FROM SCRATCH.
TO ACHIEVE THIS THE PEOPLE OF THE INDUS TURNED TO NATURE FOR INSPIRATION.
THEY LOOKED AT THE NIGHT SKY AND NOTICED THAT IT TURNED AROUND A FIXED POINT. TO THIS THEY ALIGNED THEIR STREETS.

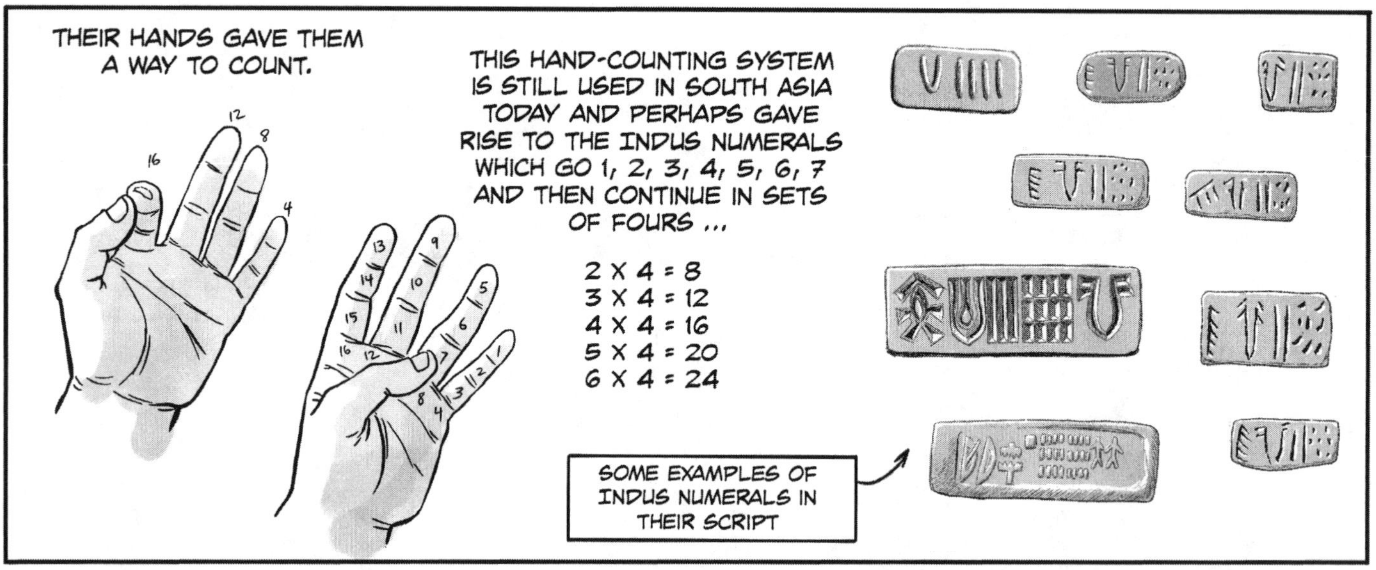
THEIR HANDS GAVE THEM A WAY TO COUNT.
THIS HAND-COUNTING SYSTEM IS STILL USED IN SOUTH ASIA TODAY AND PERHAPS GAVE RISE TO THE INDUS NUMERALS WHICH GO 1, 2, 3, 4, 5, 6, 7 AND THEN CONTINUE IN SETS OF FOURS ...
2 X 4 = 8
3 X 4 = 12
4 X 4 = 16
5 X 4 = 20
6 X 4 = 24
SOME EXAMPLES OF INDUS NUMERALS IN THEIR SCRIPT

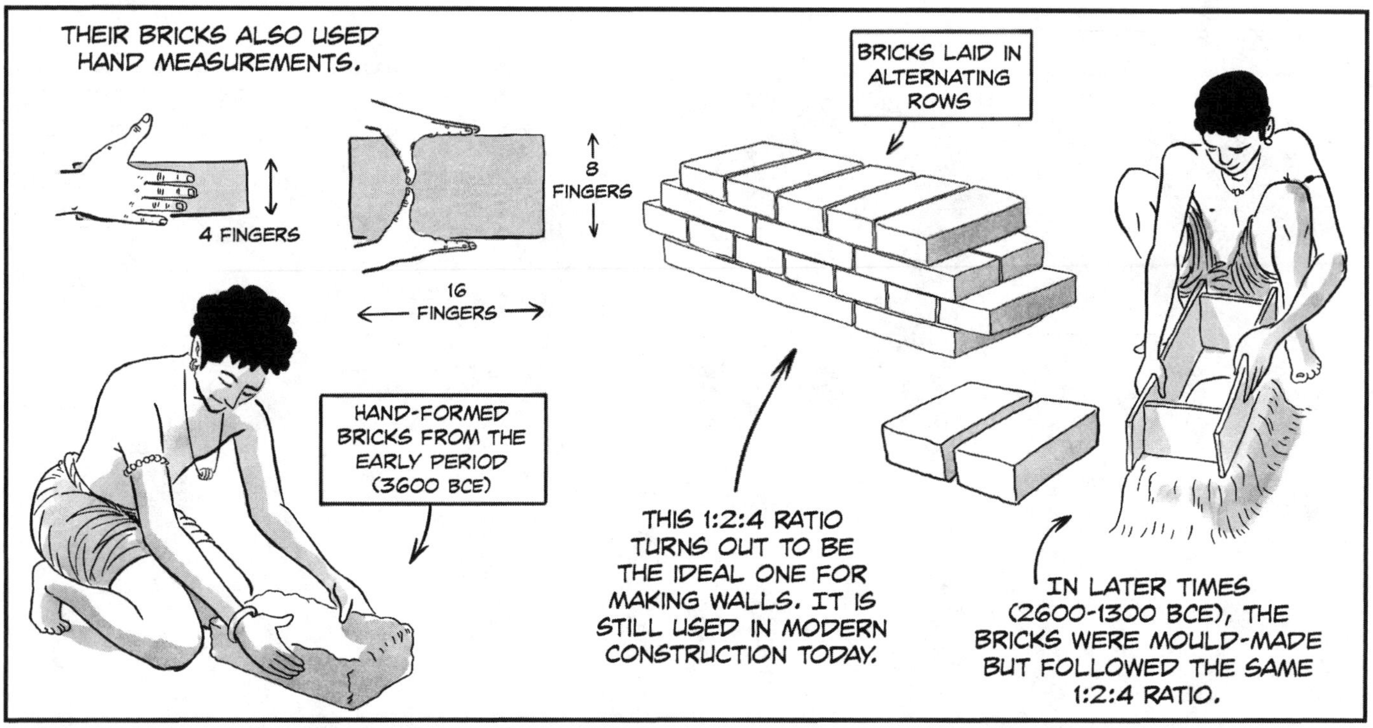
THEIR BRICKS ALSO USED HAND MEASUREMENTS.
4 FINGERS
16 FINGERS
8 FINGERS
BRICKS LAID IN ALTERNATING ROWS
HAND-FORMED BRICKS FROM THE EARLY PERIOD (3600 BCE)
THIS 1:2:4 RATIO TURNS OUT TO BE THE IDEAL ONE FOR MAKING WALLS. IT IS STILL USED IN MODERN CONSTRUCTION TODAY.
IN LATER TIMES (2600-1300 BCE), THE BRICKS WERE MOULD-MADE BUT FOLLOWED THE SAME 1:2:4 RATIO.

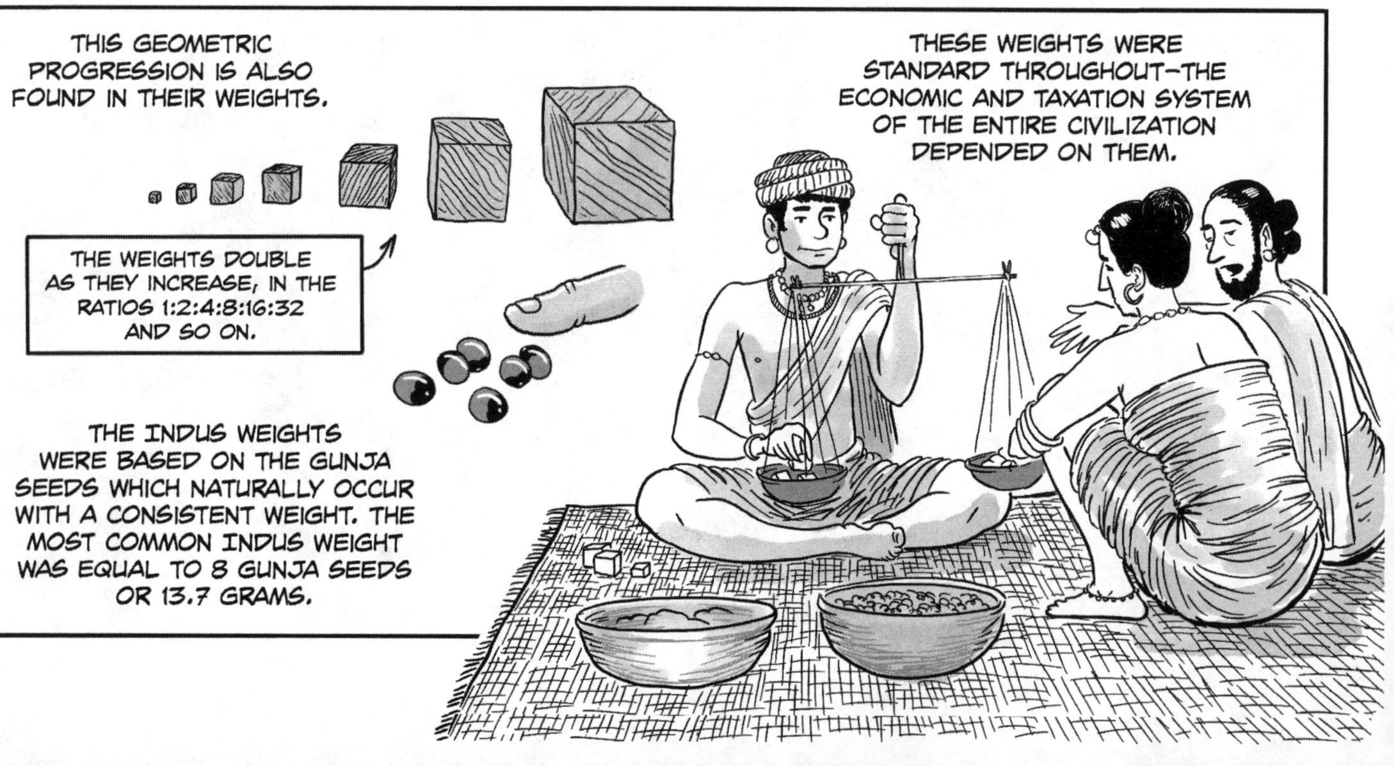
THIS GEOMETRIC PROGRESSION IS ALSO FOUND IN THEIR WEIGHTS.
THESE WEIGHTS WERE STANDARD THROUGHOUT—THE ECONOMIC AND TAXATION SYSTEM OF THE ENTIRE CIVILIZATION DEPENDED ON THEM.
THE WEIGHTS DOUBLE AS THEY INCREASE, IN THE RATIOS 1:2:4:8:16:32 AND SO ON.
THE INDUS WEIGHTS WERE BASED ON THE GUNJA SEEDS WHICH NATURALLY OCCUR WITH A CONSISTENT WEIGHT. THE MOST COMMON INDUS WEIGHT WAS EQUAL TO 8 GUNJA SEEDS OR 13.7 GRAMS.

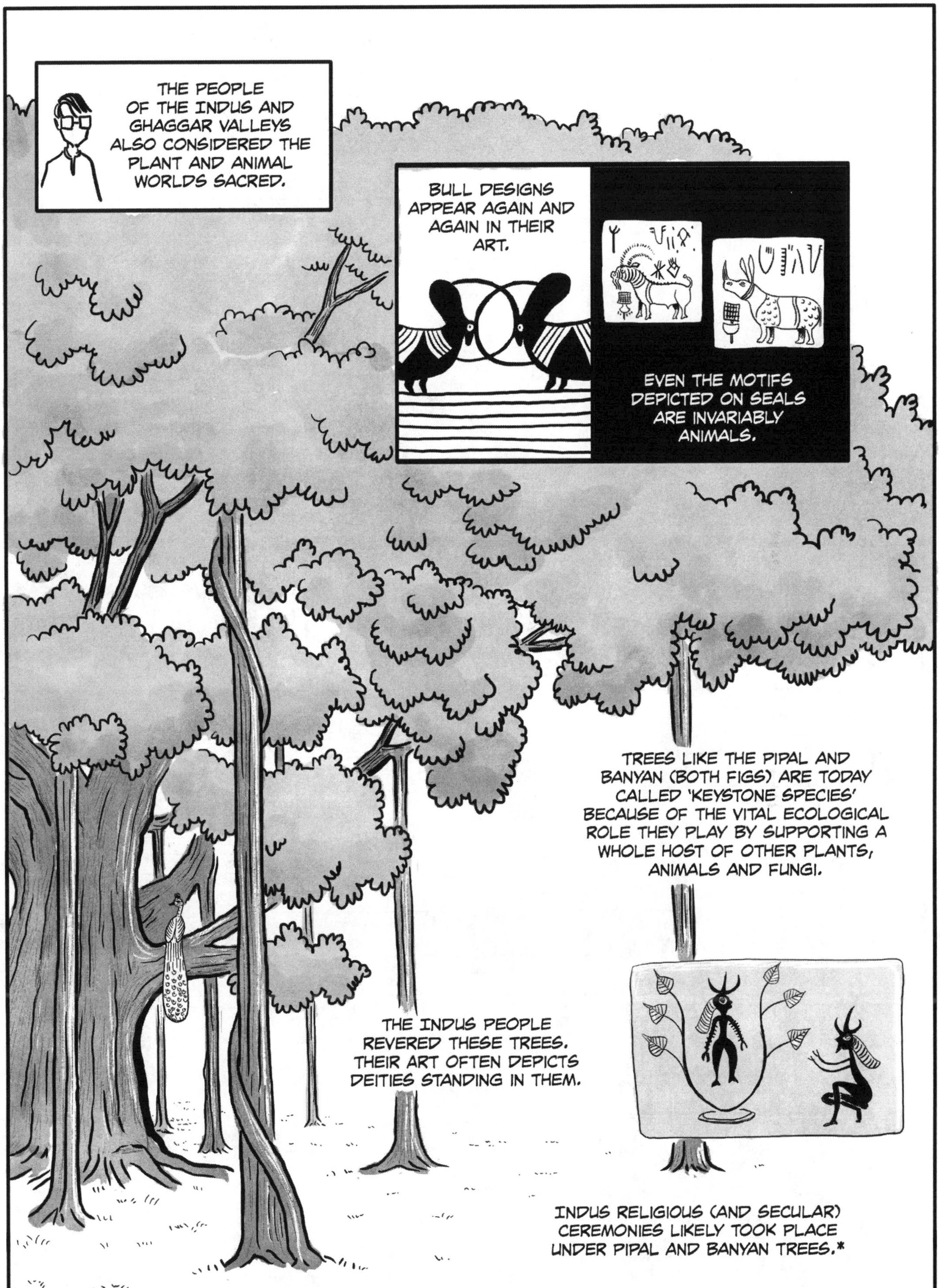
THE PEOPLE OF THE INDUS AND GHAGGAR VALLEYS ALSO CONSIDERED THE PLANT AND ANIMAL WORLDS SACRED.
BULL DESIGNS APPEAR AGAIN AND AGAIN IN THEIR ART.
EVEN THE MOTIFS DEPICTED ON SEALS ARE INVARIABLY ANIMALS.
TREES LIKE THE PIPAL AND BANYAN (BOTH FIGS) ARE TODAY CALLED 'KEYSTONE SPECIES' BECAUSE OF THE VITAL ECOLOGICAL ROLE THEY PLAY BY SUPPORTING A WHOLE HOST OF OTHER PLANTS, ANIMALS AND FUNGI.
THE INDUS PEOPLE REVERED THESE TREES. THEIR ART OFTEN DEPICTS DEITIES STANDING IN THEM.
INDUS RELIGIOUS (AND SECULAR) CEREMONIES LIKELY TOOK PLACE UNDER PIPAL AND BANYAN TREES.*

* THEY MAY HAVE ALSO HAD TEMPLES POSSIBLY MADE OF REEDS OR OTHER PERISHABLE MATERIALS.

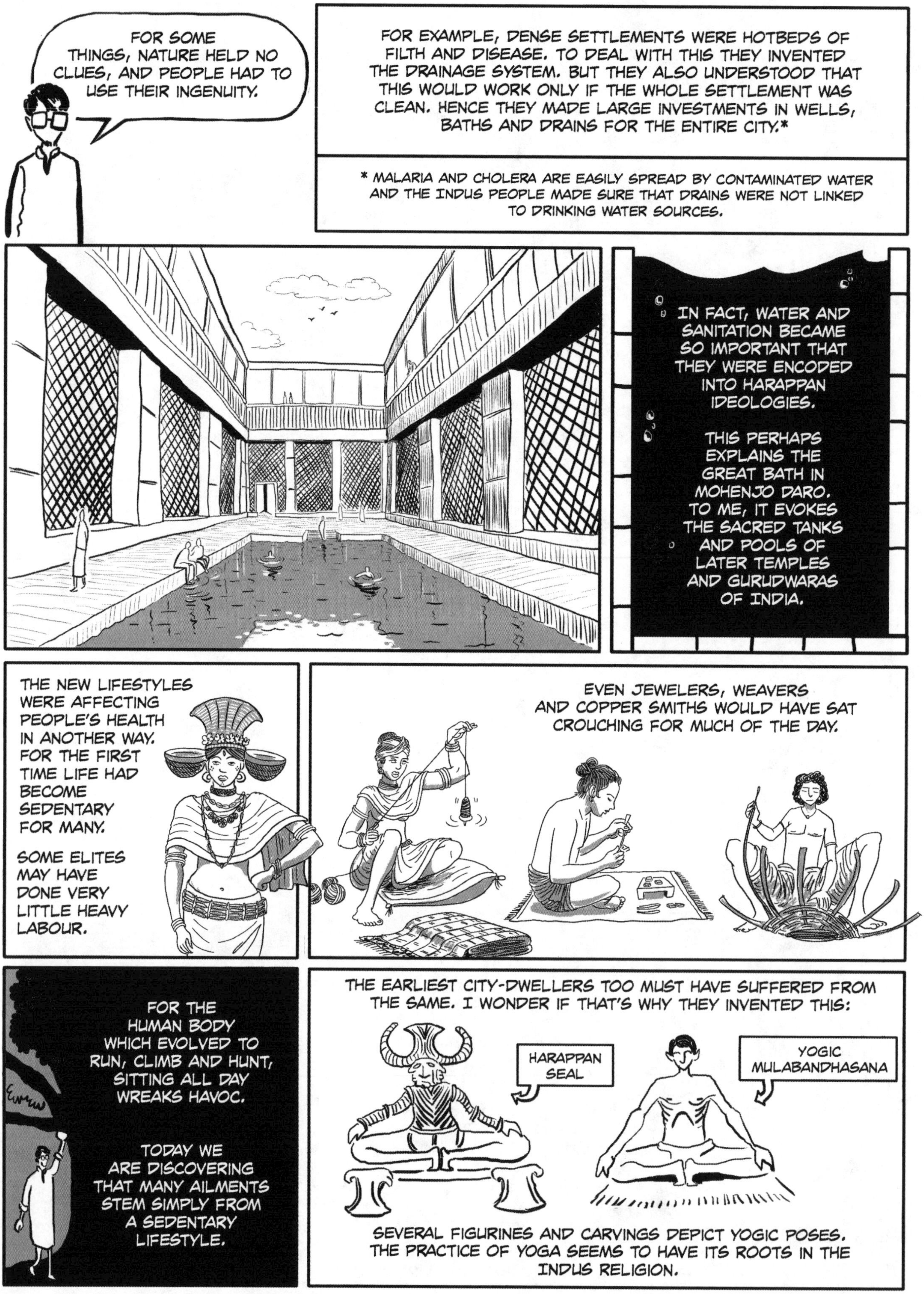

FOR SOME THINGS, NATURE HELD NO CLUES, AND PEOPLE HAD TO USE THEIR INGENUITY.
FOR EXAMPLE, DENSE SETTLEMENTS WERE HOTBEDS OF FILTH AND DISEASE. TO DEAL WITH THIS THEY INVENTED THE DRAINAGE SYSTEM. BUT THEY ALSO UNDERSTOOD THAT THIS WOULD WORK ONLY IF THE WHOLE SETTLEMENT WAS CLEAN. HENCE THEY MADE LARGE INVESTMENTS IN WELLS, BATHS AND DRAINS FOR THE ENTIRE CITY.*
* MALARIA AND CHOLERA ARE EASILY SPREAD BY CONTAMINATED WATER AND THE INDUS PEOPLE MADE SURE THAT DRAINS WERE NOT LINKED TO DRINKING WATER SOURCES.
IN FACT, WATER AND SANITATION BECAME SO IMPORTANT THAT THEY WERE ENCODED INTO HARAPPAN IDEOLOGIES.
THIS PERHAPS EXPLAINS THE GREAT BATH IN MOHENJO DARO. TO ME, IT EVOKES THE SACRED TANKS AND POOLS OF LATER TEMPLES AND GURUDWARAS OF INDIA.
THE NEW LIFESTYLES WERE AFFECTING PEOPLE'S HEALTH IN ANOTHER WAY. FOR THE FIRST TIME LIFE HAD BECOME SEDENTARY FOR MANY.
SOME ELITES MAY HAVE DONE VERY LITTLE HEAVY LABOUR.
EVEN JEWELERS, WEAVERS AND COPPER SMITHS WOULD HAVE SAT CROUCHING FOR MUCH OF THE DAY.
FOR THE HUMAN BODY WHICH EVOLVED TO RUN, CLIMB AND HUNT, SITTING ALL DAY WREAKS HAVOC.
TODAY WE ARE DISCOVERING THAT MANY AILMENTS STEM SIMPLY FROM A SEDENTARY LIFESTYLE.
THE EARLIEST CITY-DWELLERS TOO MUST HAVE SUFFERED FROM THE SAME. I WONDER IF THAT'S WHY THEY INVENTED THIS:
HARAPPAN SEAL
YOGIC MULABANDHASANA
SEVERAL FIGURINES AND CARVINGS DEPICT YOGIC POSES. THE PRACTICE OF YOGA SEEMS TO HAVE ITS ROOTS IN THE INDUS RELIGION.

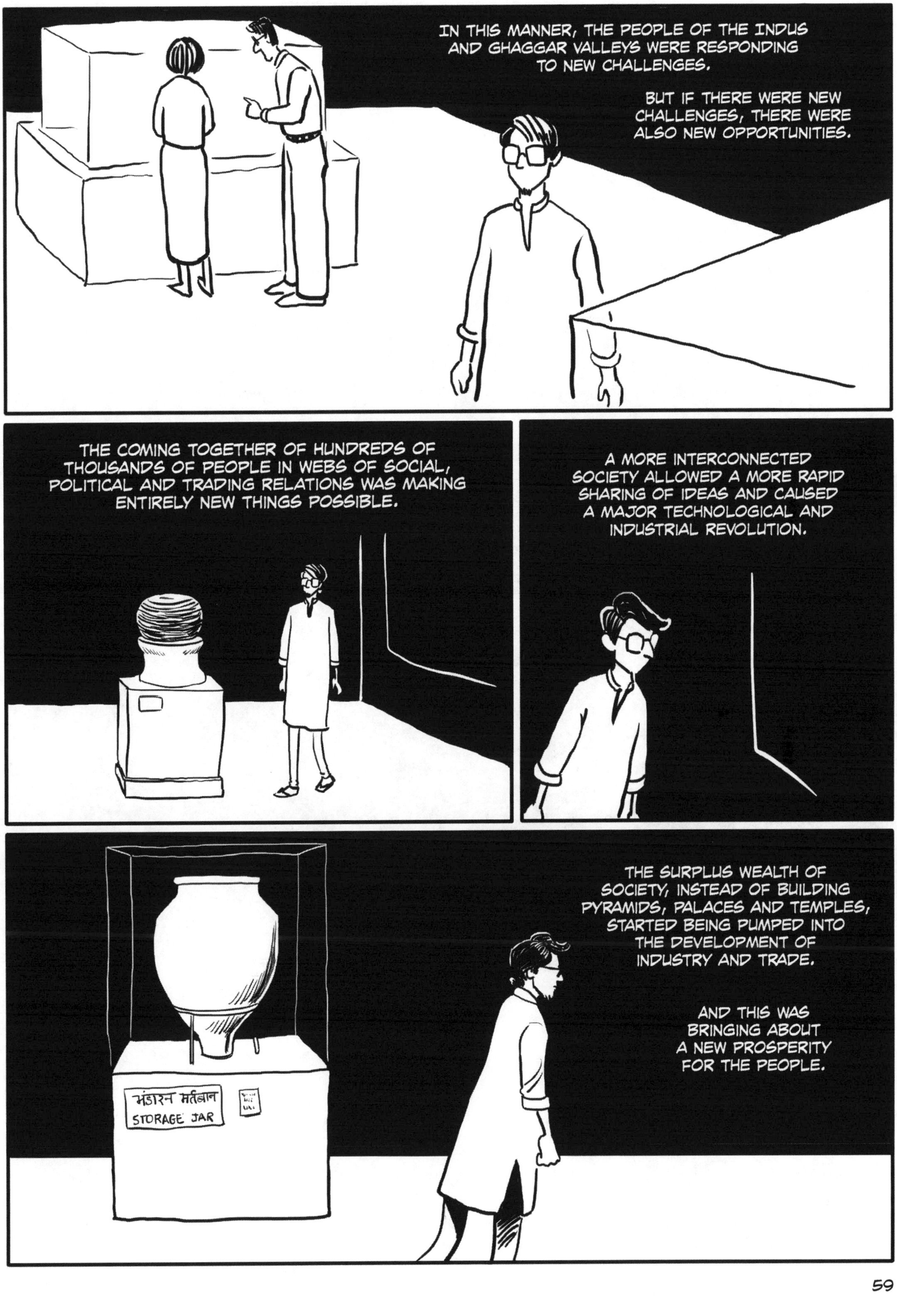
IN THIS MANNER, THE PEOPLE OF THE INDUS AND GHAGGAR VALLEYS WERE RESPONDING TO NEW CHALLENGES.
BUT IF THERE WERE NEW CHALLENGES, THERE WERE ALSO NEW OPPORTUNITIES.
THE COMING TOGETHER OF HUNDREDS OF THOUSANDS OF PEOPLE IN WEBS OF SOCIAL, POLITICAL AND TRADING RELATIONS WAS MAKING ENTIRELY NEW THINGS POSSIBLE.
A MORE INTERCONNECTED SOCIETY ALLOWED A MORE RAPID SHARING OF IDEAS AND CAUSED A MAJOR TECHNOLOGICAL AND INDUSTRIAL REVOLUTION.
THE SURPLUS WEALTH OF SOCIETY, INSTEAD OF BUILDING PYRAMIDS, PALACES AND TEMPLES, STARTED BEING PUMPED INTO THE DEVELOPMENT OF INDUSTRY AND TRADE.
AND THIS WAS BRINGING ABOUT A NEW PROSPERITY FOR THE PEOPLE.
STORAGE JAR

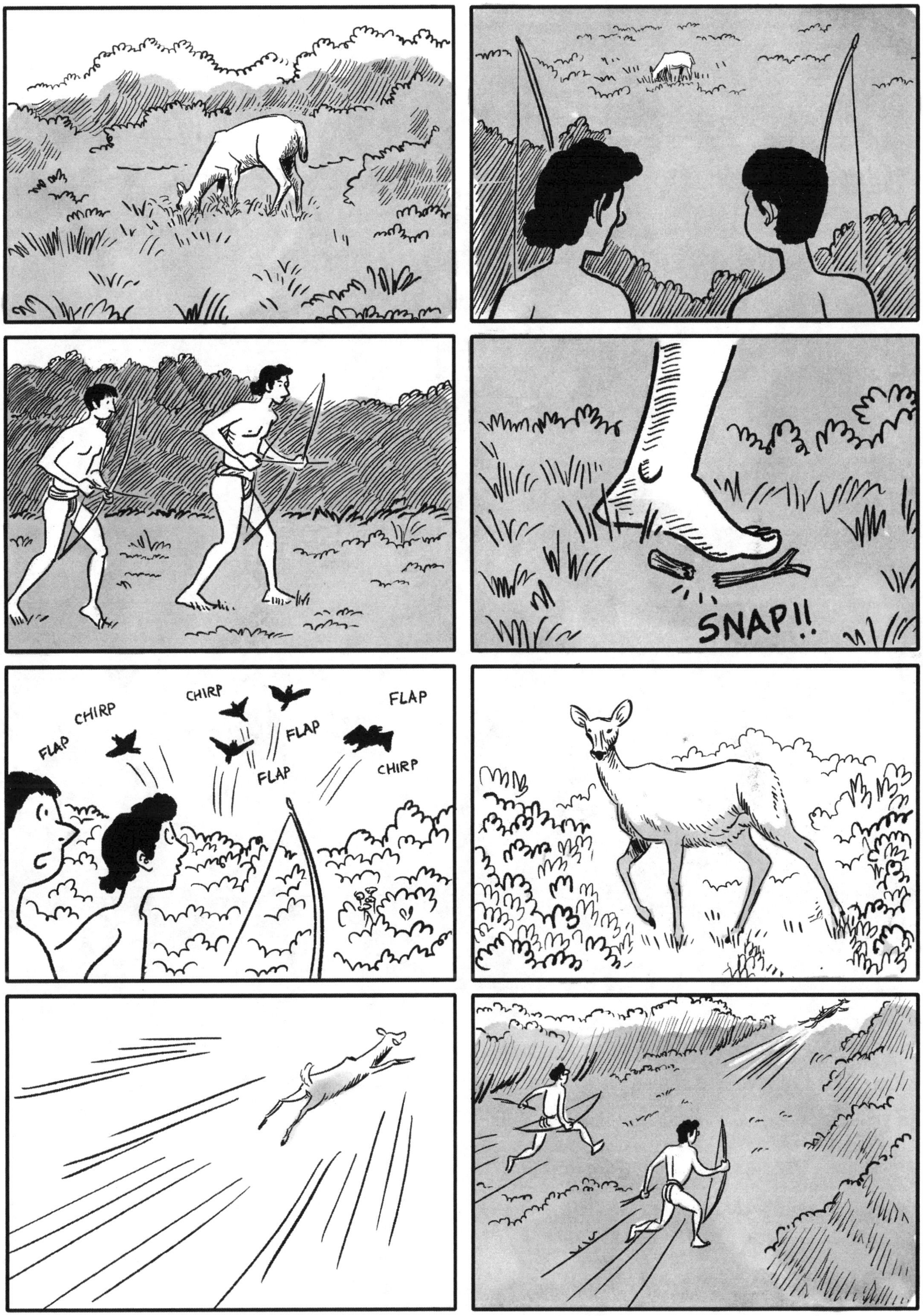
SNAP!!
FLAP
CHIRP
CHIRP
FLAP
FLAP
FLAP
CHIRP

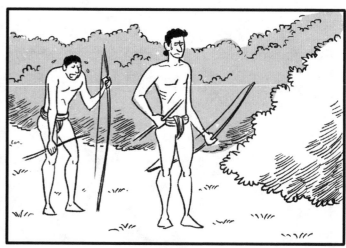

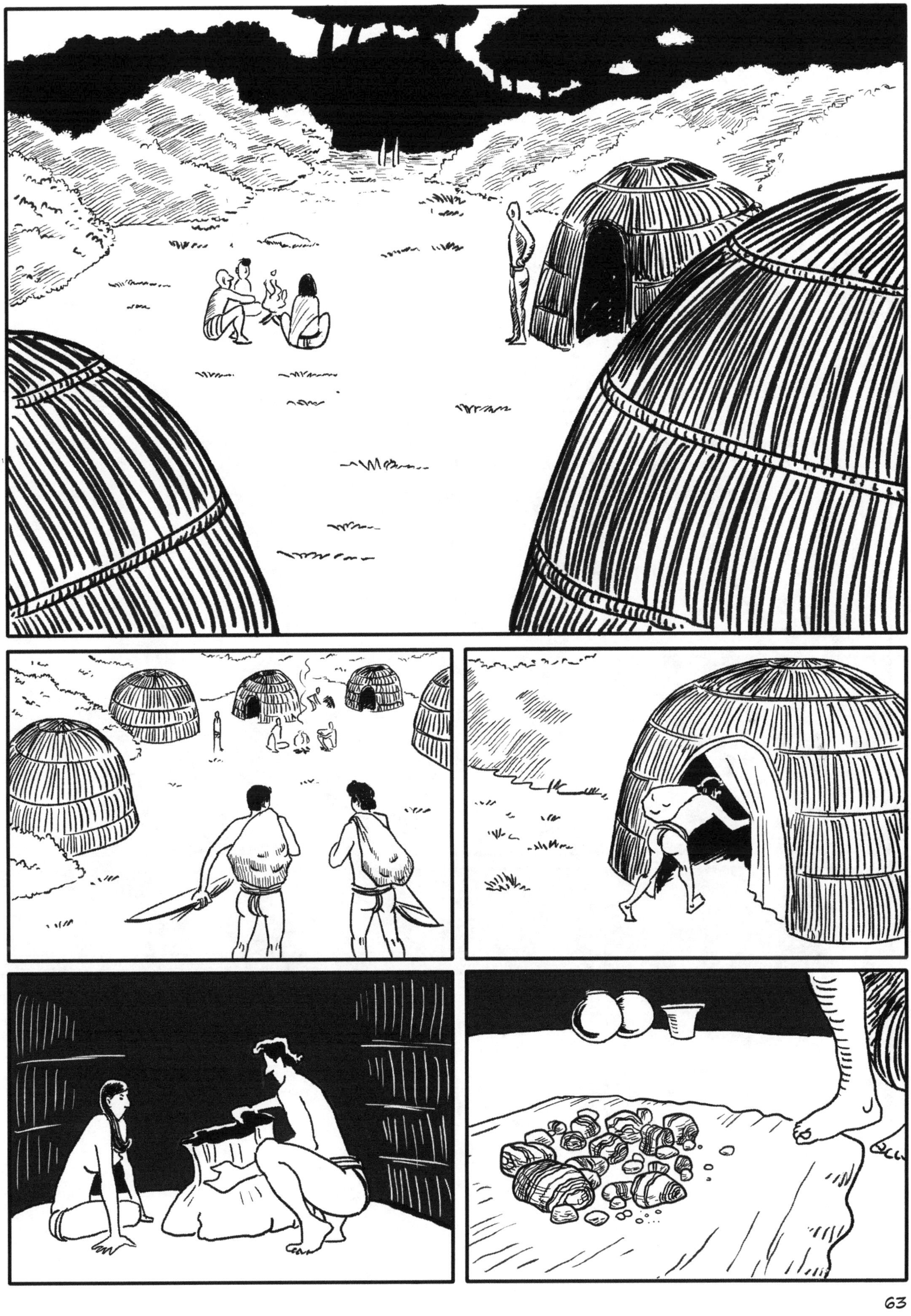

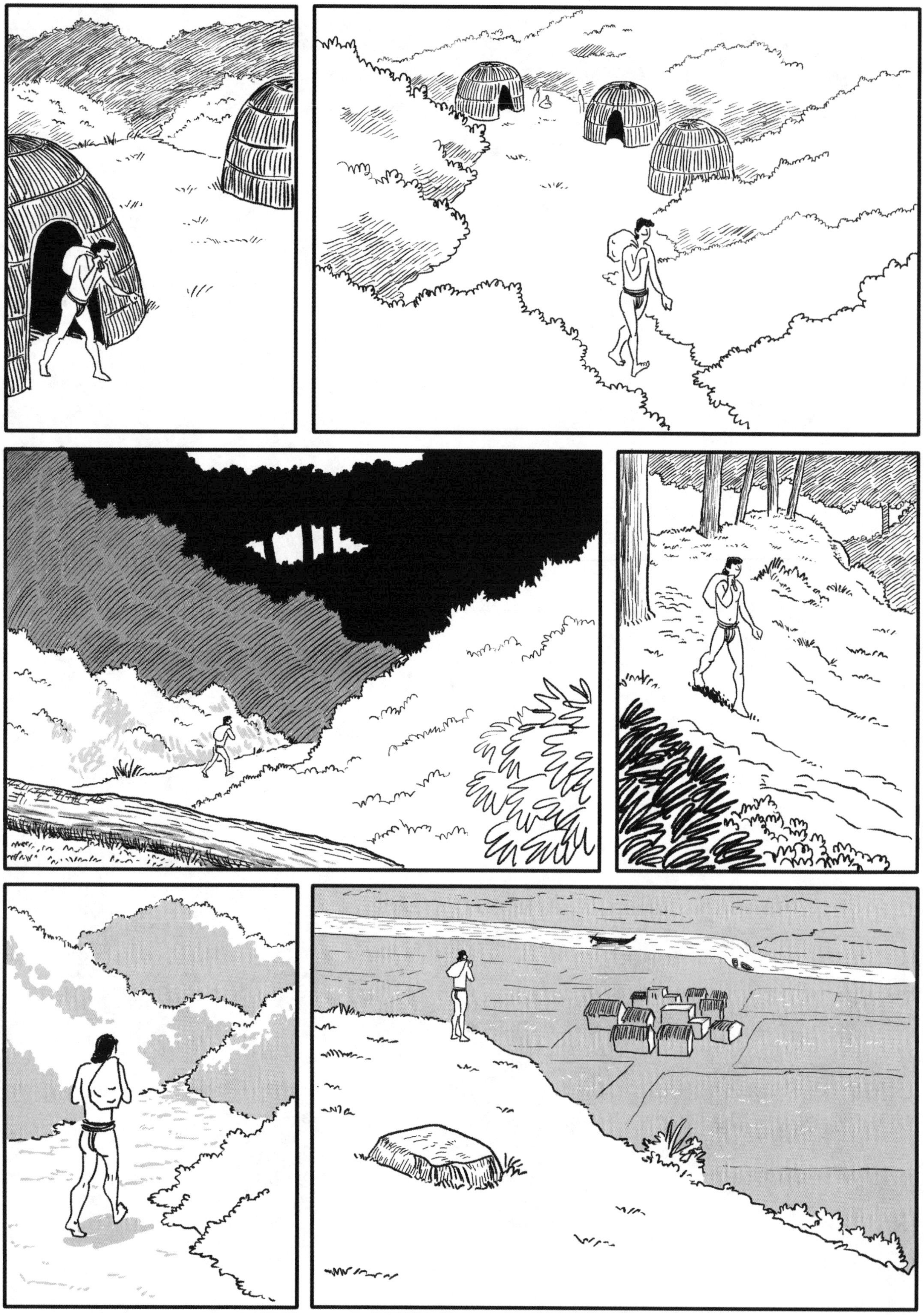

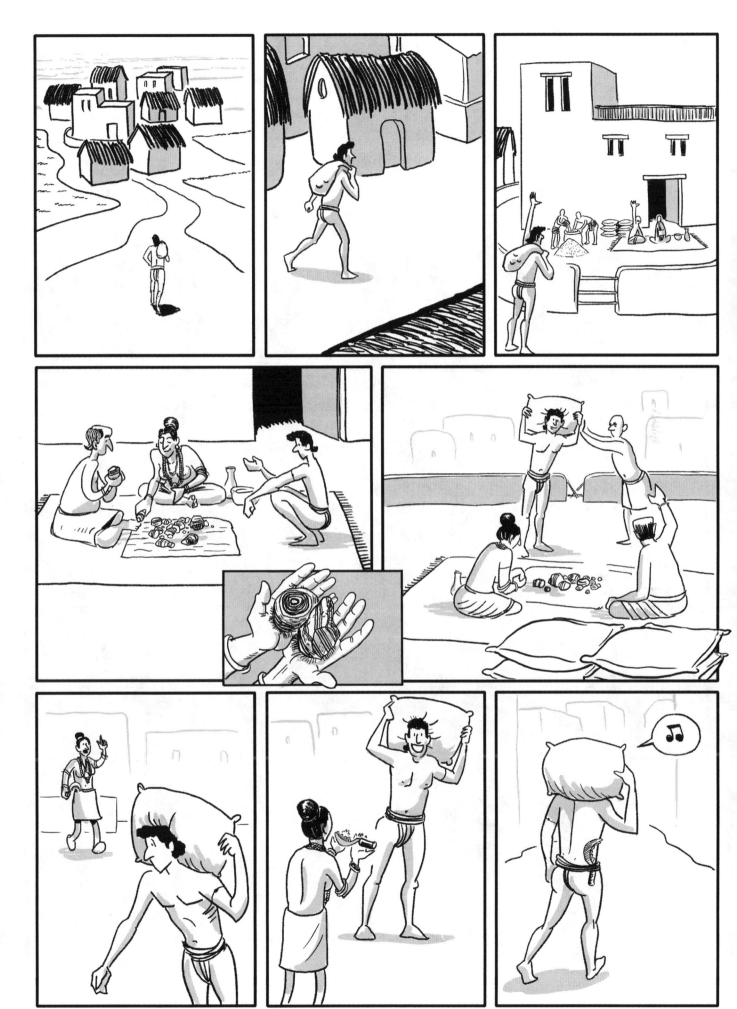

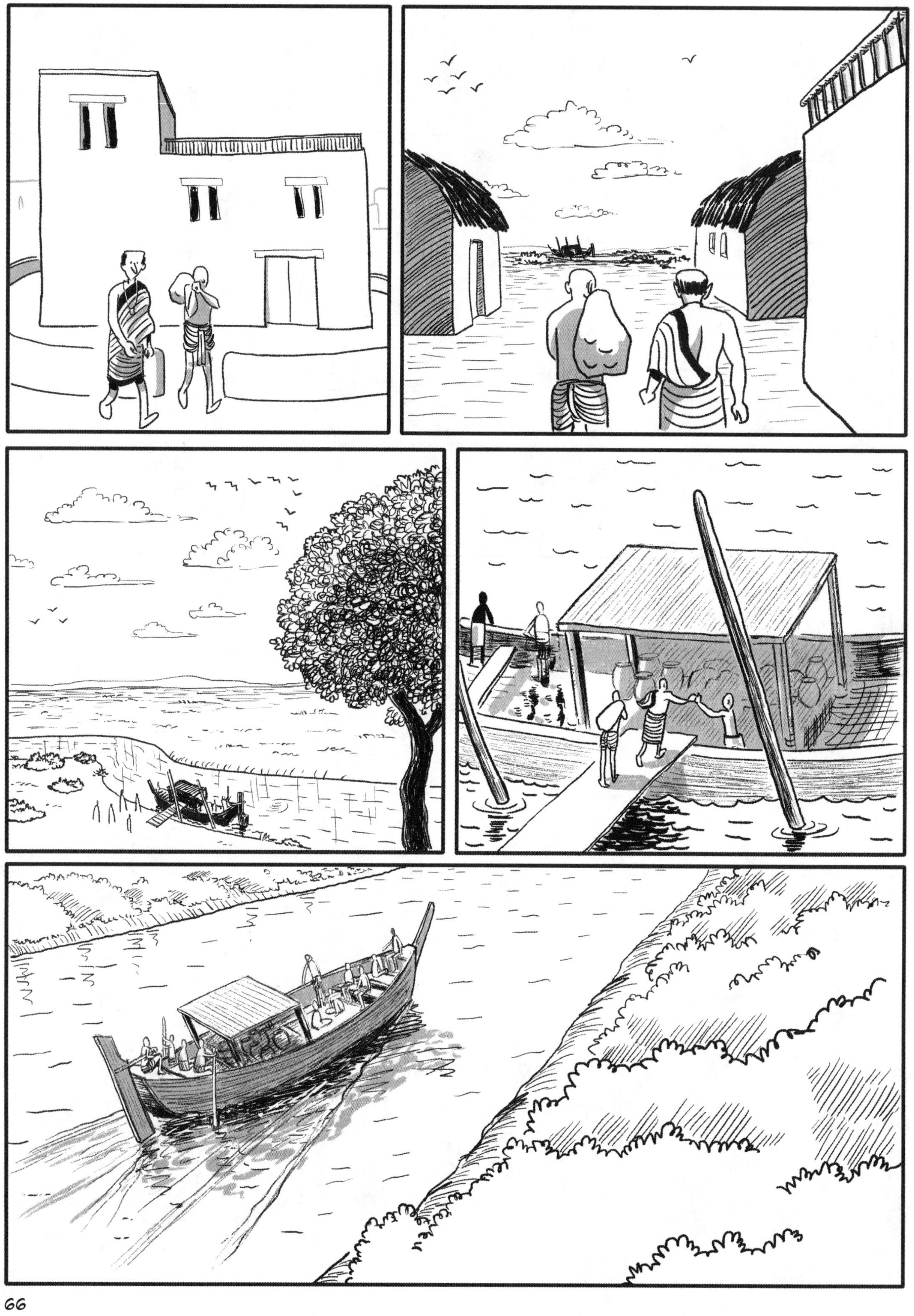

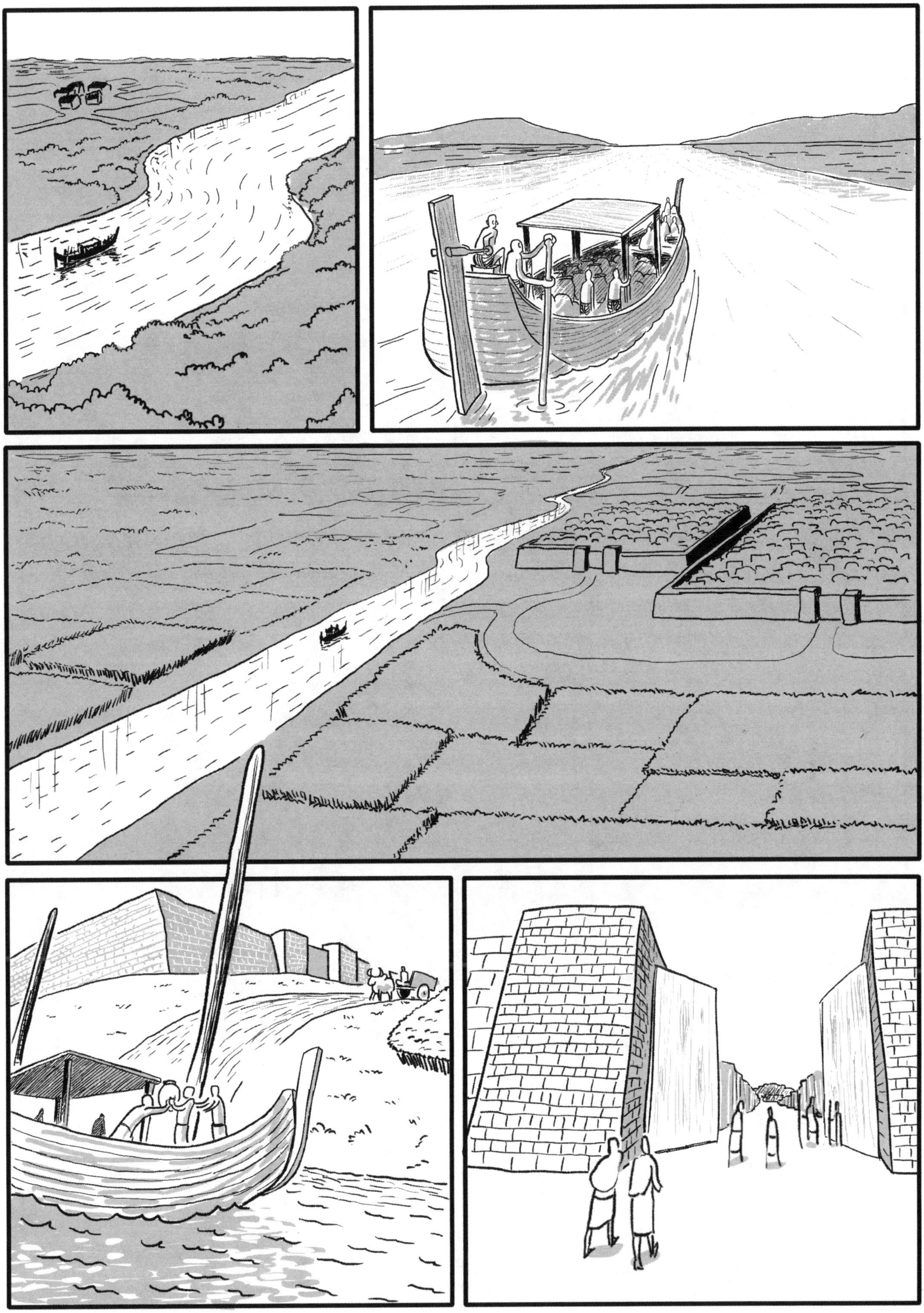

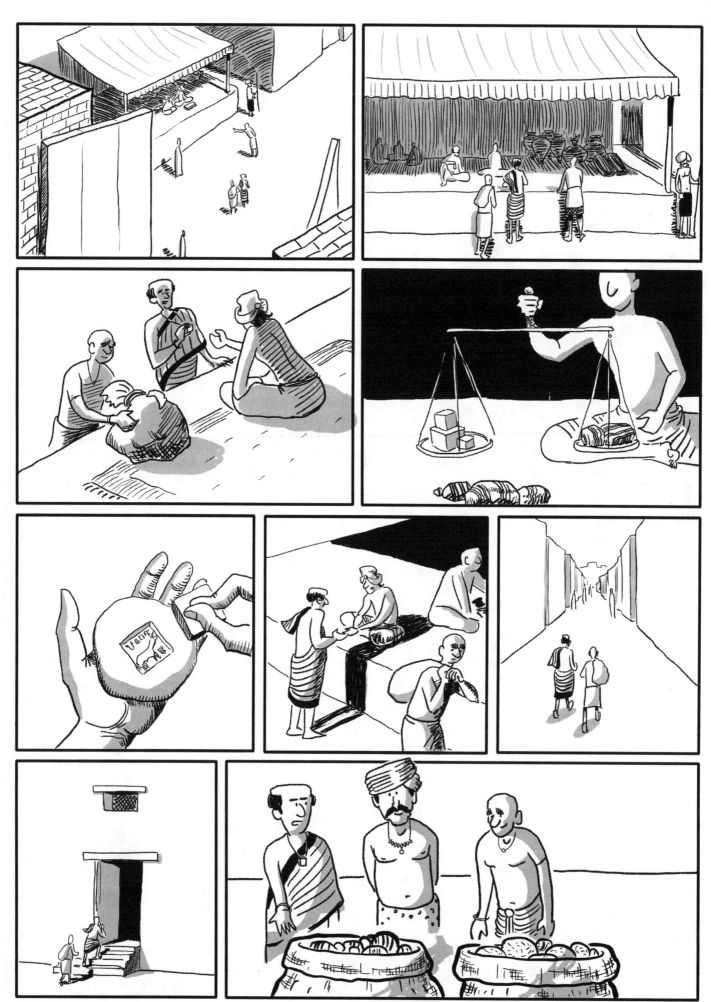

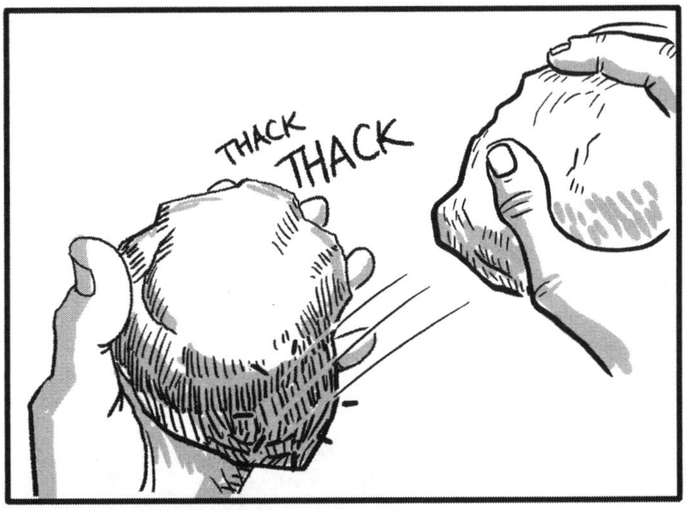
THACK
THACK
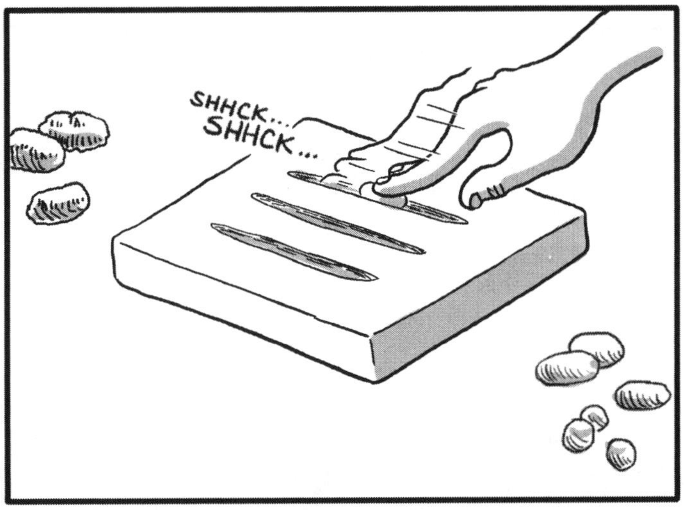
SHHCK...
SHHCK...
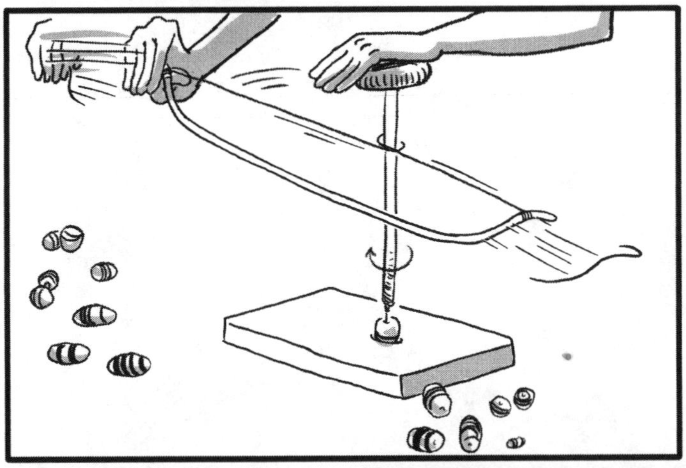
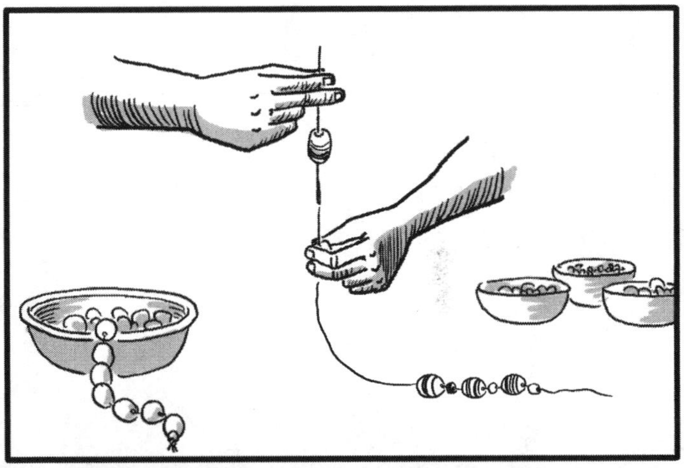
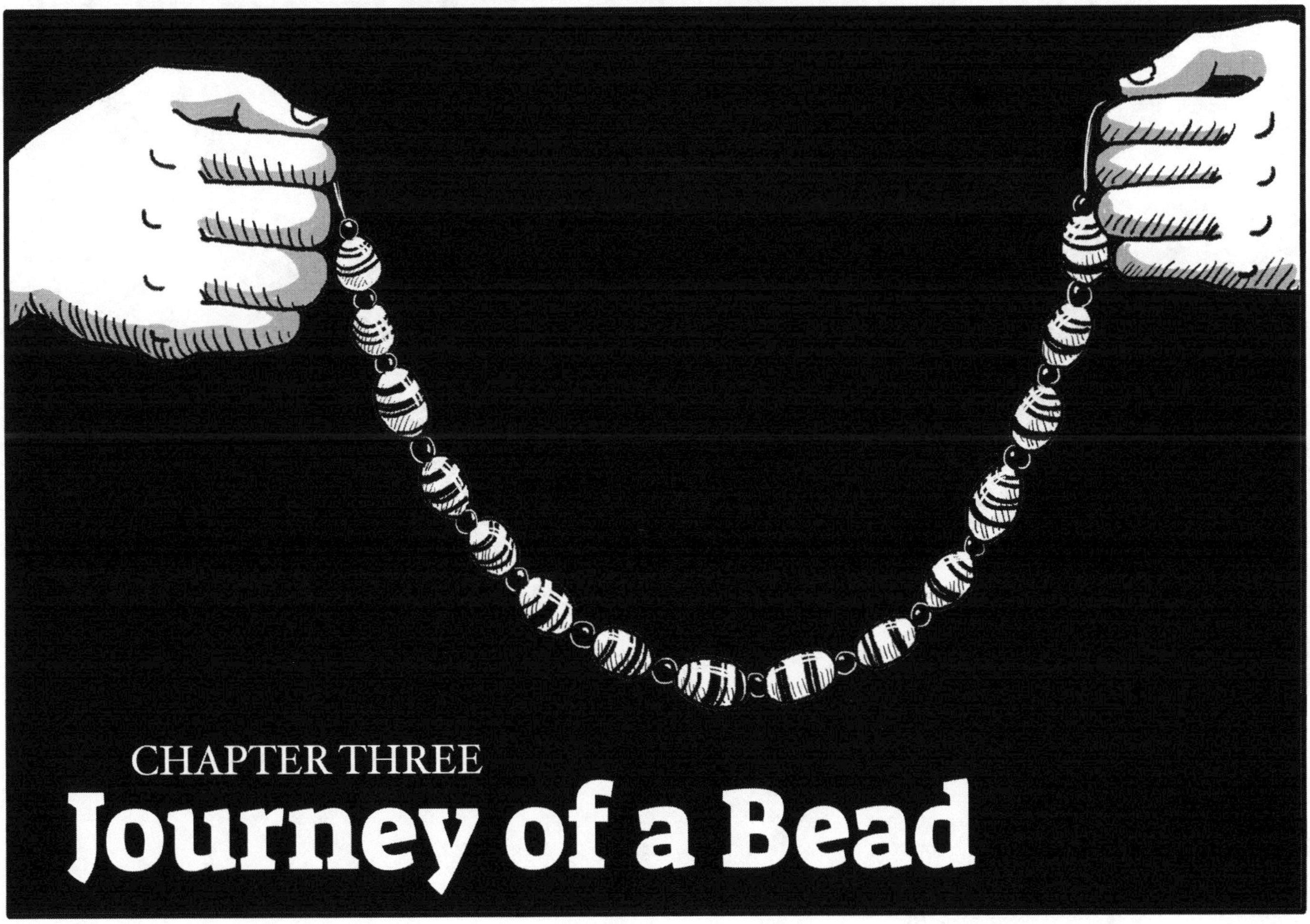

CHAPTER THREE

Journey of a Bead

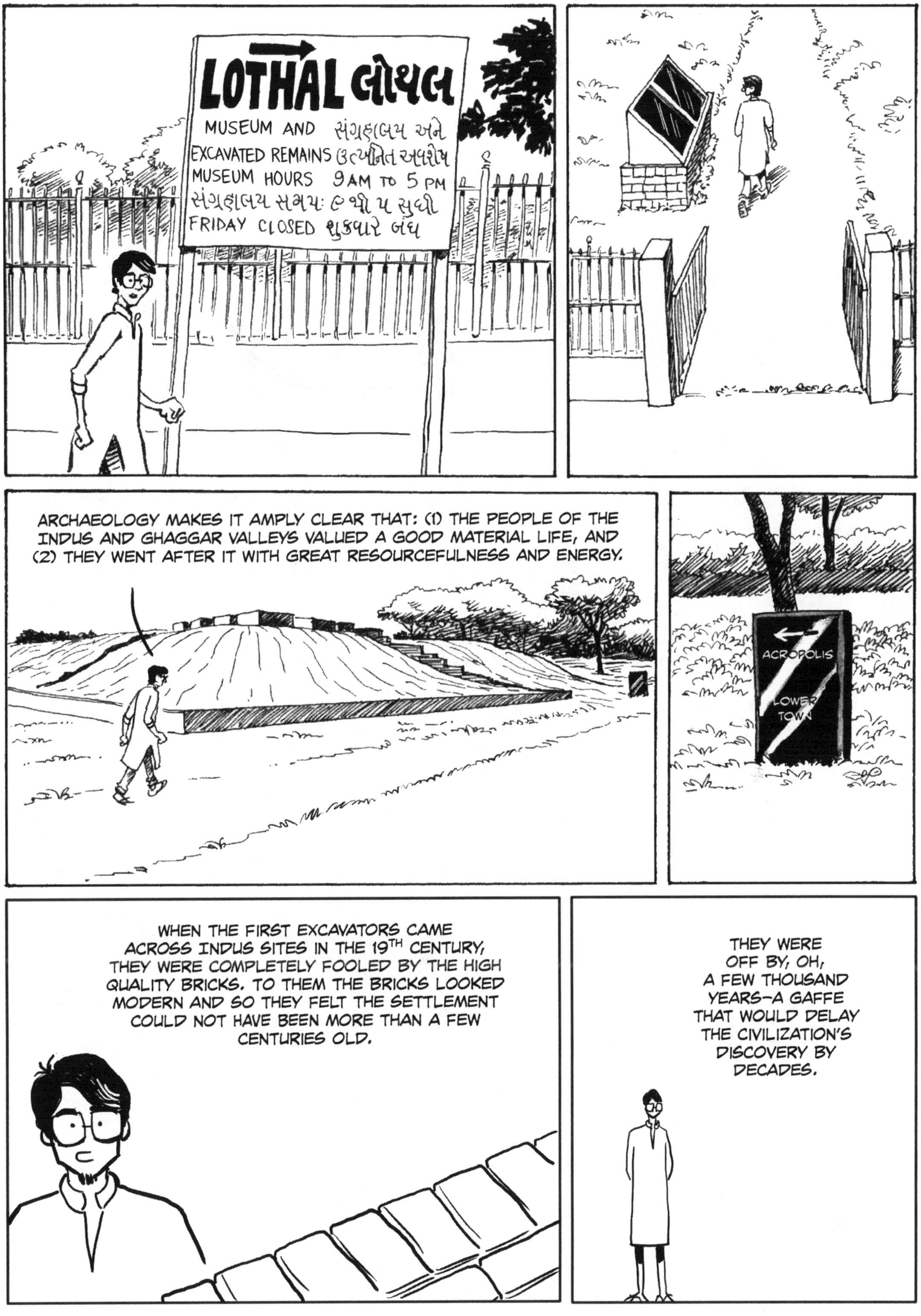

LOTHAL લોથલ
MUSEUM AND સંગ્રહાલય અને
EXCAVATED REMAINS ઉત્ખનિત અવશેષ
MUSEUM HOURS 9 AM TO 5 PM
સંગ્રહાલય સમય: ૯ થી ૫ સુધી
FRIDAY CLOSED શુક્રવારે બંધ
ARCHAEOLOGY MAKES IT AMPLY CLEAR THAT: (1) THE PEOPLE OF THE INDUS AND GHAGGAR VALLEYS VALUED A GOOD MATERIAL LIFE, AND (2) THEY WENT AFTER IT WITH GREAT RESOURCEFULNESS AND ENERGY.
ACROPOLIS
LOWER TOWN
WHEN THE FIRST EXCAVATORS CAME ACROSS INDUS SITES IN THE 19TH CENTURY, THEY WERE COMPLETELY FOOLED BY THE HIGH QUALITY BRICKS. TO THEM THE BRICKS LOOKED MODERN AND SO THEY FELT THE SETTLEMENT COULD NOT HAVE BEEN MORE THAN A FEW CENTURIES OLD.
THEY WERE OFF BY, OH, A FEW THOUSAND YEARS—A GAFFE THAT WOULD DELAY THE CIVILIZATION'S DISCOVERY BY DECADES.

THIS EXCEPTIONALLY HIGH CRAFTING PERVADES ALL MATERIAL ASPECTS OF INDUS LIFE.

FOR EXAMPLE, THEIR METAL TOOLS. THEIR AXES AND KNIVES WERE MADE OF COPPER ALLOYED WITH ARSENIC AND TIN TO PRODUCE BRONZE AS HARD AS STEEL.

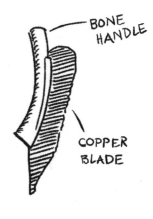

BONE HANDLE

COPPER BLADE

ALLOYS OF COPPER WITH TIN AND LEAD PRODUCED SHINY SURFACES IDEAL FOR MAKING MIRRORS AND HIGH END VESSELS.

BRONZE MIRRORS

COPPER WITH TIN WAS USED TO MAKE GOLDEN COLOURED ORNAMENTS.

ALLOYS WITH LEAD, ZINC AND ARSENIC AS WELL AS UNALLOYED COPPER WERE USED TO MAKE VASES, JARS, PANS, PENDANTS, BANGLES, BEADS AND BLADES WHICH ARE FOUND IN ABUNDANCE BY EXCAVATORS.

FOR JEWELLERY THEY USED MARINE SHELL, IVORY, SEMI-PRECIOUS STONES LIKE CARNELIAN AND AGATE, GOLD, SILVER AND AN ARTIFICIAL GLASS-LIKE MATERIAL CALLED **FAIENCE**.

SOME OF THEIR JEWELLERY WAS SO REFINED THAT EVEN MESOPOTAMIAN KINGS AND QUEENS WERE FOND OF IT—SOME OF IT HAS TURNED UP IN MESOPOTAMIAN ROYAL GRAVES DATED TO 2500 BCE.

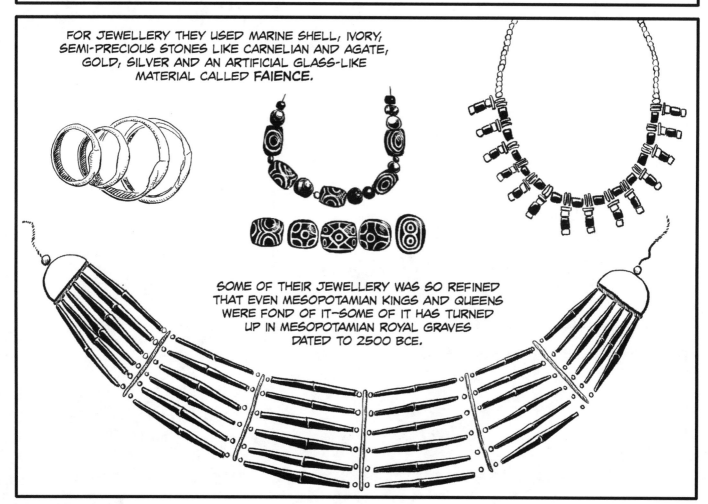

ARCHAEOLOGISTS FIND REMAINS OF NUMEROUS WORKSHOPS IN HARAPPAN CITIES AND TOWNS THAT MANUFACTURED THESE GOODS IN LARGE NUMBERS.

THERE ARE EVEN WORKSHOPS THAT MASS-PRODUCED ONLY ONE ITEM, WHICH POINTS TO THE HIGHLY SPECIALIZED NATURE OF HARAPPAN INDUSTRY.[1]

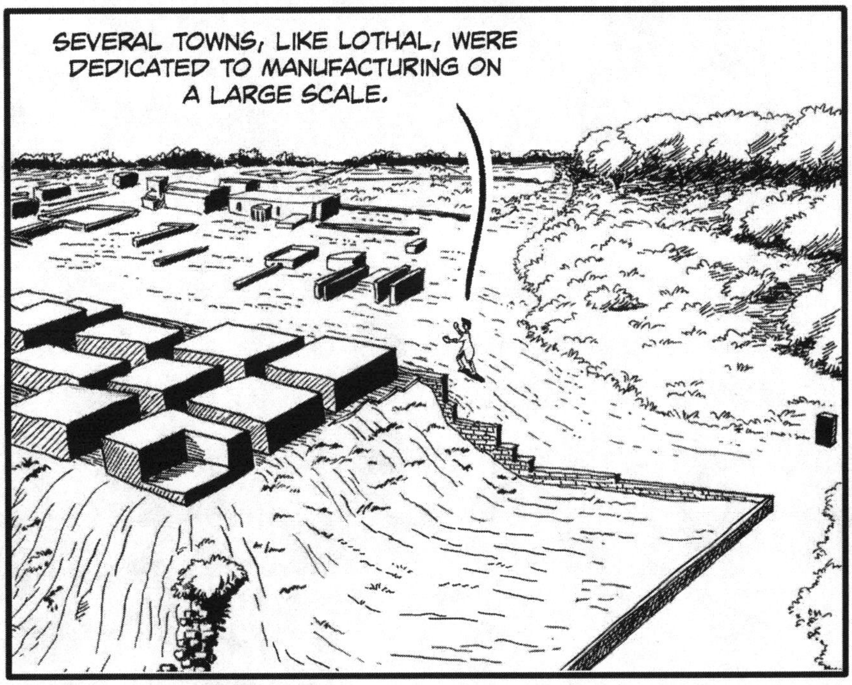

SEVERAL TOWNS, LIKE LOTHAL, WERE DEDICATED TO MANUFACTURING ON A LARGE SCALE.

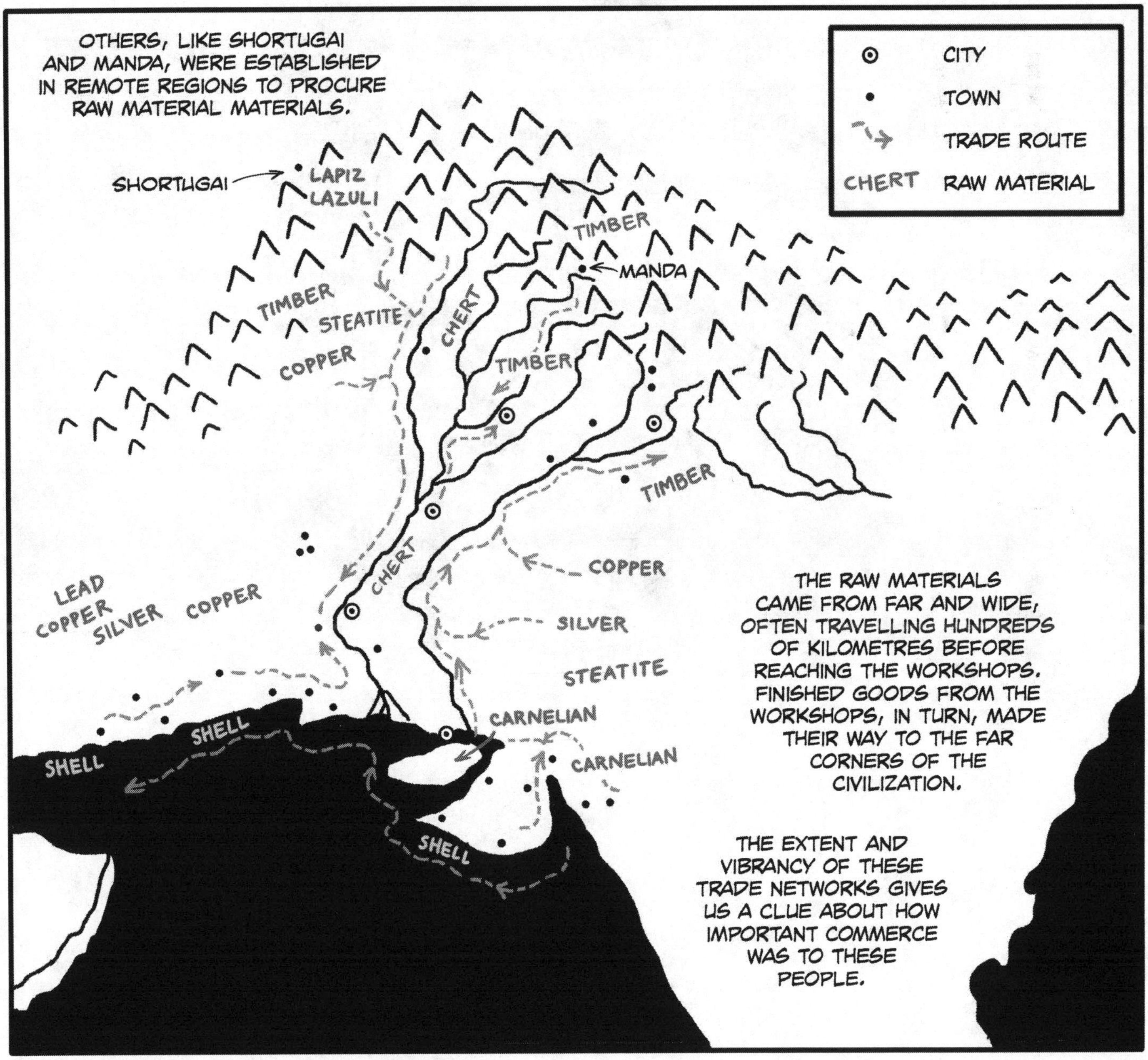

OTHERS, LIKE SHORTUGAI AND MANDA, WERE ESTABLISHED IN REMOTE REGIONS TO PROCURE RAW MATERIAL MATERIALS.
CITY
TOWN
TRADE ROUTE
CHERT RAW MATERIAL
SHORTUGAI
LAPIZ LAZULI
TIMBER
MANDA
TIMBER
STEATITE
COPPER
CHERT
TIMBER
TIMBER
LEAD
COPPER
SILVER
COPPER
CHERT
COPPER
SILVER
STEATITE
SHELL
SHELL
CARNELIAN
CARNELIAN
SHELL
THE RAW MATERIALS CAME FROM FAR AND WIDE, OFTEN TRAVELLING HUNDREDS OF KILOMETRES BEFORE REACHING THE WORKSHOPS. FINISHED GOODS FROM THE WORKSHOPS, IN TURN, MADE THEIR WAY TO THE FAR CORNERS OF THE CIVILIZATION.
THE EXTENT AND VIBRANCY OF THESE TRADE NETWORKS GIVES US A CLUE ABOUT HOW IMPORTANT COMMERCE WAS TO THESE PEOPLE.

ARCHAEOLOGY SHOWS US THAT TRADE AND INDUSTRY, RATHER THAN WARFARE, WAS THE ROUTE TO POWER AND RICHES IN HARAPPAN SOCIETY.

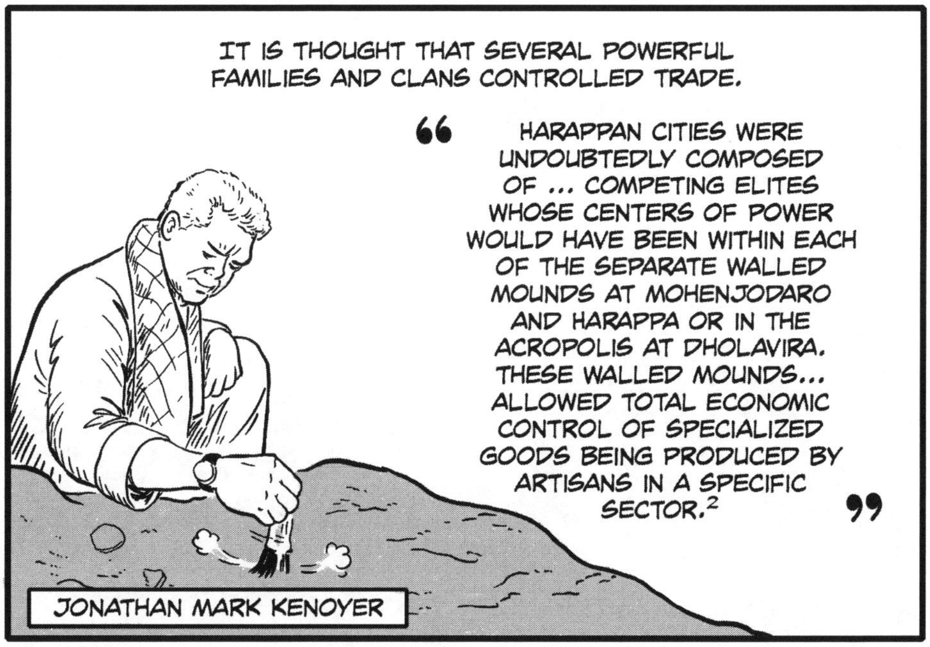
IT IS THOUGHT THAT SEVERAL POWERFUL FAMILIES AND CLANS CONTROLLED TRADE.
“HARAPPAN CITIES WERE UNDOUBTEDLY COMPOSED OF ... COMPETING ELITES WHOSE CENTERS OF POWER WOULD HAVE BEEN WITHIN EACH OF THE SEPARATE WALLED MOUNDS AT MOHENJODARO AND HARAPPA OR IN THE ACROPOLIS AT DHOLAVIRA. THESE WALLED MOUNDS... ALLOWED TOTAL ECONOMIC CONTROL OF SPECIALIZED GOODS BEING PRODUCED BY ARTISANS IN A SPECIFIC SECTOR.[2]”
JONATHAN MARK KENOYER

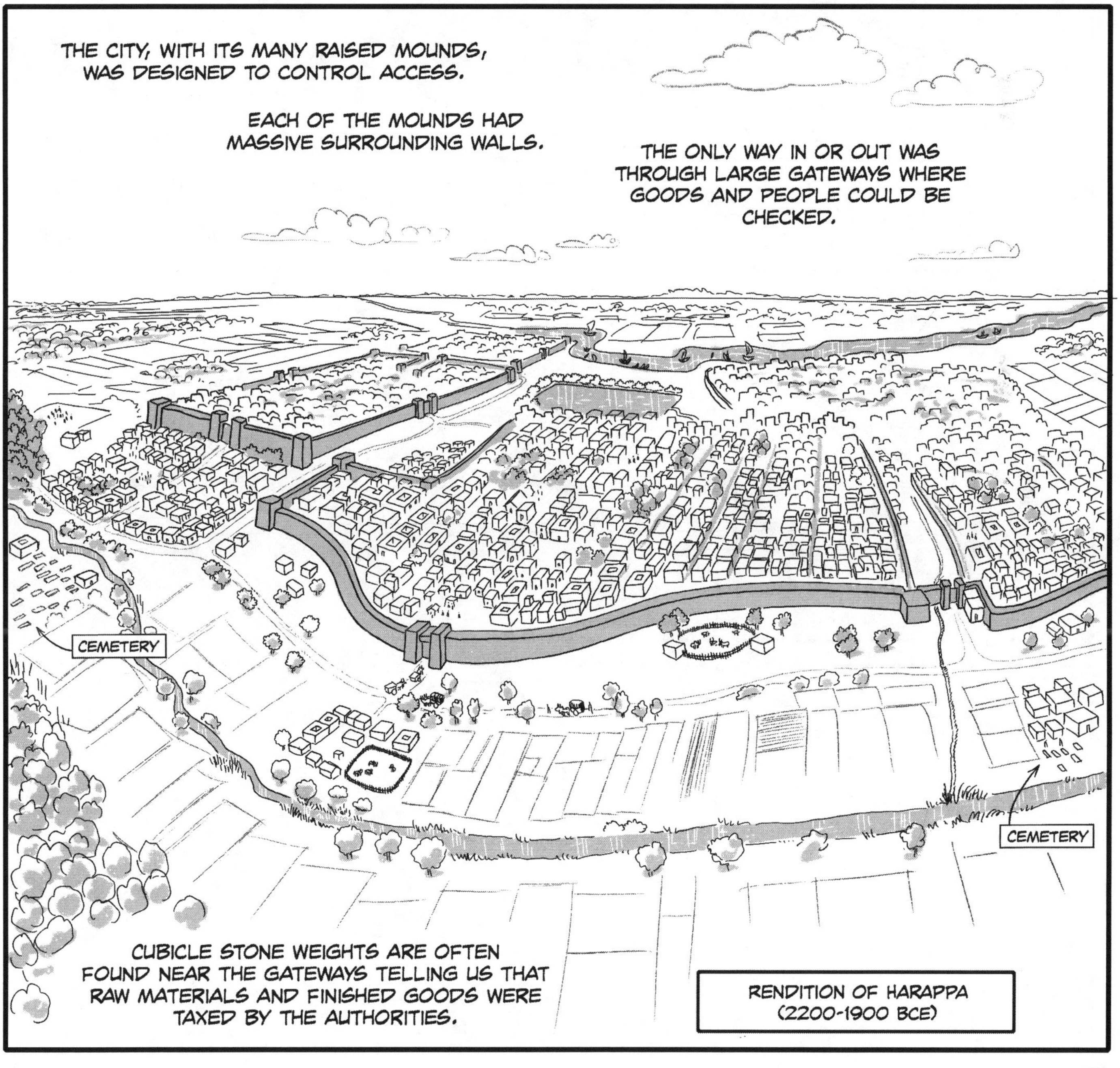
THE CITY, WITH ITS MANY RAISED MOUNDS, WAS DESIGNED TO CONTROL ACCESS.
EACH OF THE MOUNDS HAD MASSIVE SURROUNDING WALLS.
THE ONLY WAY IN OR OUT WAS THROUGH LARGE GATEWAYS WHERE GOODS AND PEOPLE COULD BE CHECKED.
CEMETERY
CEMETERY
CUBICLE STONE WEIGHTS ARE OFTEN FOUND NEAR THE GATEWAYS TELLING US THAT RAW MATERIALS AND FINISHED GOODS WERE TAXED BY THE AUTHORITIES.
RENDITION OF HARAPPA (2200-1900 BCE)

SINCE THERE WERE NO KINGS TO MONOPOLIZE TRADE HERE, COMPETITION BETWEEN THE VARIOUS RULING CLANS MUST HAVE BEEN INTENSE.

BY PROVIDING BETTER LIVING AND WORKING CONDITIONS PERHAPS THE RULING CLANS COULD ATTRACT BETTER CRAFTSPEOPLE AND WORKERS TO THEIR MOUNDS. BUSY MARKETS MADE THE ENTIRE MOUND PROSPER.

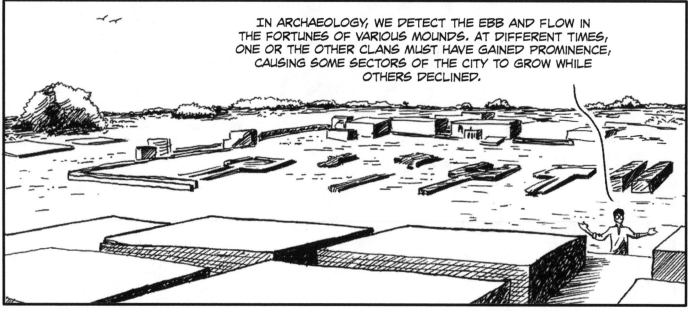

IN ARCHAEOLOGY, WE DETECT THE EBB AND FLOW IN THE FORTUNES OF VARIOUS MOUNDS. AT DIFFERENT TIMES, ONE OR THE OTHER CLANS MUST HAVE GAINED PROMINENCE, CAUSING SOME SECTORS OF THE CITY TO GROW WHILE OTHERS DECLINED.

WE DON'T KNOW MUCH ABOUT THESE RULING CLANS AND FAMILIES, BUT WE DETECT THEIR PRESENCE IN THEIR FIRED STEATITE SEALS.

UNDECIPHERED WRITING

ANIMAL MOTIFS

SEALS CONTAIN BY FAR THE BEST HARAPPAN ARTWORKS.

AND YET THEY ARE OFTEN NO BIGGER THAN THIS.

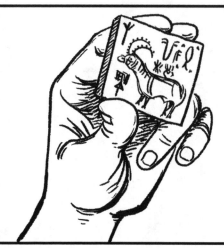

CLEARLY THEY WERE CARVED BY EXPERTS. ONLY A FEW PEOPLE WOULD HAVE OWNED OR CARRIED ONE.

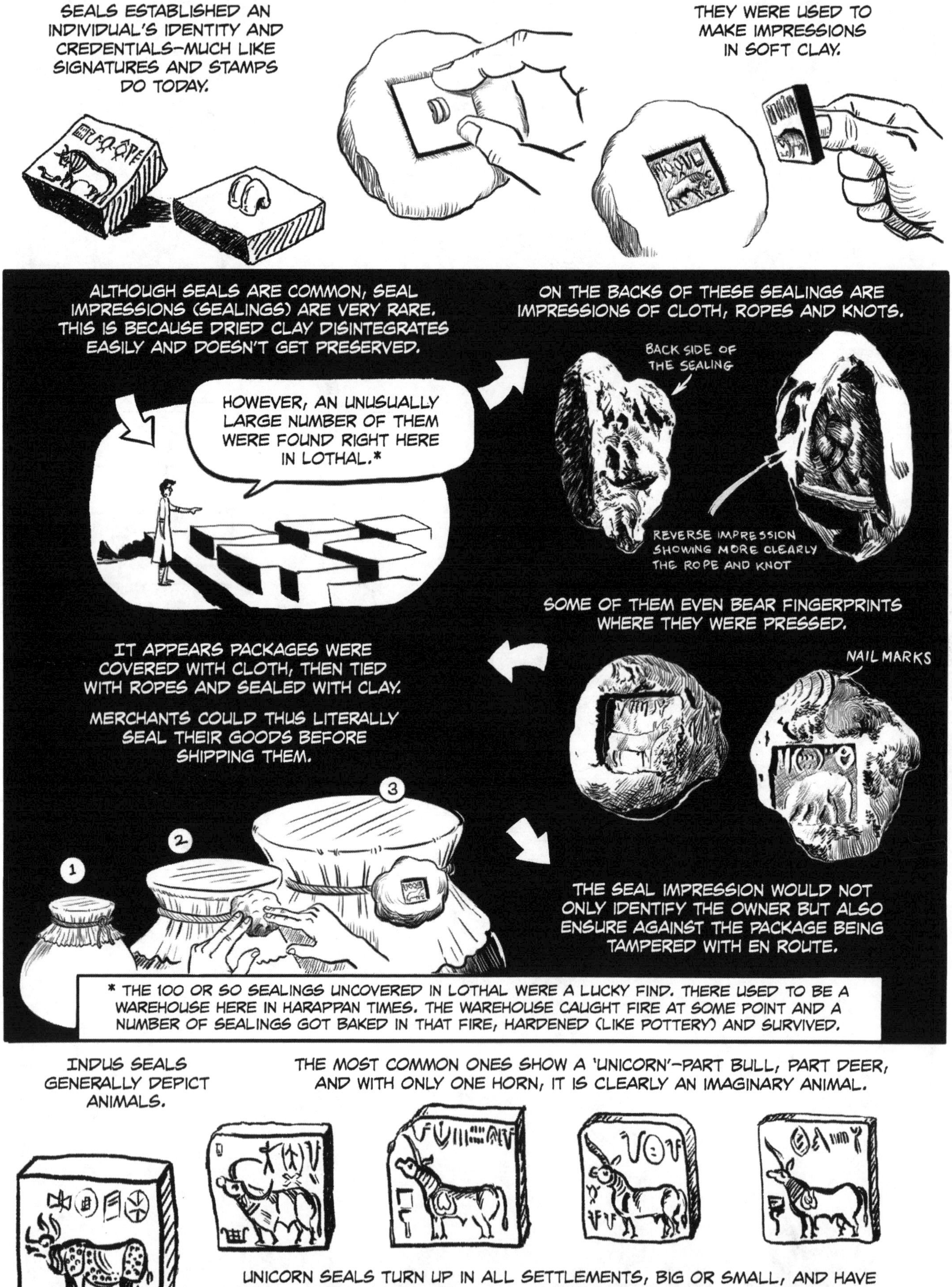
SEALS ESTABLISHED AN INDIVIDUAL'S IDENTITY AND CREDENTIALS—MUCH LIKE SIGNATURES AND STAMPS DO TODAY.
THEY WERE USED TO MAKE IMPRESSIONS IN SOFT CLAY.
ALTHOUGH SEALS ARE COMMON, SEAL IMPRESSIONS (SEALINGS) ARE VERY RARE. THIS IS BECAUSE DRIED CLAY DISINTEGRATES EASILY AND DOESN'T GET PRESERVED.
HOWEVER, AN UNUSUALLY LARGE NUMBER OF THEM WERE FOUND RIGHT HERE IN LOTHAL.*
ON THE BACKS OF THESE SEALINGS ARE IMPRESSIONS OF CLOTH, ROPES AND KNOTS.
BACK SIDE OF THE SEALING
REVERSE IMPRESSION SHOWING MORE CLEARLY THE ROPE AND KNOT
SOME OF THEM EVEN BEAR FINGERPRINTS WHERE THEY WERE PRESSED.
NAIL MARKS
IT APPEARS PACKAGES WERE COVERED WITH CLOTH, THEN TIED WITH ROPES AND SEALED WITH CLAY.
MERCHANTS COULD THUS LITERALLY SEAL THEIR GOODS BEFORE SHIPPING THEM.
1
2
3
THE SEAL IMPRESSION WOULD NOT ONLY IDENTIFY THE OWNER BUT ALSO ENSURE AGAINST THE PACKAGE BEING TAMPERED WITH EN ROUTE.
* THE 100 OR SO SEALINGS UNCOVERED IN LOTHAL WERE A LUCKY FIND. THERE USED TO BE A WAREHOUSE HERE IN HARAPPAN TIMES. THE WAREHOUSE CAUGHT FIRE AT SOME POINT AND A NUMBER OF SEALINGS GOT BAKED IN THAT FIRE, HARDENED (LIKE POTTERY) AND SURVIVED.
INDUS SEALS GENERALLY DEPICT ANIMALS.
THE MOST COMMON ONES SHOW A 'UNICORN'—PART BULL, PART DEER, AND WITH ONLY ONE HORN, IT IS CLEARLY AN IMAGINARY ANIMAL.
UNICORN SEALS TURN UP IN ALL SETTLEMENTS, BIG OR SMALL, AND HAVE BEEN FOUND EVEN IN MESOPOTAMIA. THEY ARE THOUGHT TO REPRESENT AN IMPORTANT MERCHANT CLAN. THEY FIRST APPEAR AROUND 2600 BCE BUT STOP BEING USED BY 1900 BCE.

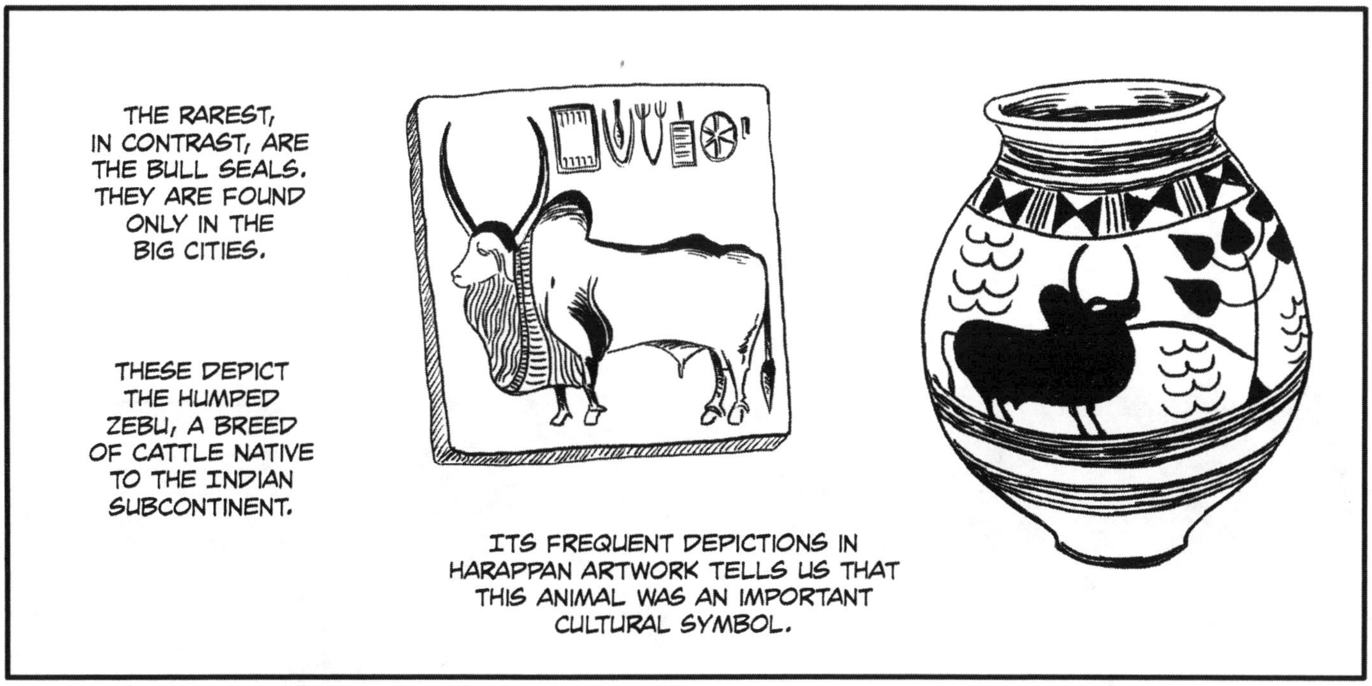
THE RAREST, IN CONTRAST, ARE THE BULL SEALS. THEY ARE FOUND ONLY IN THE BIG CITIES.
THESE DEPICT THE HUMPED ZEBU, A BREED OF CATTLE NATIVE TO THE INDIAN SUBCONTINENT.
ITS FREQUENT DEPICTIONS IN HARAPPAN ARTWORK TELLS US THAT THIS ANIMAL WAS AN IMPORTANT CULTURAL SYMBOL.

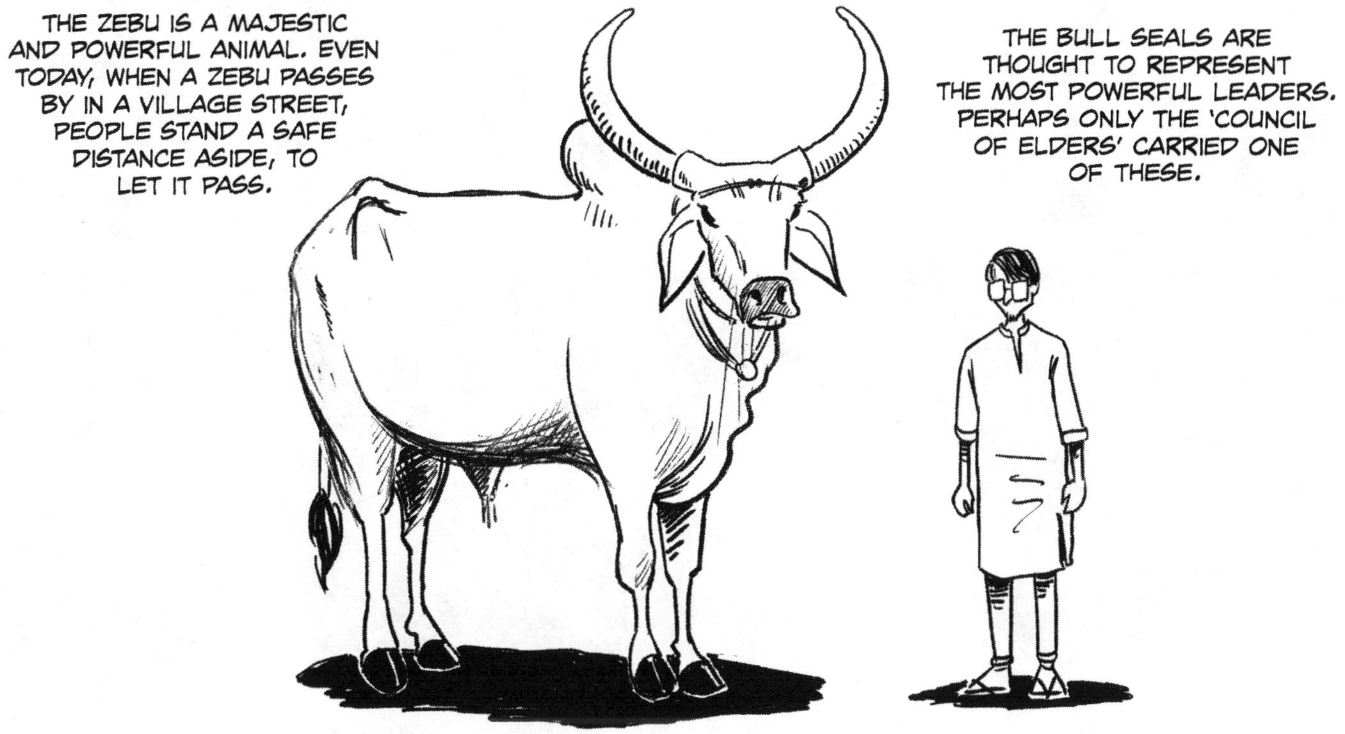
THE ZEBU IS A MAJESTIC AND POWERFUL ANIMAL. EVEN TODAY, WHEN A ZEBU PASSES BY IN A VILLAGE STREET, PEOPLE STAND A SAFE DISTANCE ASIDE, TO LET IT PASS.
THE BULL SEALS ARE THOUGHT TO REPRESENT THE MOST POWERFUL LEADERS. PERHAPS ONLY THE 'COUNCIL OF ELDERS' CARRIED ONE OF THESE.

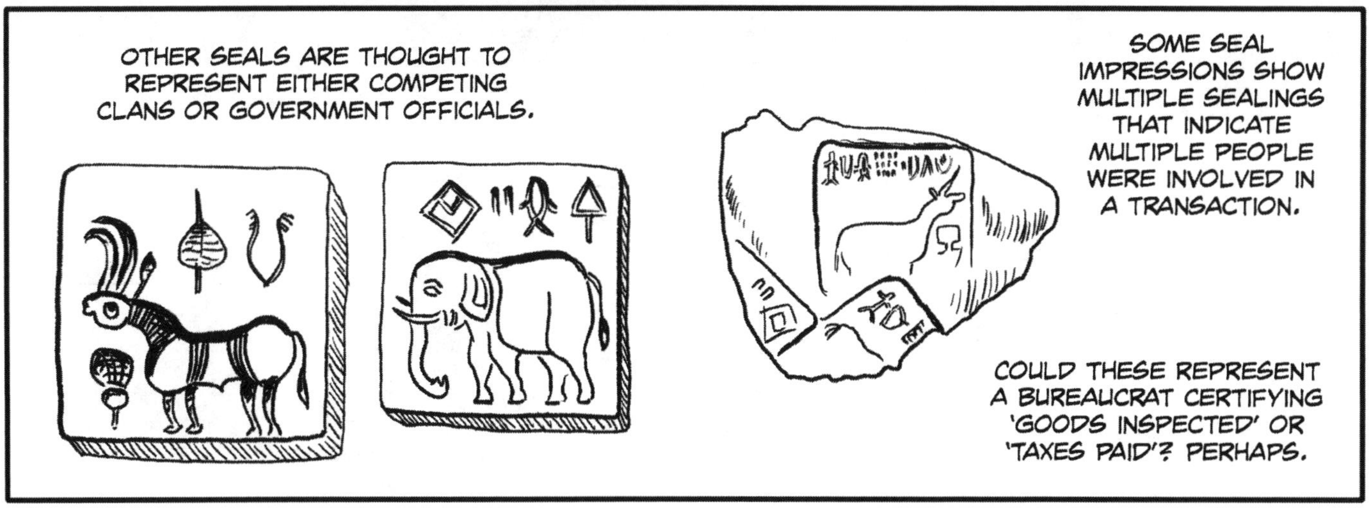
OTHER SEALS ARE THOUGHT TO REPRESENT EITHER COMPETING CLANS OR GOVERNMENT OFFICIALS.
SOME SEAL IMPRESSIONS SHOW MULTIPLE SEALINGS THAT INDICATE MULTIPLE PEOPLE WERE INVOLVED IN A TRANSACTION.
COULD THESE REPRESENT A BUREAUCRAT CERTIFYING 'GOODS INSPECTED' OR 'TAXES PAID'? PERHAPS.

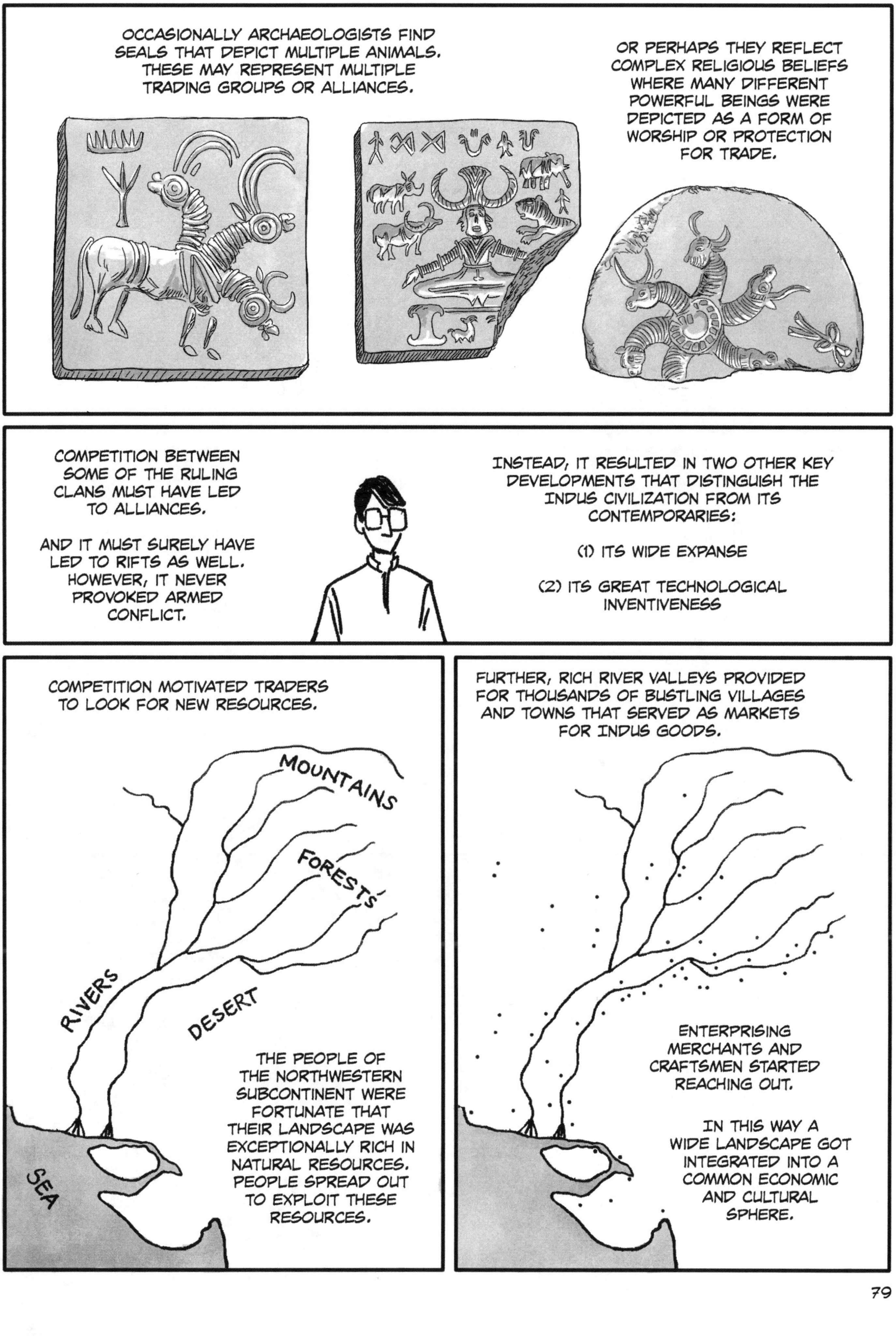

OCCASIONALLY ARCHAEOLOGISTS FIND SEALS THAT DEPICT MULTIPLE ANIMALS. THESE MAY REPRESENT MULTIPLE TRADING GROUPS OR ALLIANCES.

OR PERHAPS THEY REFLECT COMPLEX RELIGIOUS BELIEFS WHERE MANY DIFFERENT POWERFUL BEINGS WERE DEPICTED AS A FORM OF WORSHIP OR PROTECTION FOR TRADE.

COMPETITION BETWEEN SOME OF THE RULING CLANS MUST HAVE LED TO ALLIANCES.

AND IT MUST SURELY HAVE LED TO RIFTS AS WELL. HOWEVER, IT NEVER PROVOKED ARMED CONFLICT.

INSTEAD, IT RESULTED IN TWO OTHER KEY DEVELOPMENTS THAT DISTINGUISH THE INDUS CIVILIZATION FROM ITS CONTEMPORARIES:

(1) ITS WIDE EXPANSE

(2) ITS GREAT TECHNOLOGICAL INVENTIVENESS

COMPETITION MOTIVATED TRADERS TO LOOK FOR NEW RESOURCES.

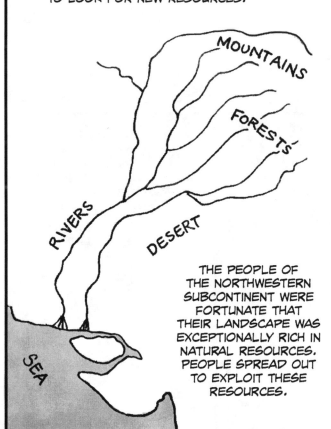

MOUNTAINS

FORESTS

RIVERS

DESERT

SEA

THE PEOPLE OF THE NORTHWESTERN SUBCONTINENT WERE FORTUNATE THAT THEIR LANDSCAPE WAS EXCEPTIONALLY RICH IN NATURAL RESOURCES. PEOPLE SPREAD OUT TO EXPLOIT THESE RESOURCES.

FURTHER, RICH RIVER VALLEYS PROVIDED FOR THOUSANDS OF BUSTLING VILLAGES AND TOWNS THAT SERVED AS MARKETS FOR INDUS GOODS.

ENTERPRISING MERCHANTS AND CRAFTSMEN STARTED REACHING OUT.

IN THIS WAY A WIDE LANDSCAPE GOT INTEGRATED INTO A COMMON ECONOMIC AND CULTURAL SPHERE.

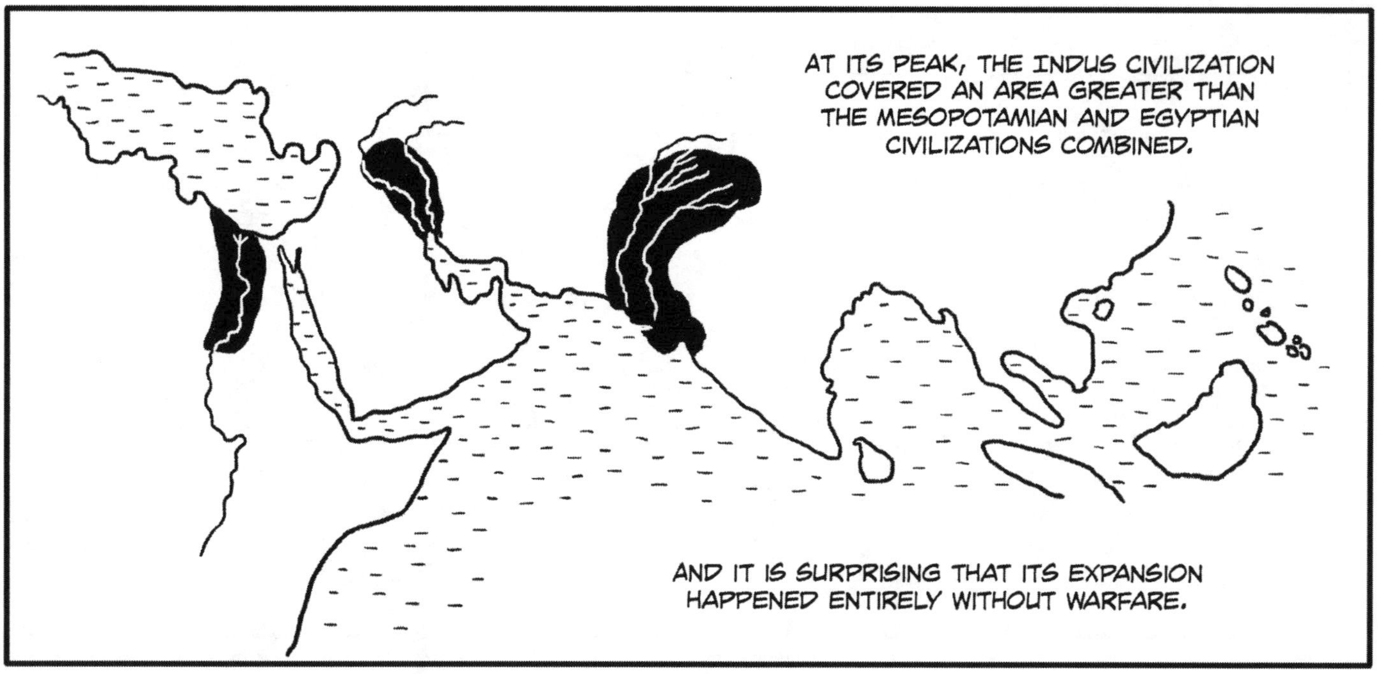
AT ITS PEAK, THE INDUS CIVILIZATION COVERED AN AREA GREATER THAN THE MESOPOTAMIAN AND EGYPTIAN CIVILIZATIONS COMBINED.
AND IT IS SURPRISING THAT ITS EXPANSION HAPPENED ENTIRELY WITHOUT WARFARE.

THE INDUS PEOPLE HAD FOUND IT PREFERABLE TO COOPERATE AND INTEGRATE DIVERSE COMMUNITIES.

THIS CAN BE SEEN IN THEIR INTERACTIONS WITH HUNTER-GATHERERS AND NOMADS WHO WERE IMPORTANT PLAYERS IN THE INDUS ECONOMIC SYSTEM BUT WERE OFTEN LOCATED ON THE PERIPHERY OF THE MAIN URBAN CENTRES.

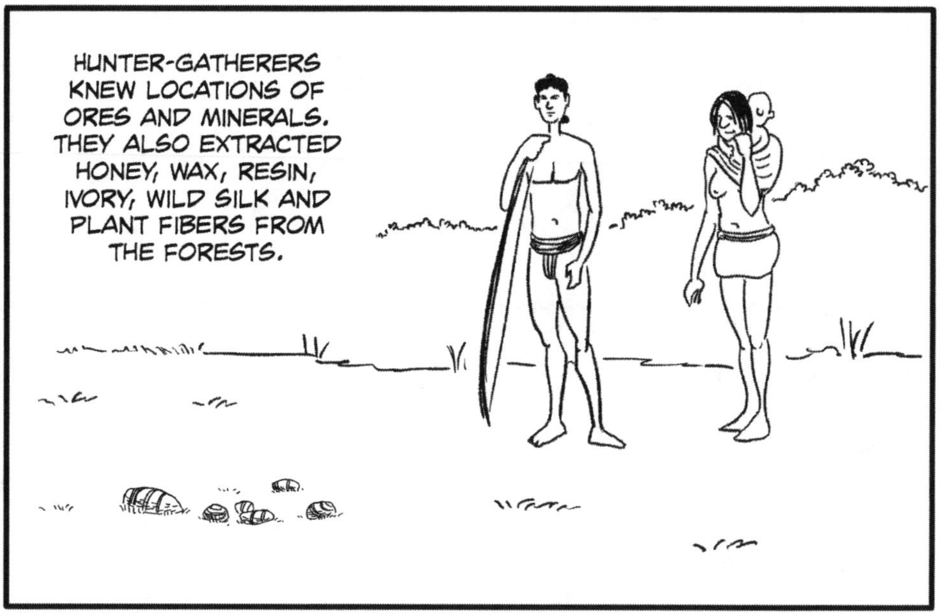
HUNTER-GATHERERS KNEW LOCATIONS OF ORES AND MINERALS. THEY ALSO EXTRACTED HONEY, WAX, RESIN, IVORY, WILD SILK AND PLANT FIBERS FROM THE FORESTS.

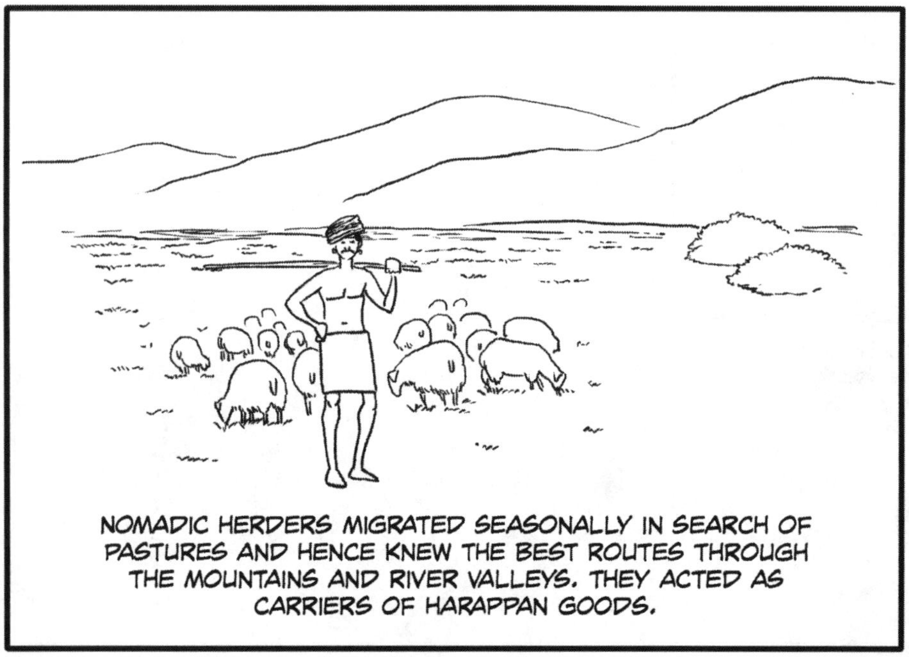
NOMADIC HERDERS MIGRATED SEASONALLY IN SEARCH OF PASTURES AND HENCE KNEW THE BEST ROUTES THROUGH THE MOUNTAINS AND RIVER VALLEYS. THEY ACTED AS CARRIERS OF HARAPPAN GOODS.

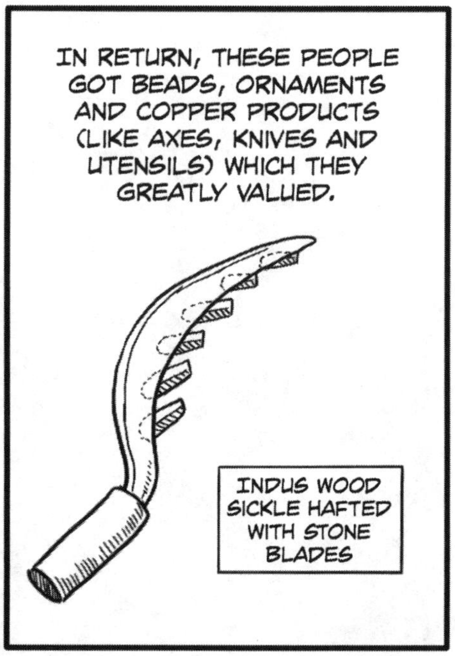
IN RETURN, THESE PEOPLE GOT BEADS, ORNAMENTS AND COPPER PRODUCTS (LIKE AXES, KNIVES AND UTENSILS) WHICH THEY GREATLY VALUED.
INDUS WOOD SICKLE HAFTED WITH STONE BLADES

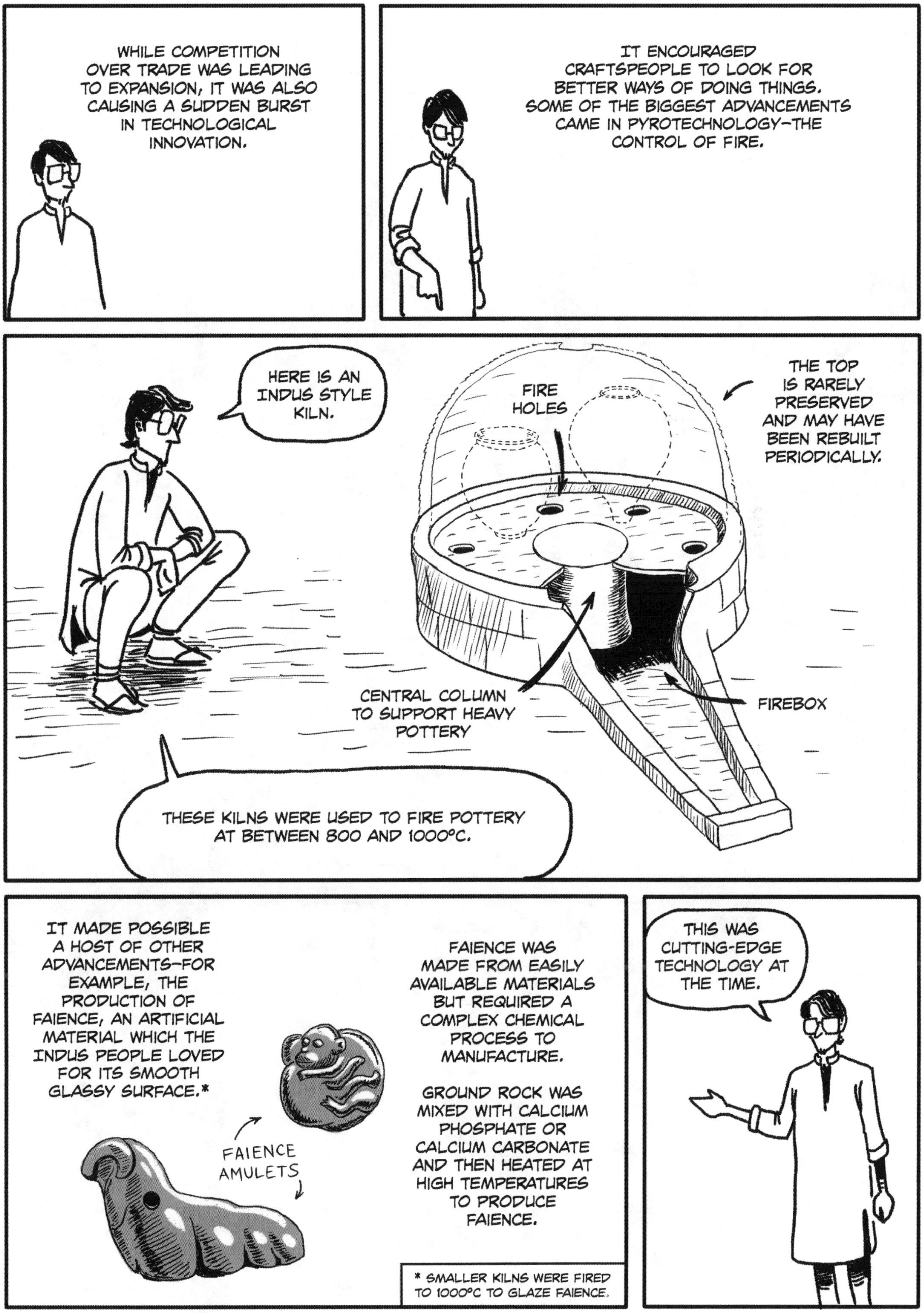

WHILE COMPETITION OVER TRADE WAS LEADING TO EXPANSION, IT WAS ALSO CAUSING A SUDDEN BURST IN TECHNOLOGICAL INNOVATION.

IT ENCOURAGED CRAFTSPEOPLE TO LOOK FOR BETTER WAYS OF DOING THINGS. SOME OF THE BIGGEST ADVANCEMENTS CAME IN PYROTECHNOLOGY—THE CONTROL OF FIRE.

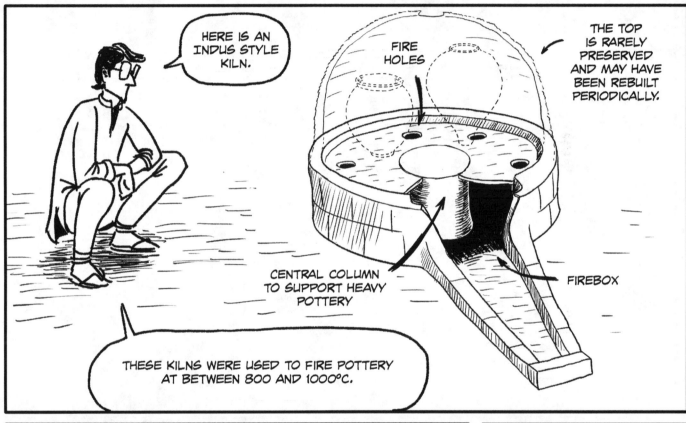

HERE IS AN INDUS STYLE KILN.

FIRE HOLES

THE TOP IS RARELY PRESERVED AND MAY HAVE BEEN REBUILT PERIODICALLY.

CENTRAL COLUMN TO SUPPORT HEAVY POTTERY

FIREBOX

THESE KILNS WERE USED TO FIRE POTTERY AT BETWEEN 800 AND 1000°C.

IT MADE POSSIBLE A HOST OF OTHER ADVANCEMENTS—FOR EXAMPLE, THE PRODUCTION OF FAIENCE, AN ARTIFICIAL MATERIAL WHICH THE INDUS PEOPLE LOVED FOR ITS SMOOTH GLASSY SURFACE.*

FAIENCE AMULETS

FAIENCE WAS MADE FROM EASILY AVAILABLE MATERIALS BUT REQUIRED A COMPLEX CHEMICAL PROCESS TO MANUFACTURE.

GROUND ROCK WAS MIXED WITH CALCIUM PHOSPHATE OR CALCIUM CARBONATE AND THEN HEATED AT HIGH TEMPERATURES TO PRODUCE FAIENCE.

* SMALLER KILNS WERE FIRED TO 1000°C TO GLAZE FAIENCE.

THIS WAS CUTTING-EDGE TECHNOLOGY AT THE TIME.

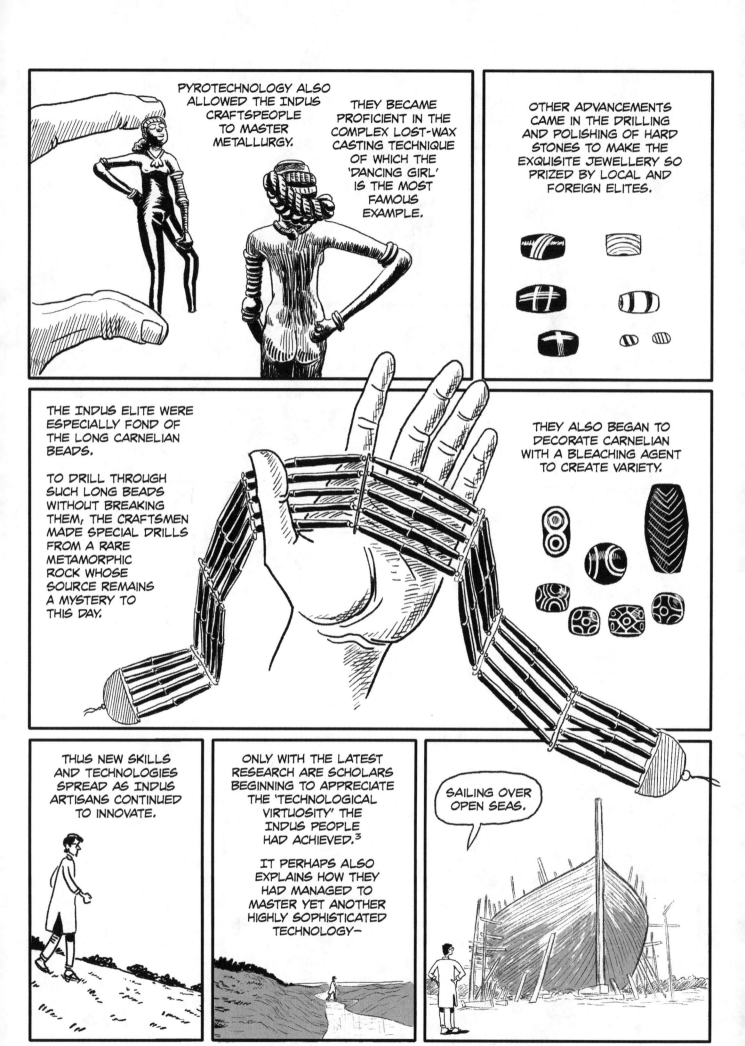

PYROTECHNOLOGY ALSO ALLOWED THE INDUS CRAFTSPEOPLE TO MASTER METALLURGY.

THEY BECAME PROFICIENT IN THE COMPLEX LOST-WAX CASTING TECHNIQUE OF WHICH THE 'DANCING GIRL' IS THE MOST FAMOUS EXAMPLE.

OTHER ADVANCEMENTS CAME IN THE DRILLING AND POLISHING OF HARD STONES TO MAKE THE EXQUISITE JEWELLERY SO PRIZED BY LOCAL AND FOREIGN ELITES.

THE INDUS ELITE WERE ESPECIALLY FOND OF THE LONG CARNELIAN BEADS.

TO DRILL THROUGH SUCH LONG BEADS WITHOUT BREAKING THEM, THE CRAFTSMEN MADE SPECIAL DRILLS FROM A RARE METAMORPHIC ROCK WHOSE SOURCE REMAINS A MYSTERY TO THIS DAY.

THEY ALSO BEGAN TO DECORATE CARNELIAN WITH A BLEACHING AGENT TO CREATE VARIETY.

THUS NEW SKILLS AND TECHNOLOGIES SPREAD AS INDUS ARTISANS CONTINUED TO INNOVATE.

ONLY WITH THE LATEST RESEARCH ARE SCHOLARS BEGINNING TO APPRECIATE THE 'TECHNOLOGICAL VIRTUOSITY' THE INDUS PEOPLE HAD ACHIEVED.[3]

IT PERHAPS ALSO EXPLAINS HOW THEY HAD MANAGED TO MASTER YET ANOTHER HIGHLY SOPHISTICATED TECHNOLOGY—

SAILING OVER OPEN SEAS.

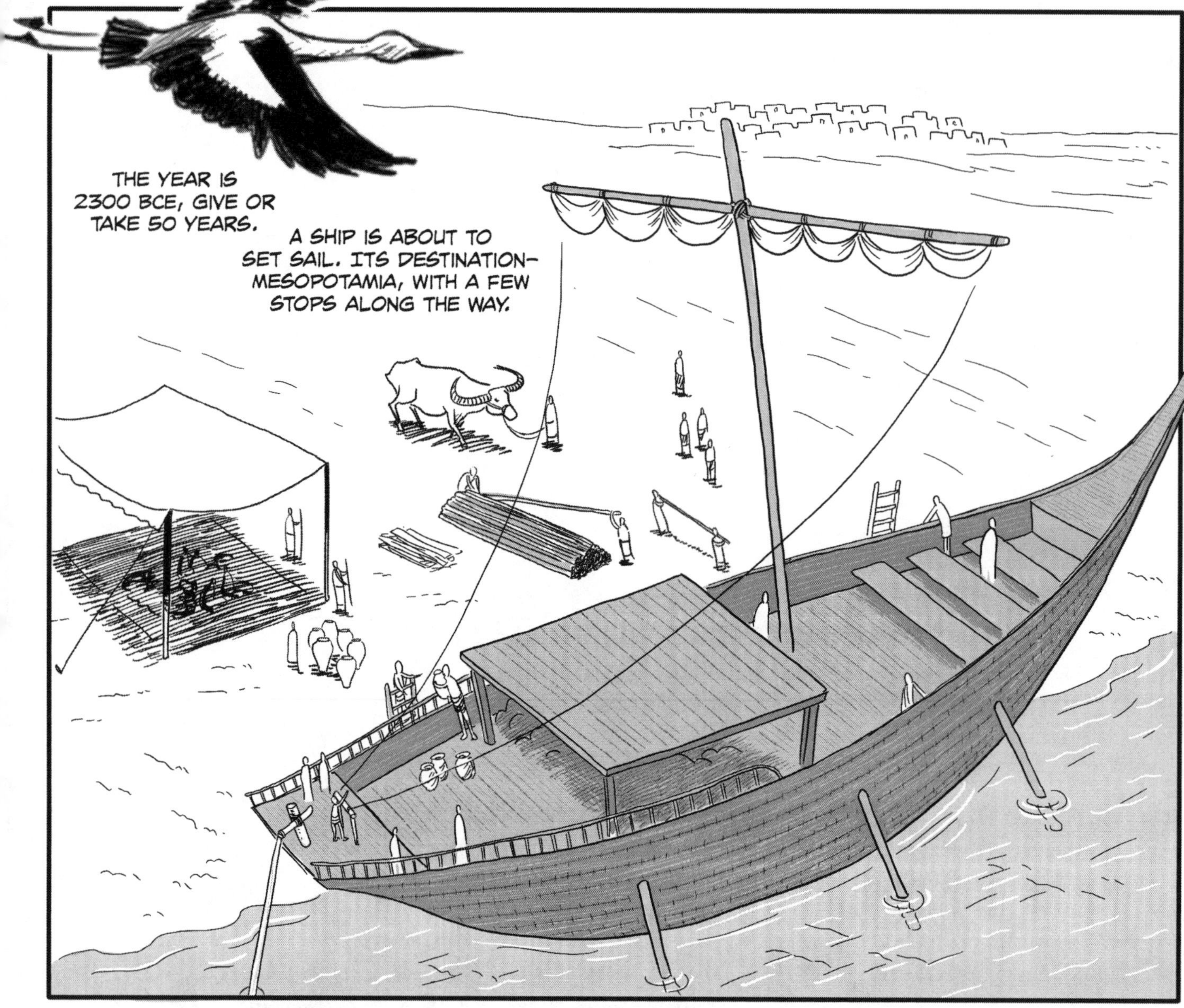
THE YEAR IS 2300 BCE, GIVE OR TAKE 50 YEARS.
A SHIP IS ABOUT TO SET SAIL. ITS DESTINATION– MESOPOTAMIA, WITH A FEW STOPS ALONG THE WAY.

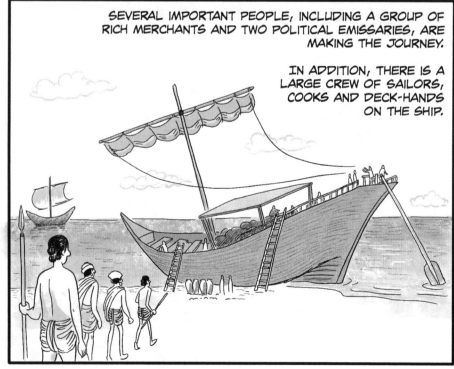

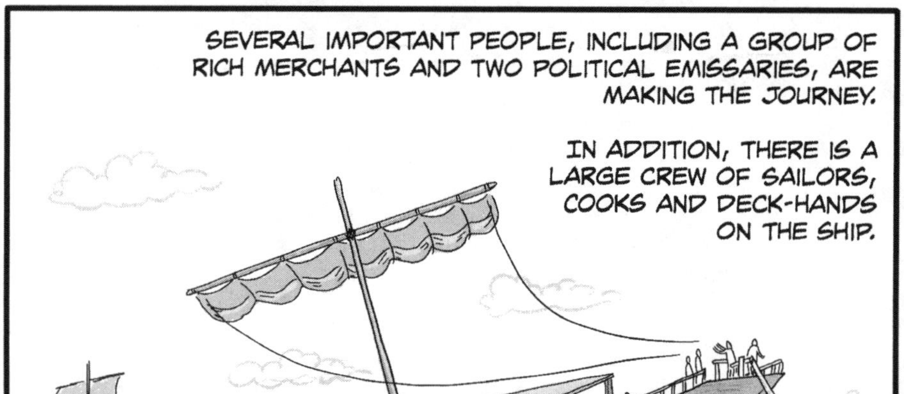
SEVERAL IMPORTANT PEOPLE, INCLUDING A GROUP OF RICH MERCHANTS AND TWO POLITICAL EMISSARIES, ARE MAKING THE JOURNEY.
IN ADDITION, THERE IS A LARGE CREW OF SAILORS, COOKS AND DECK-HANDS ON THE SHIP.

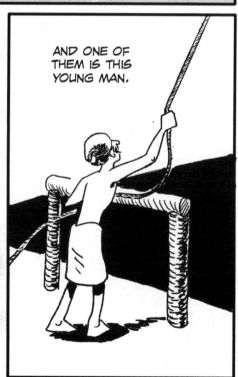

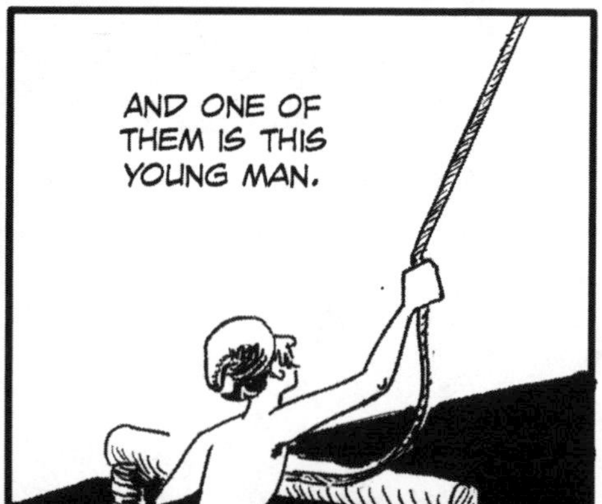
AND ONE OF THEM IS THIS YOUNG MAN.

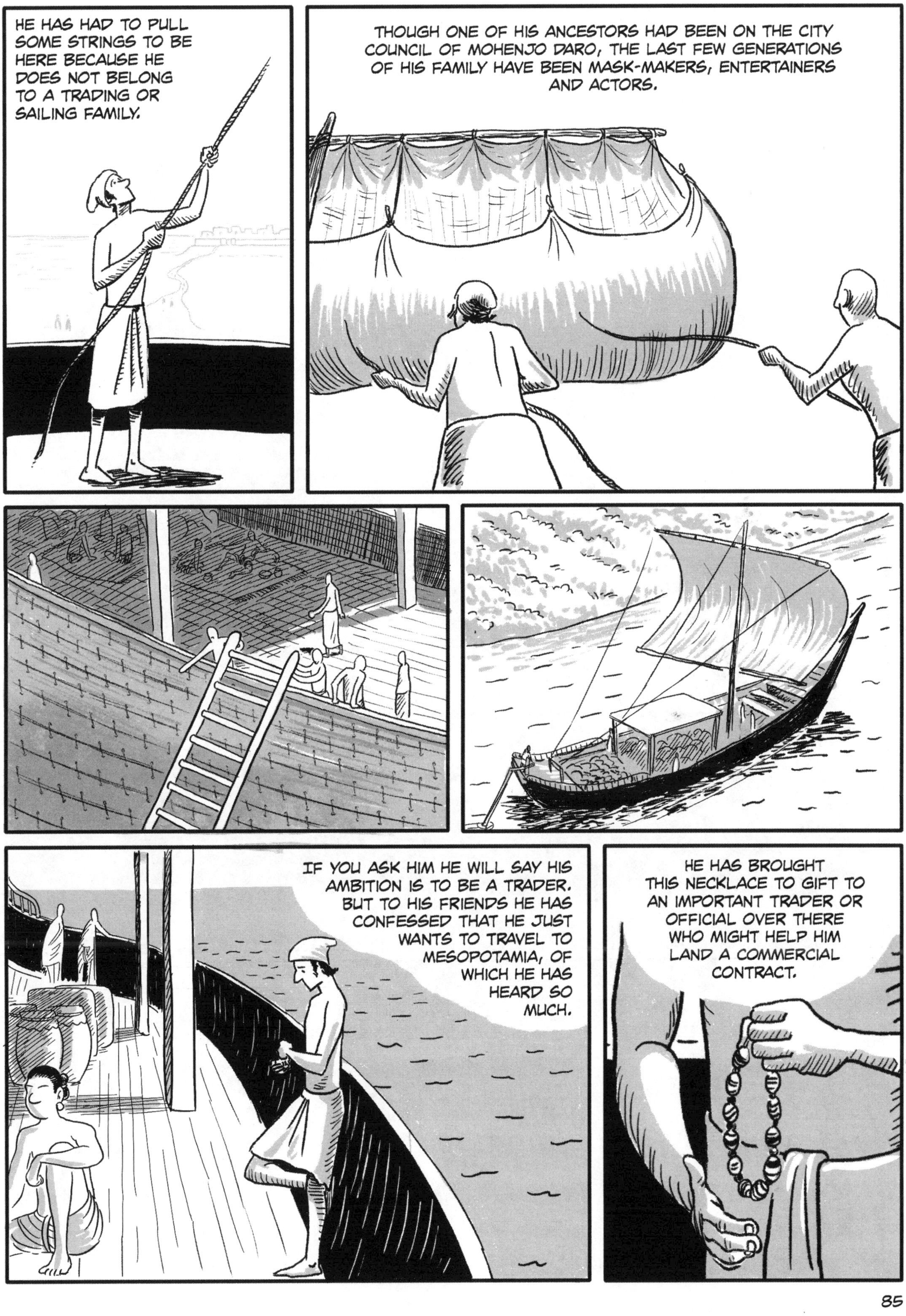
HE HAS HAD TO PULL SOME STRINGS TO BE HERE BECAUSE HE DOES NOT BELONG TO A TRADING OR SAILING FAMILY.
THOUGH ONE OF HIS ANCESTORS HAD BEEN ON THE CITY COUNCIL OF MOHENJO DARO, THE LAST FEW GENERATIONS OF HIS FAMILY HAVE BEEN MASK-MAKERS, ENTERTAINERS AND ACTORS.
IF YOU ASK HIM HE WILL SAY HIS AMBITION IS TO BE A TRADER. BUT TO HIS FRIENDS HE HAS CONFESSED THAT HE JUST WANTS TO TRAVEL TO MESOPOTAMIA, OF WHICH HE HAS HEARD SO MUCH.
HE HAS BROUGHT THIS NECKLACE TO GIFT TO AN IMPORTANT TRADER OR OFFICIAL OVER THERE WHO MIGHT HELP HIM LAND A COMMERCIAL CONTRACT.

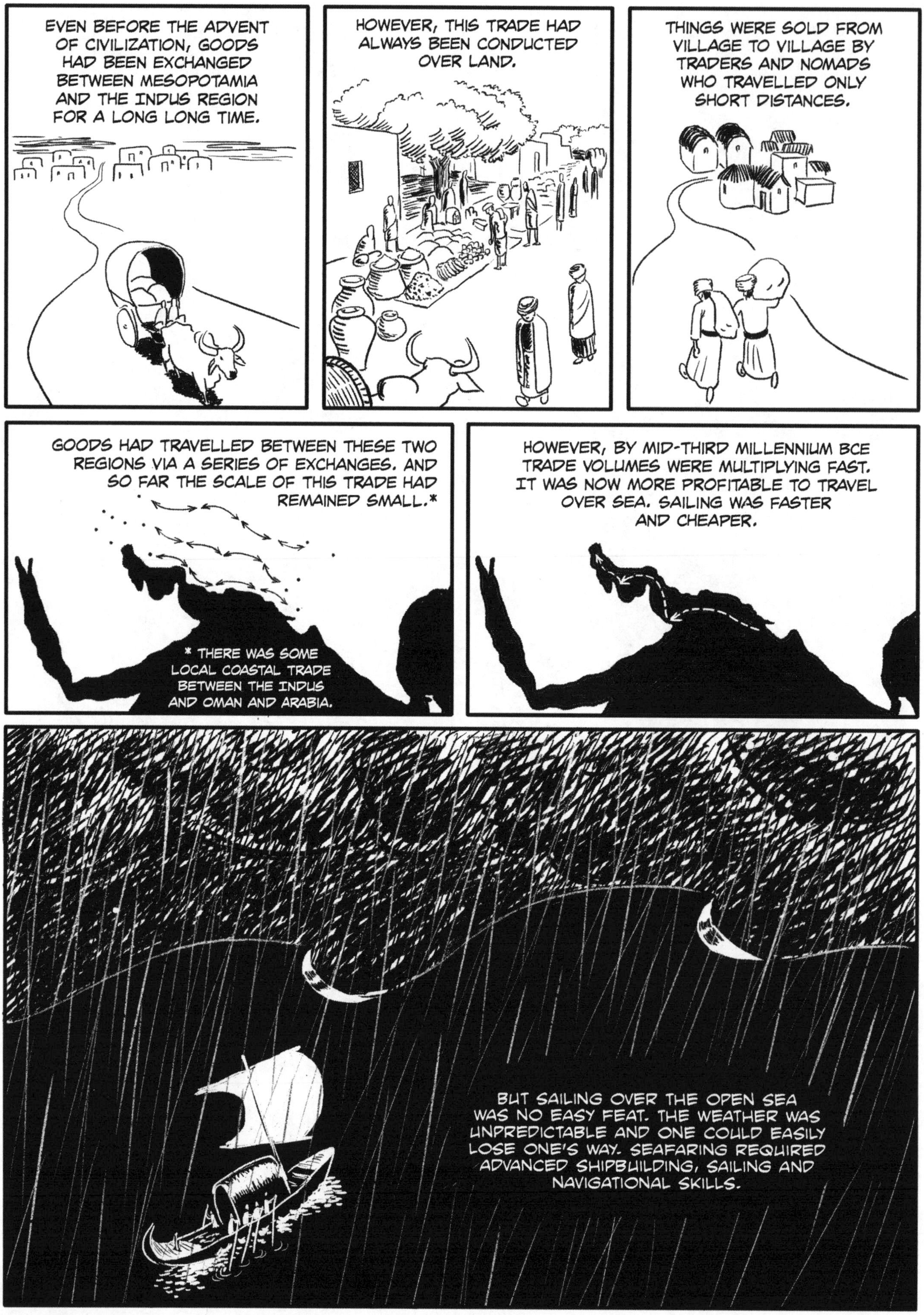
EVEN BEFORE THE ADVENT OF CIVILIZATION, GOODS HAD BEEN EXCHANGED BETWEEN MESOPOTAMIA AND THE INDUS REGION FOR A LONG LONG TIME.
HOWEVER, THIS TRADE HAD ALWAYS BEEN CONDUCTED OVER LAND.
THINGS WERE SOLD FROM VILLAGE TO VILLAGE BY TRADERS AND NOMADS WHO TRAVELLED ONLY SHORT DISTANCES.
GOODS HAD TRAVELLED BETWEEN THESE TWO REGIONS VIA A SERIES OF EXCHANGES. AND SO FAR THE SCALE OF THIS TRADE HAD REMAINED SMALL.*
* THERE WAS SOME LOCAL COASTAL TRADE BETWEEN THE INDUS AND OMAN AND ARABIA.
HOWEVER, BY MID-THIRD MILLENNIUM BCE TRADE VOLUMES WERE MULTIPLYING FAST. IT WAS NOW MORE PROFITABLE TO TRAVEL OVER SEA. SAILING WAS FASTER AND CHEAPER.
BUT SAILING OVER THE OPEN SEA WAS NO EASY FEAT. THE WEATHER WAS UNPREDICTABLE AND ONE COULD EASILY LOSE ONE'S WAY. SEAFARING REQUIRED ADVANCED SHIPBUILDING, SAILING AND NAVIGATIONAL SKILLS.

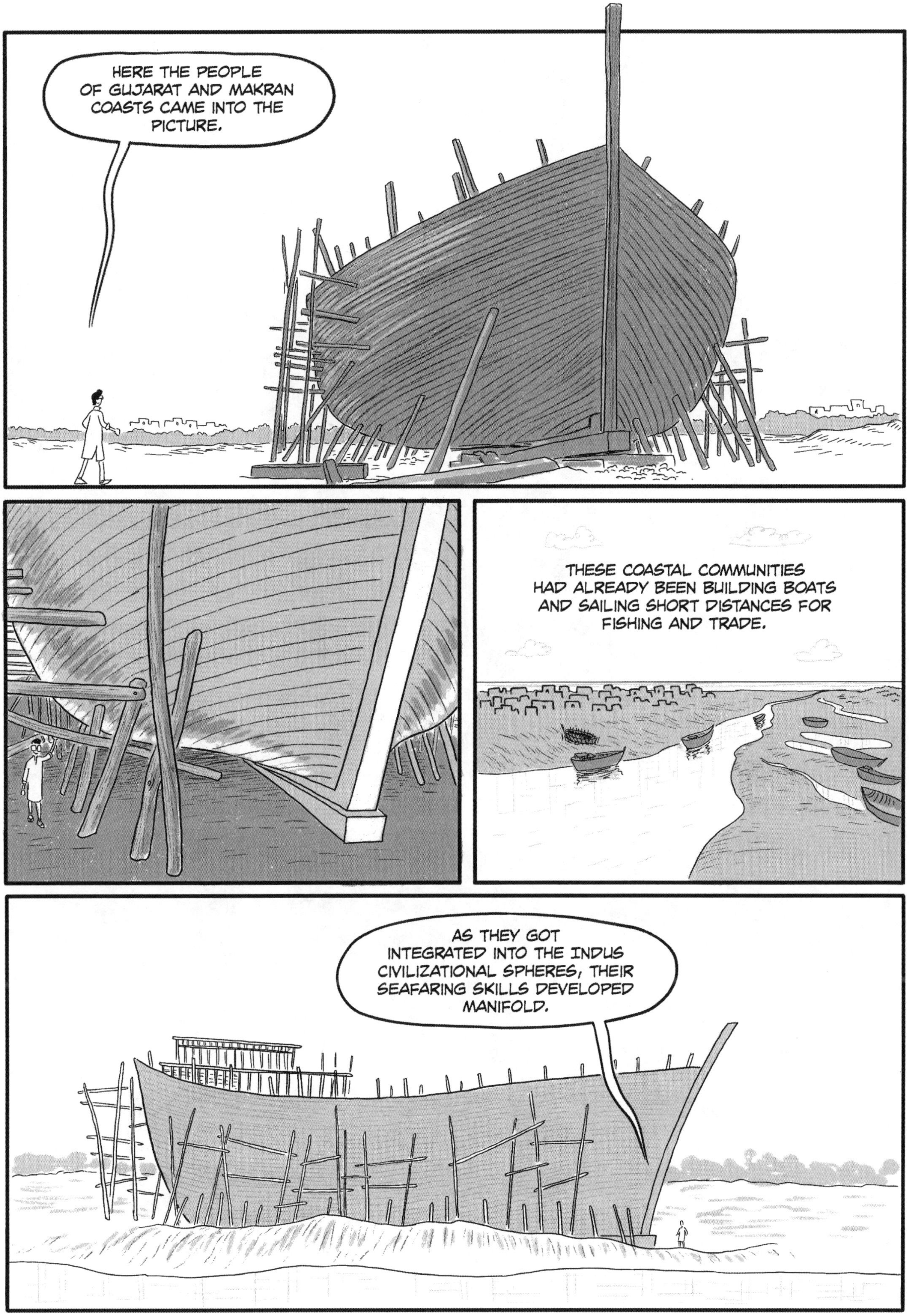
HERE THE PEOPLE OF GUJARAT AND MAKRAN COASTS CAME INTO THE PICTURE.
THESE COASTAL COMMUNITIES HAD ALREADY BEEN BUILDING BOATS AND SAILING SHORT DISTANCES FOR FISHING AND TRADE.
AS THEY GOT INTEGRATED INTO THE INDUS CIVILIZATIONAL SPHERES, THEIR SEAFARING SKILLS DEVELOPED MANIFOLD.

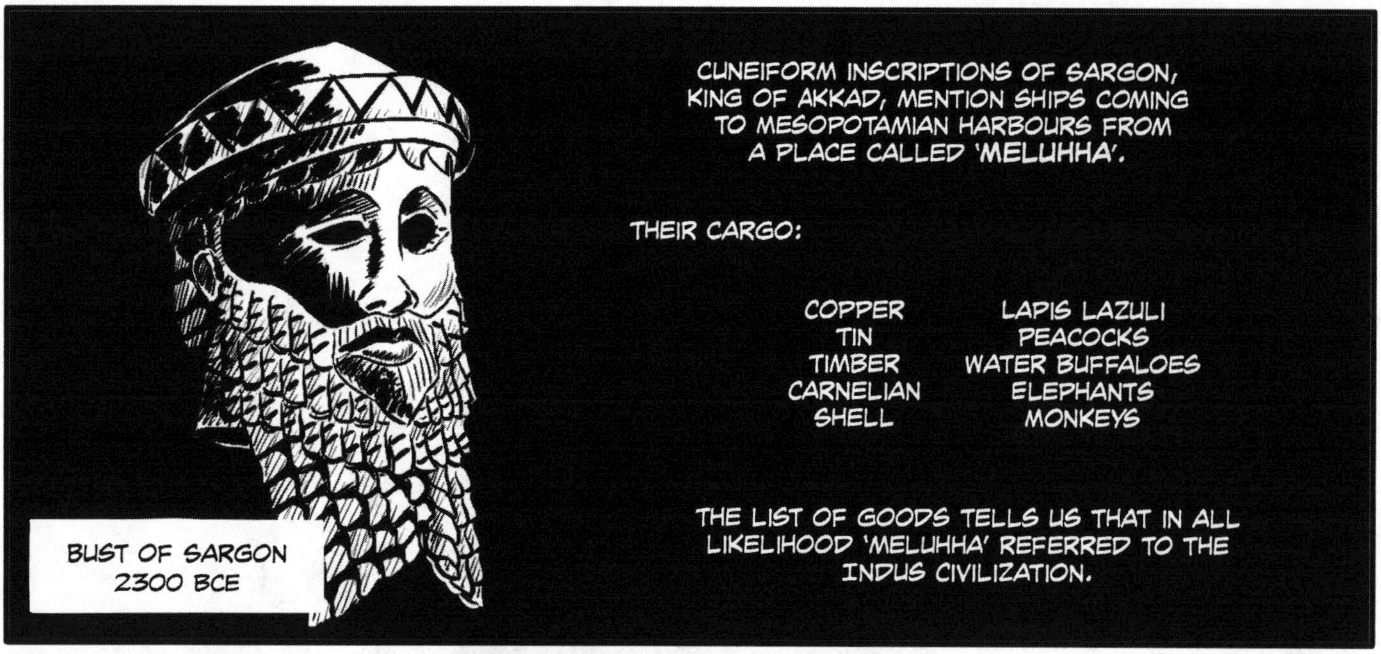

CUNEIFORM INSCRIPTIONS OF SARGON, KING OF AKKAD, MENTION SHIPS COMING TO MESOPOTAMIAN HARBOURS FROM A PLACE CALLED 'MELUHHA'.

THEIR CARGO:

COPPER	LAPIS LAZULI
TIN	PEACOCKS
TIMBER	WATER BUFFALOES
CARNELIAN	ELEPHANTS
SHELL	MONKEYS

THE LIST OF GOODS TELLS US THAT IN ALL LIKELIHOOD 'MELUHHA' REFERRED TO THE INDUS CIVILIZATION.

BUST OF SARGON
2300 BCE

'MELUHHAN' SHIPS ARE SAID TO BE LARGE AND WELL BUILT. THEY HAD TO BE, IN ORDER TO MAKE THE LONG SEA VOYAGE, AND TO CARRY BULKY GOODS LIKE TIMBER (AND ELEPHANTS).

AND THESE SHIPS WOULD HAVE SET SAIL FROM THE GUJARATI COAST WHERE SEVERAL INDUS SITES ARE FOUND.

DHOLAVIRA

← LOTHAL

THIS STRUCTURE IN LOTHAL HAS SOMETIMES BEEN CALLED A DOCKYARD FOR BOATS.

HOWEVER, MANY SCHOLARS DO NOT AGREE.

THEY FEEL THAT THIS WAS MOST LIKELY A TANK FOR STORING WATER. THE DISCOVERY OF LARGE RESERVOIRS AT DHOLAVIRA AND A POSSIBLE ONE AT HARAPPA SHOW THE IMPORTANCE OF RELIABLE WATER SOURCES TO THE INDUS CITY PLANNERS.*

* NEVERTHELESS, LOTHAL HAS SOME EVIDENCE OF MANUFACTURING AND INDUSTRY AND MAY HAVE INDIRECTLY PARTICIPATED IN INTERNATIONAL TRADE.

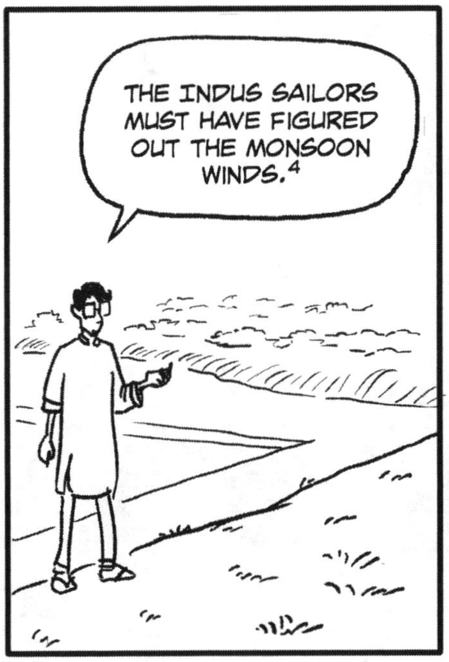
THE INDUS SAILORS MUST HAVE FIGURED OUT THE MONSOON WINDS.4

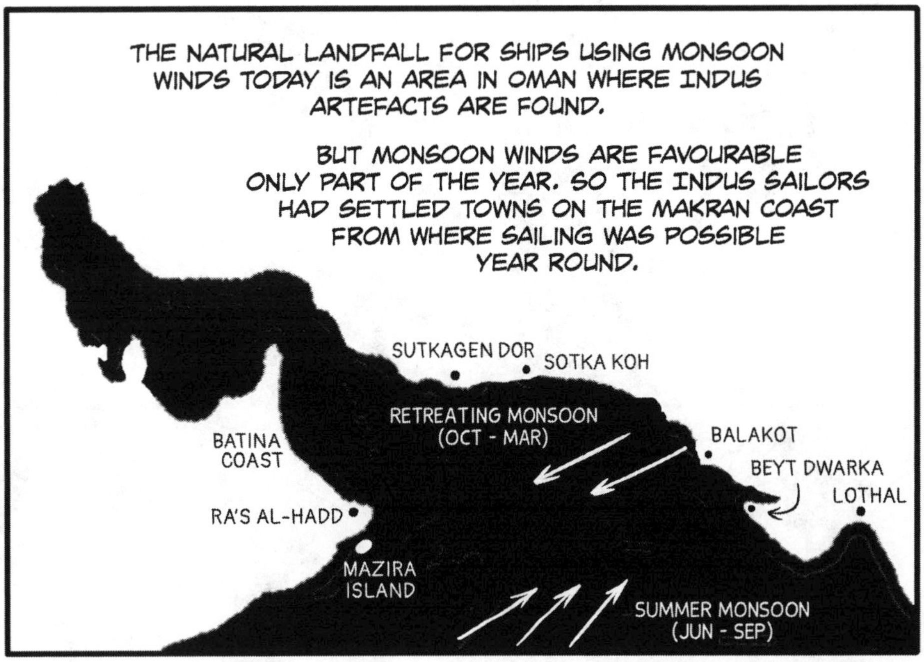
THE NATURAL LANDFALL FOR SHIPS USING MONSOON WINDS TODAY IS AN AREA IN OMAN WHERE INDUS ARTEFACTS ARE FOUND.
BUT MONSOON WINDS ARE FAVOURABLE ONLY PART OF THE YEAR. SO THE INDUS SAILORS HAD SETTLED TOWNS ON THE MAKRAN COAST FROM WHERE SAILING WAS POSSIBLE YEAR ROUND.
SUTKAGEN DOR
SOTKA KOH
RETREATING MONSOON (OCT - MAR)
BATINA COAST
BALAKOT
BEYT DWARKA
LOTHAL
RA'S AL-HADD
MAZIRA ISLAND
SUMMER MONSOON (JUN - SEP)

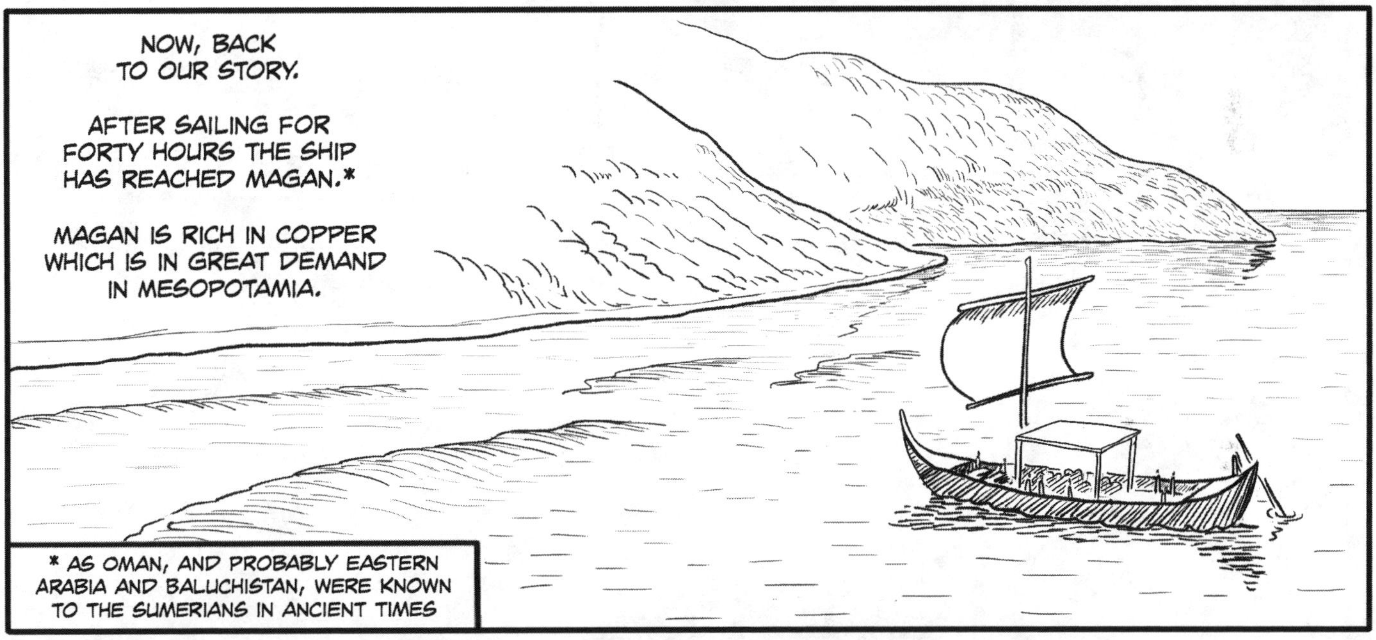
NOW, BACK TO OUR STORY.
AFTER SAILING FOR FORTY HOURS THE SHIP HAS REACHED MAGAN.*
MAGAN IS RICH IN COPPER WHICH IS IN GREAT DEMAND IN MESOPOTAMIA.
* AS OMAN, AND PROBABLY EASTERN ARABIA AND BALUCHISTAN, WERE KNOWN TO THE SUMERIANS IN ANCIENT TIMES

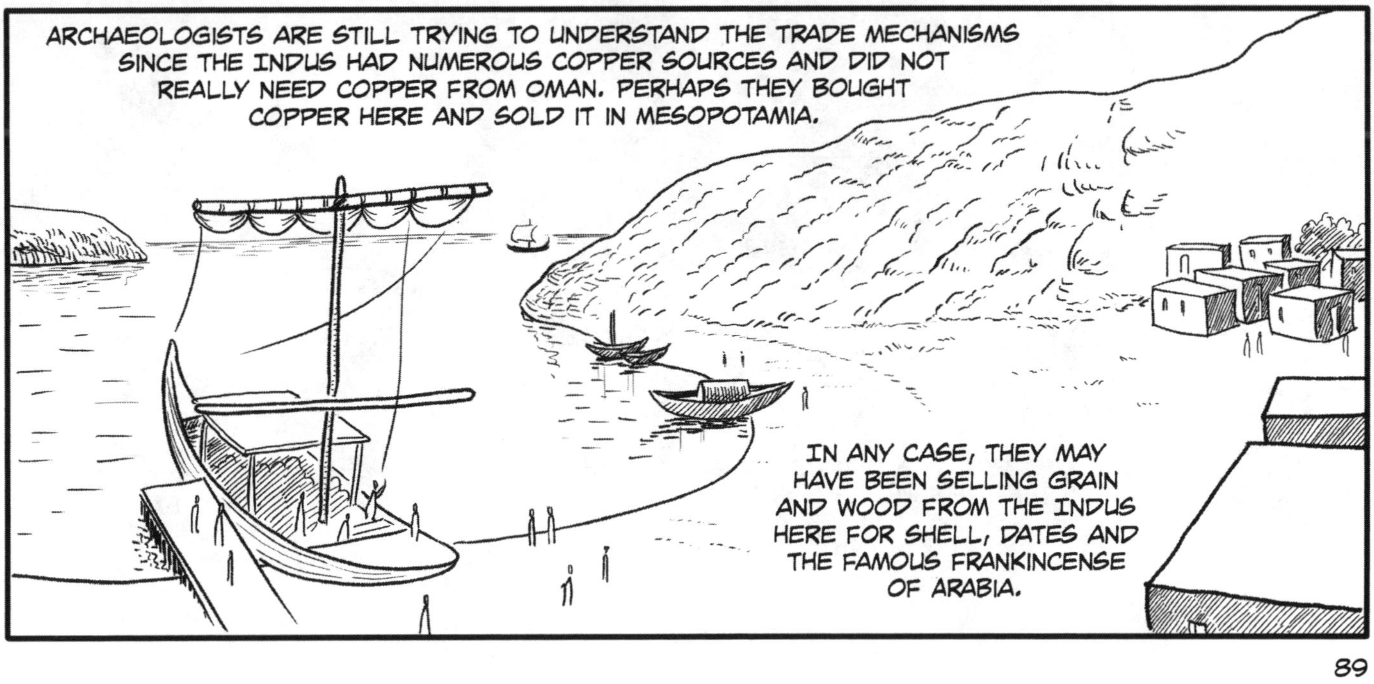
ARCHAEOLOGISTS ARE STILL TRYING TO UNDERSTAND THE TRADE MECHANISMS SINCE THE INDUS HAD NUMEROUS COPPER SOURCES AND DID NOT REALLY NEED COPPER FROM OMAN. PERHAPS THEY BOUGHT COPPER HERE AND SOLD IT IN MESOPOTAMIA.
IN ANY CASE, THEY MAY HAVE BEEN SELLING GRAIN AND WOOD FROM THE INDUS HERE FOR SHELL, DATES AND THE FAMOUS FRANKINCENSE OF ARABIA.

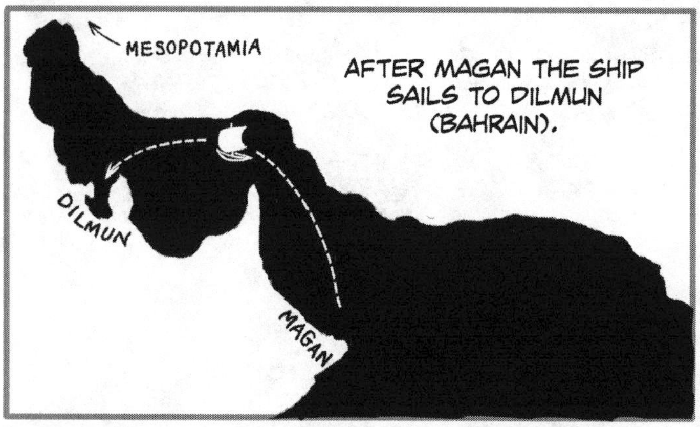
MESOPOTAMIA
AFTER MAGAN THE SHIP SAILS TO DILMUN (BAHRAIN).
DILMUN
MAGAN

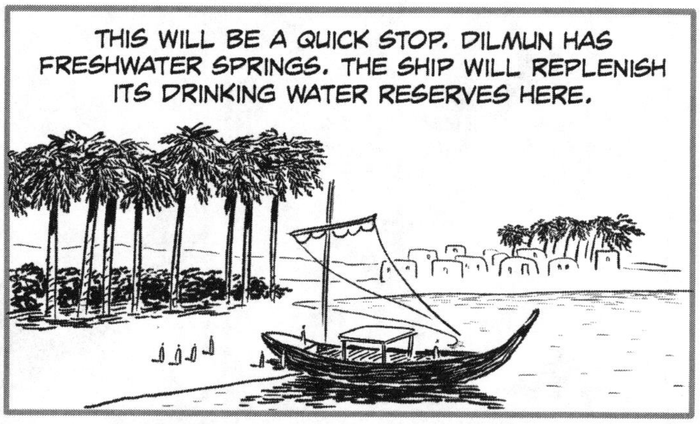
THIS WILL BE A QUICK STOP. DILMUN HAS FRESHWATER SPRINGS. THE SHIP WILL REPLENISH ITS DRINKING WATER RESERVES HERE.

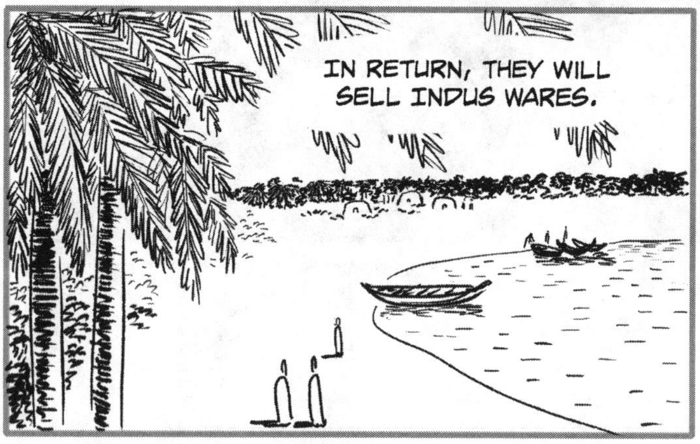
IN RETURN, THEY WILL SELL INDUS WARES.

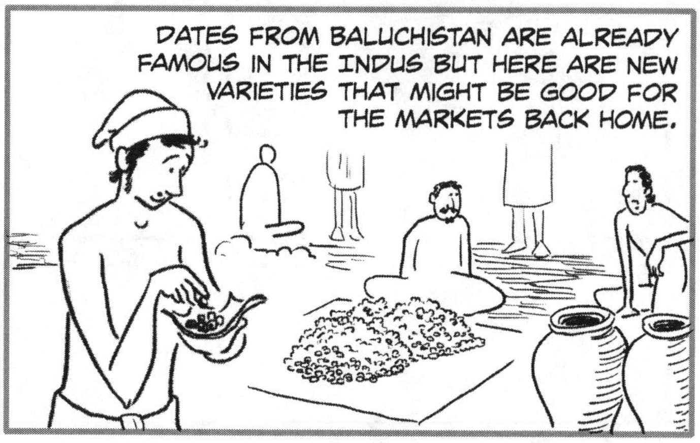
DATES FROM BALUCHISTAN ARE ALREADY FAMOUS IN THE INDUS BUT HERE ARE NEW VARIETIES THAT MIGHT BE GOOD FOR THE MARKETS BACK HOME.

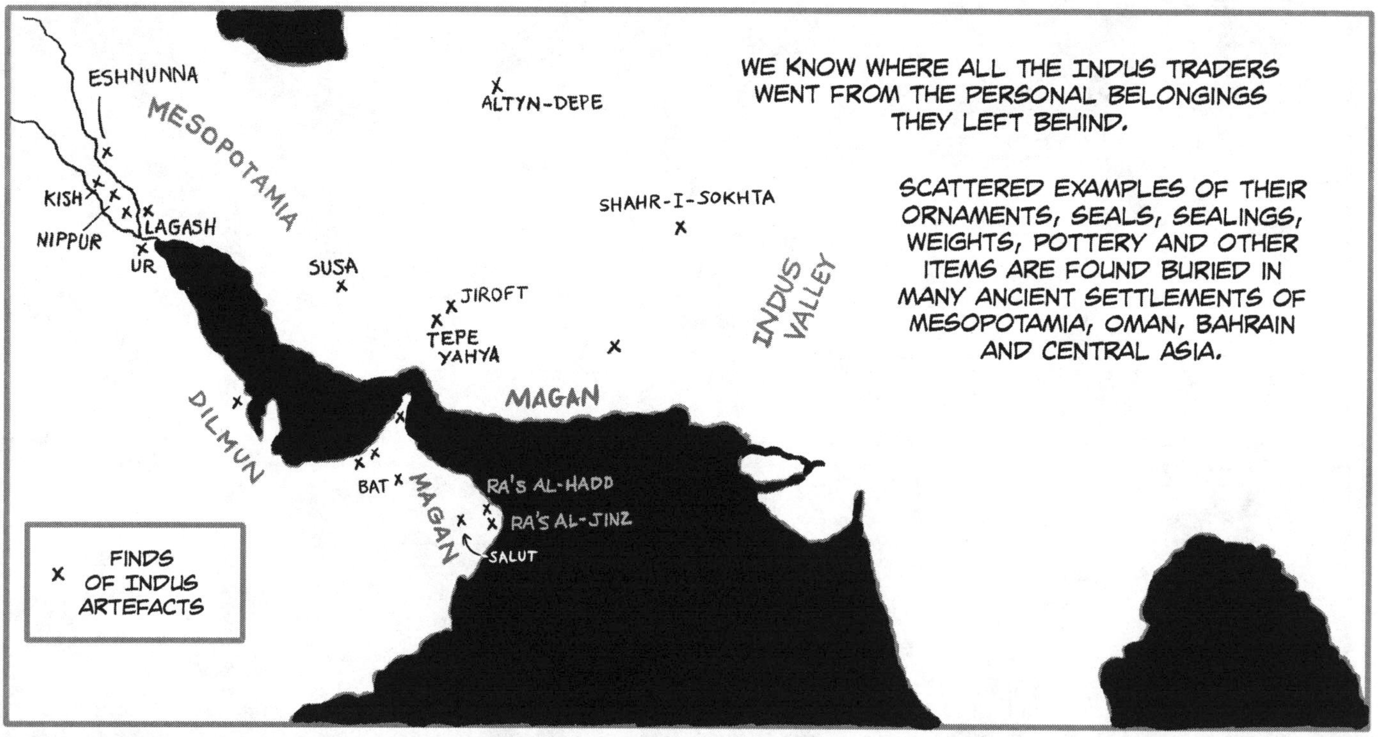
ESHNUNNA
MESOPOTAMIA
KISH
NIPPUR
LAGASH
UR
ALTYN-DEPE
SHAHR-I-SOKHTA
SUSA
JIROFT
TEPE YAHYA
INDUS VALLEY
DILMUN
MAGAN
BAT
MAGAN
RA'S AL-HADD
RA'S AL-JINZ
SALUT
FINDS OF INDUS ARTEFACTS
WE KNOW WHERE ALL THE INDUS TRADERS WENT FROM THE PERSONAL BELONGINGS THEY LEFT BEHIND.
SCATTERED EXAMPLES OF THEIR ORNAMENTS, SEALS, SEALINGS, WEIGHTS, POTTERY AND OTHER ITEMS ARE FOUND BURIED IN MANY ANCIENT SETTLEMENTS OF MESOPOTAMIA, OMAN, BAHRAIN AND CENTRAL ASIA.

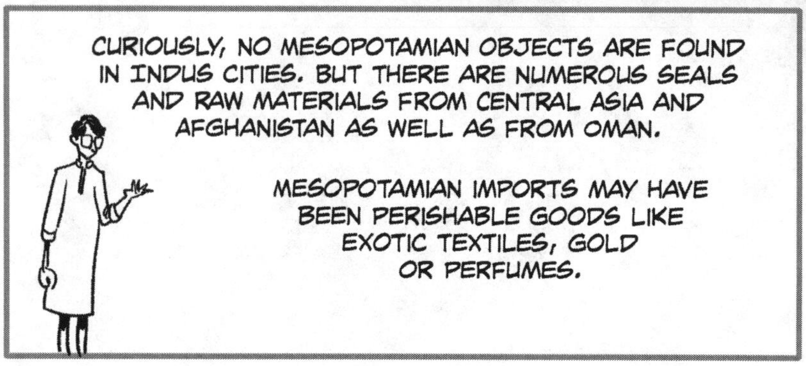
CURIOUSLY, NO MESOPOTAMIAN OBJECTS ARE FOUND IN INDUS CITIES. BUT THERE ARE NUMEROUS SEALS AND RAW MATERIALS FROM CENTRAL ASIA AND AFGHANISTAN AS WELL AS FROM OMAN.
MESOPOTAMIAN IMPORTS MAY HAVE BEEN PERISHABLE GOODS LIKE EXOTIC TEXTILES, GOLD OR PERFUMES.

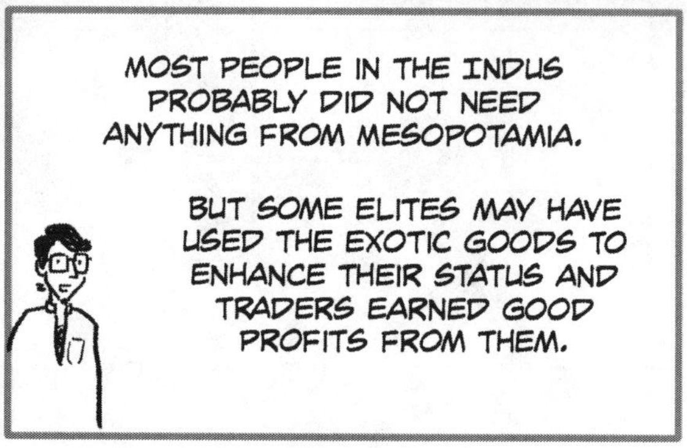
MOST PEOPLE IN THE INDUS PROBABLY DID NOT NEED ANYTHING FROM MESOPOTAMIA.
BUT SOME ELITES MAY HAVE USED THE EXOTIC GOODS TO ENHANCE THEIR STATUS AND TRADERS EARNED GOOD PROFITS FROM THEM.

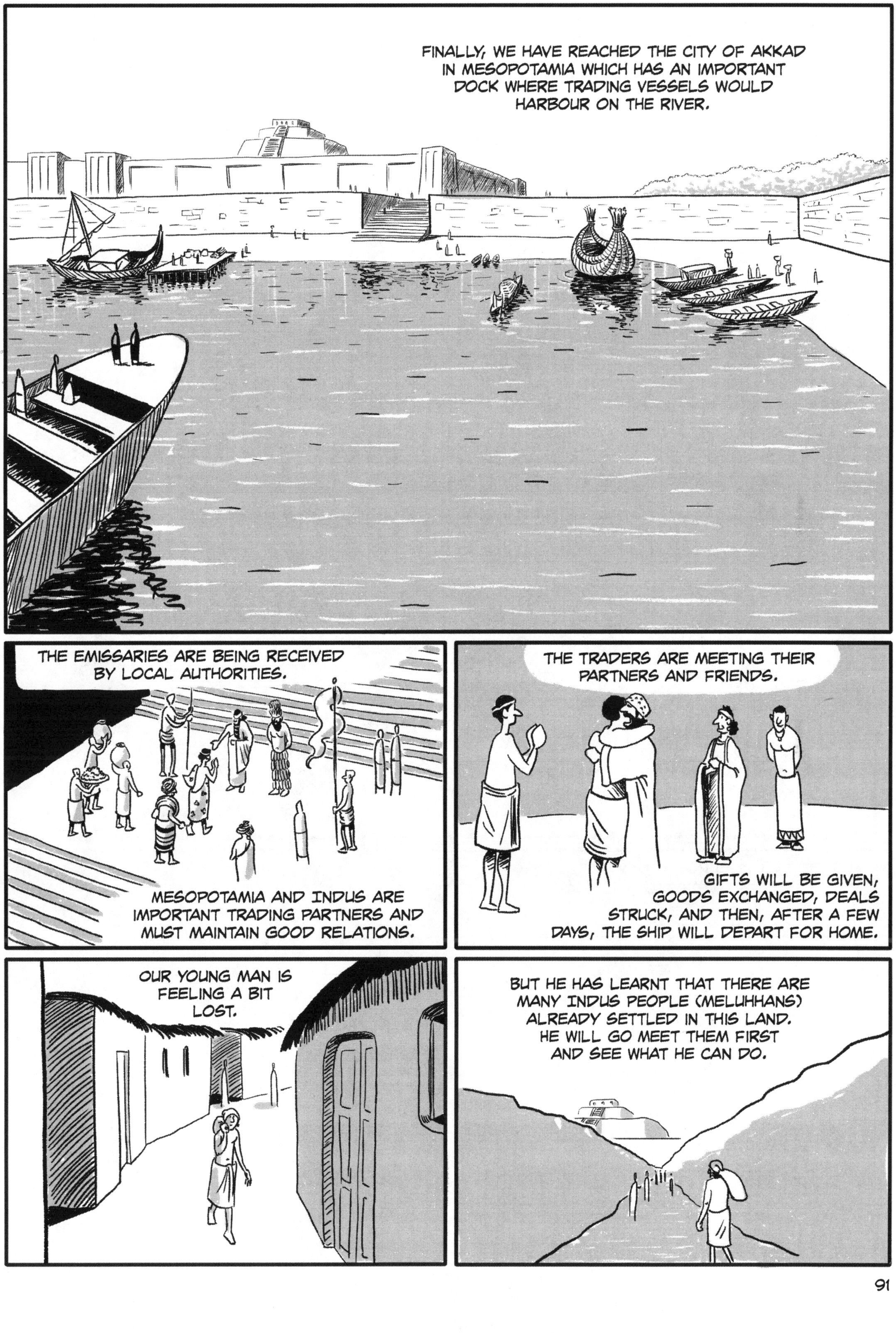
FINALLY, WE HAVE REACHED THE CITY OF AKKAD IN MESOPOTAMIA WHICH HAS AN IMPORTANT DOCK WHERE TRADING VESSELS WOULD HARBOUR ON THE RIVER.
THE EMISSARIES ARE BEING RECEIVED BY LOCAL AUTHORITIES.
MESOPOTAMIA AND INDUS ARE IMPORTANT TRADING PARTNERS AND MUST MAINTAIN GOOD RELATIONS.
THE TRADERS ARE MEETING THEIR PARTNERS AND FRIENDS.
GIFTS WILL BE GIVEN, GOODS EXCHANGED, DEALS STRUCK, AND THEN, AFTER A FEW DAYS, THE SHIP WILL DEPART FOR HOME.
OUR YOUNG MAN IS FEELING A BIT LOST.
BUT HE HAS LEARNT THAT THERE ARE MANY INDUS PEOPLE (MELUHHANS) ALREADY SETTLED IN THIS LAND. HE WILL GO MEET THEM FIRST AND SEE WHAT HE CAN DO.

CUNEIFORM INSCRIPTIONS INFORM US THAT SOME INDUS COMMUNITIES HAD PERMANENTLY SETTLED IN MESOPOTAMIA.

THERE WAS A 'VILLAGE OF MELUHHANS' IN LAGASH IN THE 21ST CENTURY BCE, INHABITED BY 'SONS OF MELUHHA'.

OLD BABYLON TEMPLE OF ISHTAR-KITITUM, 1950-1850 BCE

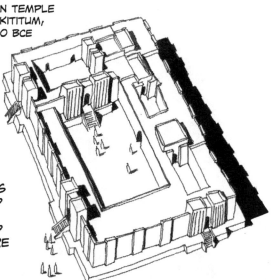

SOME OF THEM WORKED AT TEMPLES AS 'OVERSEERS IN CHARGE OF SCRIBES AND CRAFTSPERSONS'. OTHERS WERE 'KEEPERS OF SACRED GARDENS'. YET OTHERS WERE 'TRADERS TRANSPORTING CEREALS'.

A SEAL WAS FOUND THAT BELONGED TO A PERSON CALLED 'SERVANT OF NINILDUM'. NINILDUM WAS THE MESOPOTAMIAN DEITY OF TIMBER AND CARPENTRY. LARGE QUANTITIES OF TIMBER USED FOR TEMPLES, PALACES, SHIPS AND FURNITURE IS KNOWN TO HAVE COME FROM THE INDUS VALLEY; AND THIS INDIVIDUAL WAS LIKELY A MELUHHAN TRADER WHO SUPPORTED A LOCAL CULT.

FOR THE FIRST TIME WE GET GLIMPSES OF SPECIFIC INDUS INDIVIDUALS.

ONE TABLET RECORDS A LU-SUNZIDA, 'MAN OF MELUHHA', WHO HAS BEEN MADE TO PAY 10 SHEKELS AS A FINE FOR BREAKING A SERVANT'S TOOTH.[5]

A CERTAIN SHU-ILISHU FINDS EMPLOYMENT AS A MELUHHAN INTERPRETER.

WE KNOW OF HIM FROM HIS SEAL. ↷

OUR YOUNG MAN HAS ALREADY MET SOME OF THESE OVERSEAS MELUHHANS.

HOWEVER, IT SEEMS HIS PLAN OF GIVING THE NECKLACE TO A TRADING PARTNER HASN'T EXACTLY WORKED OUT.

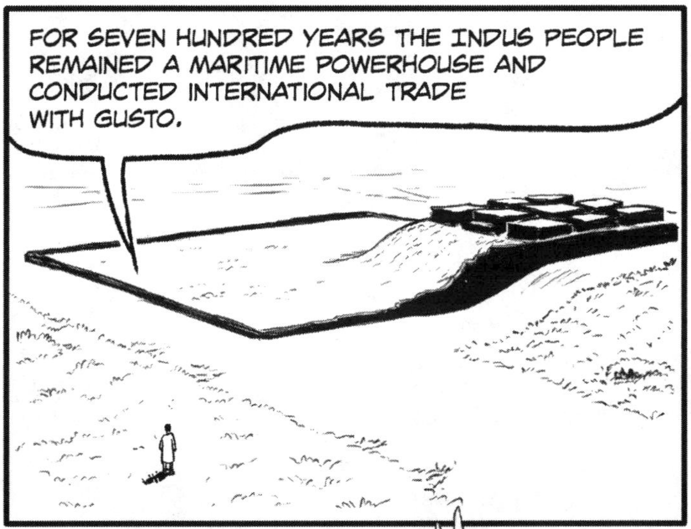
FOR SEVEN HUNDRED YEARS THE INDUS PEOPLE REMAINED A MARITIME POWERHOUSE AND CONDUCTED INTERNATIONAL TRADE WITH GUSTO.

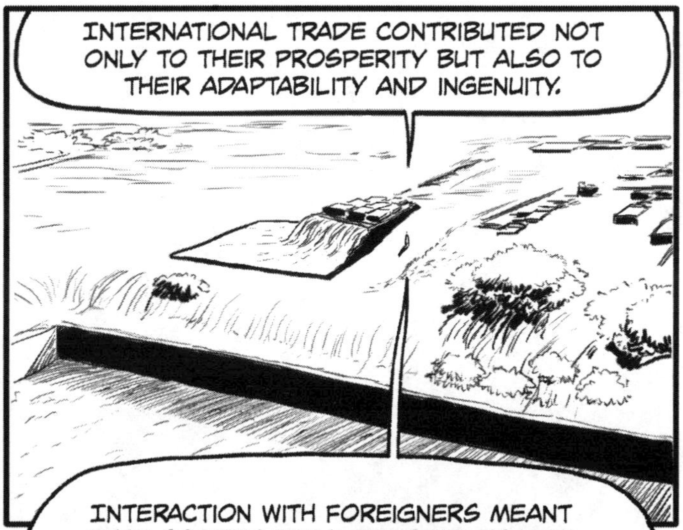
INTERNATIONAL TRADE CONTRIBUTED NOT ONLY TO THEIR PROSPERITY BUT ALSO TO THEIR ADAPTABILITY AND INGENUITY.
INTERACTION WITH FOREIGNERS MEANT THAT SOCIETY REMAINED OPEN TO NEW INFLUENCES. IN A MORE INTERCONNECTED WORLD YOU COULD BORROW AND BUILD ON OTHER PEOPLE'S IDEAS.

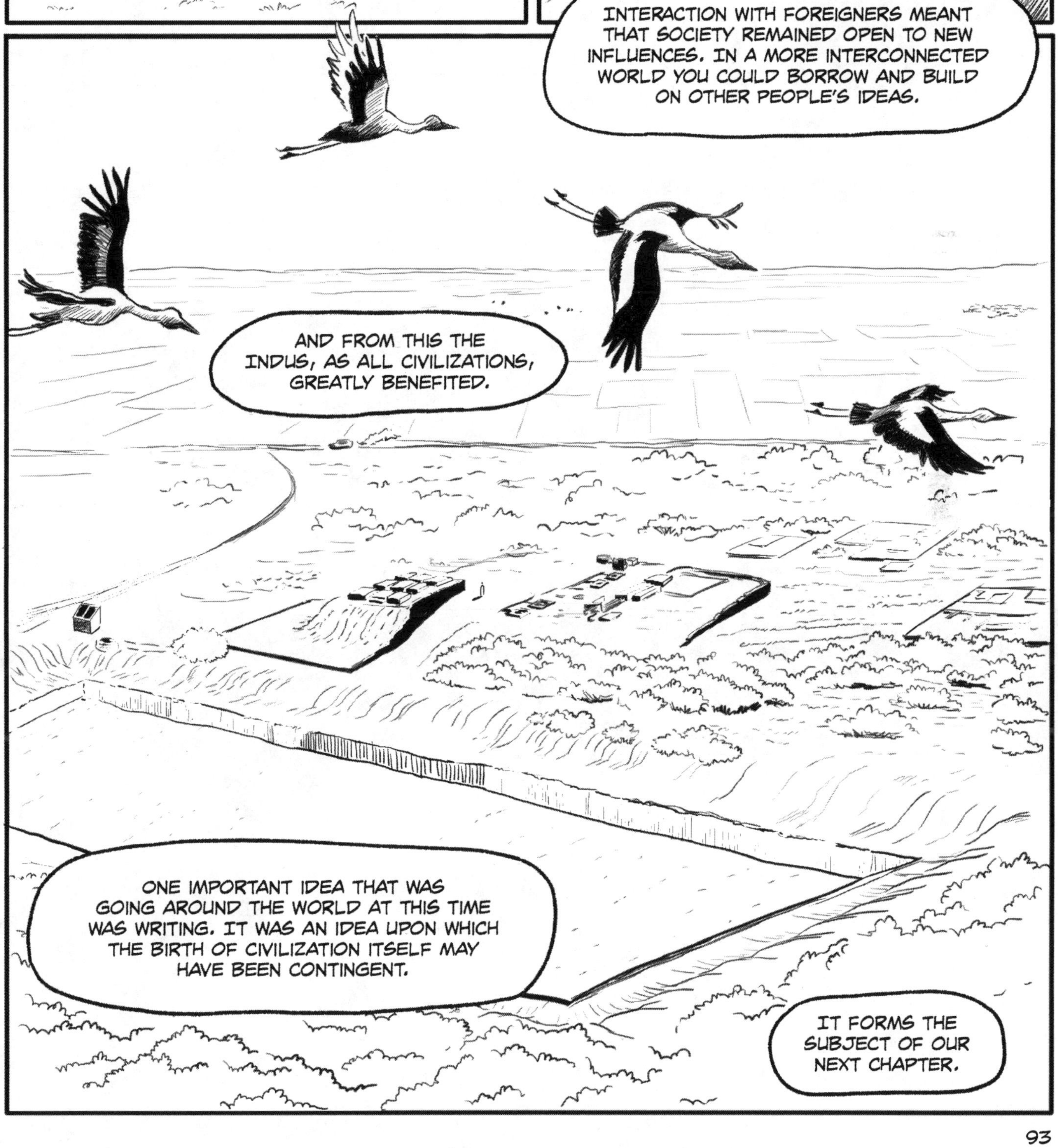
AND FROM THIS THE INDUS, AS ALL CIVILIZATIONS, GREATLY BENEFITED.
ONE IMPORTANT IDEA THAT WAS GOING AROUND THE WORLD AT THIS TIME WAS WRITING. IT WAS AN IDEA UPON WHICH THE BIRTH OF CIVILIZATION ITSELF MAY HAVE BEEN CONTINGENT.
IT FORMS THE SUBJECT OF OUR NEXT CHAPTER.

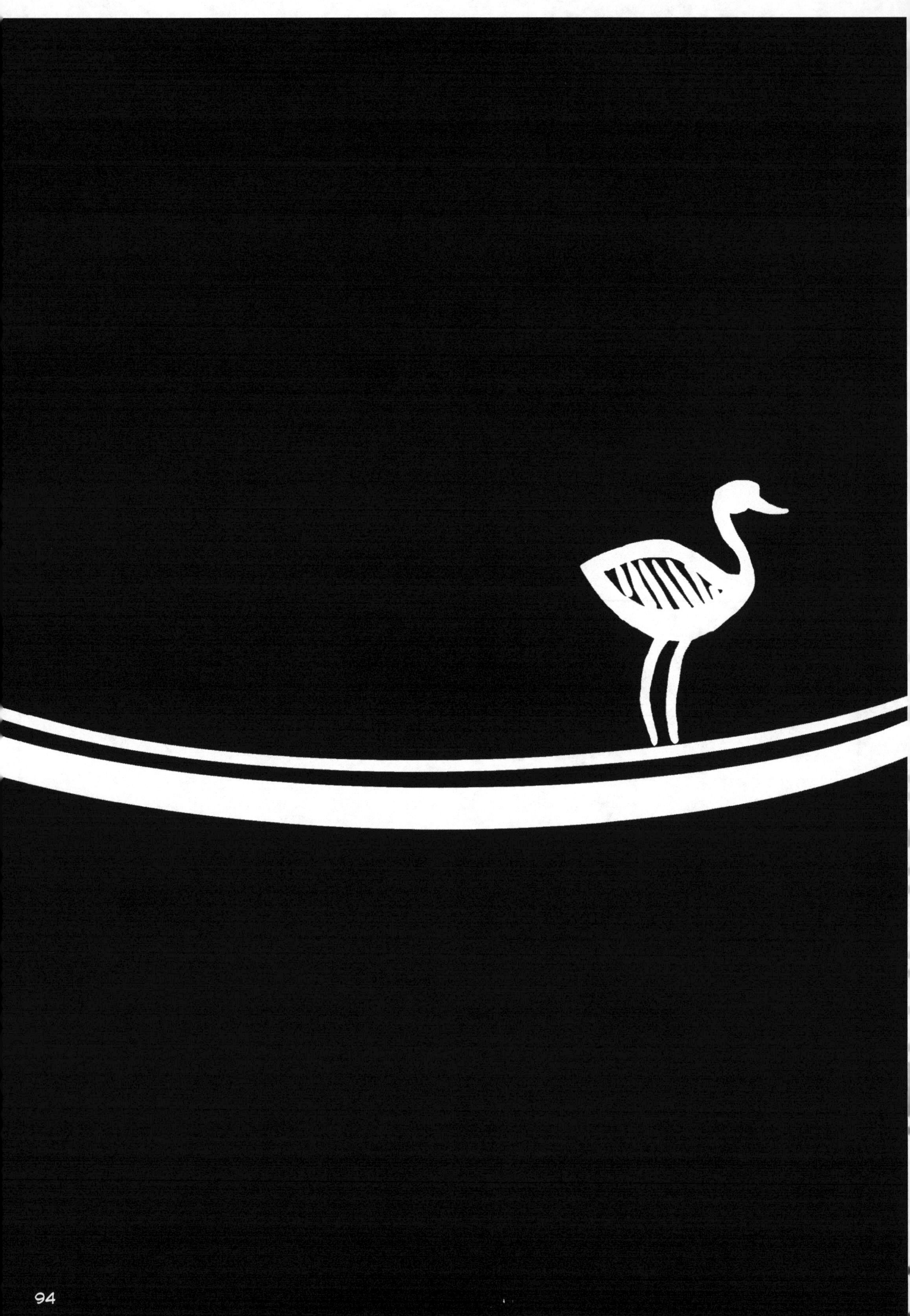

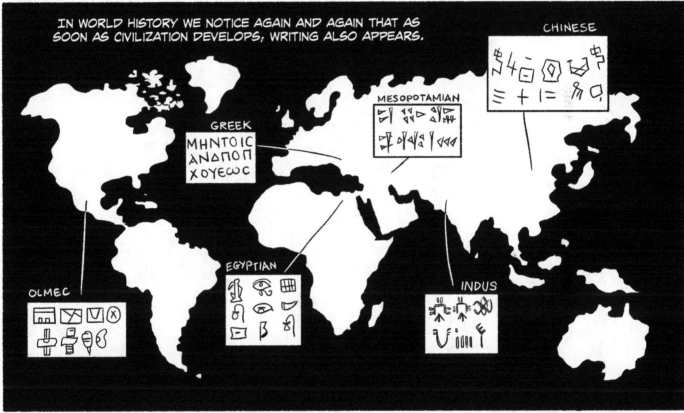

IN WORLD HISTORY WE NOTICE AGAIN AND AGAIN THAT AS SOON AS CIVILIZATION DEVELOPS, WRITING ALSO APPEARS.

CHINESE

GREEK

MHNTOIC ANΔΠOΠ XOYEωC

MESOPOTAMIAN

OLMEC

EGYPTIAN

INDUS

DID CIVILIZATION, THEN, GIVE BIRTH TO WRITING?

I USED TO THINK THAT WRITING MUST HAVE BEEN INVENTED BY A STORYTELLER, OR PERHAPS A PROPHET OR A KING.

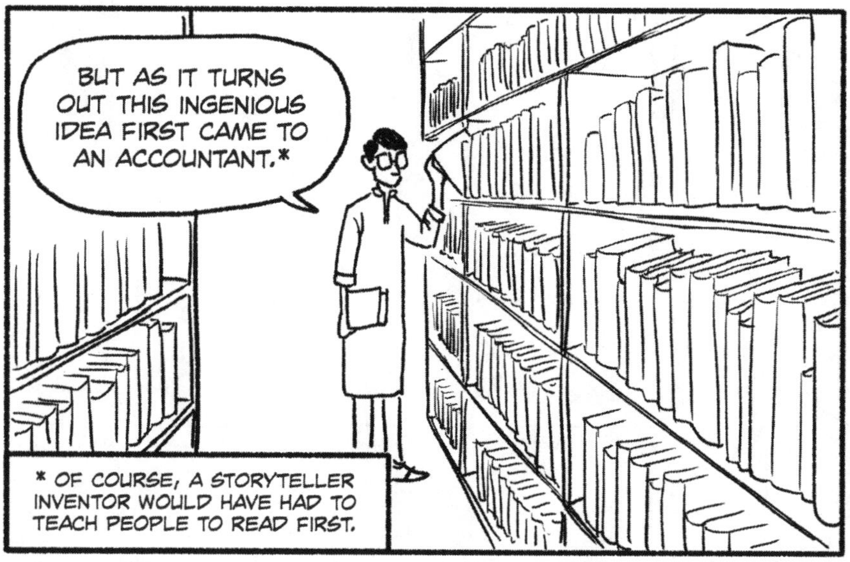
BUT AS IT TURNS OUT THIS INGENIOUS IDEA FIRST CAME TO AN ACCOUNTANT.*
* OF COURSE, A STORYTELLER INVENTOR WOULD HAVE HAD TO TEACH PEOPLE TO READ FIRST.

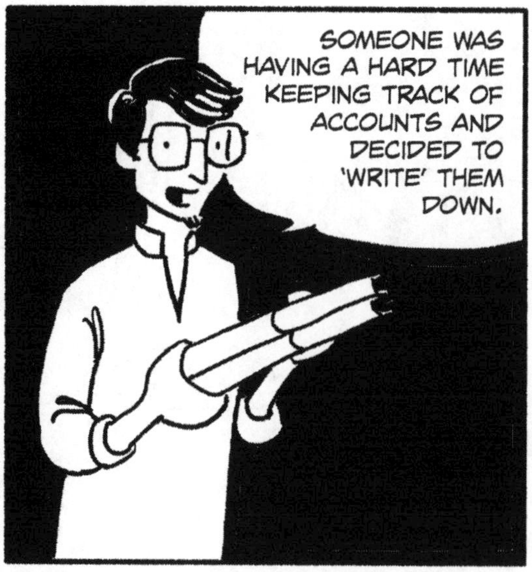
SOMEONE WAS HAVING A HARD TIME KEEPING TRACK OF ACCOUNTS AND DECIDED TO 'WRITE' THEM DOWN.

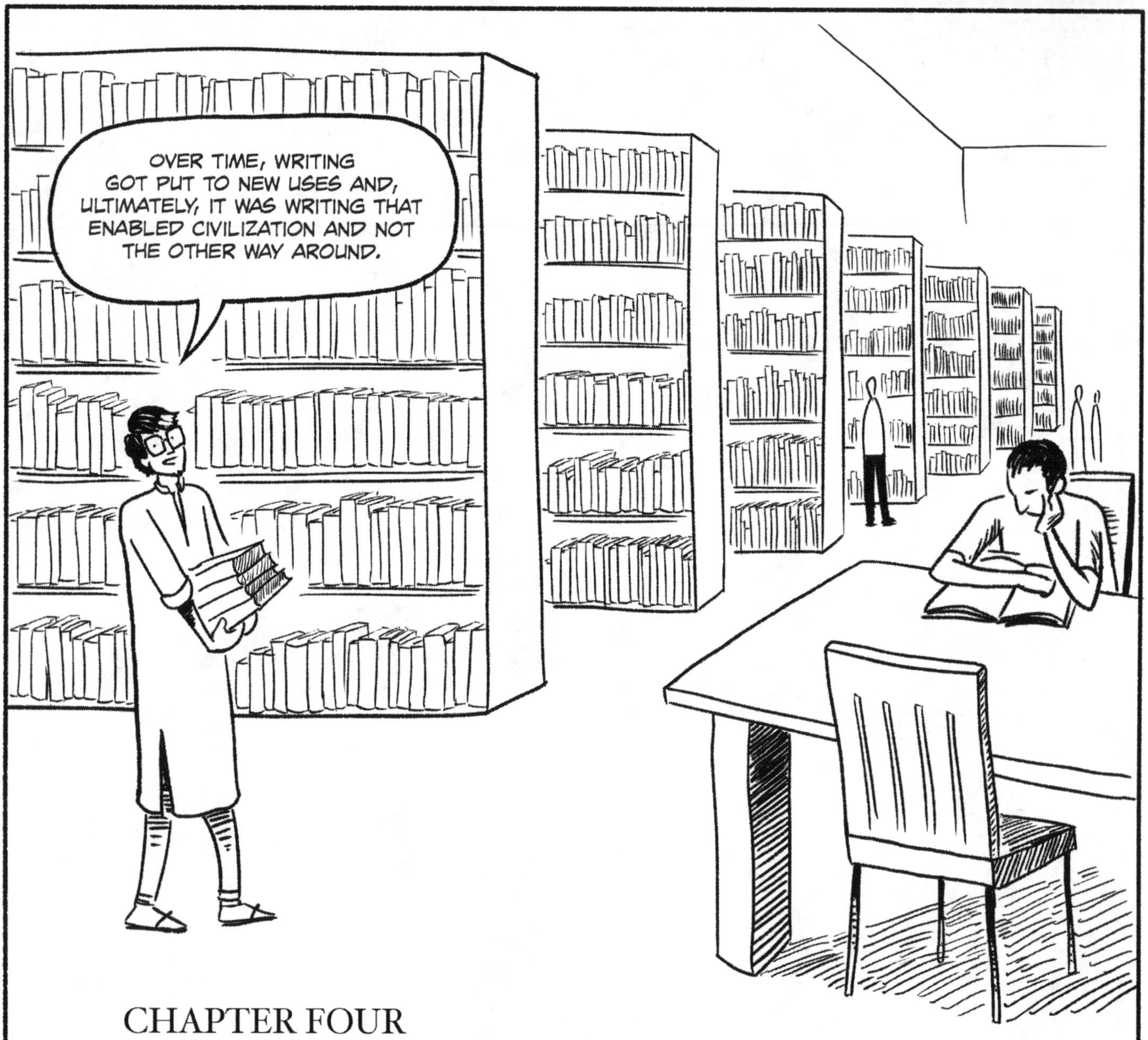
OVER TIME, WRITING GOT PUT TO NEW USES AND, ULTIMATELY, IT WAS WRITING THAT ENABLED CIVILIZATION AND NOT THE OTHER WAY AROUND.

CHAPTER FOUR

Writing Your Way to Civilization

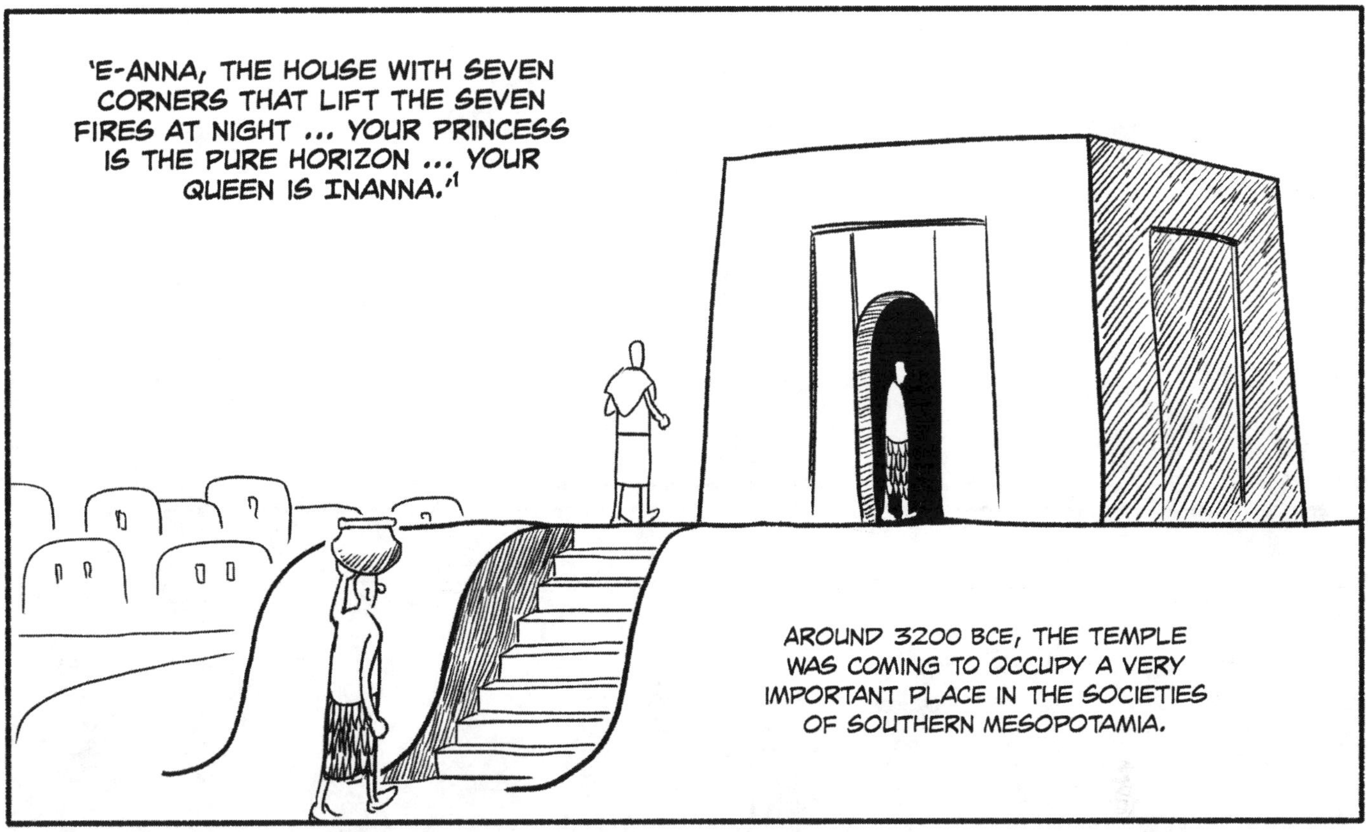
'E-ANNA, THE HOUSE WITH SEVEN CORNERS THAT LIFT THE SEVEN FIRES AT NIGHT ... YOUR PRINCESS IS THE PURE HORIZON ... YOUR QUEEN IS INANNA.'[1]
AROUND 3200 BCE, THE TEMPLE WAS COMING TO OCCUPY A VERY IMPORTANT PLACE IN THE SOCIETIES OF SOUTHERN MESOPOTAMIA.

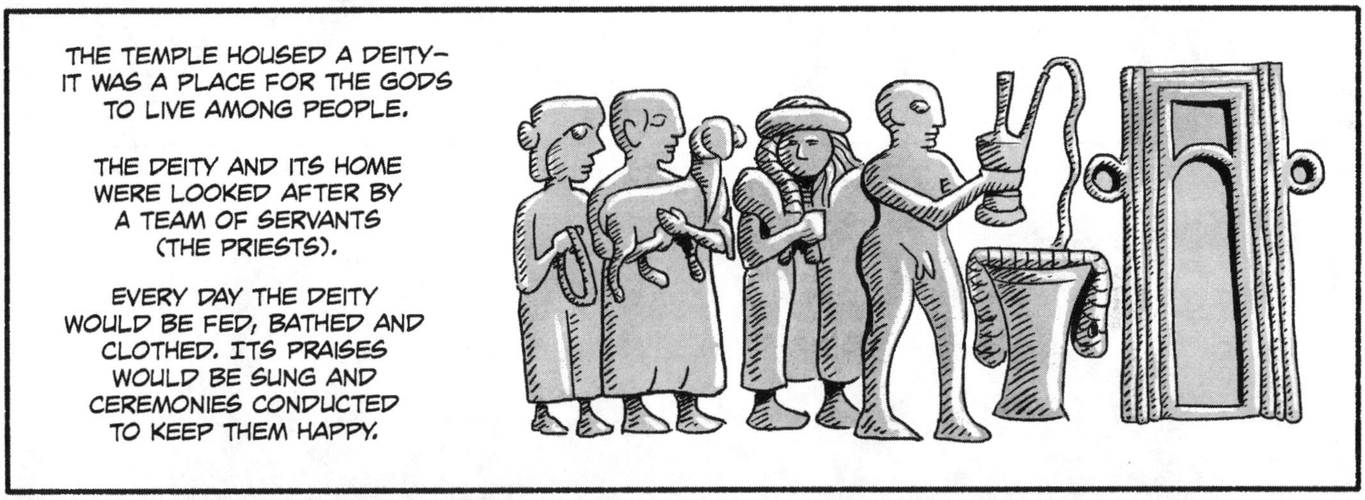
THE TEMPLE HOUSED A DEITY– IT WAS A PLACE FOR THE GODS TO LIVE AMONG PEOPLE.
THE DEITY AND ITS HOME WERE LOOKED AFTER BY A TEAM OF SERVANTS (THE PRIESTS).
EVERY DAY THE DEITY WOULD BE FED, BATHED AND CLOTHED. ITS PRAISES WOULD BE SUNG AND CEREMONIES CONDUCTED TO KEEP THEM HAPPY.

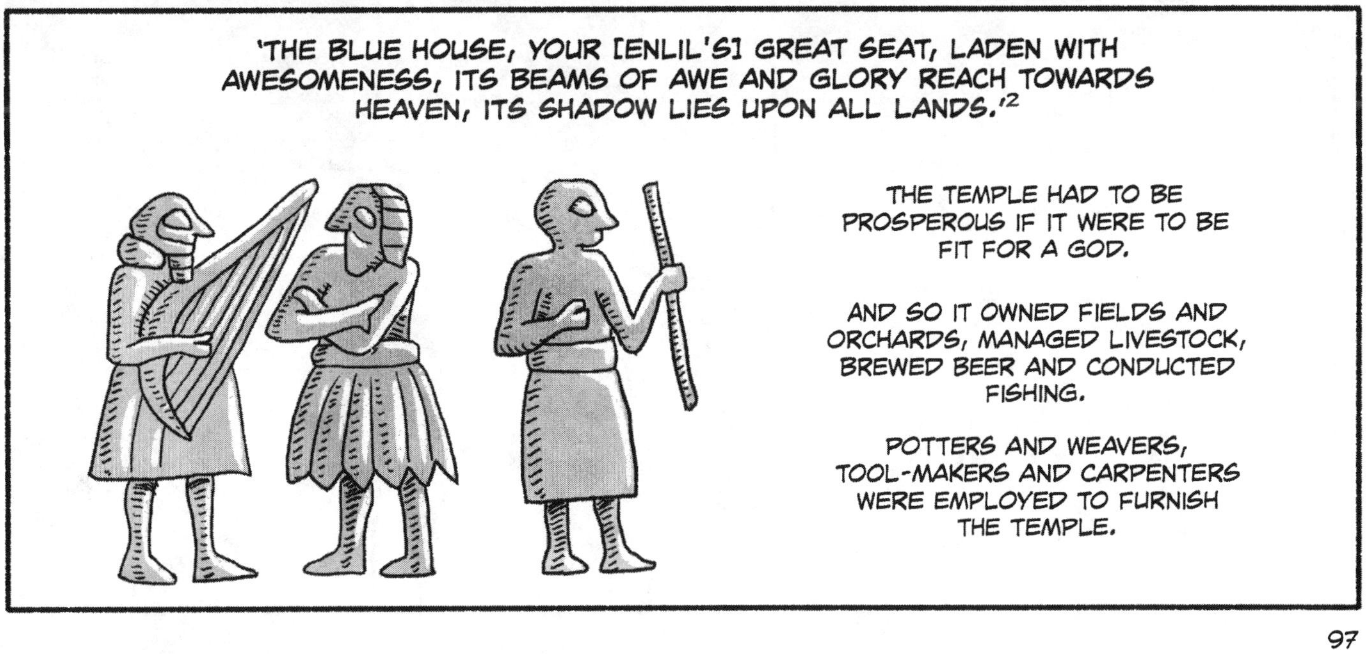
'THE BLUE HOUSE, YOUR [ENLIL'S] GREAT SEAT, LADEN WITH AWESOMENESS, ITS BEAMS OF AWE AND GLORY REACH TOWARDS HEAVEN, ITS SHADOW LIES UPON ALL LANDS.'[2]
THE TEMPLE HAD TO BE PROSPEROUS IF IT WERE TO BE FIT FOR A GOD.
AND SO IT OWNED FIELDS AND ORCHARDS, MANAGED LIVESTOCK, BREWED BEER AND CONDUCTED FISHING.
POTTERS AND WEAVERS, TOOL-MAKERS AND CARPENTERS WERE EMPLOYED TO FURNISH THE TEMPLE.

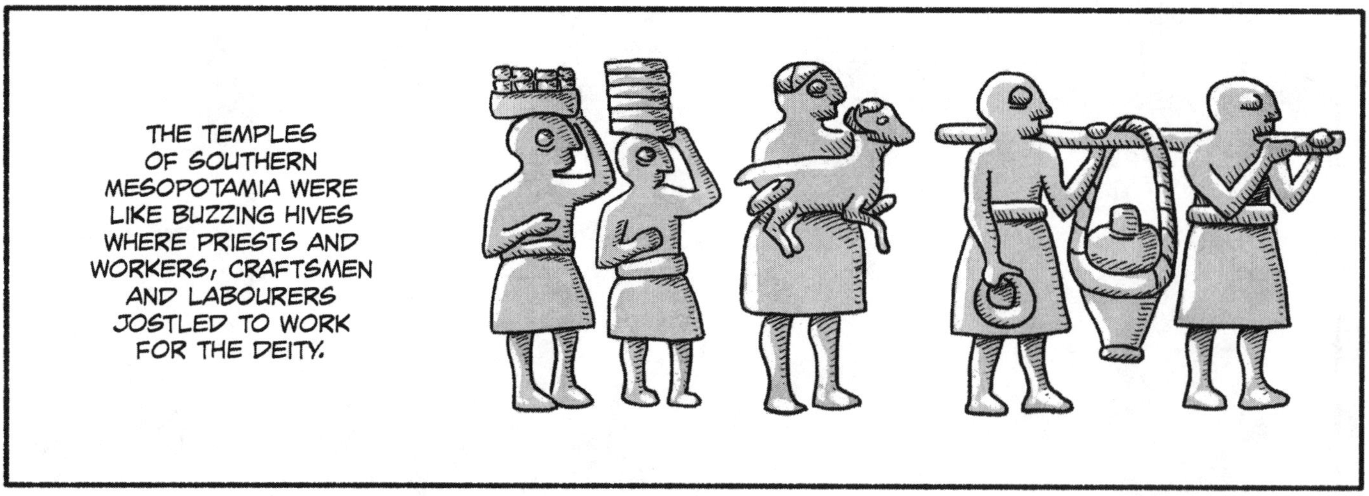
THE TEMPLES OF SOUTHERN MESOPOTAMIA WERE LIKE BUZZING HIVES WHERE PRIESTS AND WORKERS, CRAFTSMEN AND LABOURERS JOSTLED TO WORK FOR THE DEITY.

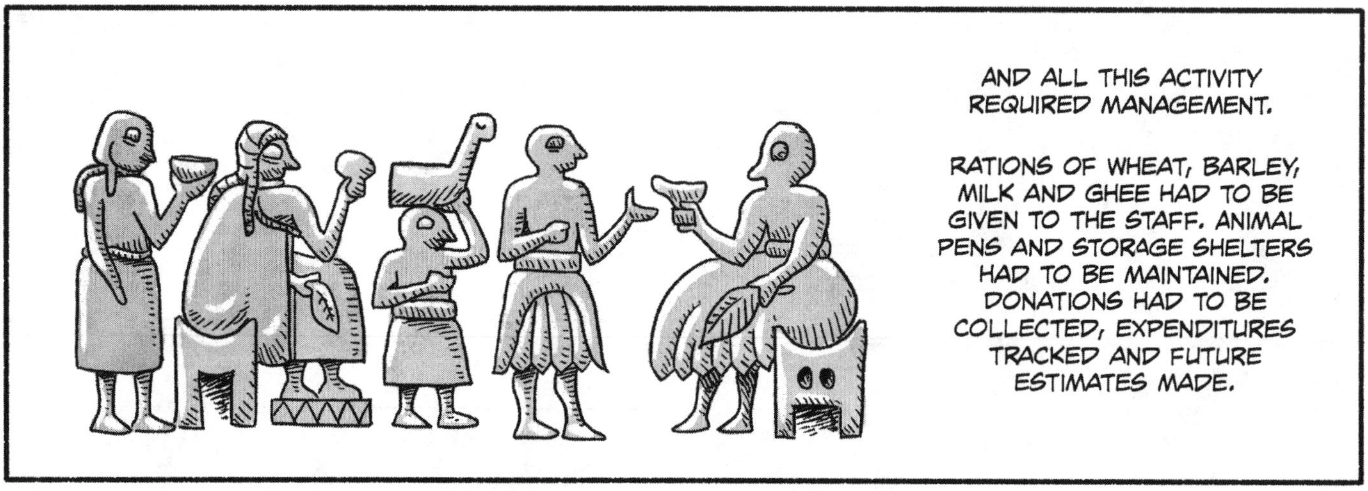
AND ALL THIS ACTIVITY REQUIRED MANAGEMENT.
RATIONS OF WHEAT, BARLEY, MILK AND GHEE HAD TO BE GIVEN TO THE STAFF. ANIMAL PENS AND STORAGE SHELTERS HAD TO BE MAINTAINED. DONATIONS HAD TO BE COLLECTED, EXPENDITURES TRACKED AND FUTURE ESTIMATES MADE.

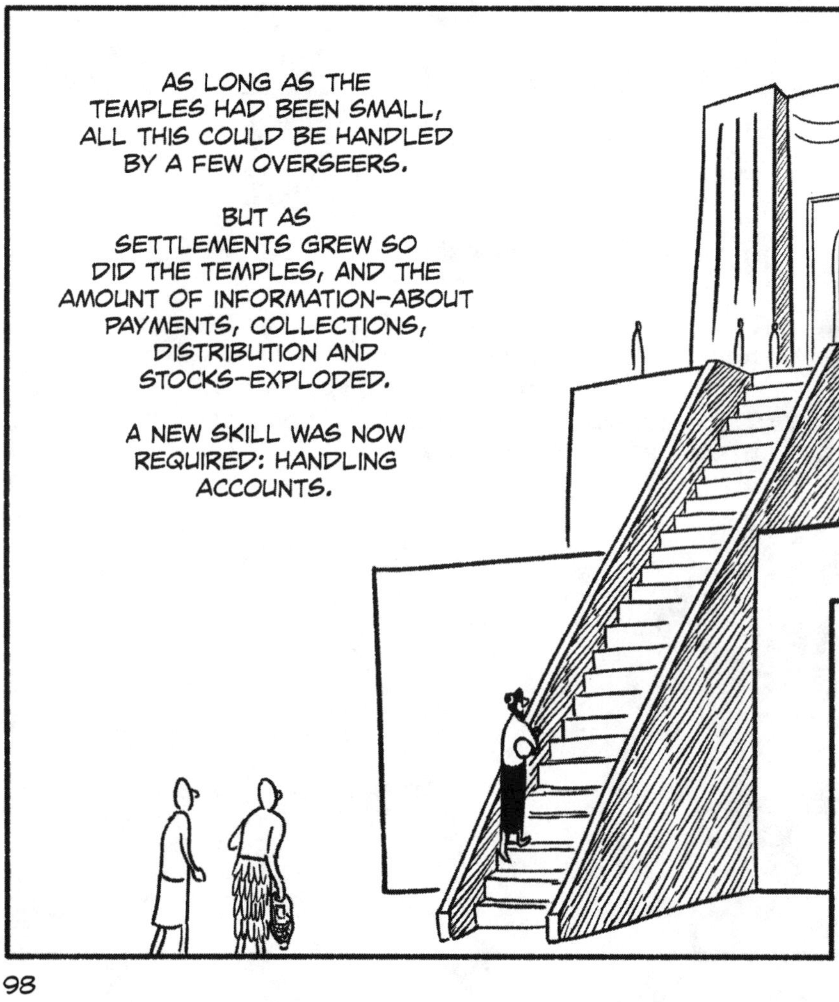
AS LONG AS THE TEMPLES HAD BEEN SMALL, ALL THIS COULD BE HANDLED BY A FEW OVERSEERS.
BUT AS SETTLEMENTS GREW SO DID THE TEMPLES, AND THE AMOUNT OF INFORMATION–ABOUT PAYMENTS, COLLECTIONS, DISTRIBUTION AND STOCKS–EXPLODED.
A NEW SKILL WAS NOW REQUIRED: HANDLING ACCOUNTS.

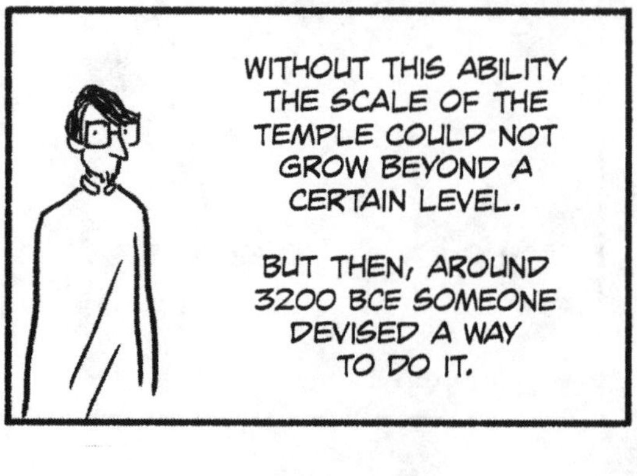
WITHOUT THIS ABILITY THE SCALE OF THE TEMPLE COULD NOT GROW BEYOND A CERTAIN LEVEL.
BUT THEN, AROUND 3200 BCE SOMEONE DEVISED A WAY TO DO IT.

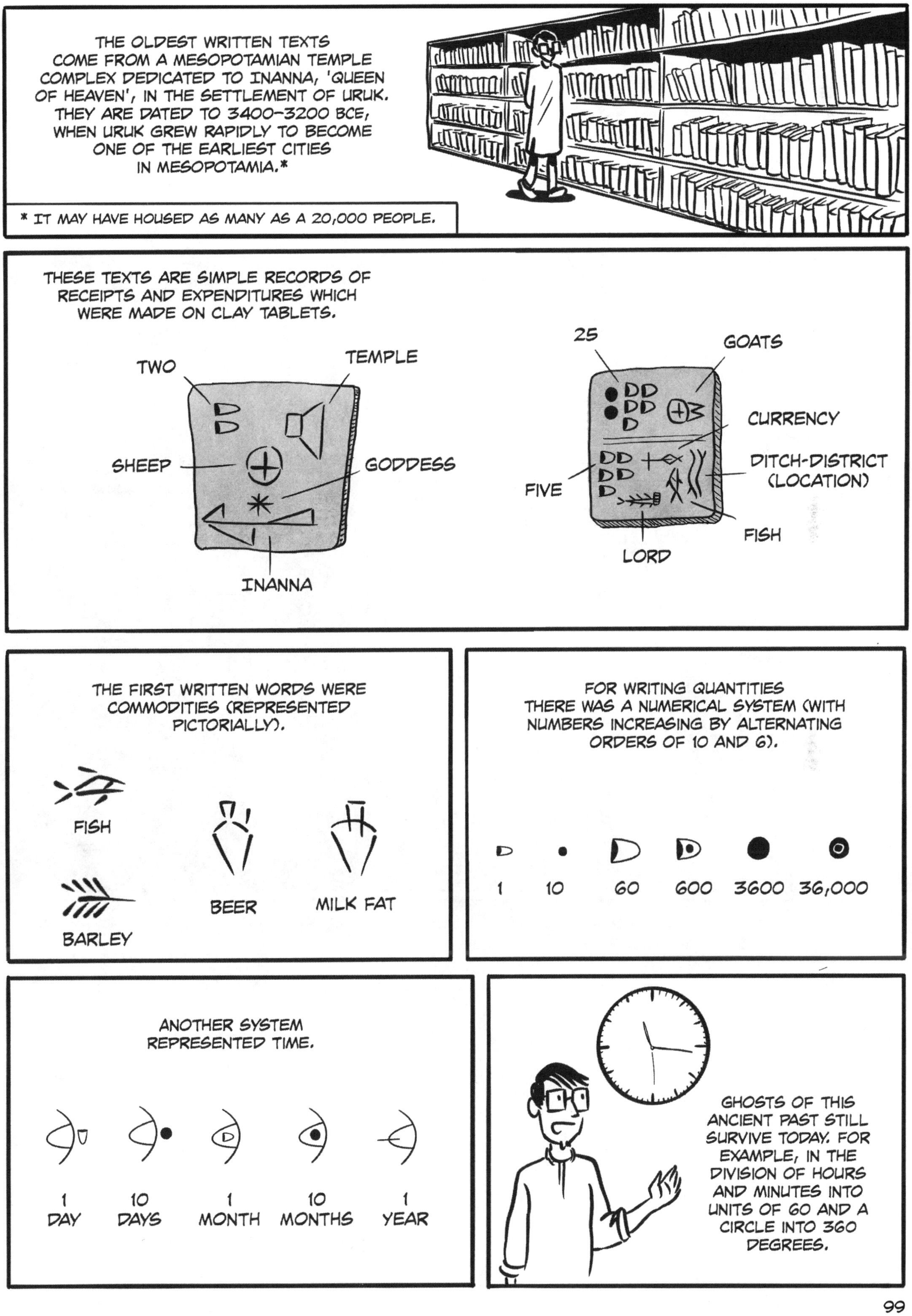

THE OLDEST WRITTEN TEXTS COME FROM A MESOPOTAMIAN TEMPLE COMPLEX DEDICATED TO INANNA, 'QUEEN OF HEAVEN', IN THE SETTLEMENT OF URUK. THEY ARE DATED TO 3400–3200 BCE, WHEN URUK GREW RAPIDLY TO BECOME ONE OF THE EARLIEST CITIES IN MESOPOTAMIA.*

* IT MAY HAVE HOUSED AS MANY AS A 20,000 PEOPLE.

THESE TEXTS ARE SIMPLE RECORDS OF RECEIPTS AND EXPENDITURES WHICH WERE MADE ON CLAY TABLETS.

TWO
TEMPLE
SHEEP
GODDESS
INANNA

25
GOATS
CURRENCY
DITCH-DISTRICT (LOCATION)
FISH
FIVE
LORD

THE FIRST WRITTEN WORDS WERE COMMODITIES (REPRESENTED PICTORIALLY).

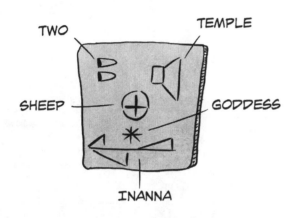

FISH

BARLEY

BEER

MILK FAT

FOR WRITING QUANTITIES THERE WAS A NUMERICAL SYSTEM (WITH NUMBERS INCREASING BY ALTERNATING ORDERS OF 10 AND 6).

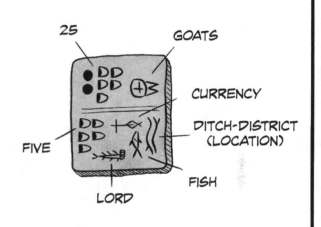

| 1 | 10 | 60 | 600 | 3600 | 36,000 |

ANOTHER SYSTEM REPRESENTED TIME.

| 1 DAY | 10 DAYS | 1 MONTH | 10 MONTHS | 1 YEAR |

GHOSTS OF THIS ANCIENT PAST STILL SURVIVE TODAY. FOR EXAMPLE, IN THE DIVISION OF HOURS AND MINUTES INTO UNITS OF 60 AND A CIRCLE INTO 360 DEGREES.

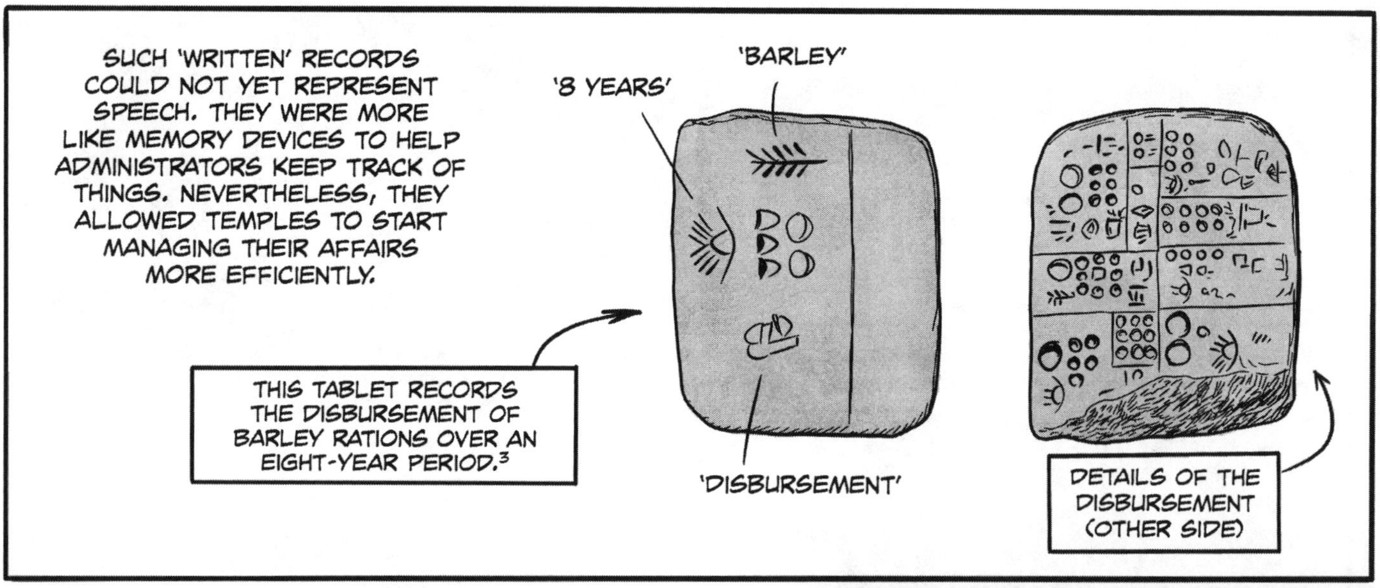
SUCH 'WRITTEN' RECORDS COULD NOT YET REPRESENT SPEECH. THEY WERE MORE LIKE MEMORY DEVICES TO HELP ADMINISTRATORS KEEP TRACK OF THINGS. NEVERTHELESS, THEY ALLOWED TEMPLES TO START MANAGING THEIR AFFAIRS MORE EFFICIENTLY.
'8 YEARS'
'BARLEY'
THIS TABLET RECORDS THE DISBURSEMENT OF BARLEY RATIONS OVER AN EIGHT-YEAR PERIOD.3
'DISBURSEMENT'
DETAILS OF THE DISBURSEMENT (OTHER SIDE)

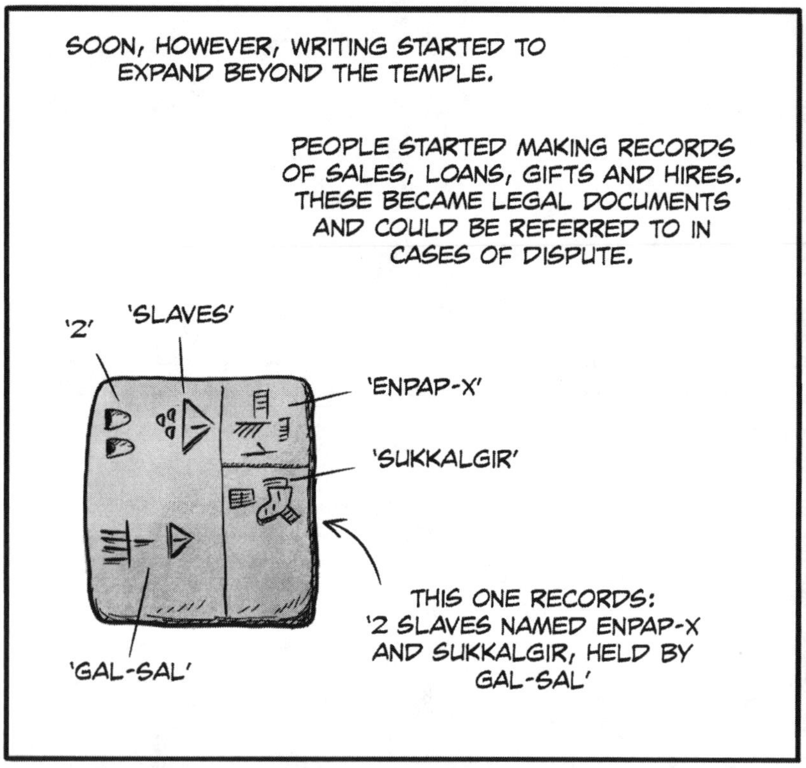
SOON, HOWEVER, WRITING STARTED TO EXPAND BEYOND THE TEMPLE.
PEOPLE STARTED MAKING RECORDS OF SALES, LOANS, GIFTS AND HIRES. THESE BECAME LEGAL DOCUMENTS AND COULD BE REFERRED TO IN CASES OF DISPUTE.
'2'
'SLAVES'
'ENPAP-X'
'SUKKALGIR'
THIS ONE RECORDS: '2 SLAVES NAMED ENPAP-X AND SUKKALGIR, HELD BY GAL-SAL'
'GAL-SAL'

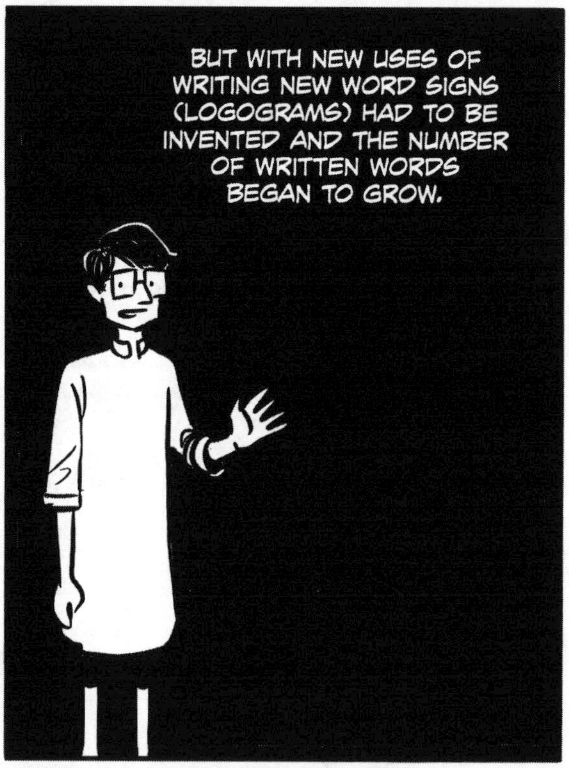
BUT WITH NEW USES OF WRITING NEW WORD SIGNS (LOGOGRAMS) HAD TO BE INVENTED AND THE NUMBER OF WRITTEN WORDS BEGAN TO GROW.

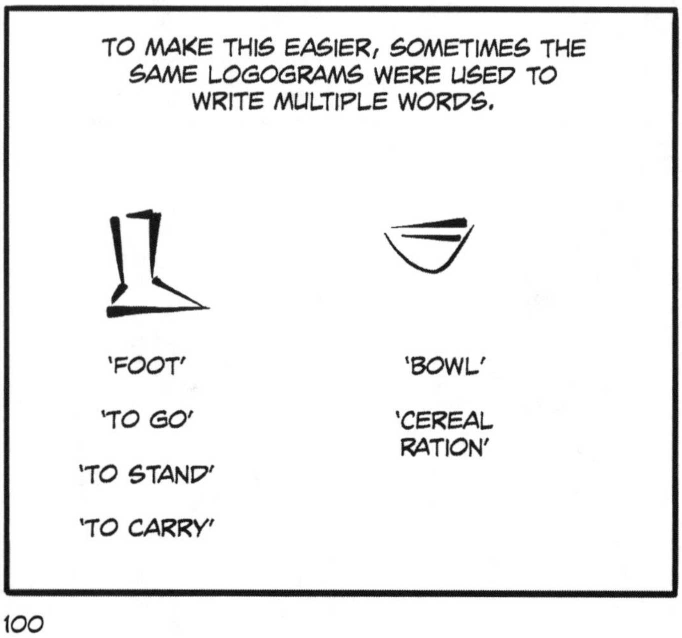
TO MAKE THIS EASIER, SOMETIMES THE SAME LOGOGRAMS WERE USED TO WRITE MULTIPLE WORDS.
'FOOT'
'TO GO'
'TO STAND'
'TO CARRY'
'BOWL'
'CEREAL RATION'

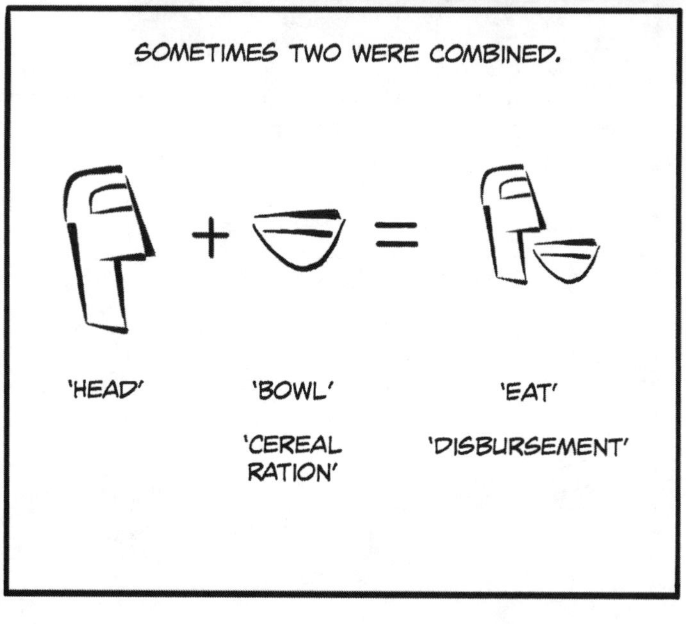
SOMETIMES TWO WERE COMBINED.
+
=
'HEAD'
'BOWL'
'CEREAL RATION'
'EAT'
'DISBURSEMENT'

BUT THERE WERE SO MANY WORDS TO BE WRITTEN. SOON THE TOTAL NUMBER HAD REACHED THE THOUSANDS.

'ACCOUNTANT'

'IRRIGATION DITCH'

'FIELD AREA'

NOW A NEW PROBLEM AROSE—HOW WOULD YOU REMEMBER SO MANY SIGNS? AND HOW WOULD EVERYONE AGREE ON THE SAME ONES?

AND WHAT IF A DOCUMENT HAD TO BE CONSULTED DECADES AFTER IT WAS MADE AND, SAY, THE ORIGINAL SCRIBE WAS DEAD?

ONE OF THE SOLUTIONS DEVISED WAS LEXICAL LISTS.

THESE WERE LONG LISTS OF WORDS CATEGORIZED BY SUBJECT.

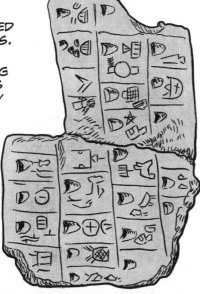

THEY LISTED THINGS LIKE PROFESSIONS, NAMES OF METALS, CITY NAMES, OFFICIAL TITLES, TYPES OF GRAINS, ANIMALS, AND SO ON.

WITH 'OFFICIAL' LISTS MESOPOTAMIAN TEMPLES COULD STANDARDIZE WORD SIGNS AND TEACH THEM TO NEW GENERATIONS.

A NEW PROFESSION OF SCRIBES CAME UP.

BUT EVEN THIS WASN'T ENOUGH. CONSIDER WORDS LIKE 'OUTSIDE', 'MORE', 'LESS', 'HEAVEN', 'SUBLIME'. HOW DO YOU DEPICT THESE PICTORIALLY?

IT WAS A BIG CHALLENGE. LOGOGRAMS WERE BECOMING NOT ONLY MORE NUMEROUS BUT ALSO MORE ABSTRACT.

WRITING HAD TO BE SIMPLIFIED.

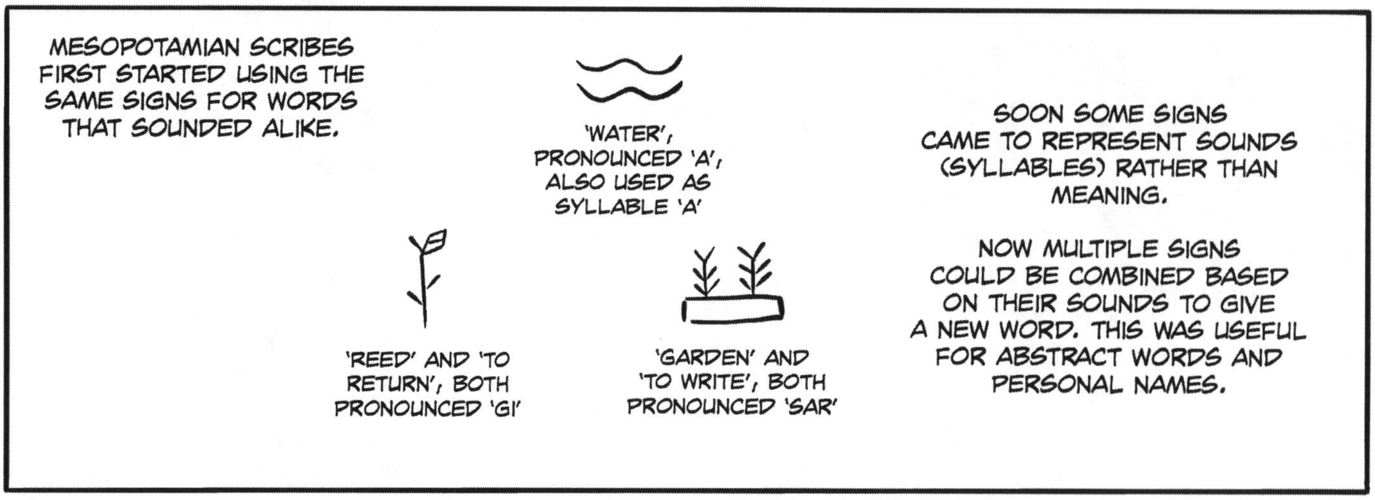
MESOPOTAMIAN SCRIBES FIRST STARTED USING THE SAME SIGNS FOR WORDS THAT SOUNDED ALIKE.
'WATER', PRONOUNCED 'A', ALSO USED AS SYLLABLE 'A'
'REED' AND 'TO RETURN', BOTH PRONOUNCED 'GI'
'GARDEN' AND 'TO WRITE', BOTH PRONOUNCED 'SAR'
SOON SOME SIGNS CAME TO REPRESENT SOUNDS (SYLLABLES) RATHER THAN MEANING.
NOW MULTIPLE SIGNS COULD BE COMBINED BASED ON THEIR SOUNDS TO GIVE A NEW WORD. THIS WAS USEFUL FOR ABSTRACT WORDS AND PERSONAL NAMES.

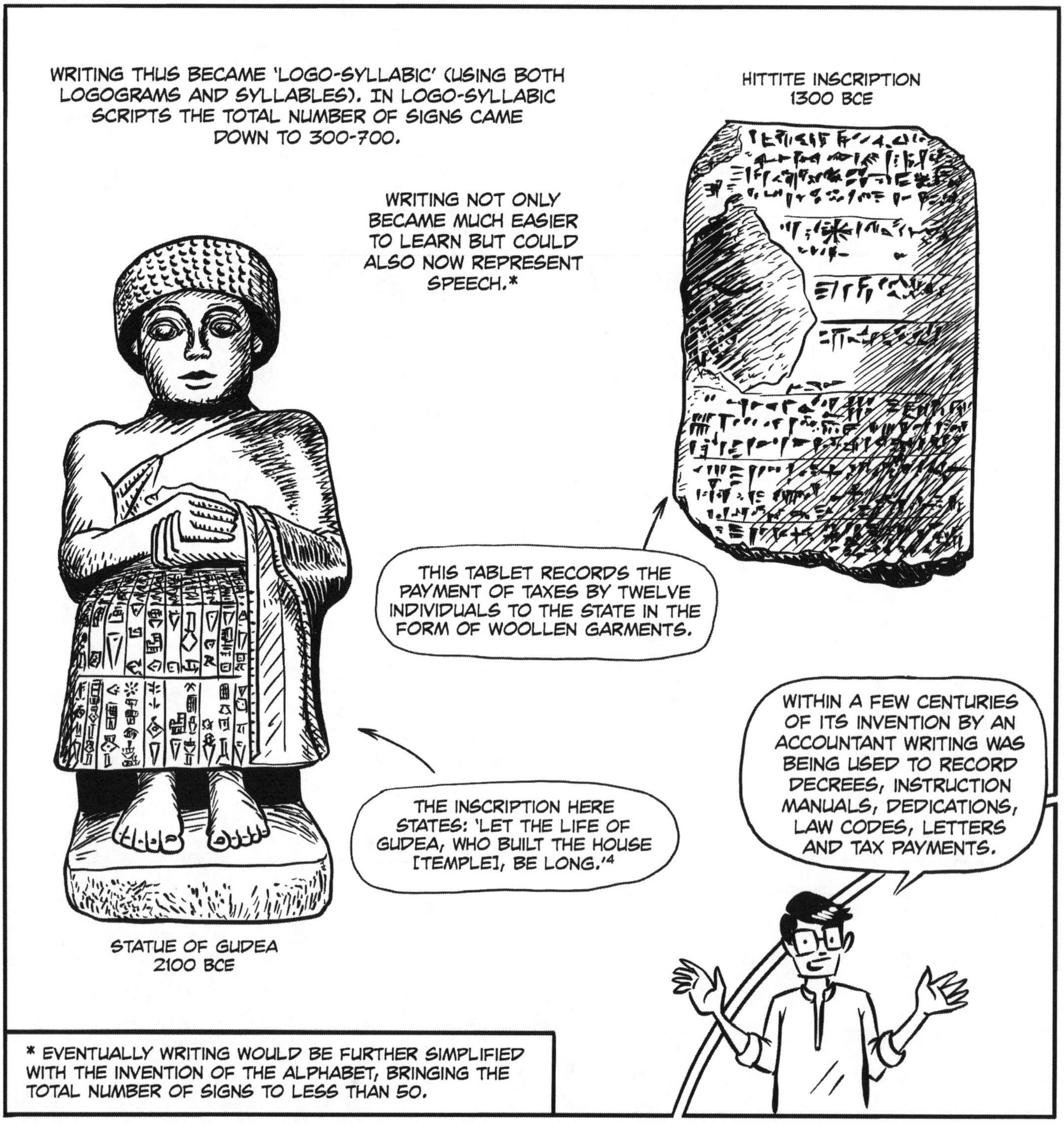
WRITING THUS BECAME 'LOGO-SYLLABIC' (USING BOTH LOGOGRAMS AND SYLLABLES). IN LOGO-SYLLABIC SCRIPTS THE TOTAL NUMBER OF SIGNS CAME DOWN TO 300-700.
HITTITE INSCRIPTION 1300 BCE
WRITING NOT ONLY BECAME MUCH EASIER TO LEARN BUT COULD ALSO NOW REPRESENT SPEECH.*
THIS TABLET RECORDS THE PAYMENT OF TAXES BY TWELVE INDIVIDUALS TO THE STATE IN THE FORM OF WOOLLEN GARMENTS.
WITHIN A FEW CENTURIES OF ITS INVENTION BY AN ACCOUNTANT WRITING WAS BEING USED TO RECORD DECREES, INSTRUCTION MANUALS, DEDICATIONS, LAW CODES, LETTERS AND TAX PAYMENTS.
THE INSCRIPTION HERE STATES: 'LET THE LIFE OF GUDEA, WHO BUILT THE HOUSE [TEMPLE], BE LONG.'[4]
STATUE OF GUDEA 2100 BCE
* EVENTUALLY WRITING WOULD BE FURTHER SIMPLIFIED WITH THE INVENTION OF THE ALPHABET, BRINGING THE TOTAL NUMBER OF SIGNS TO LESS THAN 50.

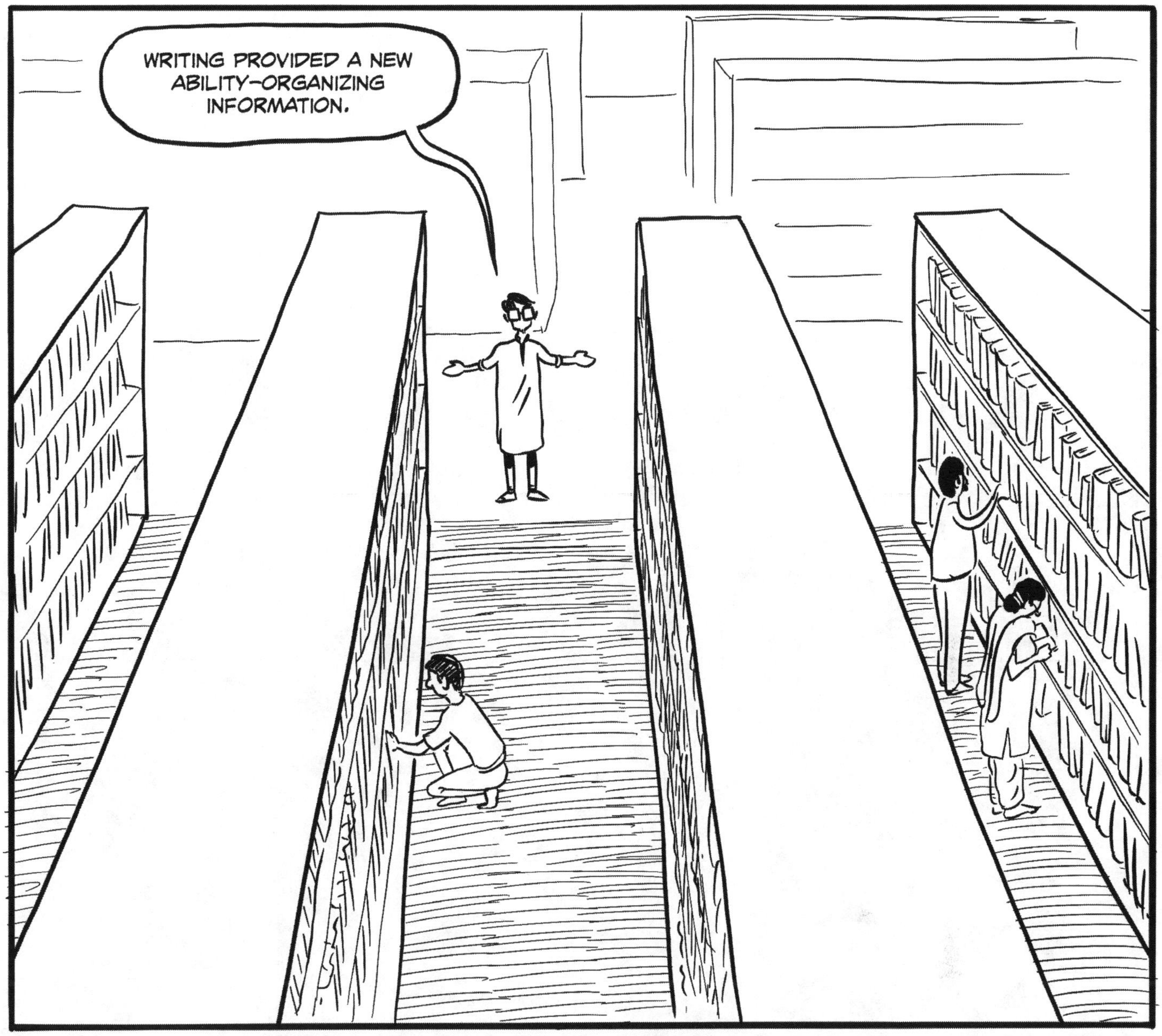
WRITING PROVIDED A NEW ABILITY—ORGANIZING INFORMATION.

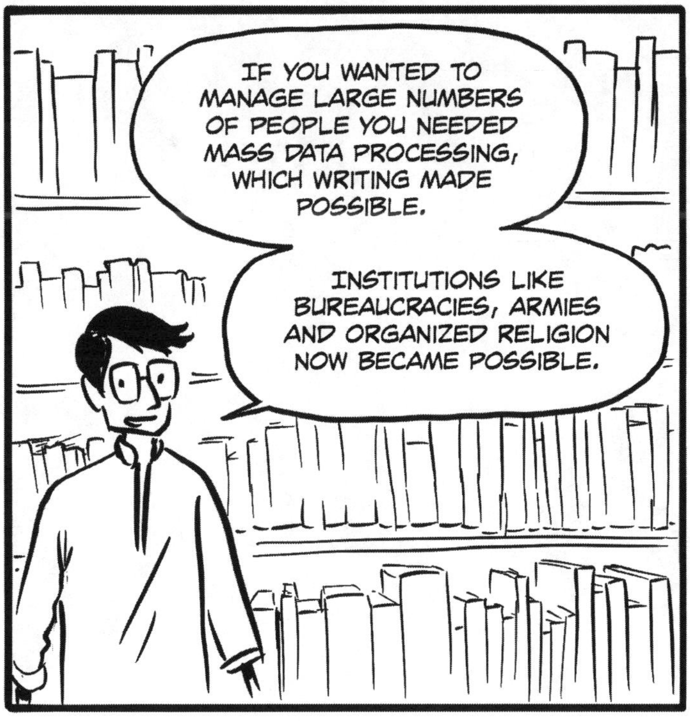
IF YOU WANTED TO MANAGE LARGE NUMBERS OF PEOPLE YOU NEEDED MASS DATA PROCESSING, WHICH WRITING MADE POSSIBLE.
INSTITUTIONS LIKE BUREAUCRACIES, ARMIES AND ORGANIZED RELIGION NOW BECAME POSSIBLE.

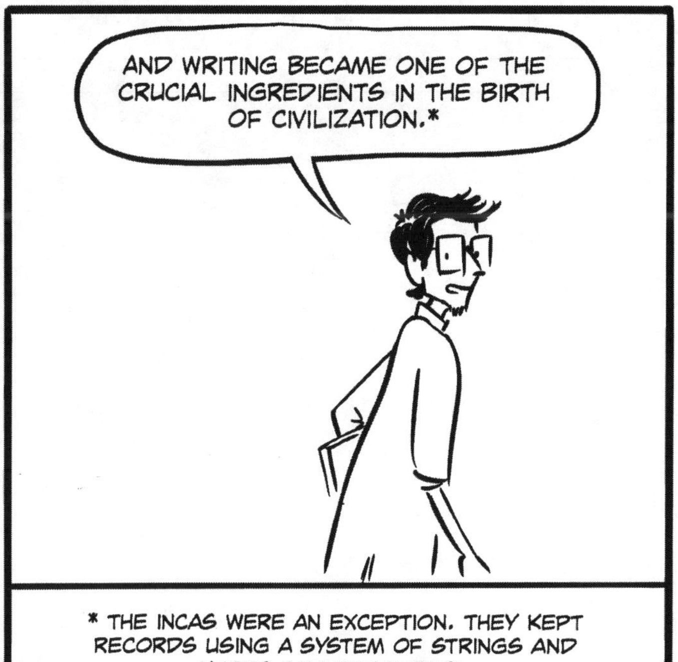
AND WRITING BECAME ONE OF THE CRUCIAL INGREDIENTS IN THE BIRTH OF CIVILIZATION.*

* THE INCAS WERE AN EXCEPTION. THEY KEPT RECORDS USING A SYSTEM OF STRINGS AND KNOTS CALLED 'QUIPUS'.

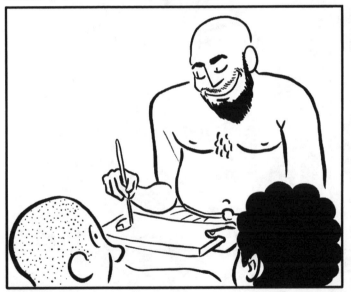

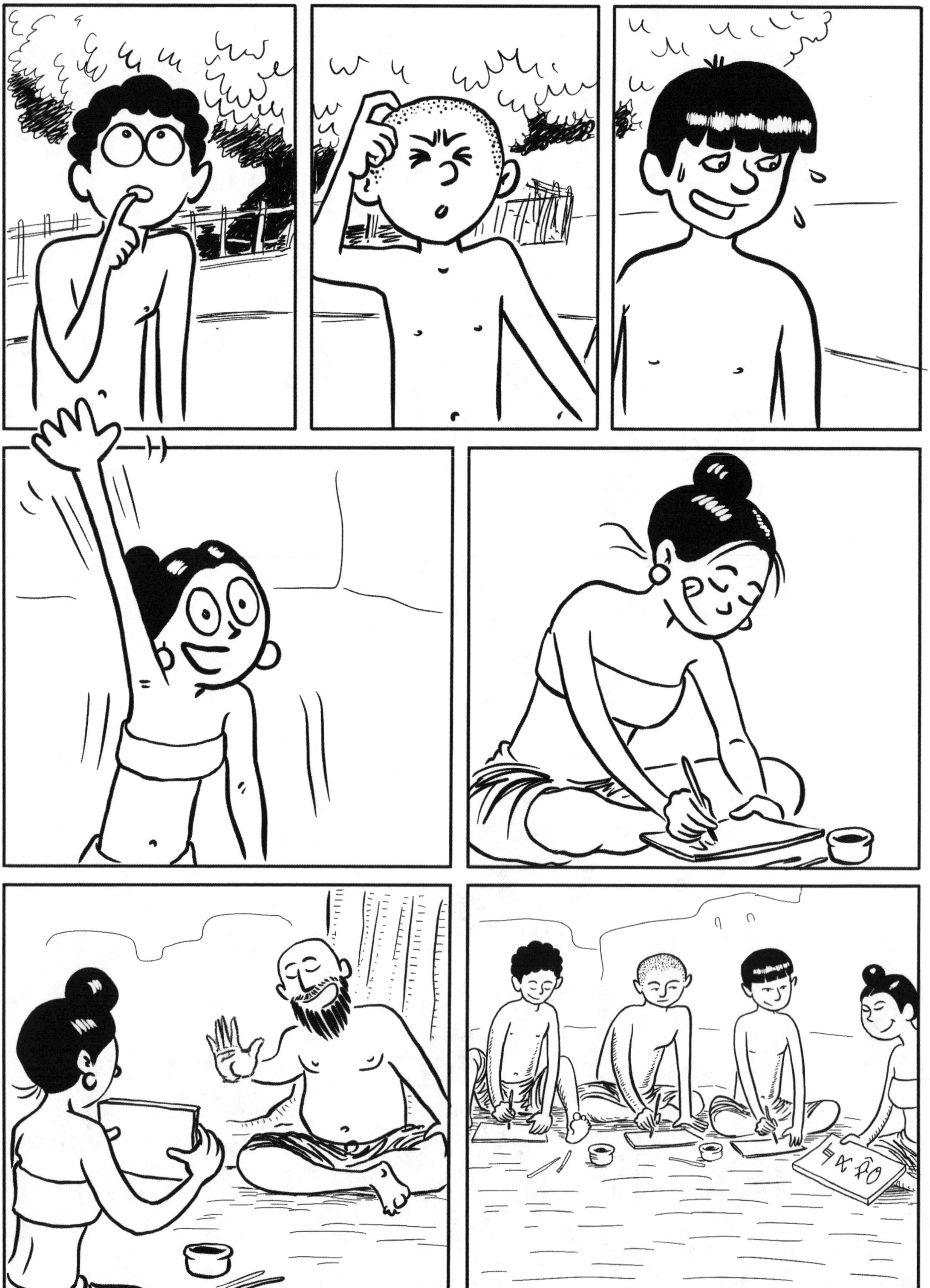

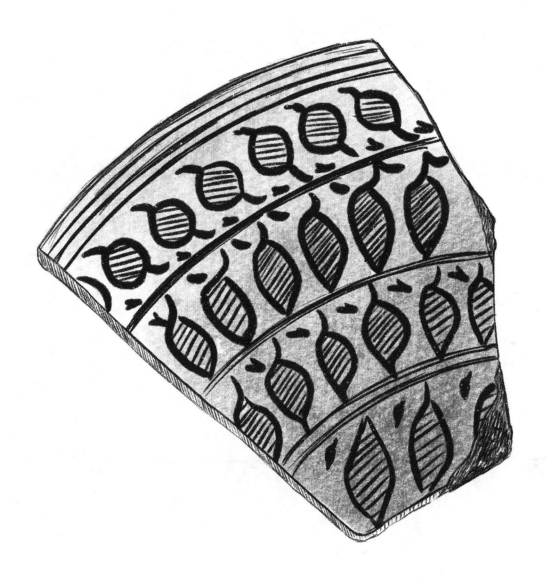

 WRITING APPEARED IN THE INDUS REGION OF NORTHWESTERN SOUTH ASIA AROUND 2600 BCE, JUST AS CITIES WERE BEING BORN.

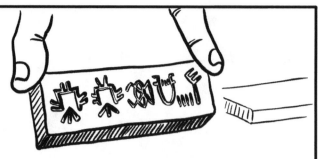 IT SURVIVES IN THE FORM OF THOUSANDS OF INSCRIPTIONS, MOST OF WHICH ARE SHORT, AVERAGING 5-7 SYMBOLS. IT IS POSSIBLE THAT LONGER TEXTS EXISTED ON WOOD OR CLOTH BUT NONE HAVE SURVIVED.

INDUS WRITING APPEARS MOST COMMONLY ON POTTERY BUT ALSO ON SEALS, COPPER TABLETS, GOLD JEWELLERY, AND IN ONE CASE EVEN AS INLAY IN A WOODEN SIGNBOARD.

THESE LETTERS WERE FOUND IN DHOLAVIRA, RIGHT NEXT TO A GATEWAY. BUT, CURIOUSLY, THEY APPEARED IN REVERSE ORDER TO HOW THEY ARE NORMALLY SEEN.

 IT TURNS OUT THEY WERE PART OF A LARGE WOODEN SIGN BOARD WHICH, AT SOME POINT, FELL WITH THE WRITING FACING DOWN. THE WOOD DECAYED, BUT THE LETTERS, MADE FROM GYPSUM, A CHALK LIKE MATERIAL, SURVIVED.

THE ORIGINS OF THE INDUS SCRIPT CAN BE TRACED TO AS EARLY AS 3300 BCE AT THE SITE OF HARAPPA.

SOME SIGNS MAY HAVE BEEN LINKED TO PLANT MOTIFS SUCH AS THE PIPAL LEAF THAT ALSO APPEAR ON POTTERY.

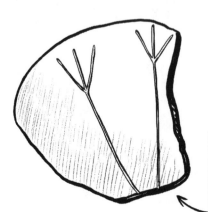

BY AROUND 2800 BCE MANY DISTINCT SIGNS WERE BEING USED ON SEALS AND POTTERY AT THE SITE OF HARAPPA AND THROUGHOUT THE GREATER INDUS REGION.

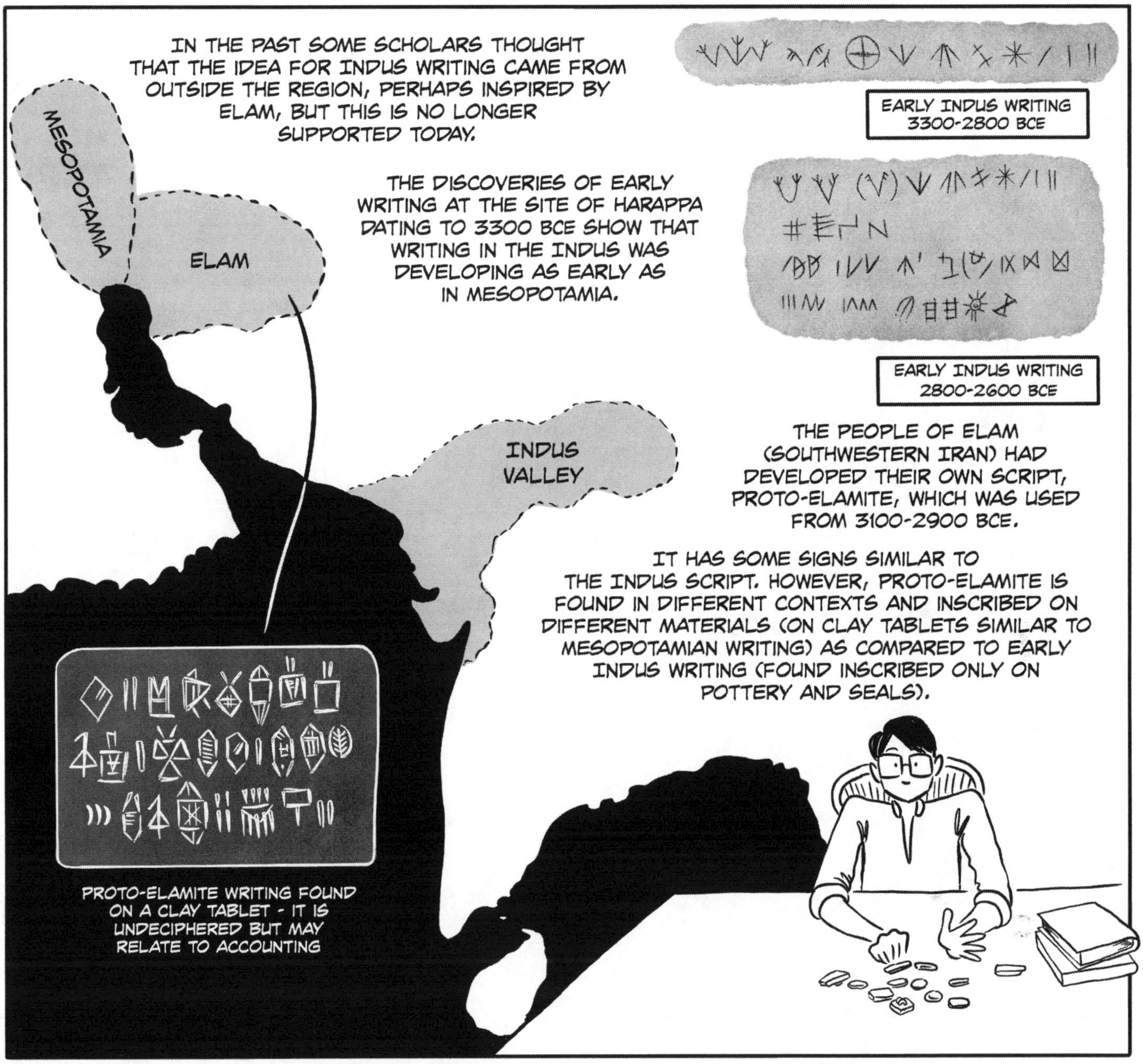
IN THE PAST SOME SCHOLARS THOUGHT THAT THE IDEA FOR INDUS WRITING CAME FROM OUTSIDE THE REGION, PERHAPS INSPIRED BY ELAM, BUT THIS IS NO LONGER SUPPORTED TODAY.
MESOPOTAMIA
ELAM
THE DISCOVERIES OF EARLY WRITING AT THE SITE OF HARAPPA DATING TO 3300 BCE SHOW THAT WRITING IN THE INDUS WAS DEVELOPING AS EARLY AS IN MESOPOTAMIA.
EARLY INDUS WRITING 3300-2800 BCE
EARLY INDUS WRITING 2800-2600 BCE
INDUS VALLEY
THE PEOPLE OF ELAM (SOUTHWESTERN IRAN) HAD DEVELOPED THEIR OWN SCRIPT, PROTO-ELAMITE, WHICH WAS USED FROM 3100-2900 BCE.
IT HAS SOME SIGNS SIMILAR TO THE INDUS SCRIPT. HOWEVER, PROTO-ELAMITE IS FOUND IN DIFFERENT CONTEXTS AND INSCRIBED ON DIFFERENT MATERIALS (ON CLAY TABLETS SIMILAR TO MESOPOTAMIAN WRITING) AS COMPARED TO EARLY INDUS WRITING (FOUND INSCRIBED ONLY ON POTTERY AND SEALS).
PROTO-ELAMITE WRITING FOUND ON A CLAY TABLET - IT IS UNDECIPHERED BUT MAY RELATE TO ACCOUNTING

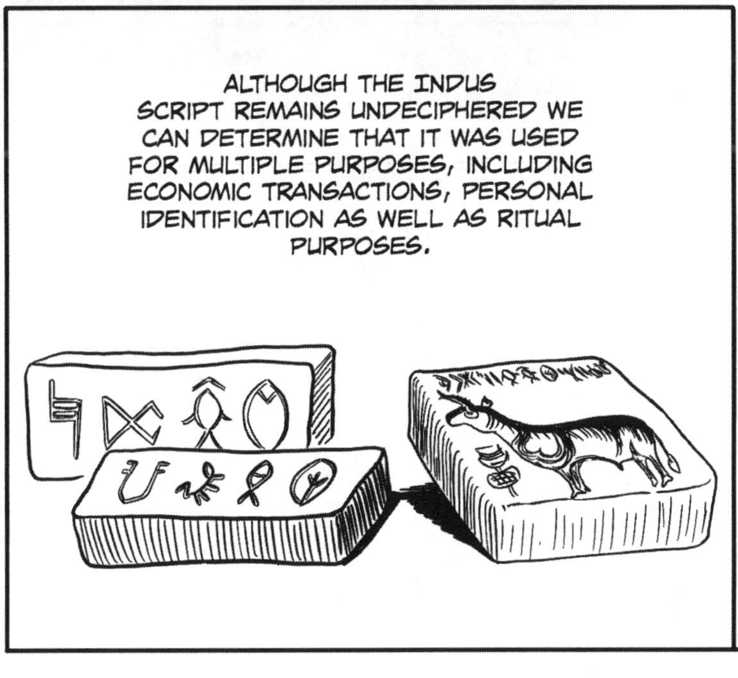
ALTHOUGH THE INDUS SCRIPT REMAINS UNDECIPHERED WE CAN DETERMINE THAT IT WAS USED FOR MULTIPLE PURPOSES, INCLUDING ECONOMIC TRANSACTIONS, PERSONAL IDENTIFICATION AS WELL AS RITUAL PURPOSES.

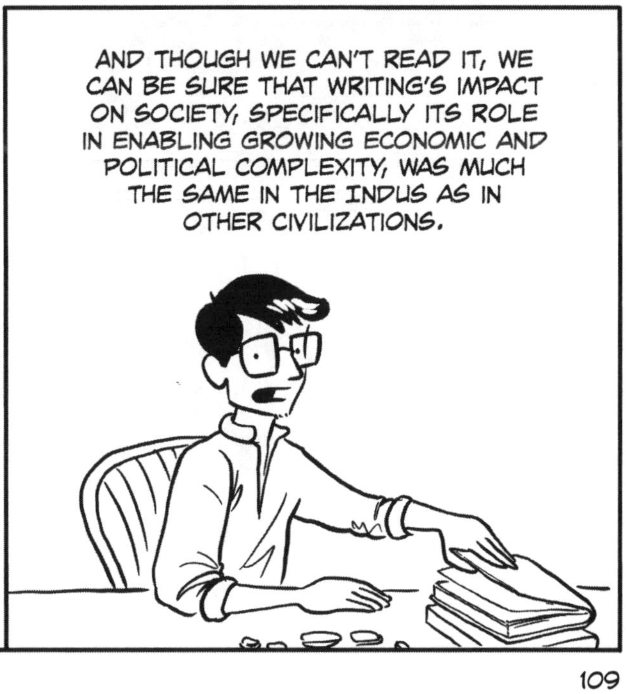
AND THOUGH WE CAN'T READ IT, WE CAN BE SURE THAT WRITING'S IMPACT ON SOCIETY, SPECIFICALLY ITS ROLE IN ENABLING GROWING ECONOMIC AND POLITICAL COMPLEXITY, WAS MUCH THE SAME IN THE INDUS AS IN OTHER CIVILIZATIONS.

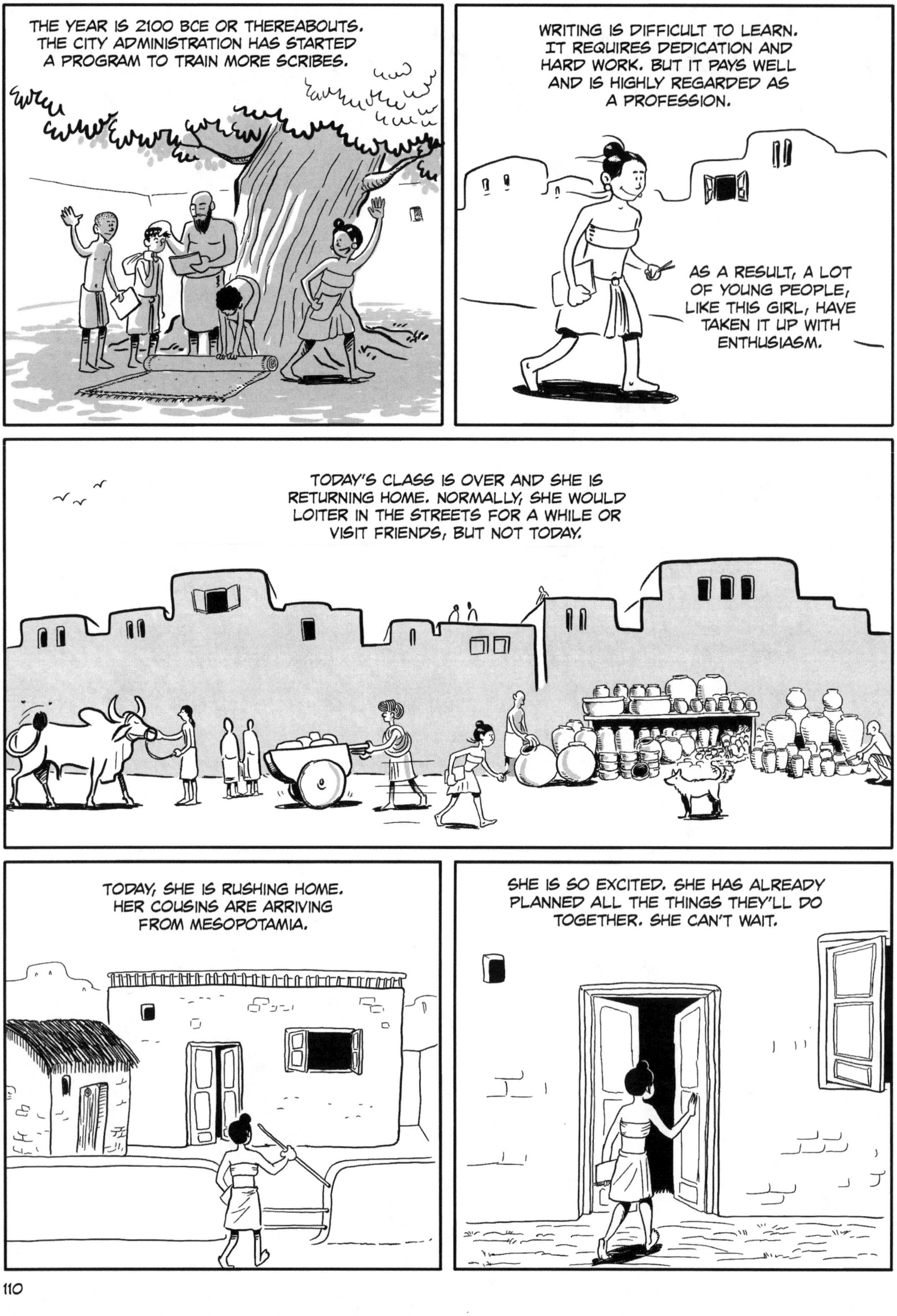
THE YEAR IS 2100 BCE OR THEREABOUTS. THE CITY ADMINISTRATION HAS STARTED A PROGRAM TO TRAIN MORE SCRIBES.
WRITING IS DIFFICULT TO LEARN. IT REQUIRES DEDICATION AND HARD WORK. BUT IT PAYS WELL AND IS HIGHLY REGARDED AS A PROFESSION.
AS A RESULT, A LOT OF YOUNG PEOPLE, LIKE THIS GIRL, HAVE TAKEN IT UP WITH ENTHUSIASM.
TODAY'S CLASS IS OVER AND SHE IS RETURNING HOME. NORMALLY, SHE WOULD LOITER IN THE STREETS FOR A WHILE OR VISIT FRIENDS, BUT NOT TODAY.
TODAY, SHE IS RUSHING HOME. HER COUSINS ARE ARRIVING FROM MESOPOTAMIA.
SHE IS SO EXCITED. SHE HAS ALREADY PLANNED ALL THE THINGS THEY'LL DO TOGETHER. SHE CAN'T WAIT.

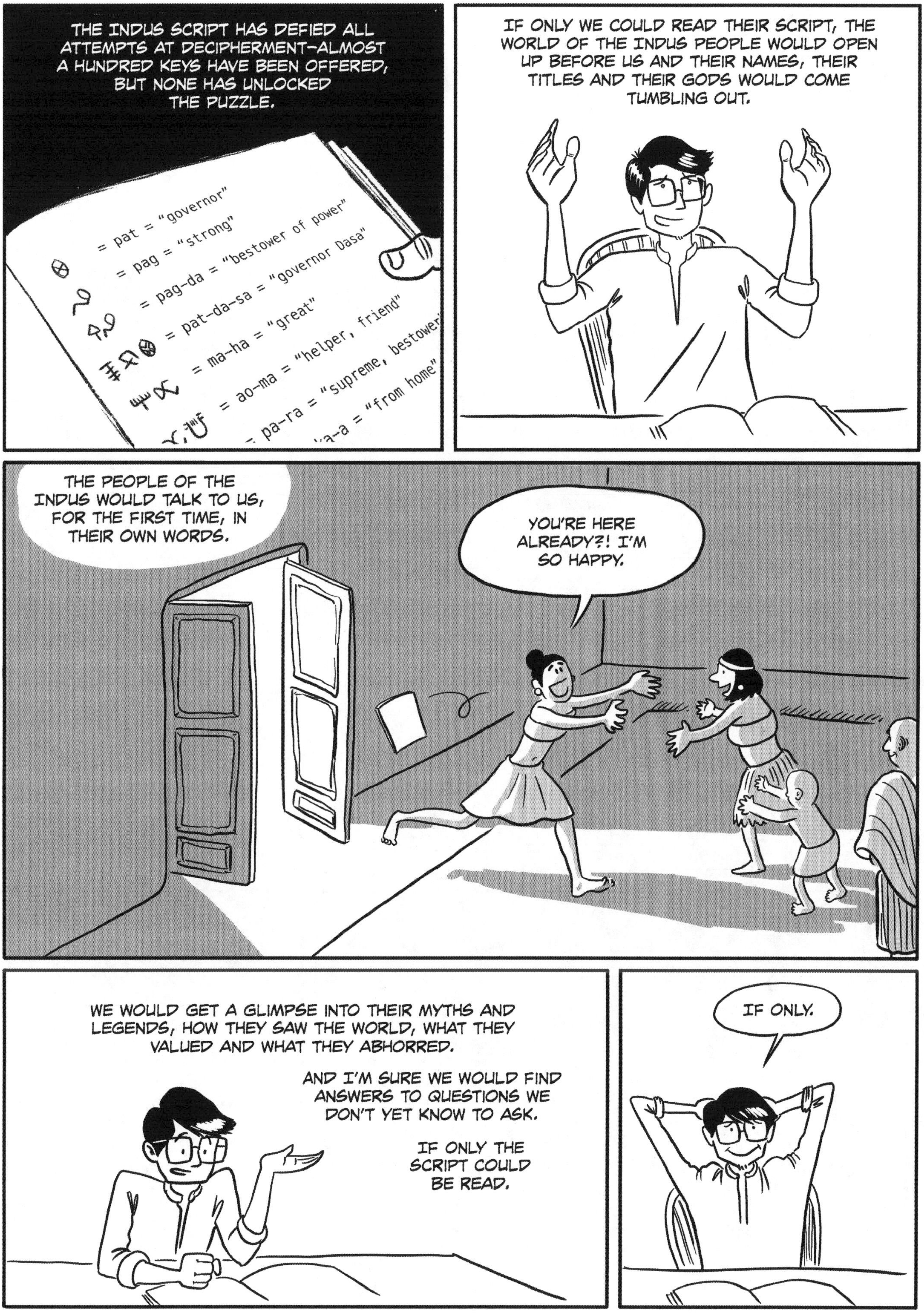
THE INDUS SCRIPT HAS DEFIED ALL ATTEMPTS AT DECIPHERMENT—ALMOST A HUNDRED KEYS HAVE BEEN OFFERED, BUT NONE HAS UNLOCKED THE PUZZLE.
= pat = "governor"
= pag = "strong"
= pag-da = "bestower of power"
= pat-da-sa = "governor Dasa"
= ma-ha = "great"
= ao-ma = "helper, friend"
= pa-ra = "supreme, bestower
= "from home"
IF ONLY WE COULD READ THEIR SCRIPT, THE WORLD OF THE INDUS PEOPLE WOULD OPEN UP BEFORE US AND THEIR NAMES, THEIR TITLES AND THEIR GODS WOULD COME TUMBLING OUT.
THE PEOPLE OF THE INDUS WOULD TALK TO US, FOR THE FIRST TIME, IN THEIR OWN WORDS.
YOU'RE HERE ALREADY?! I'M SO HAPPY.
WE WOULD GET A GLIMPSE INTO THEIR MYTHS AND LEGENDS, HOW THEY SAW THE WORLD, WHAT THEY VALUED AND WHAT THEY ABHORRED.
AND I'M SURE WE WOULD FIND ANSWERS TO QUESTIONS WE DON'T YET KNOW TO ASK.
IF ONLY THE SCRIPT COULD BE READ.
IF ONLY.

BUT DECIPHERMENT HAS PROVEN ELUSIVE, AND FOR GOOD REASONS.
THE INDUS SCRIPT, FOR ONE, BEARS NO RESEMBLANCE TO ANY OTHER KNOWN SCRIPTS.
THE ANCIENT CHINESE SCRIPT, FOR EXAMPLE, COULD BE DECIPHERED BECAUSE IT EVOLVED INTO THE MODERN CHINESE SCRIPT.
AS A RESULT, SYMBOL SHAPES COULD BE RELIABLY TRACED BACKWARDS.
IN SOUTH ASIA, THE SCRIPTS TO COME LATER SHOW NO CLEAR LINKS TO THE INDUS SCRIPT.
BRAHMI
KHAROSHTI
FURTHER, WE LACK BILINGUAL OR MULTILINGUAL TEXTS.
MANY ANCIENT SCRIPTS WERE DECIPHERED ONLY AFTER THE DISCOVERY OF INSCRIPTIONS WRITTEN IN MULTIPLE SCRIPTS, OF WHICH AT LEAST ONE WAS ALREADY UNDERSTOOD.
EGYPTIAN HIEROGLYPHS
DEMOTIC SCRIPT
GREEK SCRIPT
ROSETTA STONE, 196 BCE
BABYLONIAN CUNEIFORM
ELAMITE
OLD PERSIAN
BEHISTUN INSCRIPTION 500 BCE
THIS IS NOT THE CASE WITH THE INDUS.
SO IS THERE NO HOPE FOR DECIPHERMENT THEN?
WELL, IF INTERPRETERS LIKE SHU-ILISHU EXISTED, THEN ISN'T IT POSSIBLE BILINGUAL TEXTS ALSO EXISTED?
WE MAY YET FIND SOME. I'M KEEPING MY FINGERS CROSSED.*
* SOME INDUS STYLE SEALS WITH CUNEIFORM INSCRIPTIONS IN AKKADIAN MAY PROVIDE A KEY TO THE TYPES OF NAMES OR TITLES FOUND ON INDUS SEALS.
WHILE WE CAN STILL LEARN A LOT FROM THE CONTEXTS IN WHICH THE INDUS WRITING WAS USED, ITS DECIPHERMENT SEEMS UNLIKELY WITHOUT A BILINGUAL TEXT.
MANY EXPERTS BELIEVE THAT WITH THE GIVEN CORPUS OF 4000 SHORT INSCRIPTIONS, WE ARE OUT OF LUCK.

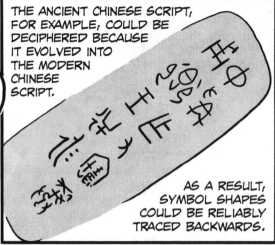

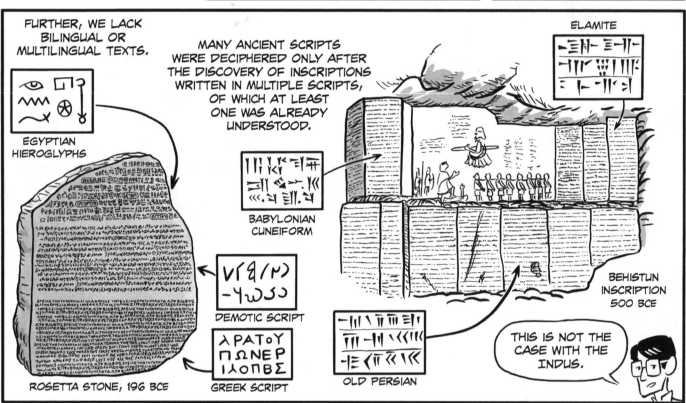

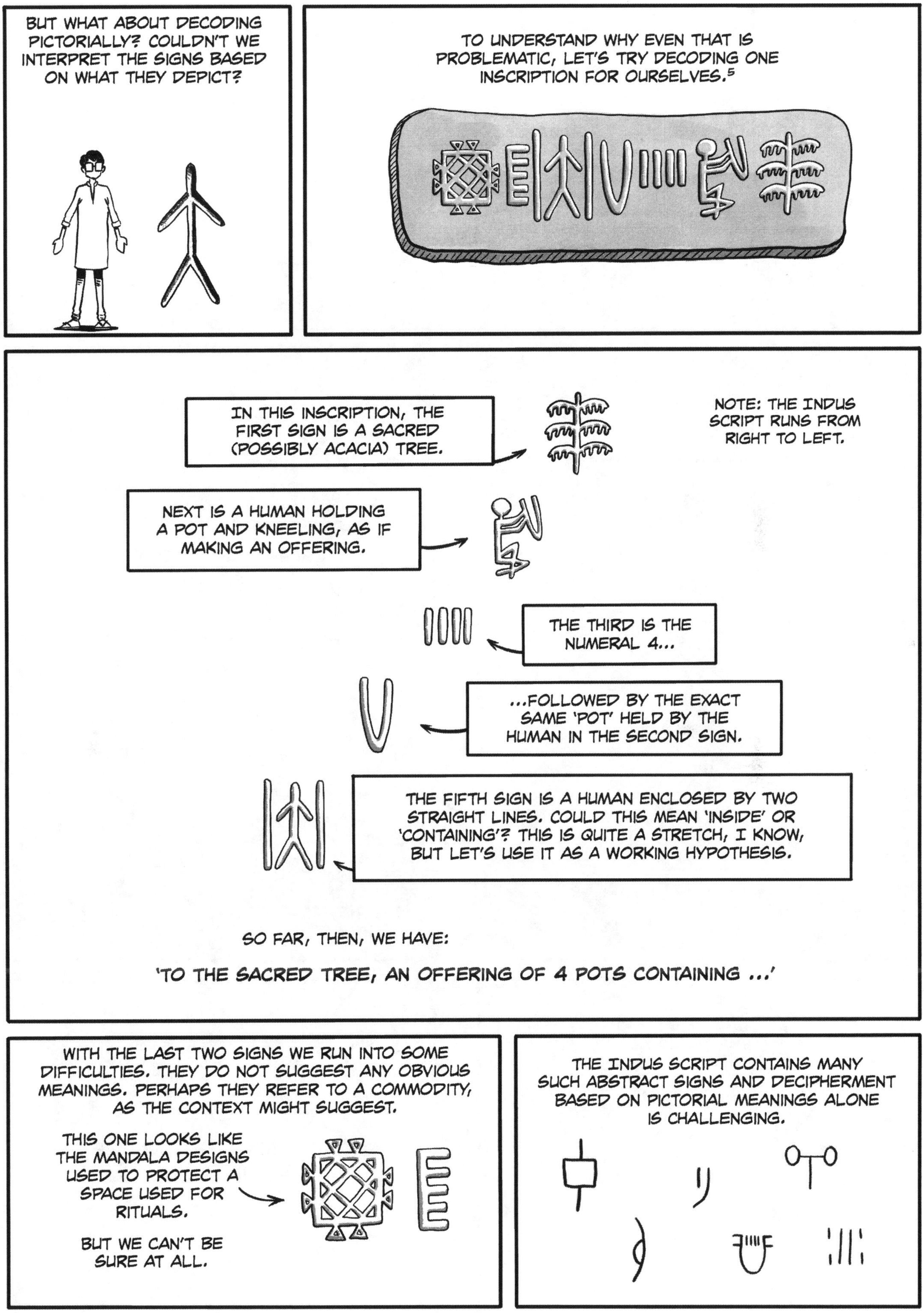
BUT WHAT ABOUT DECODING PICTORIALLY? COULDN'T WE INTERPRET THE SIGNS BASED ON WHAT THEY DEPICT?
TO UNDERSTAND WHY EVEN THAT IS PROBLEMATIC, LET'S TRY DECODING ONE INSCRIPTION FOR OURSELVES.[5]
IN THIS INSCRIPTION, THE FIRST SIGN IS A SACRED (POSSIBLY ACACIA) TREE.
NOTE: THE INDUS SCRIPT RUNS FROM RIGHT TO LEFT.
NEXT IS A HUMAN HOLDING A POT AND KNEELING, AS IF MAKING AN OFFERING.
THE THIRD IS THE NUMERAL 4...
...FOLLOWED BY THE EXACT SAME 'POT' HELD BY THE HUMAN IN THE SECOND SIGN.
THE FIFTH SIGN IS A HUMAN ENCLOSED BY TWO STRAIGHT LINES. COULD THIS MEAN 'INSIDE' OR 'CONTAINING'? THIS IS QUITE A STRETCH, I KNOW, BUT LET'S USE IT AS A WORKING HYPOTHESIS.
SO FAR, THEN, WE HAVE:
'TO THE SACRED TREE, AN OFFERING OF 4 POTS CONTAINING ...'
WITH THE LAST TWO SIGNS WE RUN INTO SOME DIFFICULTIES. THEY DO NOT SUGGEST ANY OBVIOUS MEANINGS. PERHAPS THEY REFER TO A COMMODITY, AS THE CONTEXT MIGHT SUGGEST.
THIS ONE LOOKS LIKE THE MANDALA DESIGNS USED TO PROTECT A SPACE USED FOR RITUALS.
BUT WE CAN'T BE SURE AT ALL.
THE INDUS SCRIPT CONTAINS MANY SUCH ABSTRACT SIGNS AND DECIPHERMENT BASED ON PICTORIAL MEANINGS ALONE IS CHALLENGING.

THERE IS, ANYWAY, ANOTHER MAJOR HURDLE.

MANY EARLY SCRIPTS WERE LOGO-SYLLABIC, CONTAINING SIGNS FOR NOT JUST WORDS (LOGOGRAMS) BUT ALSO SOUNDS (SYLLABLES).

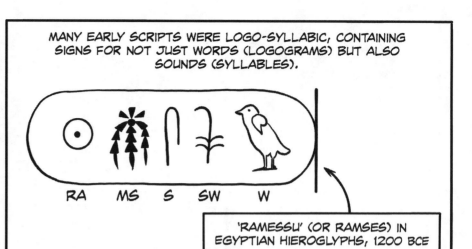

RA   MS   S   SW   W

'RAMESSU' (OR RAMSES) IN EGYPTIAN HIEROGLYPHS, 1200 BCE

THE INDUS SCRIPT SEEMS TO BE LOGO-SYLLABIC TOO. IT CONTAINS 400 SIGNS, WHICH FALLS PERFECTLY WITHIN THE RANGE (300-700 SIGNS) OF MOST LOGO-SYLLABIC SCRIPTS. MOREOVER, WORDS IN SUCH SCRIPTS RANGE FROM 1-3 SIGNS. THIS SEEMS THE CASE FOR THE INDUS SCRIPT AS WELL.

TO READ SUCH SCRIPTS, KNOWING THE SOUNDS OF THE SIGNS BECOMES CRITICAL.

IN THE INSCRIPTION DISCUSSED ON THE LAST PAGE, THE 'V' SIGN COULD EITHER MEAN 'POT' OR SOMETHING THAT SOUNDED LIKE THE HARAPPAN WORD FOR POT.

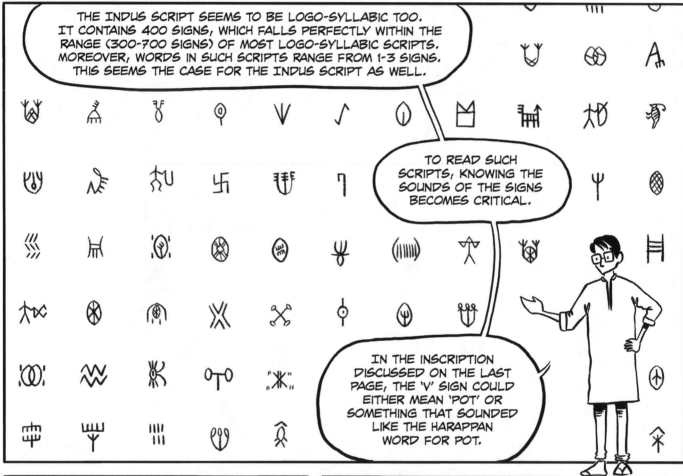

BUT WHAT WAS THE INDUS WORD FOR POT?

AND HERE WE REACH ONE OF THE MOST VEXING PROBLEMS IN THE STUDY OF THE INDUS CIVILIZATION:

WHAT LANGUAGE DID THE INDUS PEOPLE SPEAK?

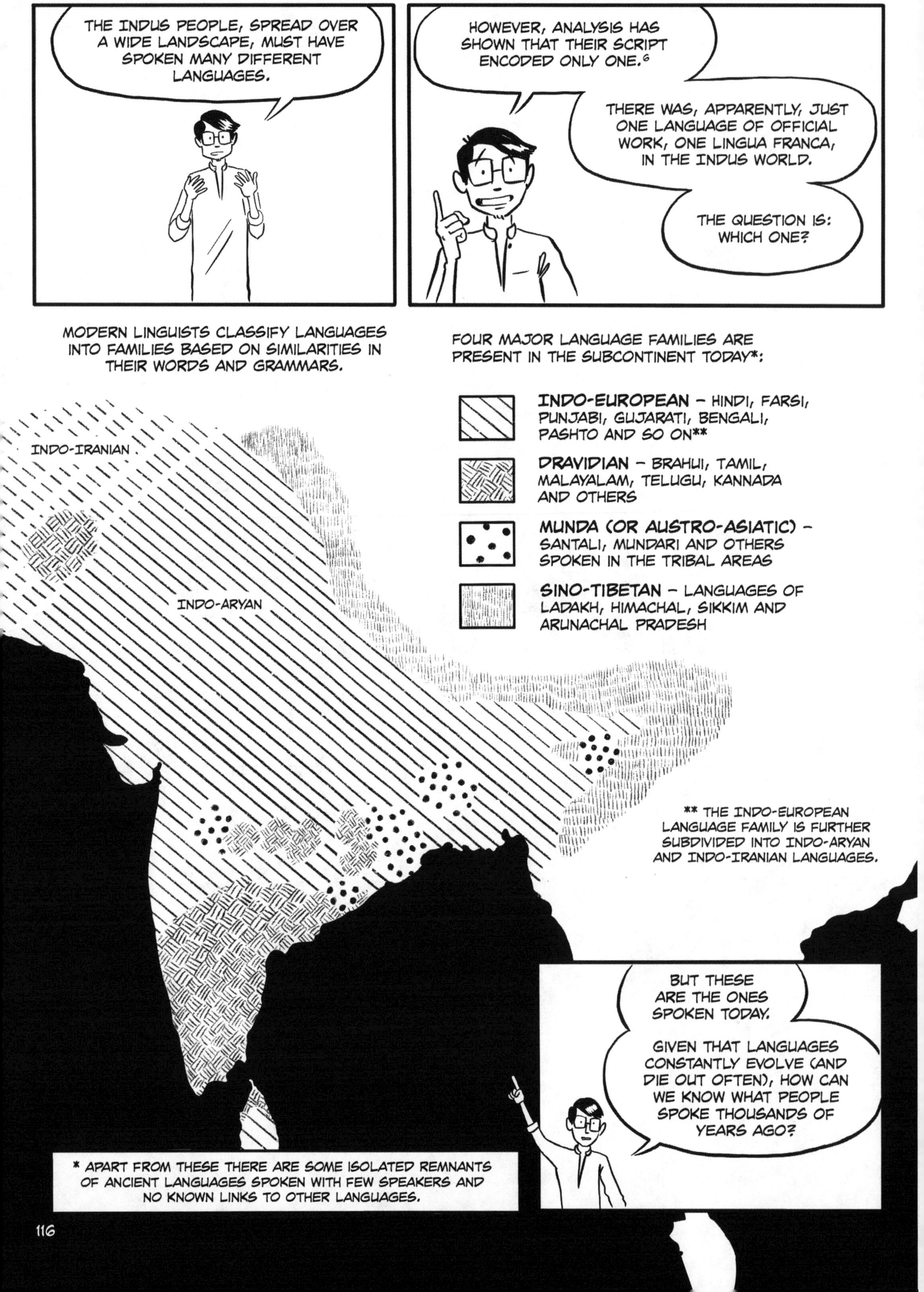

THE INDUS PEOPLE, SPREAD OVER A WIDE LANDSCAPE, MUST HAVE SPOKEN MANY DIFFERENT LANGUAGES.

HOWEVER, ANALYSIS HAS SHOWN THAT THEIR SCRIPT ENCODED ONLY ONE.[6]

THERE WAS, APPARENTLY, JUST ONE LANGUAGE OF OFFICIAL WORK, ONE LINGUA FRANCA, IN THE INDUS WORLD.

THE QUESTION IS: WHICH ONE?

MODERN LINGUISTS CLASSIFY LANGUAGES INTO FAMILIES BASED ON SIMILARITIES IN THEIR WORDS AND GRAMMARS.

FOUR MAJOR LANGUAGE FAMILIES ARE PRESENT IN THE SUBCONTINENT TODAY*:

INDO-EUROPEAN – HINDI, FARSI, PUNJABI, GUJARATI, BENGALI, PASHTO AND SO ON**

DRAVIDIAN – BRAHUI, TAMIL, MALAYALAM, TELUGU, KANNADA AND OTHERS

MUNDA (OR AUSTRO-ASIATIC) – SANTALI, MUNDARI AND OTHERS SPOKEN IN THE TRIBAL AREAS

SINO-TIBETAN – LANGUAGES OF LADAKH, HIMACHAL, SIKKIM AND ARUNACHAL PRADESH

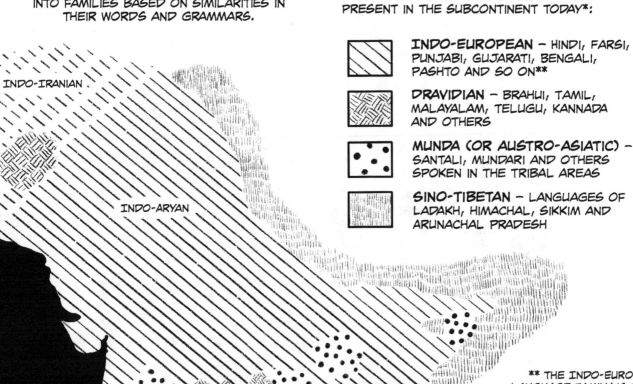

INDO-IRANIAN

INDO-ARYAN

** THE INDO-EUROPEAN LANGUAGE FAMILY IS FURTHER SUBDIVIDED INTO INDO-ARYAN AND INDO-IRANIAN LANGUAGES.

BUT THESE ARE THE ONES SPOKEN TODAY.

GIVEN THAT LANGUAGES CONSTANTLY EVOLVE (AND DIE OUT OFTEN), HOW CAN WE KNOW WHAT PEOPLE SPOKE THOUSANDS OF YEARS AGO?

* APART FROM THESE THERE ARE SOME ISOLATED REMNANTS OF ANCIENT LANGUAGES SPOKEN WITH FEW SPEAKERS AND NO KNOWN LINKS TO OTHER LANGUAGES.

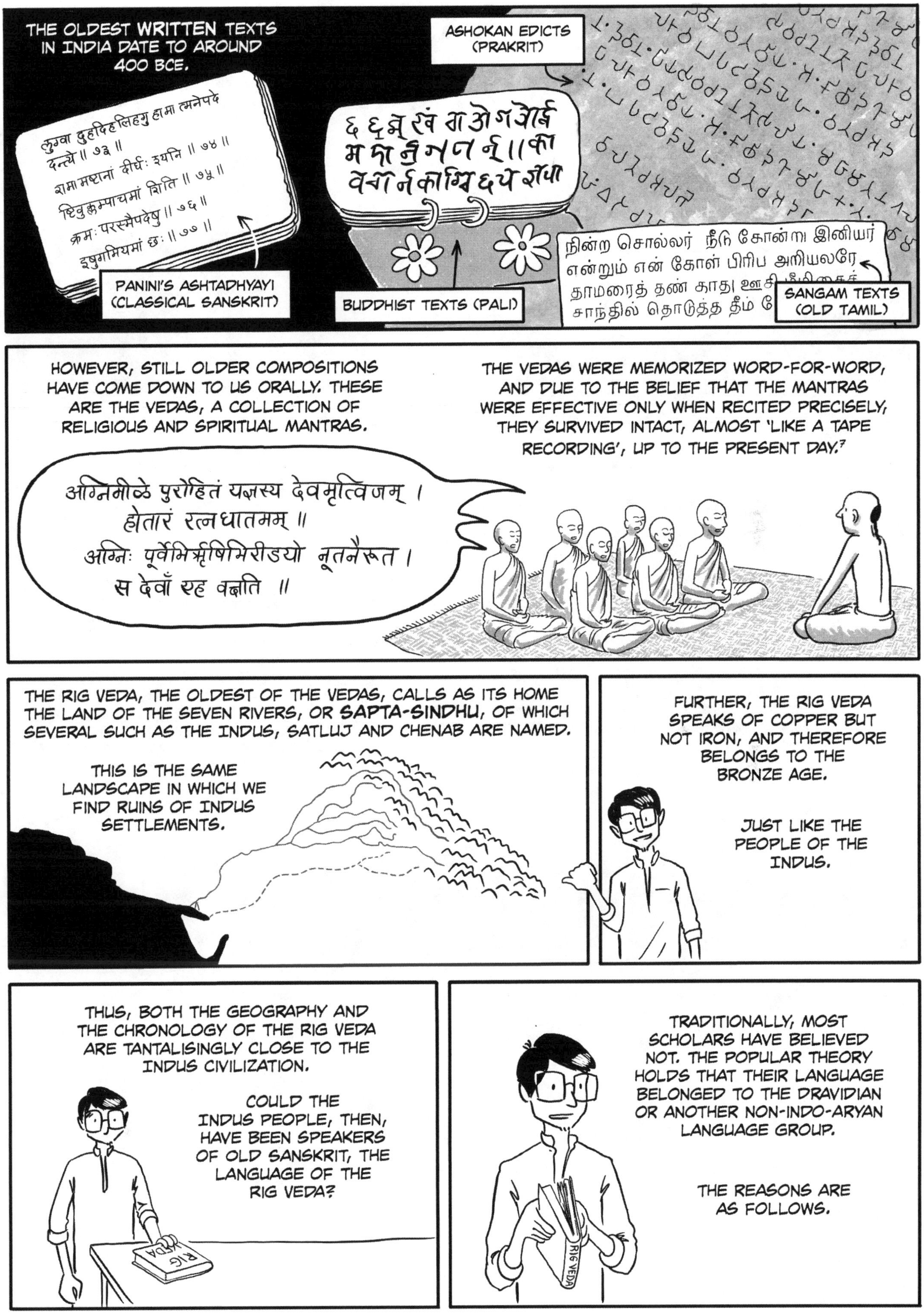
THE OLDEST WRITTEN TEXTS IN INDIA DATE TO AROUND 400 BCE.
ASHOKAN EDICTS (PRAKRIT)
PANINI'S ASHTADHYAYI (CLASSICAL SANSKRIT)
BUDDHIST TEXTS (PALI)
SANGAM TEXTS (OLD TAMIL)
HOWEVER, STILL OLDER COMPOSITIONS HAVE COME DOWN TO US ORALLY. THESE ARE THE VEDAS, A COLLECTION OF RELIGIOUS AND SPIRITUAL MANTRAS.
THE VEDAS WERE MEMORIZED WORD-FOR-WORD, AND DUE TO THE BELIEF THAT THE MANTRAS WERE EFFECTIVE ONLY WHEN RECITED PRECISELY, THEY SURVIVED INTACT, ALMOST 'LIKE A TAPE RECORDING', UP TO THE PRESENT DAY.[7]
अग्निमीळे पुरोहितं यज्ञस्य देवमृत्विजम् । होतारं रत्नधातमम् ॥ अग्निः पूर्वेभिर्ऋषिभिरीड्यो नूतनैरुत । स देवाँ एह वक्षति ॥
THE RIG VEDA, THE OLDEST OF THE VEDAS, CALLS AS ITS HOME THE LAND OF THE SEVEN RIVERS, OR SAPTA-SINDHU, OF WHICH SEVERAL SUCH AS THE INDUS, SATLUJ AND CHENAB ARE NAMED.
THIS IS THE SAME LANDSCAPE IN WHICH WE FIND RUINS OF INDUS SETTLEMENTS.
FURTHER, THE RIG VEDA SPEAKS OF COPPER BUT NOT IRON, AND THEREFORE BELONGS TO THE BRONZE AGE.
JUST LIKE THE PEOPLE OF THE INDUS.
THUS, BOTH THE GEOGRAPHY AND THE CHRONOLOGY OF THE RIG VEDA ARE TANTALISINGLY CLOSE TO THE INDUS CIVILIZATION.
COULD THE INDUS PEOPLE, THEN, HAVE BEEN SPEAKERS OF OLD SANSKRIT, THE LANGUAGE OF THE RIG VEDA?
RIG VEDA
TRADITIONALLY, MOST SCHOLARS HAVE BELIEVED NOT. THE POPULAR THEORY HOLDS THAT THEIR LANGUAGE BELONGED TO THE DRAVIDIAN OR ANOTHER NON-INDO-ARYAN LANGUAGE GROUP.
THE REASONS ARE AS FOLLOWS.
RIG VEDA

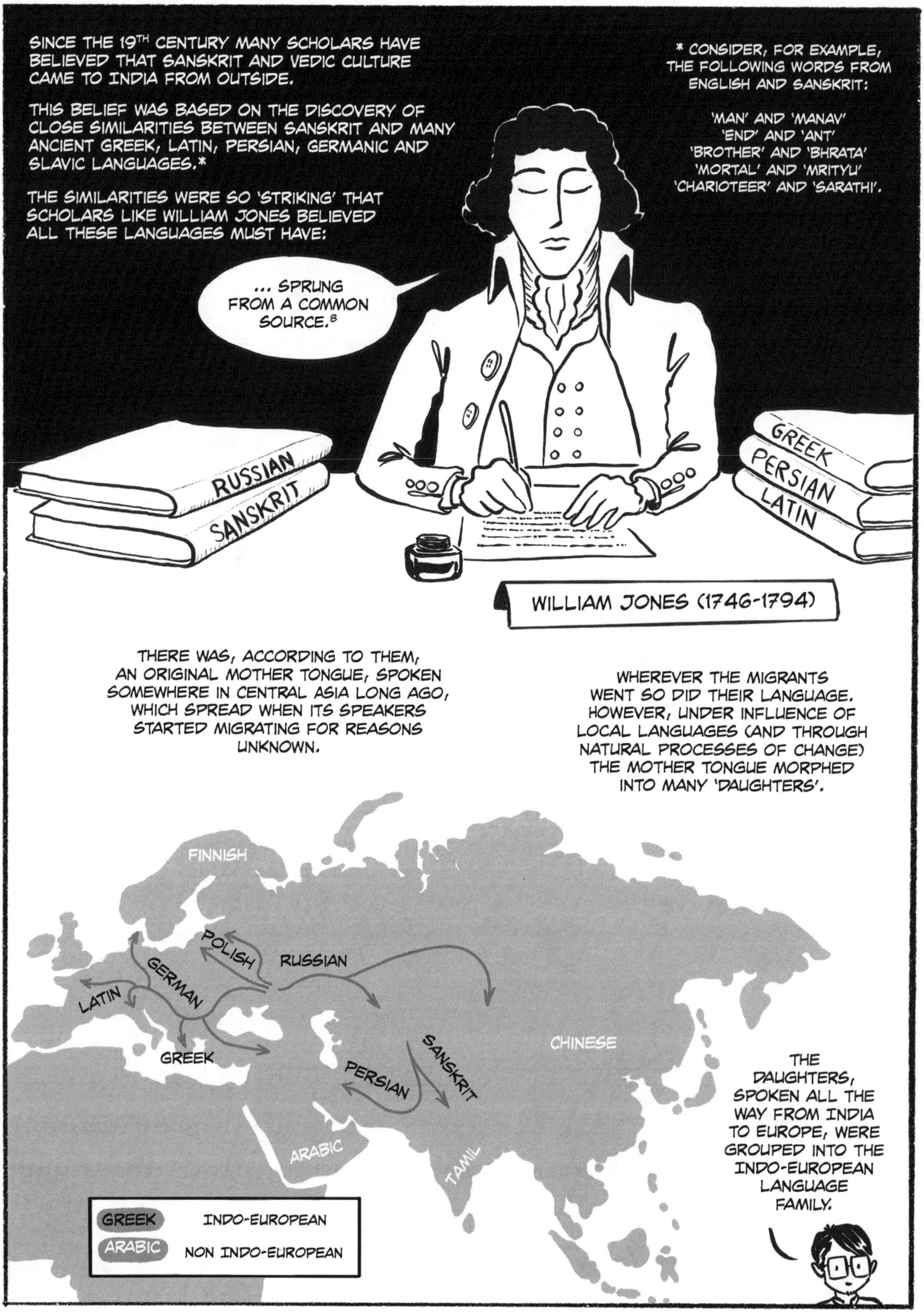
SINCE THE 19TH CENTURY MANY SCHOLARS HAVE BELIEVED THAT SANSKRIT AND VEDIC CULTURE CAME TO INDIA FROM OUTSIDE.
THIS BELIEF WAS BASED ON THE DISCOVERY OF CLOSE SIMILARITIES BETWEEN SANSKRIT AND MANY ANCIENT GREEK, LATIN, PERSIAN, GERMANIC AND SLAVIC LANGUAGES.*
THE SIMILARITIES WERE SO 'STRIKING' THAT SCHOLARS LIKE WILLIAM JONES BELIEVED ALL THESE LANGUAGES MUST HAVE:
* CONSIDER, FOR EXAMPLE, THE FOLLOWING WORDS FROM ENGLISH AND SANSKRIT:
'MAN' AND 'MANAV'
'END' AND 'ANT'
'BROTHER' AND 'BHRATA'
'MORTAL' AND 'MRITYU'
'CHARIOTEER' AND 'SARATHI'.
... SPRUNG FROM A COMMON SOURCE.[8]
RUSSIAN
SANSKRIT
GREEK
PERSIAN
LATIN
WILLIAM JONES (1746-1794)
THERE WAS, ACCORDING TO THEM, AN ORIGINAL MOTHER TONGUE, SPOKEN SOMEWHERE IN CENTRAL ASIA LONG AGO, WHICH SPREAD WHEN ITS SPEAKERS STARTED MIGRATING FOR REASONS UNKNOWN.
WHEREVER THE MIGRANTS WENT SO DID THEIR LANGUAGE. HOWEVER, UNDER INFLUENCE OF LOCAL LANGUAGES (AND THROUGH NATURAL PROCESSES OF CHANGE) THE MOTHER TONGUE MORPHED INTO MANY 'DAUGHTERS'.
FINNISH
POLISH
RUSSIAN
GERMAN
LATIN
GREEK
CHINESE
SANSKRIT
PERSIAN
ARABIC
TAMIL
GREEK INDO-EUROPEAN
ARABIC NON INDO-EUROPEAN
THE DAUGHTERS, SPOKEN ALL THE WAY FROM INDIA TO EUROPE, WERE GROUPED INTO THE INDO-EUROPEAN LANGUAGE FAMILY.

IT WAS NOT JUST THE LANGUAGES, HOWEVER, THAT SHARED SIMILARITIES BUT CULTURES AS WELL.

ZEUS, GREEK GOD OF THE SKY, WIELDS A THUNDERBOLT

INDRA, VEDIC GOD OF THE SKY, WIELDS THE VAJRA, A THUNDERBOLT WEAPON.

THE GREEK **ZEUS PATER**, THE VEDIC **DIYAUS PITAR** AND THE LATIN **JUPITER** WERE ALL FATHER GODS OF THEIR RESPECTIVE PANTHEONS.

THE AVESTAN (OLD PERSIAN) 'YASNA' (WORSHIP/SACRIFICE) AND 'MANTHRA' (PRAYER/SPELL) PARALLELED THE VEDIC 'YAGNYA' AND 'MANTRA'.

AND THERE ARE MANY SIMILAR PARALLELS AMONGST THE VARIOUS INDO-EUROPEAN CULTURES.

THE FACT THAT INDO-EUROPEAN LANGUAGES AND TRADITIONS HAD BECOME SO WIDESPREAD LED SCHOLARS TO FURTHER DEDUCE THAT THEIR SPEAKERS, THE 'INDO-EUROPEANS', MUST HAVE DOMINATED MILITARILY WHEREVER THEY WENT.

THIS WOULD EXPLAIN WHY THEY DID NOT ADOPT LOCAL LANGUAGES BUT INSTEAD IMPOSED THEIR OWN.

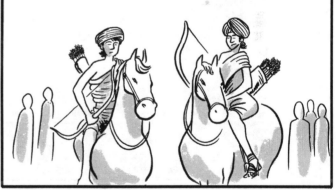

BY THE 19TH CENTURY, IT HAD BECOME CONVENTIONAL WISDOM THAT THE INDO-EUROPEAN SPEAKERS HAD COME TO INDIA AS INVADERS TOO.*

* MORE SPECIFICALLY, THE SPEAKERS OF INDO-ARYAN LANGUAGES, A SUB-BRANCH OF THE INDO-EUROPEAN FAMILY

COULD IT BE POSSIBLE THAT MEMORIES OF THIS INVASION WERE RECORDED IN THE RIG VEDA, THE OLDEST INDO-EUROPEAN TEXT?

SUCH MEMORIES WERE INDEED FOUND.

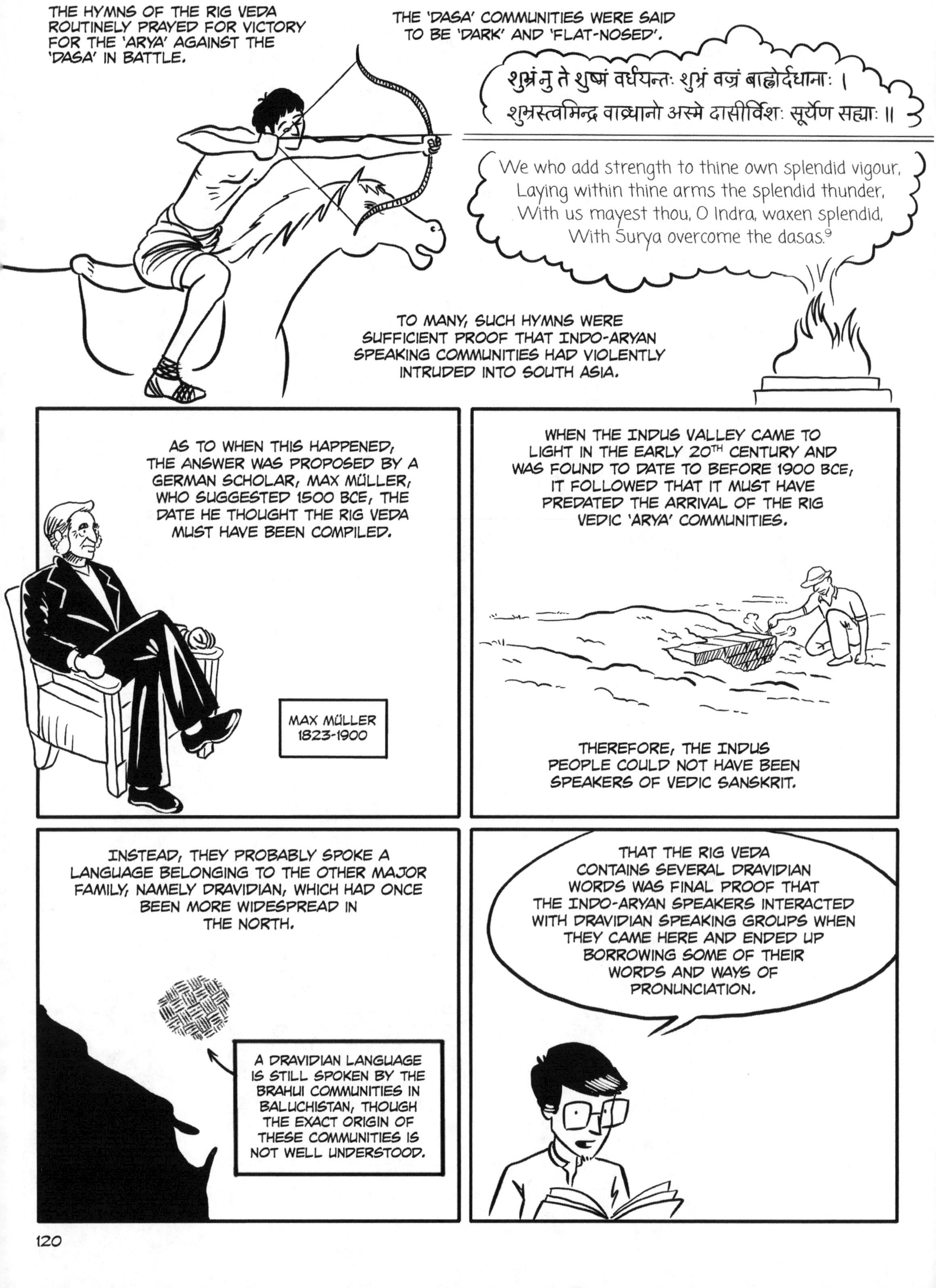
THE HYMNS OF THE RIG VEDA ROUTINELY PRAYED FOR VICTORY FOR THE 'ARYA' AGAINST THE 'DASA' IN BATTLE.
THE 'DASA' COMMUNITIES WERE SAID TO BE 'DARK' AND 'FLAT-NOSED'.
शुभ्रं नु ते शुष्मं वर्धयन्तः शुभ्रं वज्रं बाह्वोर्दधानाः ।
शुभ्रस्त्वमिन्द्र वावृधानो अस्मे दासीर्विशः सूर्येण सह्याः ॥
We who add strength to thine own splendid vigour,
Laying within thine arms the splendid thunder,
With us mayest thou, O Indra, waxen splendid,
With Surya overcome the dasas.[9]
TO MANY, SUCH HYMNS WERE SUFFICIENT PROOF THAT INDO-ARYAN SPEAKING COMMUNITIES HAD VIOLENTLY INTRUDED INTO SOUTH ASIA.
AS TO WHEN THIS HAPPENED, THE ANSWER WAS PROPOSED BY A GERMAN SCHOLAR, MAX MÜLLER, WHO SUGGESTED 1500 BCE, THE DATE HE THOUGHT THE RIG VEDA MUST HAVE BEEN COMPILED.
MAX MÜLLER 1823-1900
WHEN THE INDUS VALLEY CAME TO LIGHT IN THE EARLY 20TH CENTURY AND WAS FOUND TO DATE TO BEFORE 1900 BCE, IT FOLLOWED THAT IT MUST HAVE PREDATED THE ARRIVAL OF THE RIG VEDIC 'ARYA' COMMUNITIES.
THEREFORE, THE INDUS PEOPLE COULD NOT HAVE BEEN SPEAKERS OF VEDIC SANSKRIT.
INSTEAD, THEY PROBABLY SPOKE A LANGUAGE BELONGING TO THE OTHER MAJOR FAMILY, NAMELY DRAVIDIAN, WHICH HAD ONCE BEEN MORE WIDESPREAD IN THE NORTH.
A DRAVIDIAN LANGUAGE IS STILL SPOKEN BY THE BRAHUI COMMUNITIES IN BALUCHISTAN, THOUGH THE EXACT ORIGIN OF THESE COMMUNITIES IS NOT WELL UNDERSTOOD.
THAT THE RIG VEDA CONTAINS SEVERAL DRAVIDIAN WORDS WAS FINAL PROOF THAT THE INDO-ARYAN SPEAKERS INTERACTED WITH DRAVIDIAN SPEAKING GROUPS WHEN THEY CAME HERE AND ENDED UP BORROWING SOME OF THEIR WORDS AND WAYS OF PRONUNCIATION.

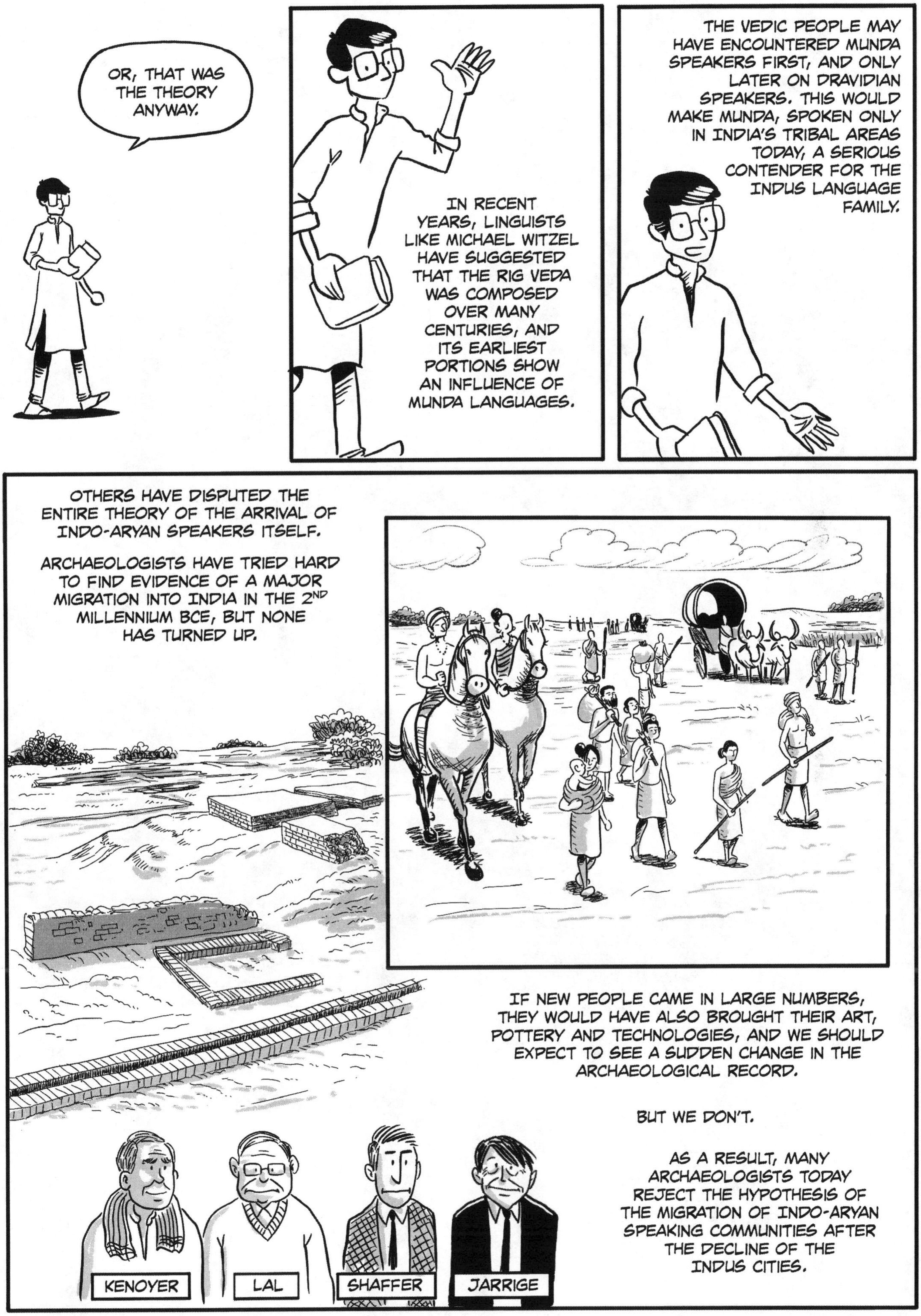
OR, THAT WAS THE THEORY ANYWAY.
IN RECENT YEARS, LINGUISTS LIKE MICHAEL WITZEL HAVE SUGGESTED THAT THE RIG VEDA WAS COMPOSED OVER MANY CENTURIES, AND ITS EARLIEST PORTIONS SHOW AN INFLUENCE OF MUNDA LANGUAGES.
THE VEDIC PEOPLE MAY HAVE ENCOUNTERED MUNDA SPEAKERS FIRST, AND ONLY LATER ON DRAVIDIAN SPEAKERS. THIS WOULD MAKE MUNDA, SPOKEN ONLY IN INDIA'S TRIBAL AREAS TODAY, A SERIOUS CONTENDER FOR THE INDUS LANGUAGE FAMILY.
OTHERS HAVE DISPUTED THE ENTIRE THEORY OF THE ARRIVAL OF INDO-ARYAN SPEAKERS ITSELF.
ARCHAEOLOGISTS HAVE TRIED HARD TO FIND EVIDENCE OF A MAJOR MIGRATION INTO INDIA IN THE 2ND MILLENNIUM BCE, BUT NONE HAS TURNED UP.
IF NEW PEOPLE CAME IN LARGE NUMBERS, THEY WOULD HAVE ALSO BROUGHT THEIR ART, POTTERY AND TECHNOLOGIES, AND WE SHOULD EXPECT TO SEE A SUDDEN CHANGE IN THE ARCHAEOLOGICAL RECORD.
BUT WE DON'T.
AS A RESULT, MANY ARCHAEOLOGISTS TODAY REJECT THE HYPOTHESIS OF THE MIGRATION OF INDO-ARYAN SPEAKING COMMUNITIES AFTER THE DECLINE OF THE INDUS CITIES.
KENOYER
LAL
SHAFFER
JARRIGE

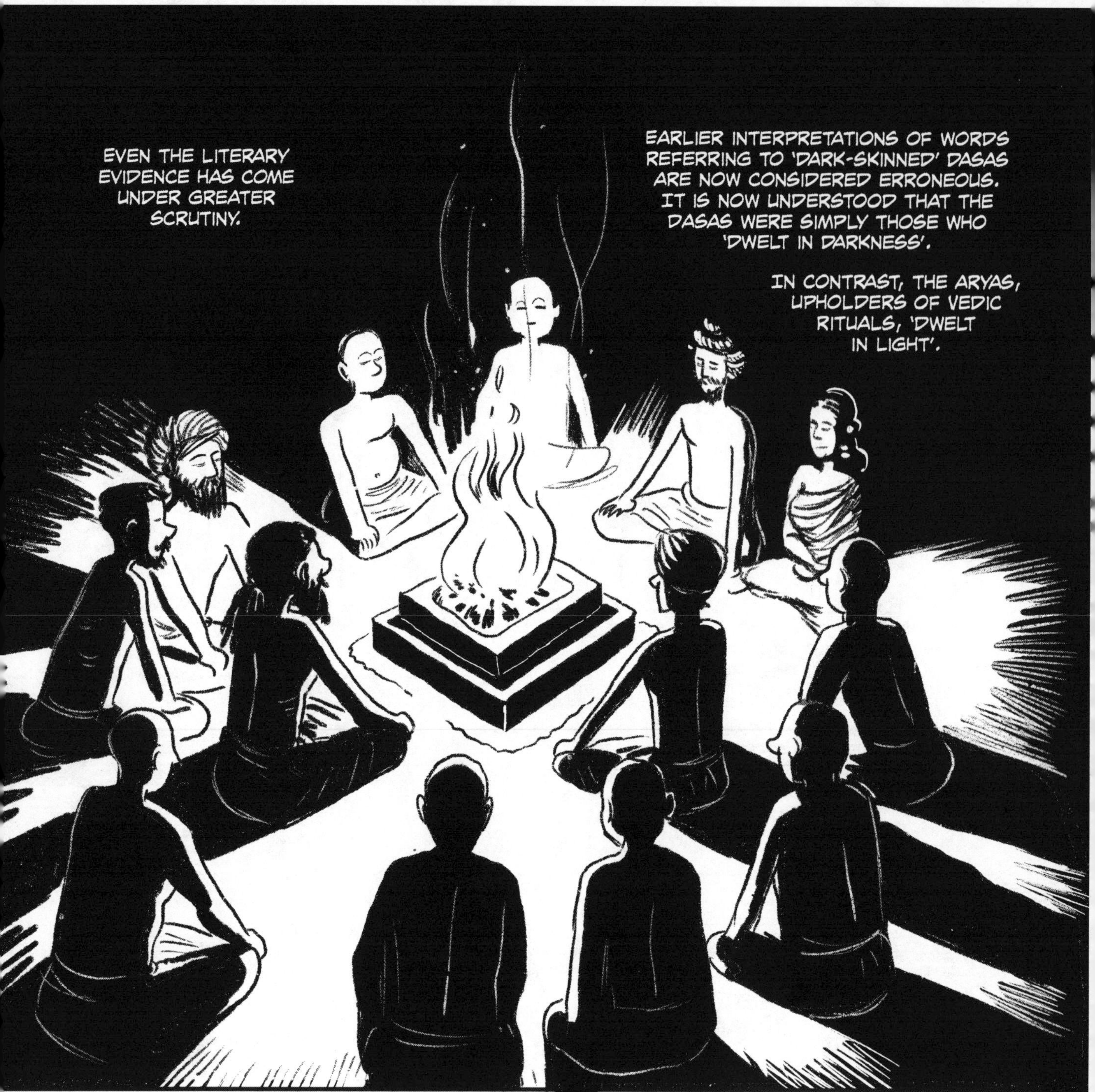
EVEN THE LITERARY EVIDENCE HAS COME UNDER GREATER SCRUTINY.
EARLIER INTERPRETATIONS OF WORDS REFERRING TO 'DARK-SKINNED' DASAS ARE NOW CONSIDERED ERRONEOUS. IT IS NOW UNDERSTOOD THAT THE DASAS WERE SIMPLY THOSE WHO 'DWELT IN DARKNESS'.
IN CONTRAST, THE ARYAS, UPHOLDERS OF VEDIC RITUALS, 'DWELT IN LIGHT'.

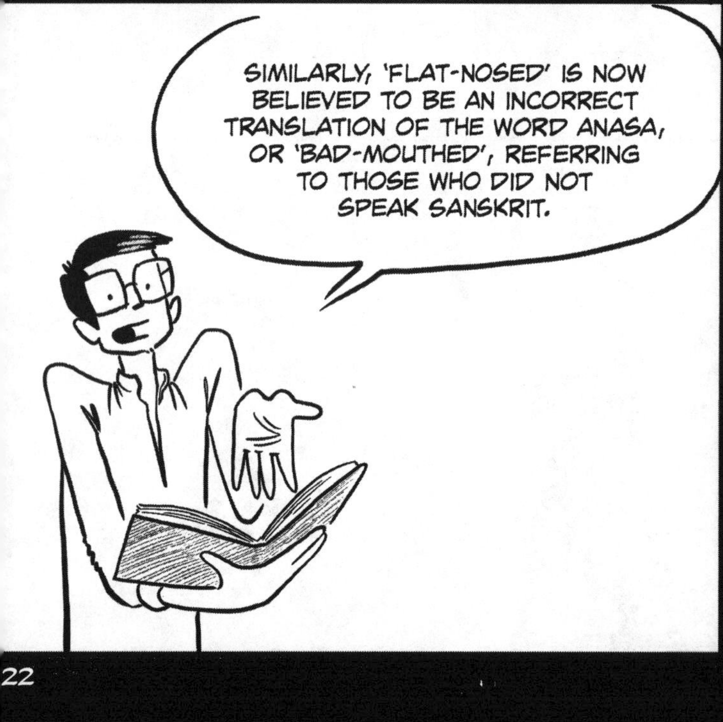
SIMILARLY, 'FLAT-NOSED' IS NOW BELIEVED TO BE AN INCORRECT TRANSLATION OF THE WORD ANASA, OR 'BAD-MOUTHED', REFERRING TO THOSE WHO DID NOT SPEAK SANSKRIT.

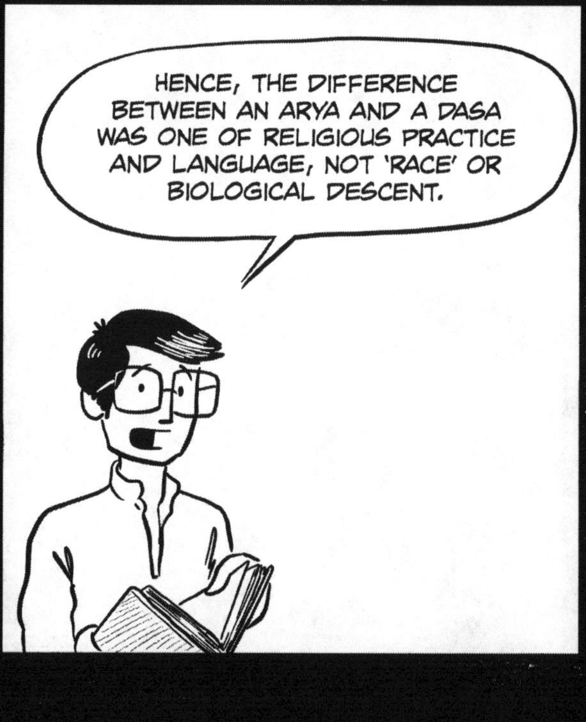
HENCE, THE DIFFERENCE BETWEEN AN ARYA AND A DASA WAS ONE OF RELIGIOUS PRACTICE AND LANGUAGE, NOT 'RACE' OR BIOLOGICAL DESCENT.

OTHER DOUBTS HAVE ALSO BEEN RAISED.

WHY DOES THE RIG VEDA NOT SPEAK OF AN ORIGINAL HOMELAND, IF ITS AUTHORS WERE ONLY RECENT ARRIVALS IN INDIA?

IN FACT, WHY IS NO LOCATION OUTSIDE THE SUBCONTINENT MENTIONED AT ALL?

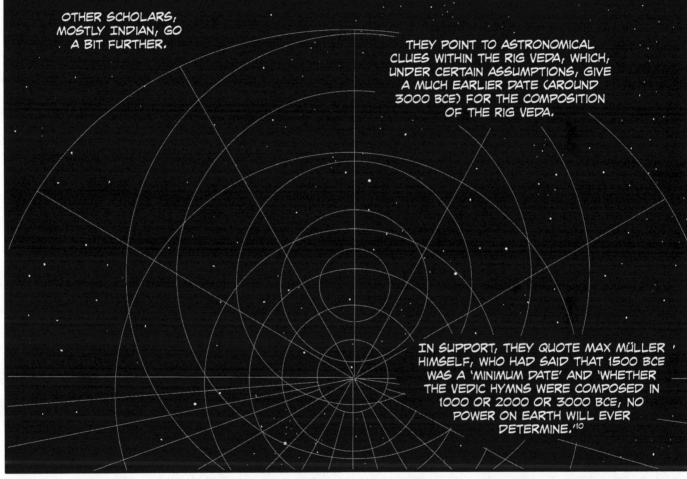

OTHER SCHOLARS, MOSTLY INDIAN, GO A BIT FURTHER.

THEY POINT TO ASTRONOMICAL CLUES WITHIN THE RIG VEDA, WHICH, UNDER CERTAIN ASSUMPTIONS, GIVE A MUCH EARLIER DATE (AROUND 3000 BCE) FOR THE COMPOSITION OF THE RIG VEDA.

IN SUPPORT, THEY QUOTE MAX MÜLLER HIMSELF, WHO HAD SAID THAT 1500 BCE WAS A 'MINIMUM DATE' AND 'WHETHER THE VEDIC HYMNS WERE COMPOSED IN 1000 OR 2000 OR 3000 BCE, NO POWER ON EARTH WILL EVER DETERMINE.'[10]

HENCE, THE CONVENTIONAL DATING MUST BE REVISED, SOME SAY.

AND IF THE RIG VEDA WAS COMPOSED MUCH EARLIER THAN 1500 BCE, THEN THE CASE CAN BE MADE THAT THE INDUS CIVILIZATION WAS VEDIC AND SPOKE OLD SANSKRIT.

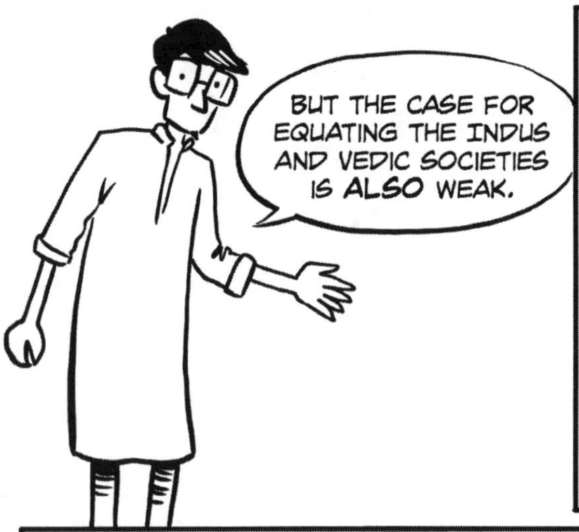
BUT THE CASE FOR EQUATING THE INDUS AND VEDIC SOCIETIES IS **ALSO** WEAK.

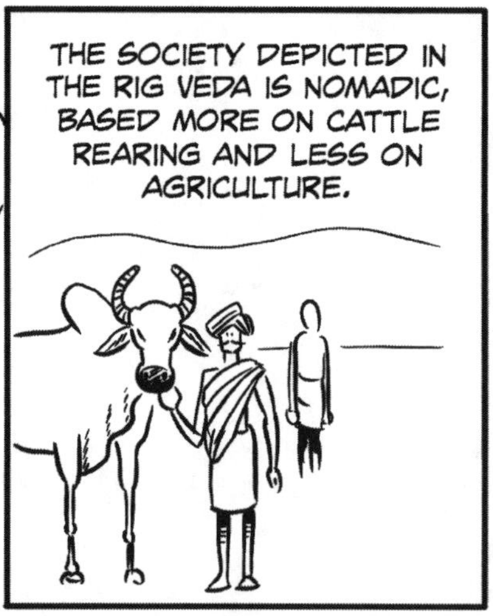
THE SOCIETY DEPICTED IN THE RIG VEDA IS NOMADIC, BASED MORE ON CATTLE REARING AND LESS ON AGRICULTURE.

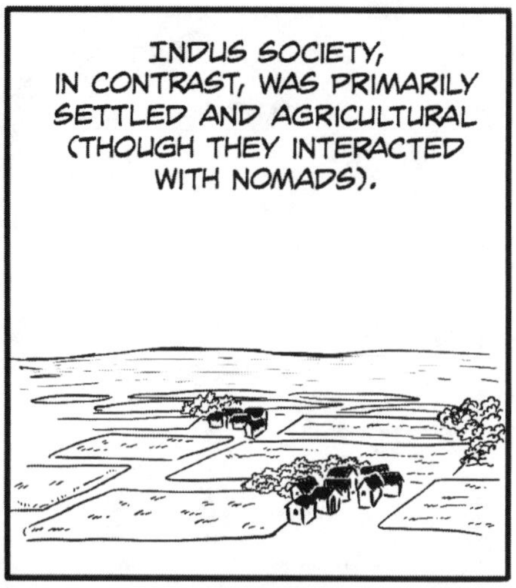
INDUS SOCIETY, IN CONTRAST, WAS PRIMARILY SETTLED AND AGRICULTURAL (THOUGH THEY INTERACTED WITH NOMADS).

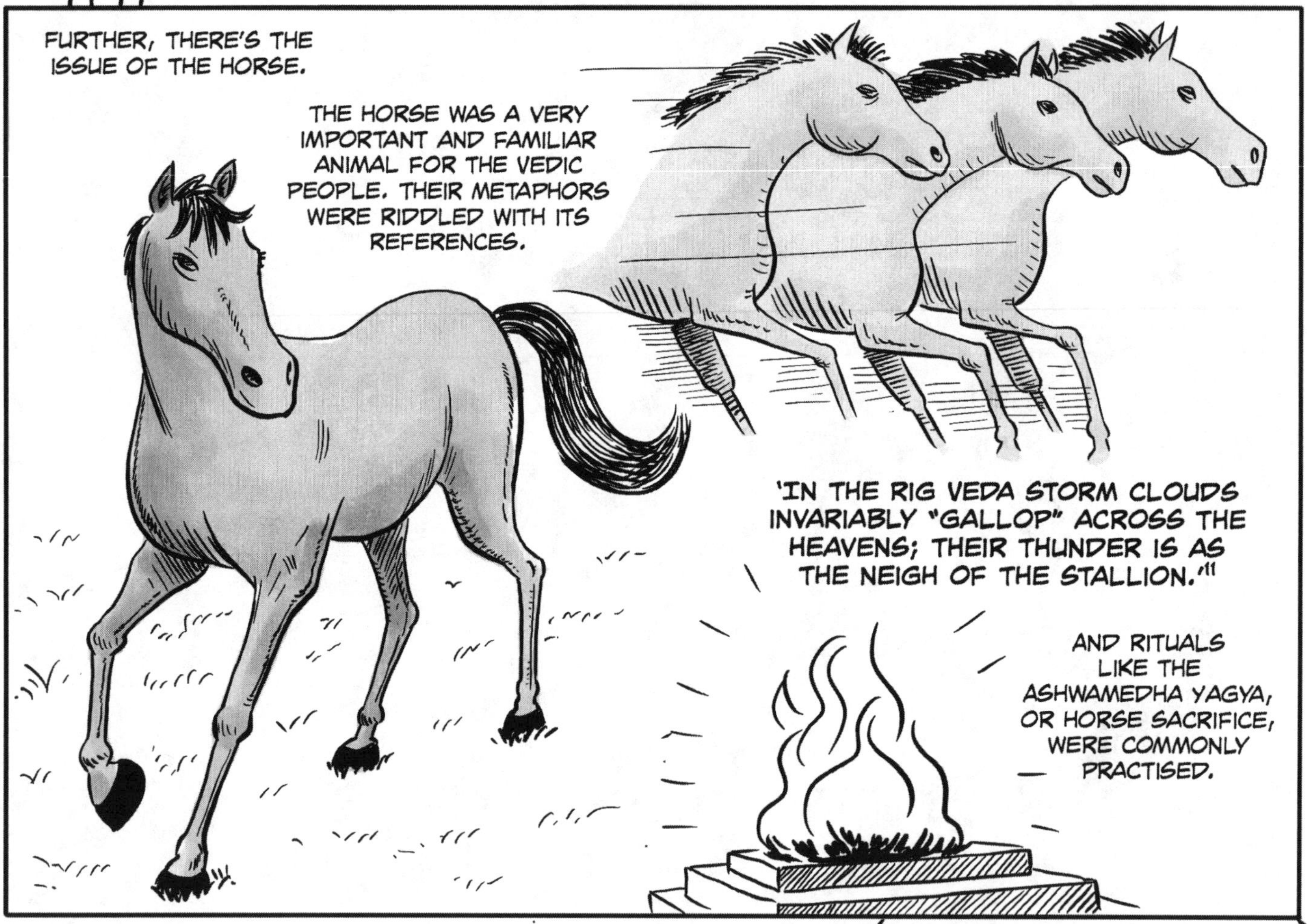
FURTHER, THERE'S THE ISSUE OF THE HORSE.
THE HORSE WAS A VERY IMPORTANT AND FAMILIAR ANIMAL FOR THE VEDIC PEOPLE. THEIR METAPHORS WERE RIDDLED WITH ITS REFERENCES.
'IN THE RIG VEDA STORM CLOUDS INVARIABLY "GALLOP" ACROSS THE HEAVENS; THEIR THUNDER IS AS THE NEIGH OF THE STALLION.'[11]
AND RITUALS LIKE THE ASHWAMEDHA YAGYA, OR HORSE SACRIFICE, WERE COMMONLY PRACTISED.

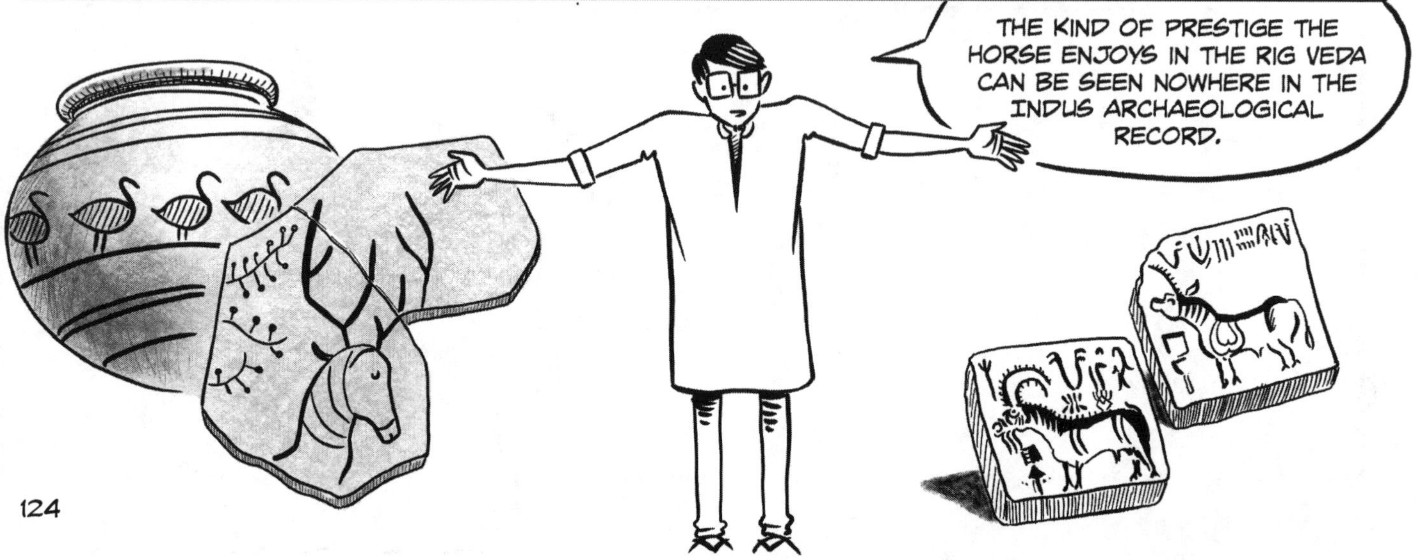
THE KIND OF PRESTIGE THE HORSE ENJOYS IN THE RIG VEDA CAN BE SEEN NOWHERE IN THE INDUS ARCHAEOLOGICAL RECORD.

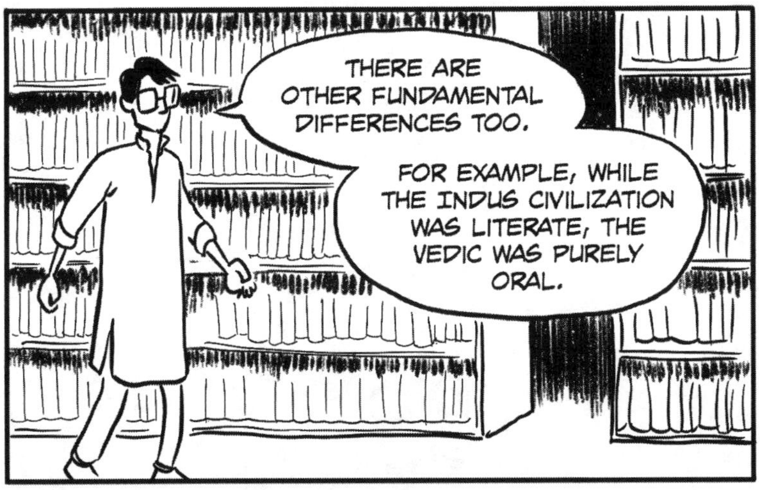
THERE ARE OTHER FUNDAMENTAL DIFFERENCES TOO.
FOR EXAMPLE, WHILE THE INDUS CIVILIZATION WAS LITERATE, THE VEDIC WAS PURELY ORAL.

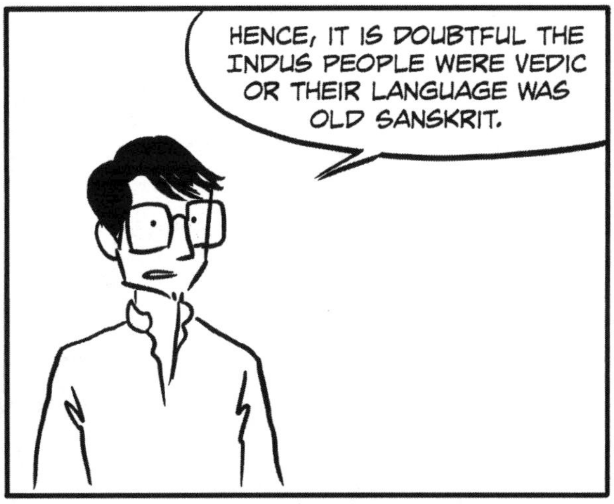
HENCE, IT IS DOUBTFUL THE INDUS PEOPLE WERE VEDIC OR THEIR LANGUAGE WAS OLD SANSKRIT.

AND MODERN LINGUISTS CONTINUE TO STRESS SANSKRIT'S DEEP CONNECTIONS TO OTHER EURASIAN LANGUAGES.

English	Sanskrit	Old Persian	Greek
Mother	Matr	Matar	Meter
Father	Pitr	Patar	Pater
New	Nava	Nava	Neos
Mead	Madhu	Madhu	Methu
Tree	Daru	Daru	Doru
Warm	Garmah	Garama	Thermos
Mind	Manas	Manah	Menos
Star	Tara	Star	Aster
Over	Upari	Upairi	Huper
	Dwar	Dar	Thura

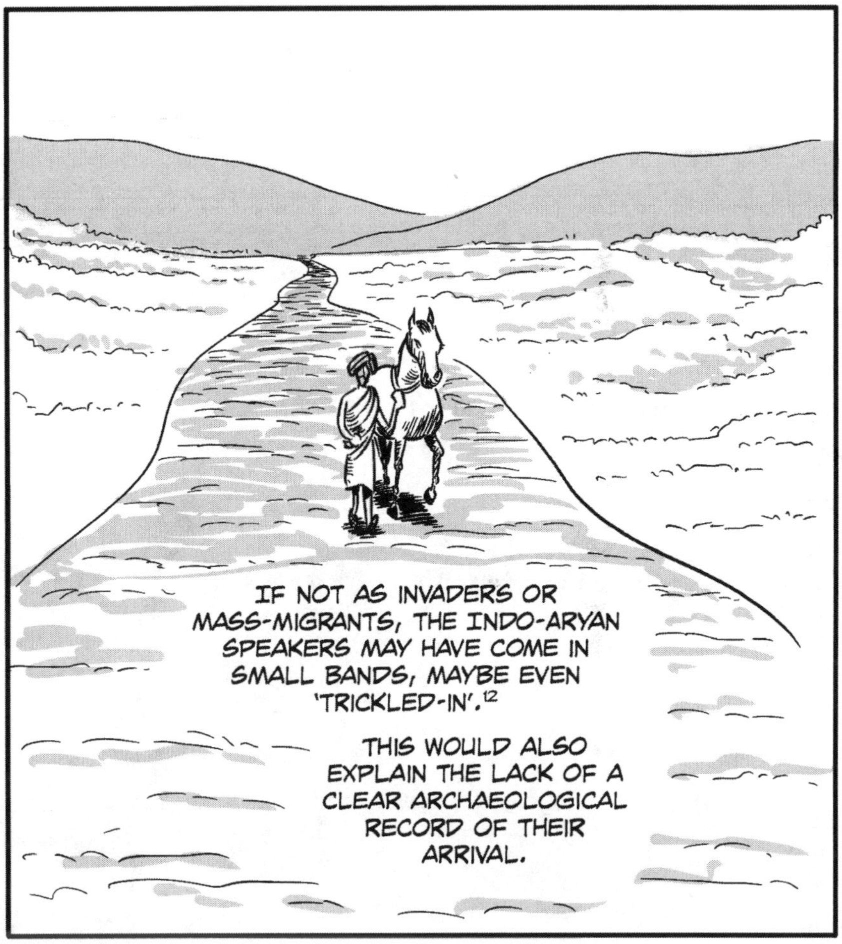
IF NOT AS INVADERS OR MASS-MIGRANTS, THE INDO-ARYAN SPEAKERS MAY HAVE COME IN SMALL BANDS, MAYBE EVEN 'TRICKLED-IN'.[12]
THIS WOULD ALSO EXPLAIN THE LACK OF A CLEAR ARCHAEOLOGICAL RECORD OF THEIR ARRIVAL.

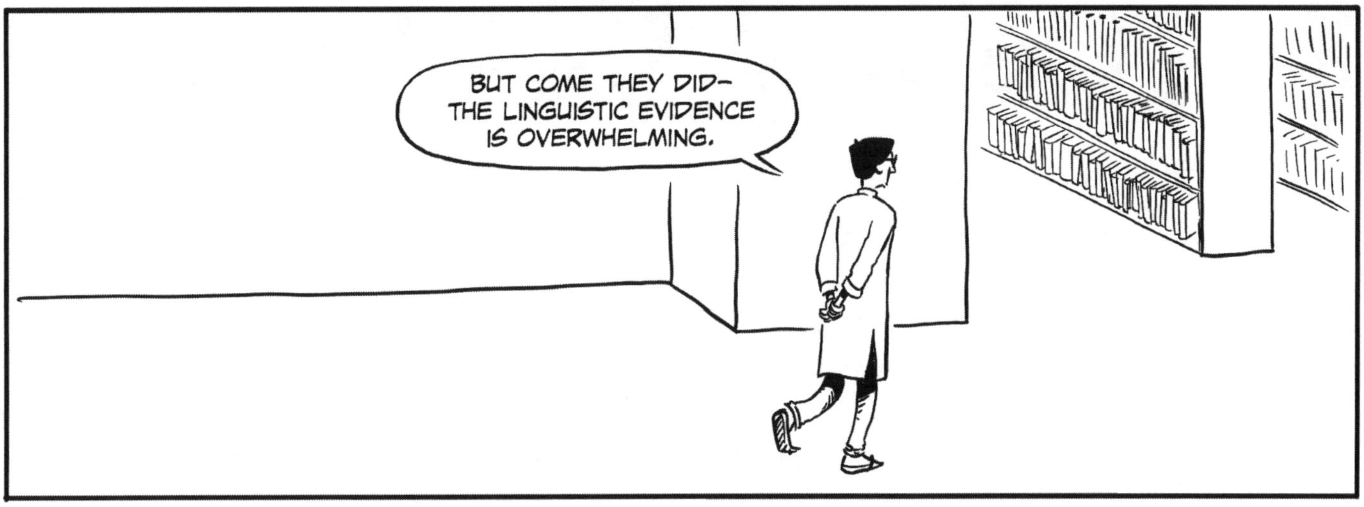
BUT COME THEY DID– THE LINGUISTIC EVIDENCE IS OVERWHELMING.

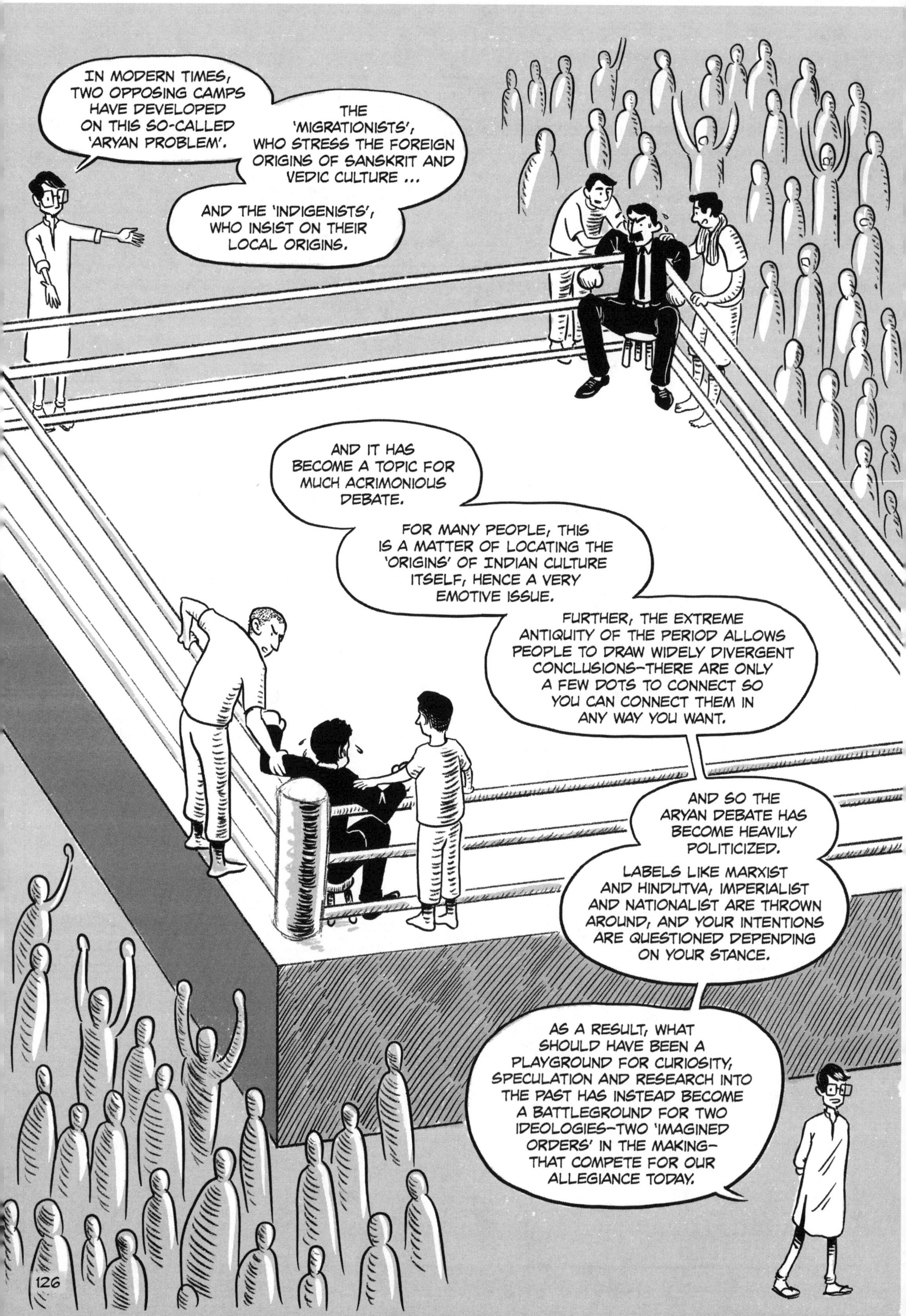
IN MODERN TIMES, TWO OPPOSING CAMPS HAVE DEVELOPED ON THIS SO-CALLED 'ARYAN PROBLEM'.
THE 'MIGRATIONISTS', WHO STRESS THE FOREIGN ORIGINS OF SANSKRIT AND VEDIC CULTURE ...
AND THE 'INDIGENISTS', WHO INSIST ON THEIR LOCAL ORIGINS.
AND IT HAS BECOME A TOPIC FOR MUCH ACRIMONIOUS DEBATE.
FOR MANY PEOPLE, THIS IS A MATTER OF LOCATING THE 'ORIGINS' OF INDIAN CULTURE ITSELF, HENCE A VERY EMOTIVE ISSUE.
FURTHER, THE EXTREME ANTIQUITY OF THE PERIOD ALLOWS PEOPLE TO DRAW WIDELY DIVERGENT CONCLUSIONS—THERE ARE ONLY A FEW DOTS TO CONNECT SO YOU CAN CONNECT THEM IN ANY WAY YOU WANT.
AND SO THE ARYAN DEBATE HAS BECOME HEAVILY POLITICIZED.
LABELS LIKE MARXIST AND HINDUTVA, IMPERIALIST AND NATIONALIST ARE THROWN AROUND, AND YOUR INTENTIONS ARE QUESTIONED DEPENDING ON YOUR STANCE.
AS A RESULT, WHAT SHOULD HAVE BEEN A PLAYGROUND FOR CURIOSITY, SPECULATION AND RESEARCH INTO THE PAST HAS INSTEAD BECOME A BATTLEGROUND FOR TWO IDEOLOGIES—TWO 'IMAGINED ORDERS' IN THE MAKING—THAT COMPETE FOR OUR ALLEGIANCE TODAY.

IF WE CAN RISE ABOVE THE POLITICS, THE ONLY THING WE MUST ACCEPT IS THAT OUR CURRENT MODELS FOR DESCRIBING THE PAST ARE INADEQUATE.

AND NEW RESEARCH IS SUGGESTING EXACTLY THIS.

THE LAST FEW DECADES HAVE SEEN MUCH MORE INTENSIVE RESEARCH INTO THE PERIOD WHEN URBANISM IN THE INDUS AND GHAGGAR VALLEYS DECLINED (THE PERIOD WHEN INDO-ARYAN SPEAKING COMMUNITIES BECAME DOMINANT).

LIBRARY HOURS 6 AM - 11 PM

ESPECIALLY INTERESTING IS THE ARCHAEOLOGY OF THE GHAGGAR RIVER, WHERE HUNDREDS OF INDUS RELATED SETTLEMENTS HAVE COME TO LIGHT, AND THE GHAGGAR'S IDENTIFICATION WITH THE SARASWATI RIVER OF VEDIC LORE.

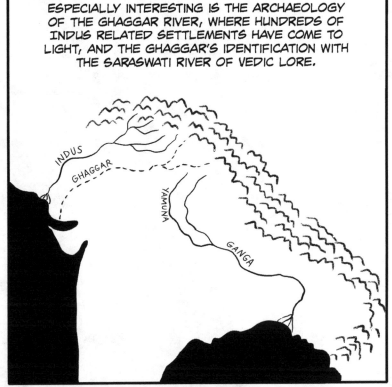

INDUS

GHAGGAR

YAMUNA

GANGA

WHAT EXACTLY HAPPENED DURING THIS PERIOD? HOW DID THE PEOPLE AND THEIR CULTURE CHANGE?

WHAT STIMULATED THE GRADUAL SHIFT FROM THE INDUS-GHAGGAR TO THE GANGA-JAMUNA?

THE ANSWERS ARE ONLY NOW STARTING TO COME TO LIGHT.

DEPT. OF ARCHAEOLOGY

THE QUESTION OF LANGUAGE STILL REMAINS STUBBORNLY UNSETTLED.

BUT NEW DISCOVERIES ARE TELLING US THAT WHAT REALLY HAPPENED IN THE 2ND MILLENNIUM BCE WAS FAR MORE COMPLEX THAN EITHER SIDE IN THE 'ARYAN DEBATE' IS WILLING TO ADMIT.

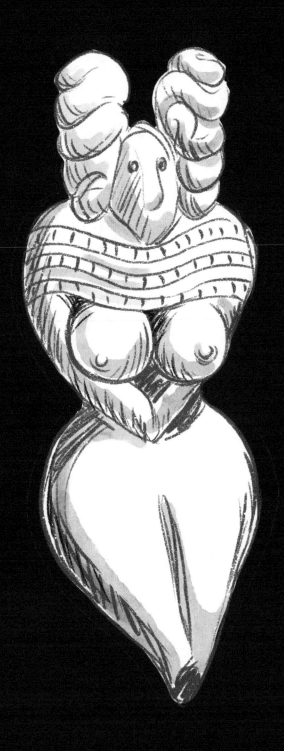

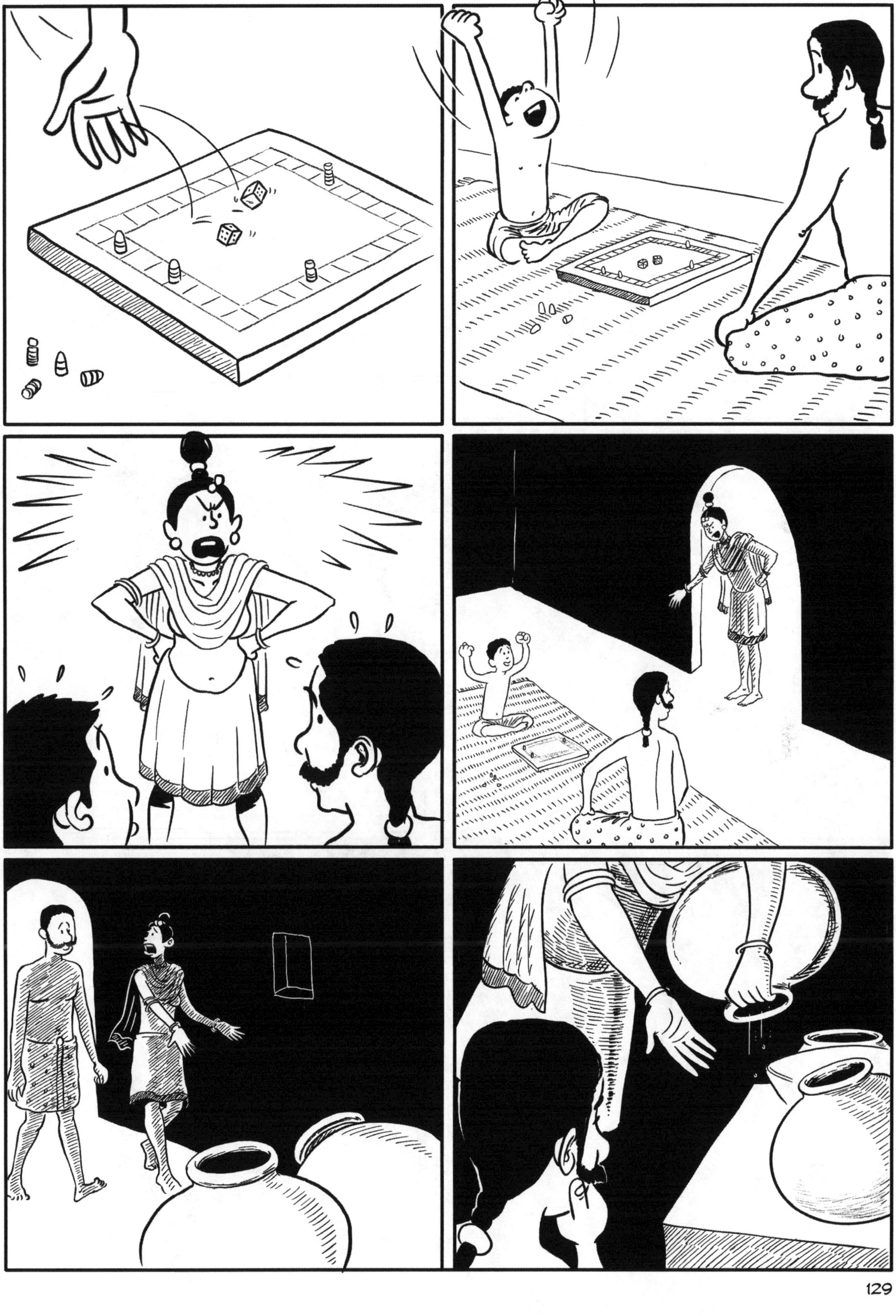

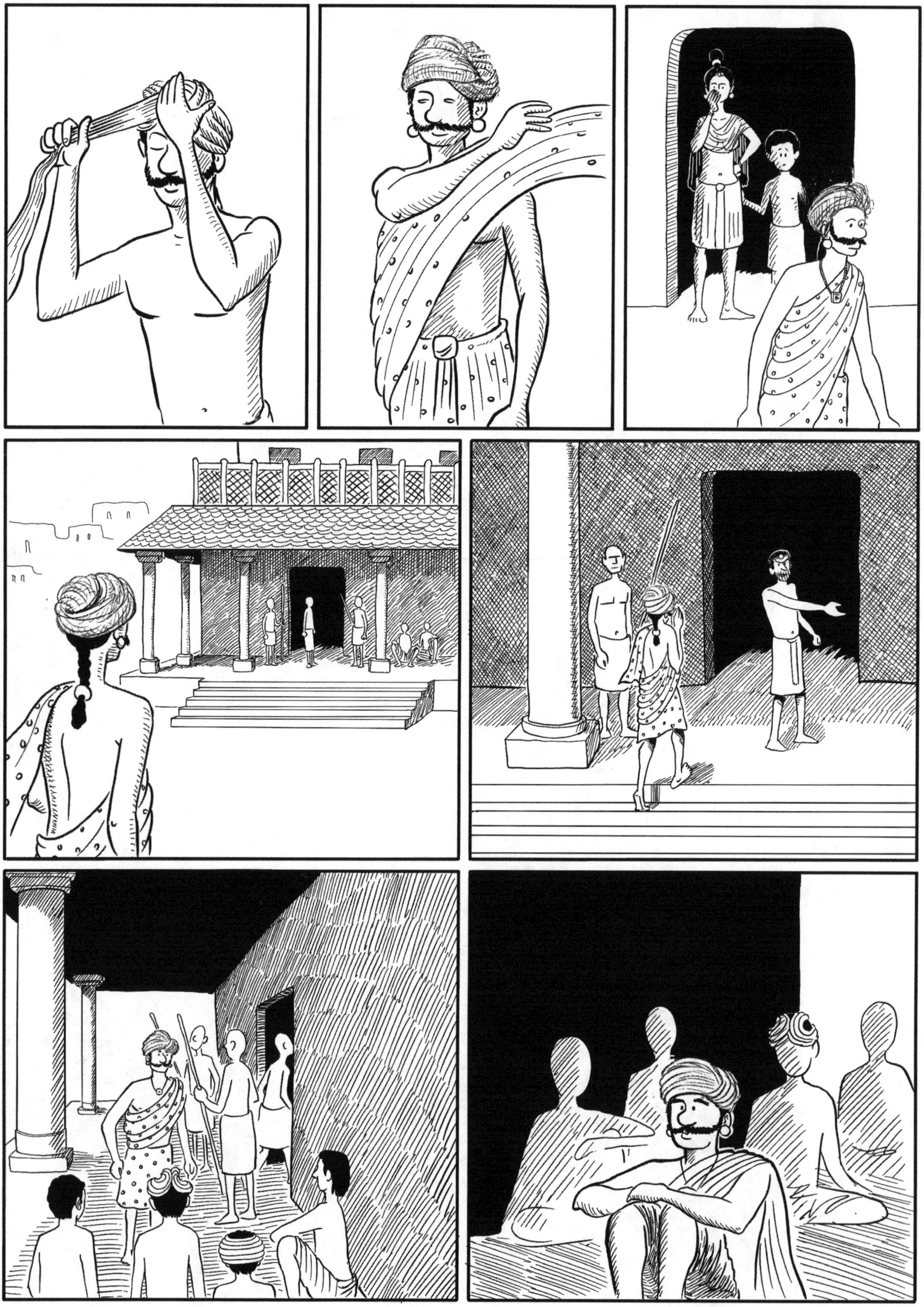

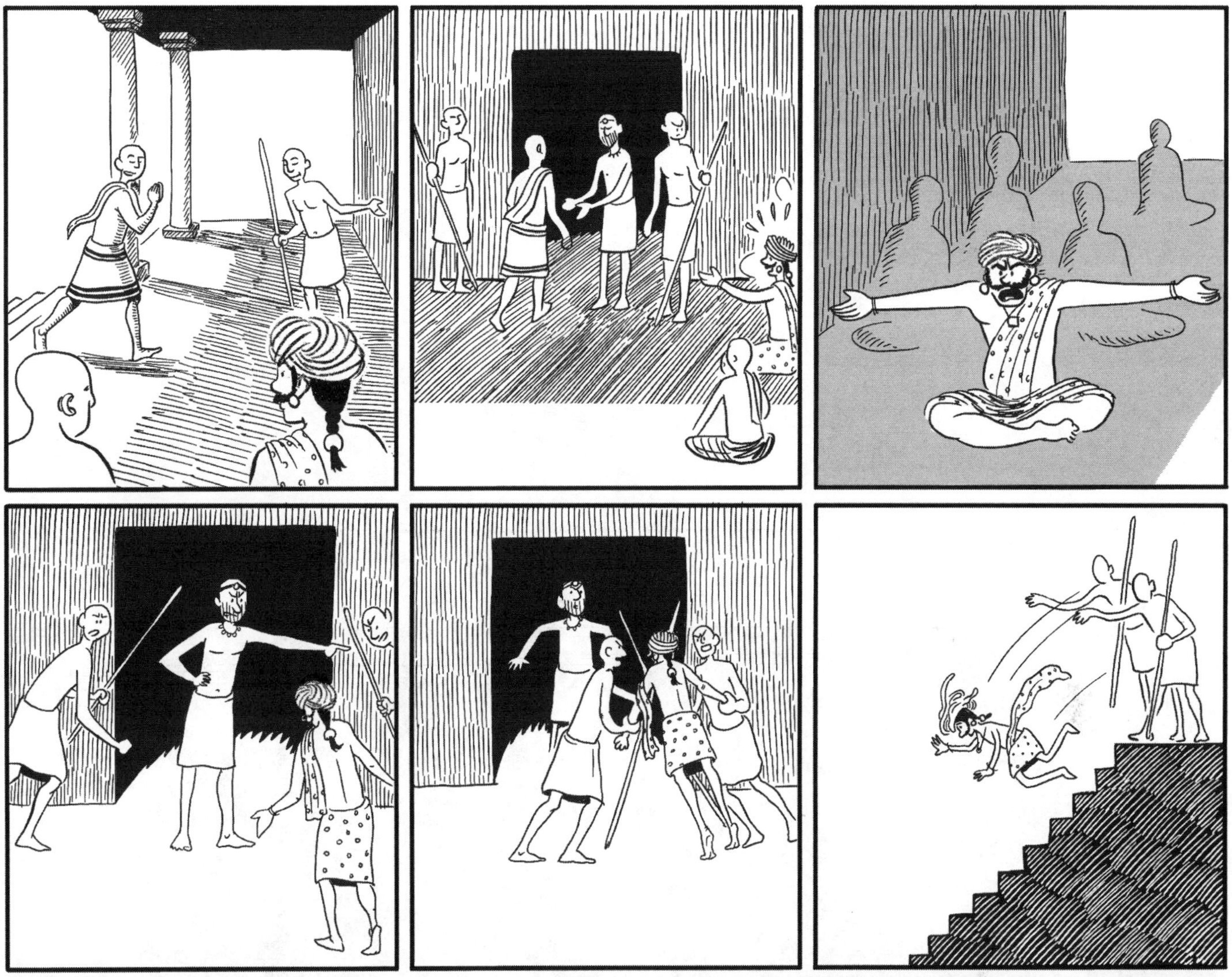

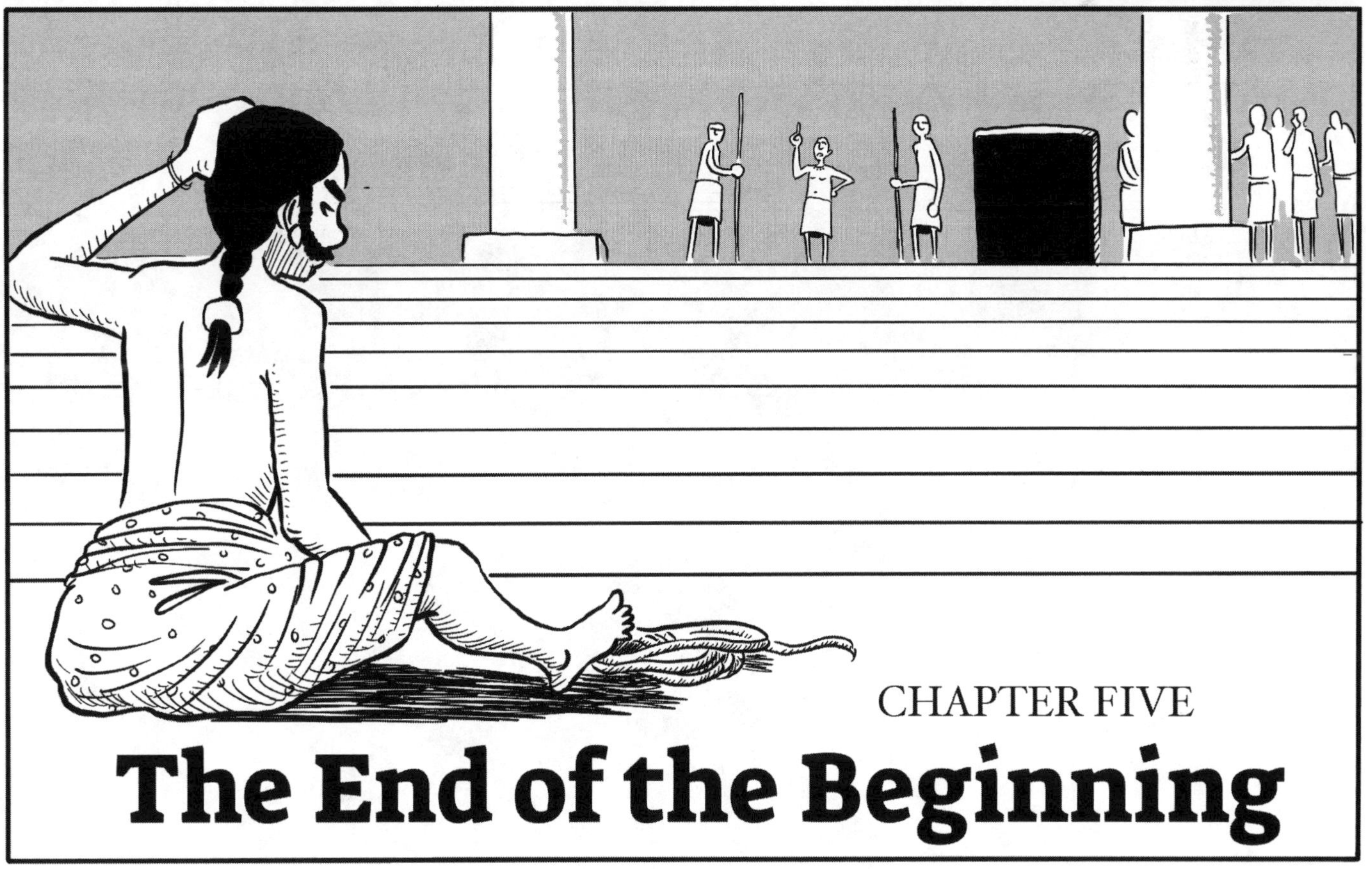

CHAPTER FIVE

The End of the Beginning

“ THE DISINTEGRATION OF THE INDUS CIVILIZATION ... AND THE SUBSEQUENT DISAPPEARANCE OF ITS CULTURE ARE IN STARK CONTRAST TO OTHER EARLY CIVILIZATIONS, WHICH WERE GENERALLY REPLACED BY THEIR RIVALS OR DEVELOPED NEW FOCI BUT ROSE AGAIN.

WHEN CIVILIZATION RE-EMERGED IN INDIA, IT WAS IN QUITE A DIFFERENT AREA, ON THE GANGES... ”

- JANE MCINTOSH[1]

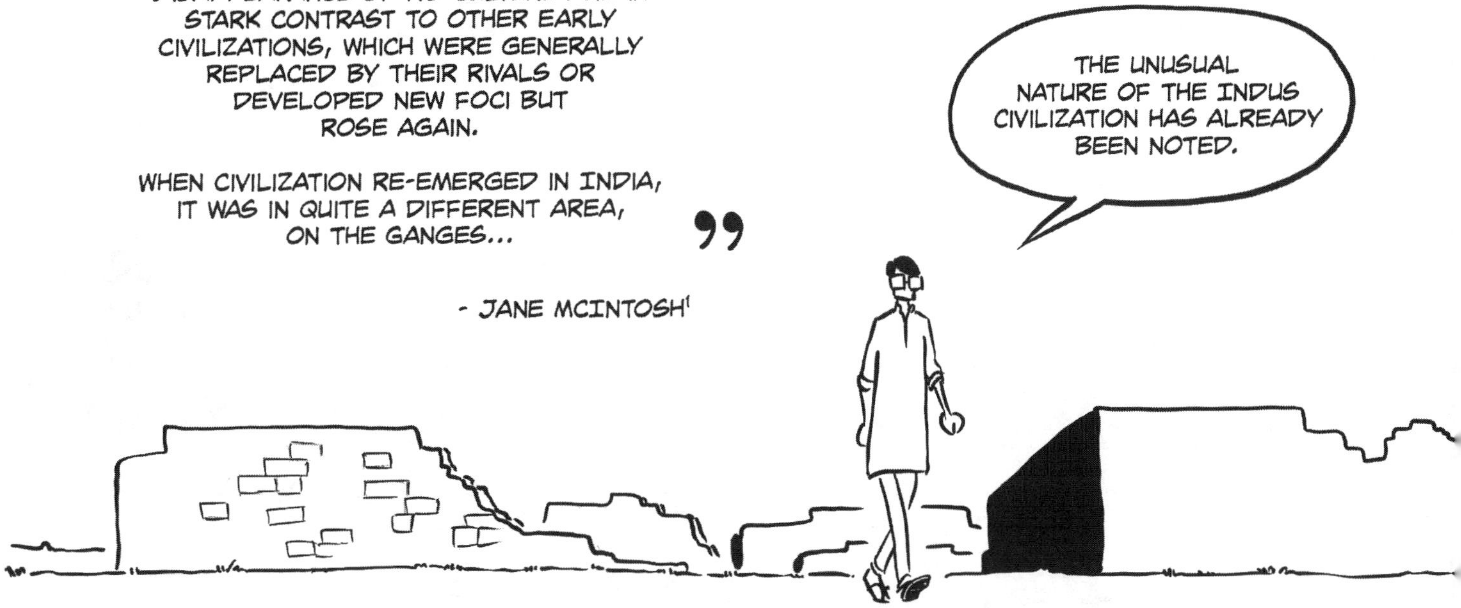
THE UNUSUAL NATURE OF THE INDUS CIVILIZATION HAS ALREADY BEEN NOTED.

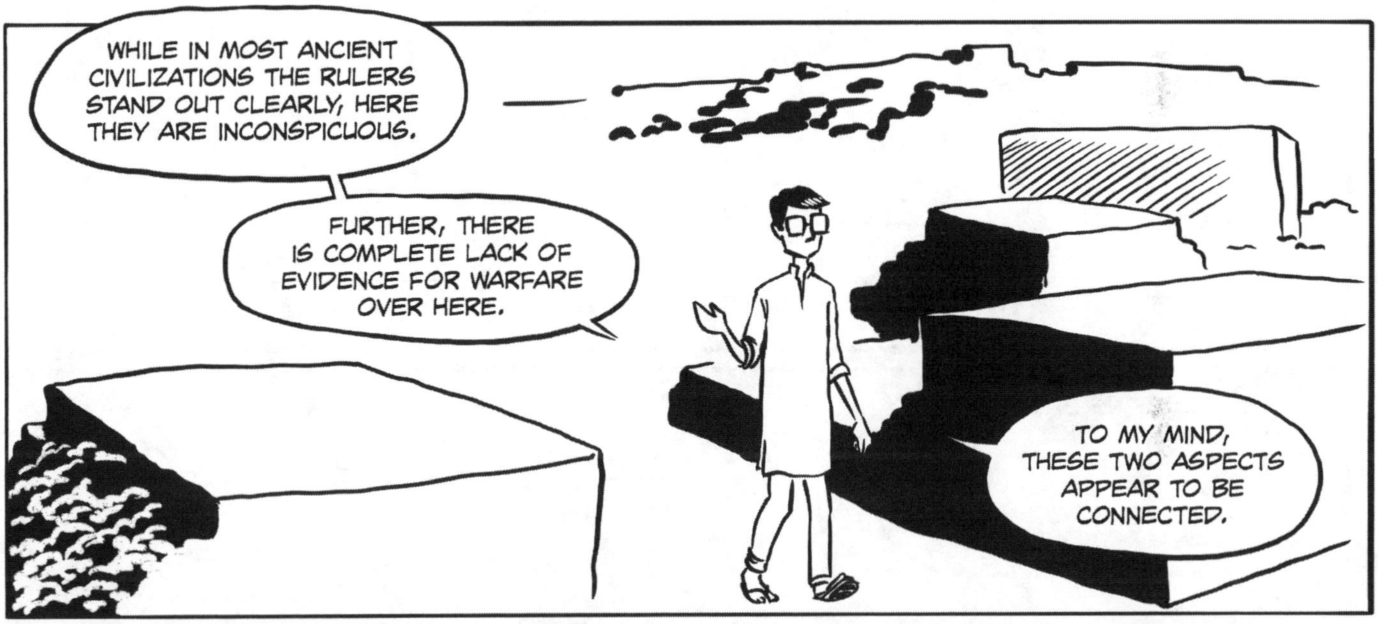
WHILE IN MOST ANCIENT CIVILIZATIONS THE RULERS STAND OUT CLEARLY, HERE THEY ARE INCONSPICUOUS.
FURTHER, THERE IS COMPLETE LACK OF EVIDENCE FOR WARFARE OVER HERE.
TO MY MIND, THESE TWO ASPECTS APPEAR TO BE CONNECTED.

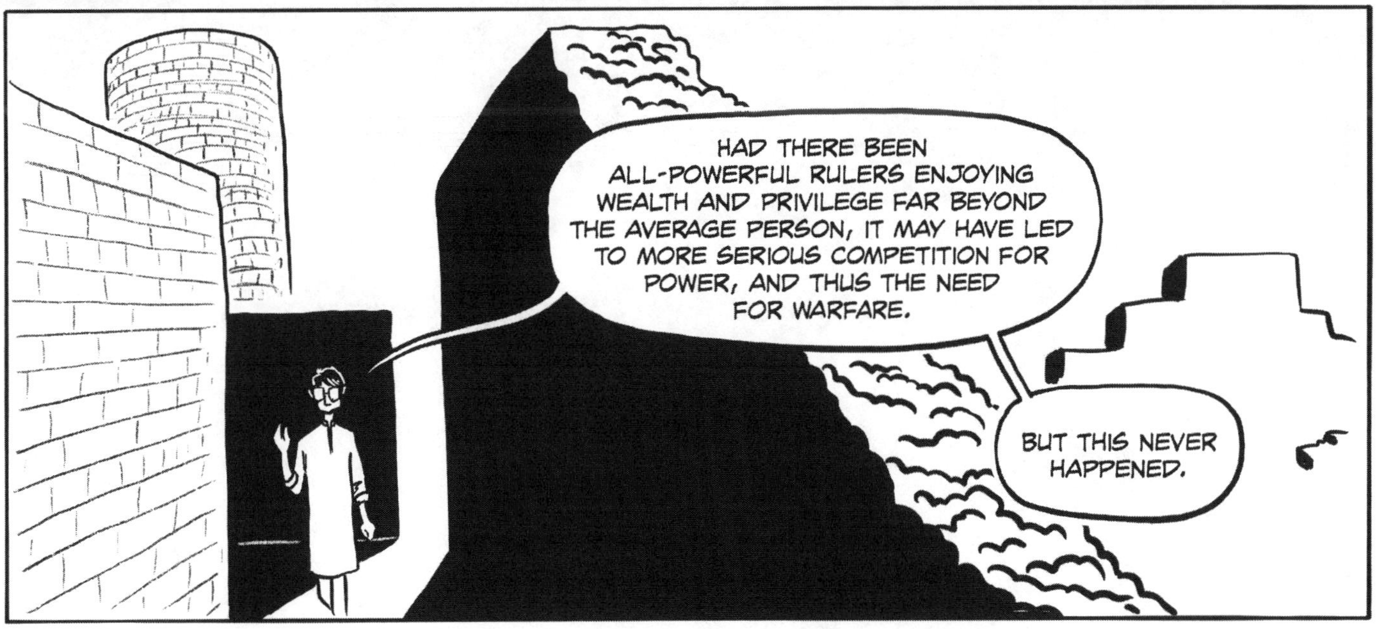
HAD THERE BEEN ALL-POWERFUL RULERS ENJOYING WEALTH AND PRIVILEGE FAR BEYOND THE AVERAGE PERSON, IT MAY HAVE LED TO MORE SERIOUS COMPETITION FOR POWER, AND THUS THE NEED FOR WARFARE.
BUT THIS NEVER HAPPENED.

THIS IS STRANGE BECAUSE THE INDUS PEOPLE MUST HAVE KNOWN OF WARFARE, GIVEN THEIR EXTENSIVE CONTACTS WITH MESOPOTAMIA AND CENTRAL ASIA.

AND YET, FOR SOME REASON, THEY DID NOT ADOPT IT.

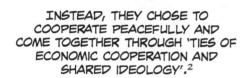

INSTEAD, THEY CHOSE TO COOPERATE PEACEFULLY AND COME TOGETHER THROUGH 'TIES OF ECONOMIC COOPERATION AND SHARED IDEOLOGY'.[2]

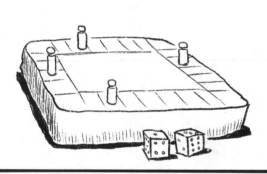

THIS MODEL OF ORGANIZATION ALLOWED THEM TO NOT ONLY EXPAND PRODIGIOUSLY BUT ALSO EXCEL IN TECHNOLOGY AND TRADE.

IT WAS UNDOUBTEDLY ONE OF THEIR GREATEST STRENGTHS.

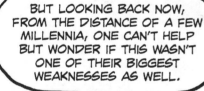

BUT LOOKING BACK NOW, FROM THE DISTANCE OF A FEW MILLENNIA, ONE CAN'T HELP BUT WONDER IF THIS WASN'T ONE OF THEIR BIGGEST WEAKNESSES AS WELL.

FOR AFTER PROSPERING FOR MORE THAN 700 YEARS, THE INDUS CIVILIZATION BEGAN TO DECLINE.

THERE IS EVIDENCE THAT BY 1900 BCE THE SOCIAL AND ECONOMIC FABRIC HAD STARTED TO FRAY.

IN THE FOLLOWING CENTURIES IT WOULD COMPLETELY COLLAPSE.

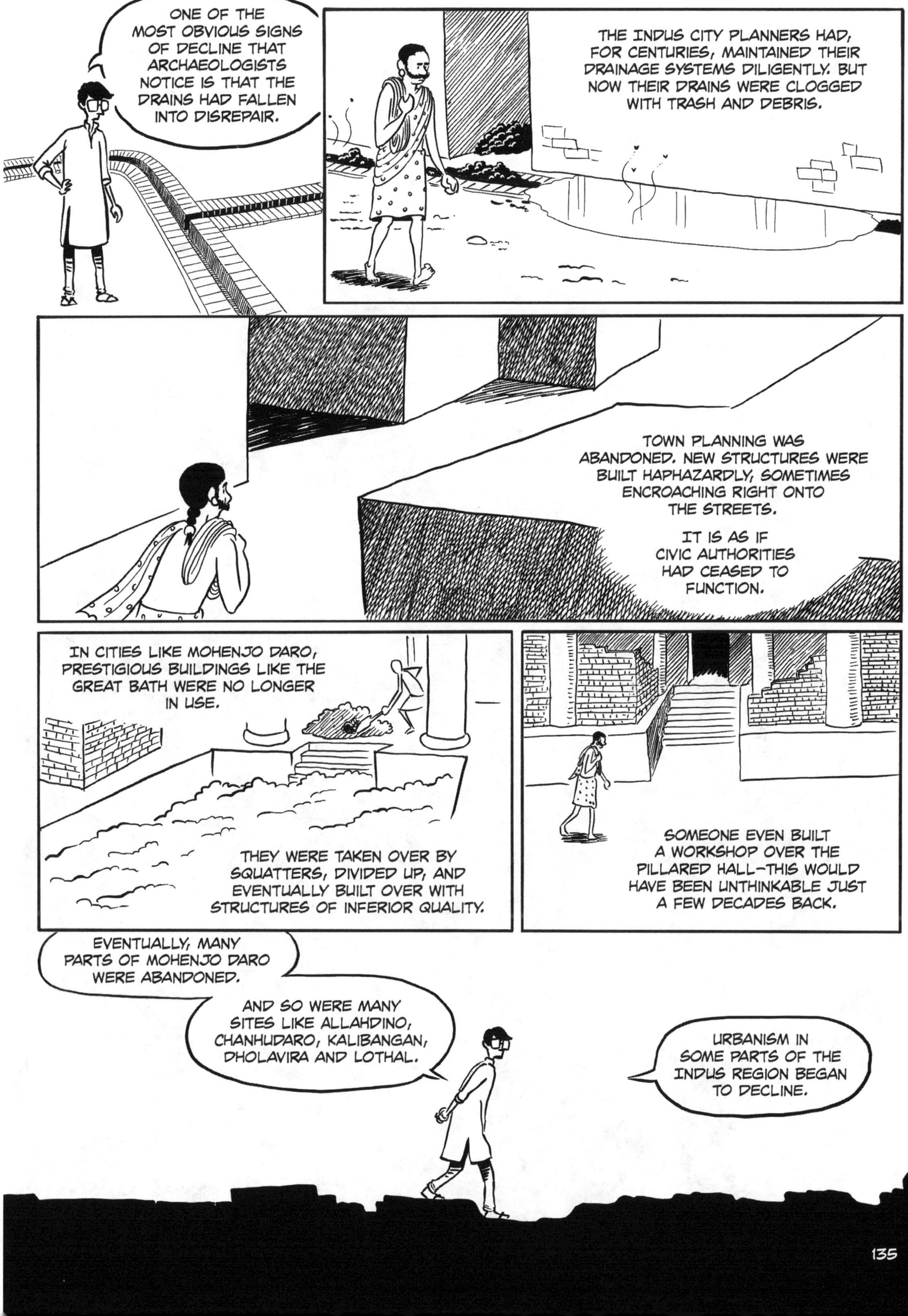
ONE OF THE MOST OBVIOUS SIGNS OF DECLINE THAT ARCHAEOLOGISTS NOTICE IS THAT THE DRAINS HAD FALLEN INTO DISREPAIR.
THE INDUS CITY PLANNERS HAD, FOR CENTURIES, MAINTAINED THEIR DRAINAGE SYSTEMS DILIGENTLY. BUT NOW THEIR DRAINS WERE CLOGGED WITH TRASH AND DEBRIS.
TOWN PLANNING WAS ABANDONED. NEW STRUCTURES WERE BUILT HAPHAZARDLY, SOMETIMES ENCROACHING RIGHT ONTO THE STREETS.
IT IS AS IF CIVIC AUTHORITIES HAD CEASED TO FUNCTION.
IN CITIES LIKE MOHENJO DARO, PRESTIGIOUS BUILDINGS LIKE THE GREAT BATH WERE NO LONGER IN USE.
THEY WERE TAKEN OVER BY SQUATTERS, DIVIDED UP, AND EVENTUALLY BUILT OVER WITH STRUCTURES OF INFERIOR QUALITY.
SOMEONE EVEN BUILT A WORKSHOP OVER THE PILLARED HALL—THIS WOULD HAVE BEEN UNTHINKABLE JUST A FEW DECADES BACK.
EVENTUALLY, MANY PARTS OF MOHENJO DARO WERE ABANDONED.
AND SO WERE MANY SITES LIKE ALLAHDINO, CHANHUDARO, KALIBANGAN, DHOLAVIRA AND LOTHAL.
URBANISM IN SOME PARTS OF THE INDUS REGION BEGAN TO DECLINE.

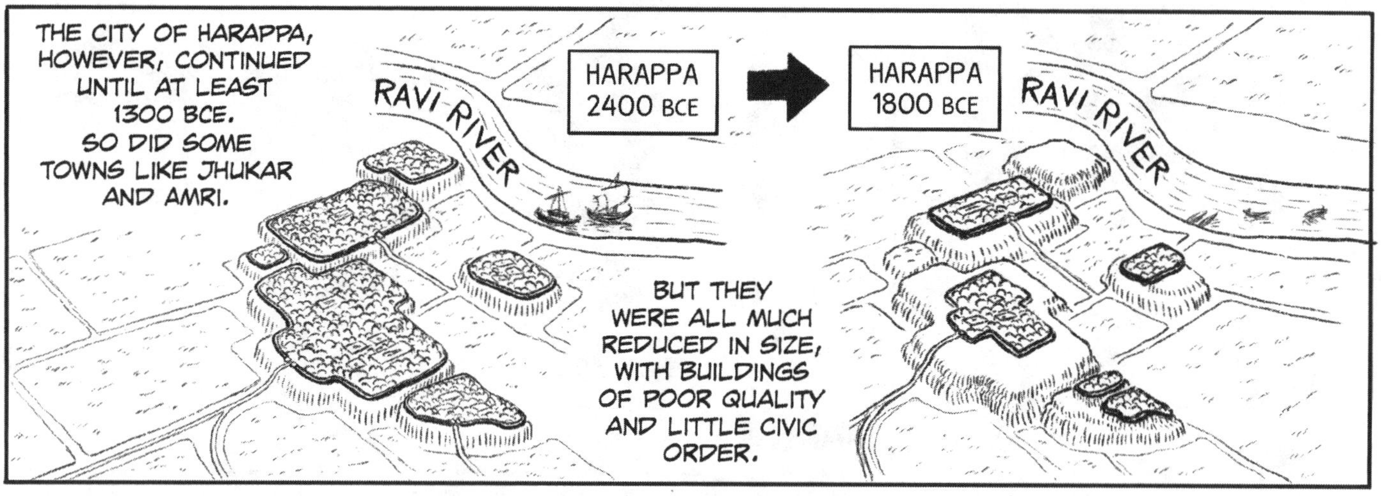
THE CITY OF HARAPPA, HOWEVER, CONTINUED UNTIL AT LEAST 1300 BCE. SO DID SOME TOWNS LIKE JHUKAR AND AMRI.
RAVI RIVER
HARAPPA 2400 BCE
HARAPPA 1800 BCE
RAVI RIVER
BUT THEY WERE ALL MUCH REDUCED IN SIZE, WITH BUILDINGS OF POOR QUALITY AND LITTLE CIVIC ORDER.

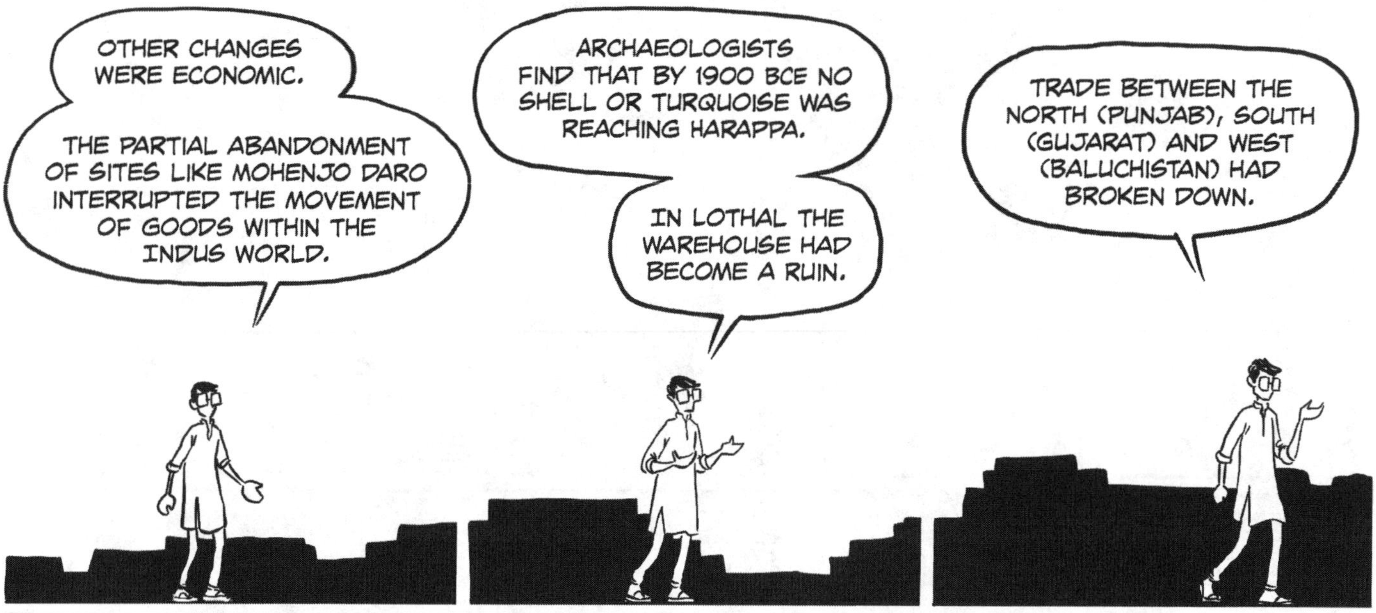
OTHER CHANGES WERE ECONOMIC.
THE PARTIAL ABANDONMENT OF SITES LIKE MOHENJO DARO INTERRUPTED THE MOVEMENT OF GOODS WITHIN THE INDUS WORLD.
ARCHAEOLOGISTS FIND THAT BY 1900 BCE NO SHELL OR TURQUOISE WAS REACHING HARAPPA.
IN LOTHAL THE WAREHOUSE HAD BECOME A RUIN.
TRADE BETWEEN THE NORTH (PUNJAB), SOUTH (GUJARAT) AND WEST (BALUCHISTAN) HAD BROKEN DOWN.

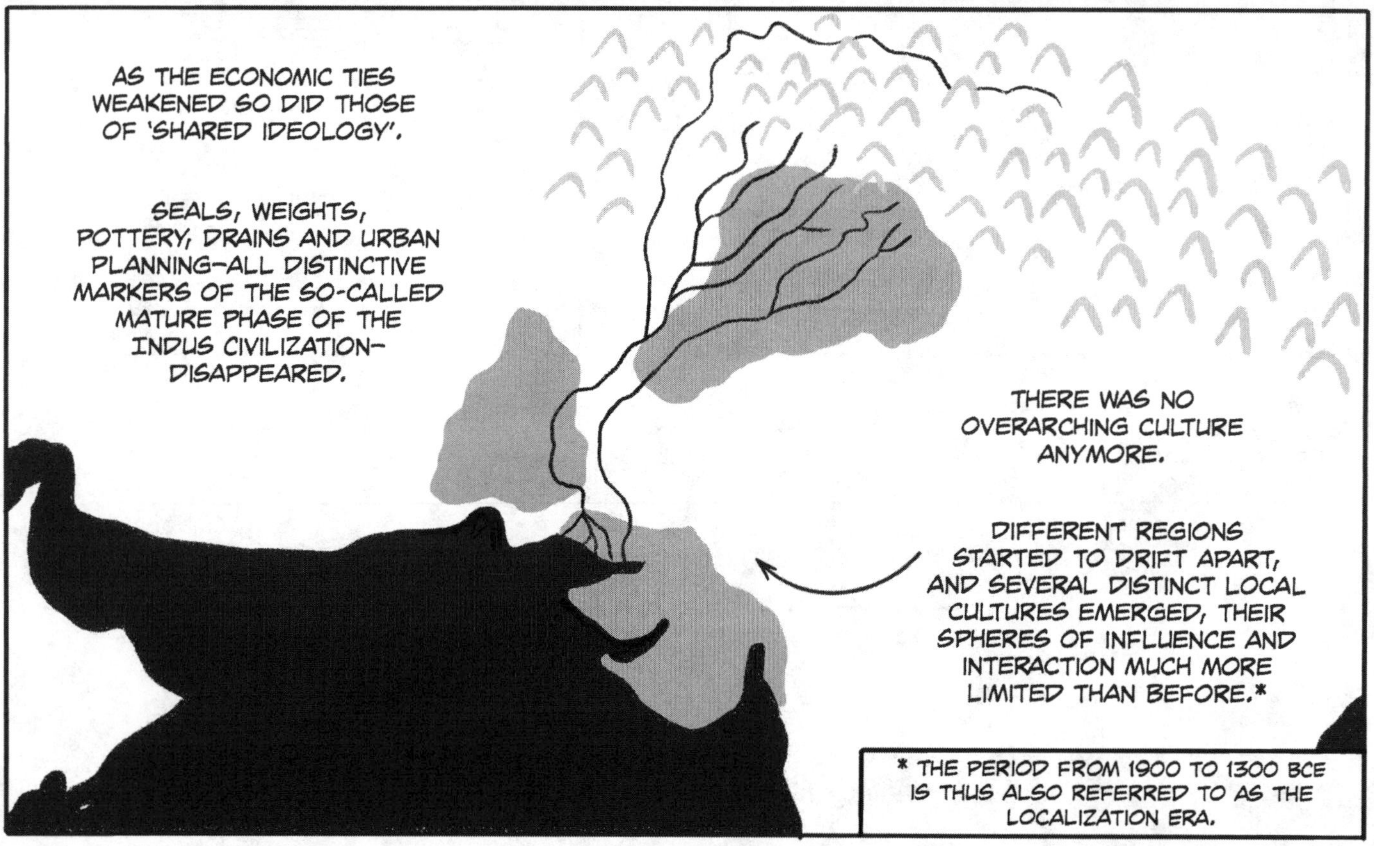
AS THE ECONOMIC TIES WEAKENED SO DID THOSE OF 'SHARED IDEOLOGY'.
SEALS, WEIGHTS, POTTERY, DRAINS AND URBAN PLANNING—ALL DISTINCTIVE MARKERS OF THE SO-CALLED MATURE PHASE OF THE INDUS CIVILIZATION—DISAPPEARED.
THERE WAS NO OVERARCHING CULTURE ANYMORE.
DIFFERENT REGIONS STARTED TO DRIFT APART, AND SEVERAL DISTINCT LOCAL CULTURES EMERGED, THEIR SPHERES OF INFLUENCE AND INTERACTION MUCH MORE LIMITED THAN BEFORE.*
* THE PERIOD FROM 1900 TO 1300 BCE IS THUS ALSO REFERRED TO AS THE LOCALIZATION ERA.

THIS CAN BE SEEN MOST CLEARLY IN THE EVOLVING POTTERY STYLES WHICH WERE TAKING DIFFERENT TRAJECTORIES IN DIFFERENT REGIONS.

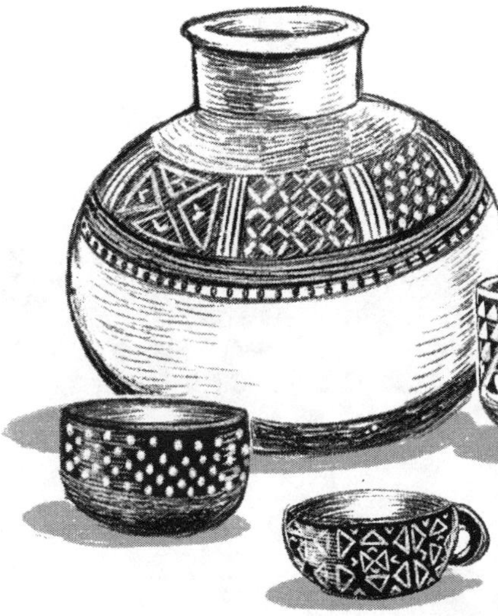

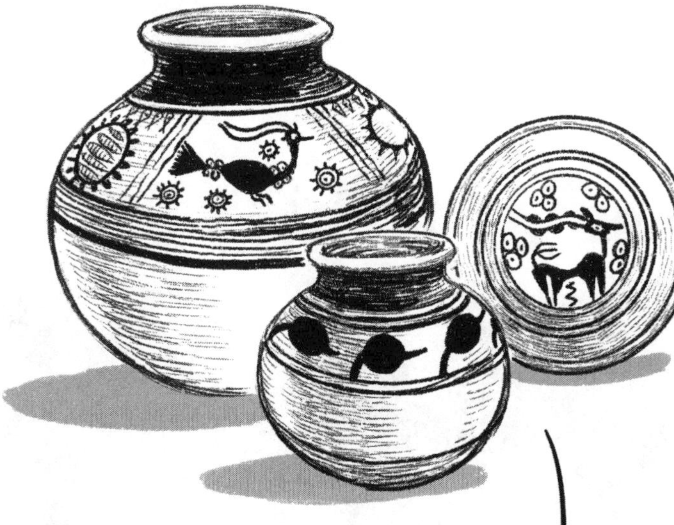

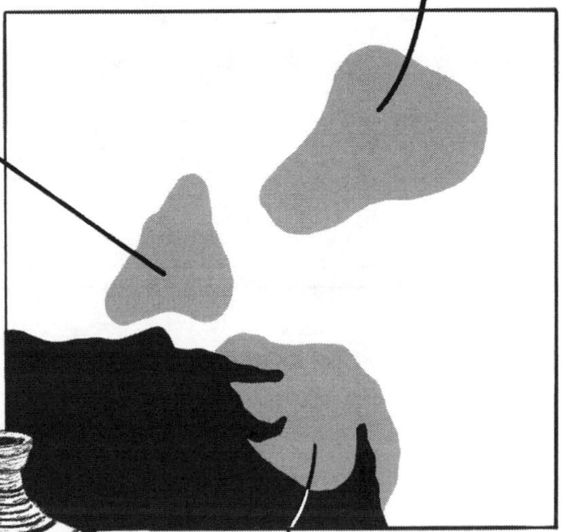

THE NEW DESIGNS BORROWED THEMES FROM THE OLDER POTTERY BUT AT THE SAME TIME REFLECTED DIVERGING CULTURAL IDEAS.

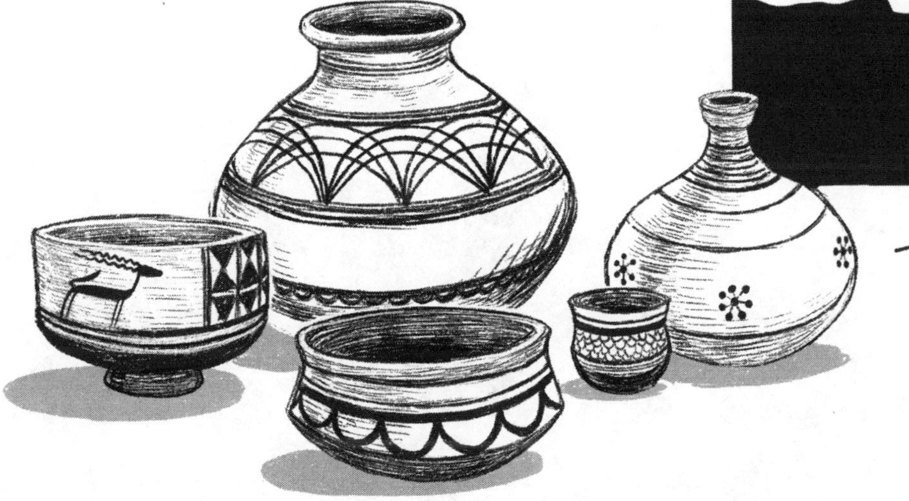

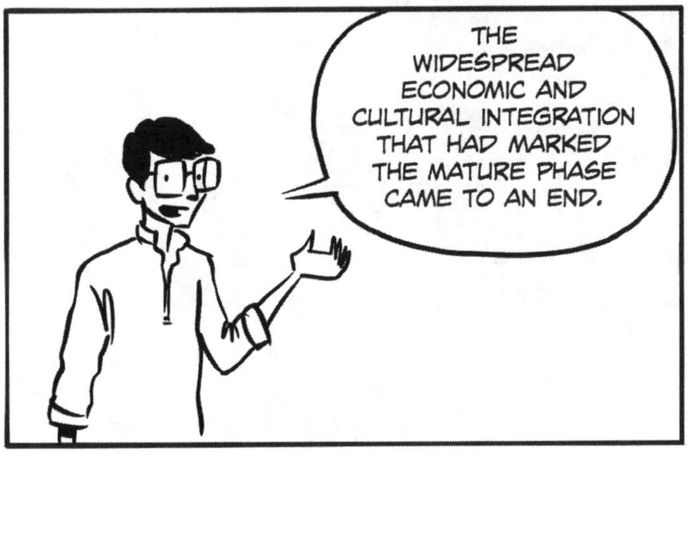
THE WIDESPREAD ECONOMIC AND CULTURAL INTEGRATION THAT HAD MARKED THE MATURE PHASE CAME TO AN END.

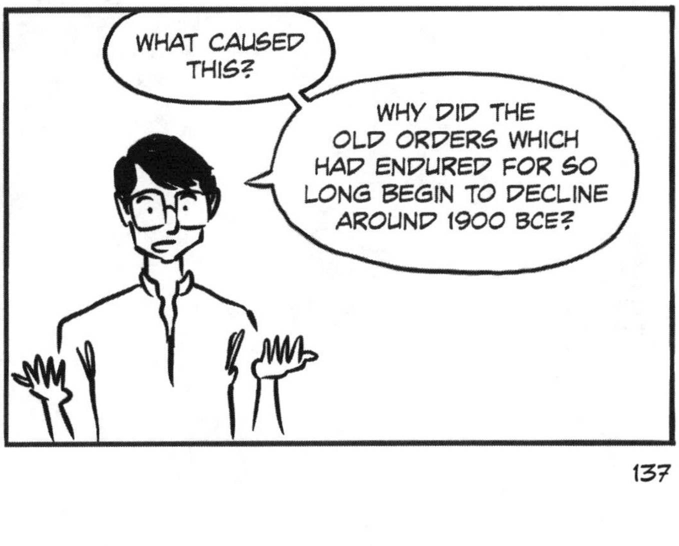
WHAT CAUSED THIS?
WHY DID THE OLD ORDERS WHICH HAD ENDURED FOR SO LONG BEGIN TO DECLINE AROUND 1900 BCE?

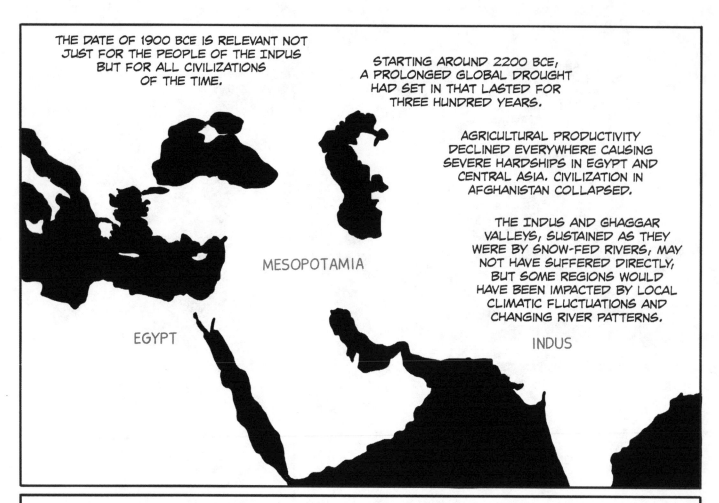

THE DATE OF 1900 BCE IS RELEVANT NOT JUST FOR THE PEOPLE OF THE INDUS BUT FOR ALL CIVILIZATIONS OF THE TIME.

STARTING AROUND 2200 BCE, A PROLONGED GLOBAL DROUGHT HAD SET IN THAT LASTED FOR THREE HUNDRED YEARS.

AGRICULTURAL PRODUCTIVITY DECLINED EVERYWHERE CAUSING SEVERE HARDSHIPS IN EGYPT AND CENTRAL ASIA. CIVILIZATION IN AFGHANISTAN COLLAPSED.

THE INDUS AND GHAGGAR VALLEYS, SUSTAINED AS THEY WERE BY SNOW-FED RIVERS, MAY NOT HAVE SUFFERED DIRECTLY; BUT SOME REGIONS WOULD HAVE BEEN IMPACTED BY LOCAL CLIMATIC FLUCTUATIONS AND CHANGING RIVER PATTERNS.

MESOPOTAMIA

EGYPT

INDUS

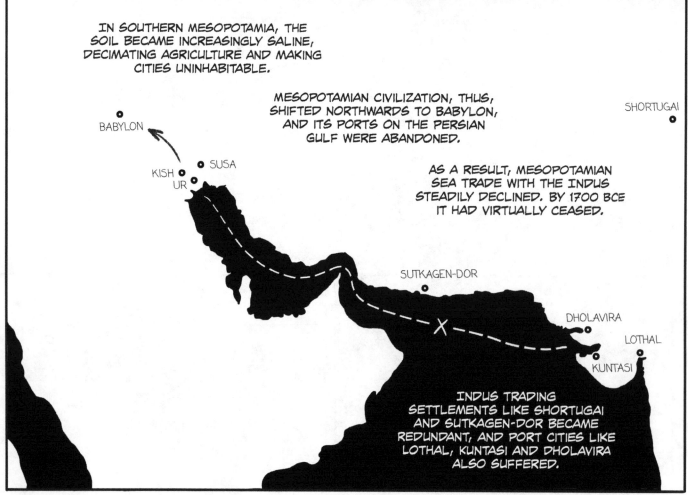

IN SOUTHERN MESOPOTAMIA, THE SOIL BECAME INCREASINGLY SALINE, DECIMATING AGRICULTURE AND MAKING CITIES UNINHABITABLE.

MESOPOTAMIAN CIVILIZATION, THUS, SHIFTED NORTHWARDS TO BABYLON, AND ITS PORTS ON THE PERSIAN GULF WERE ABANDONED.

AS A RESULT, MESOPOTAMIAN SEA TRADE WITH THE INDUS STEADILY DECLINED. BY 1700 BCE IT HAD VIRTUALLY CEASED.

SHORTUGAI

BABYLON

KISH
UR
SUSA

SUTKAGEN-DOR

DHOLAVIRA

LOTHAL

KUNTASI

INDUS TRADING SETTLEMENTS LIKE SHORTUGAI AND SUTKAGEN-DOR BECAME REDUNDANT, AND PORT CITIES LIKE LOTHAL, KUNTASI AND DHOLAVIRA ALSO SUFFERED.

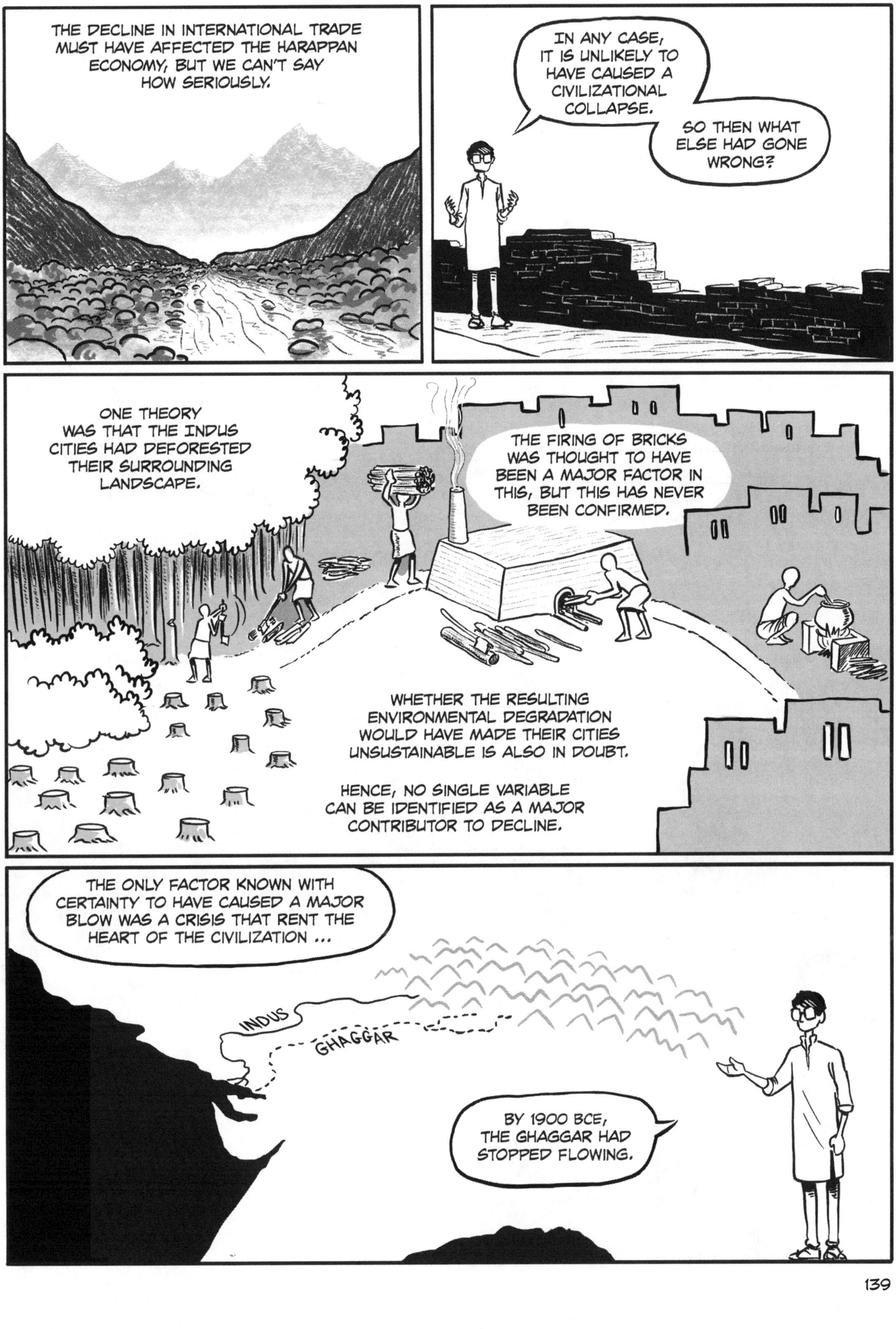
THE DECLINE IN INTERNATIONAL TRADE MUST HAVE AFFECTED THE HARAPPAN ECONOMY, BUT WE CAN'T SAY HOW SERIOUSLY.
IN ANY CASE, IT IS UNLIKELY TO HAVE CAUSED A CIVILIZATIONAL COLLAPSE.
SO THEN WHAT ELSE HAD GONE WRONG?
ONE THEORY WAS THAT THE INDUS CITIES HAD DEFORESTED THEIR SURROUNDING LANDSCAPE.
THE FIRING OF BRICKS WAS THOUGHT TO HAVE BEEN A MAJOR FACTOR IN THIS, BUT THIS HAS NEVER BEEN CONFIRMED.
WHETHER THE RESULTING ENVIRONMENTAL DEGRADATION WOULD HAVE MADE THEIR CITIES UNSUSTAINABLE IS ALSO IN DOUBT.
HENCE, NO SINGLE VARIABLE CAN BE IDENTIFIED AS A MAJOR CONTRIBUTOR TO DECLINE.
THE ONLY FACTOR KNOWN WITH CERTAINTY TO HAVE CAUSED A MAJOR BLOW WAS A CRISIS THAT RENT THE HEART OF THE CIVILIZATION ...
INDUS
GHAGGAR
BY 1900 BCE, THE GHAGGAR HAD STOPPED FLOWING.

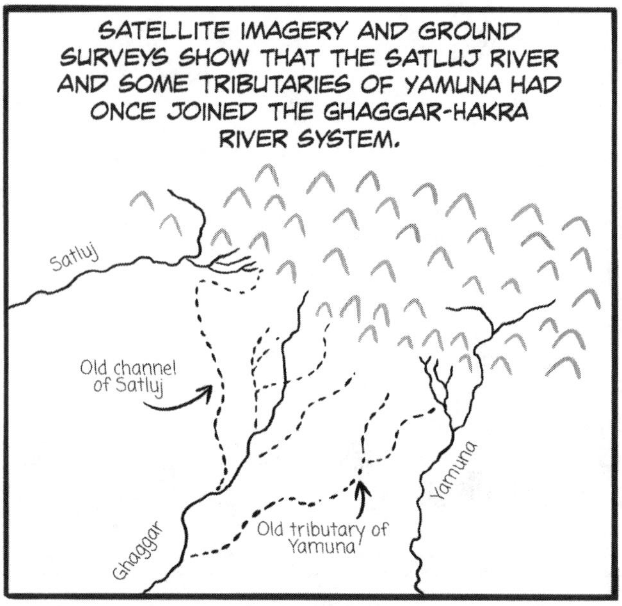
SATELLITE IMAGERY AND GROUND SURVEYS SHOW THAT THE SATLUJ RIVER AND SOME TRIBUTARIES OF YAMUNA HAD ONCE JOINED THE GHAGGAR-HAKRA RIVER SYSTEM.
Satluj
Old channel of Satluj
Yamuna
Ghaggar
Old tributary of Yamuna

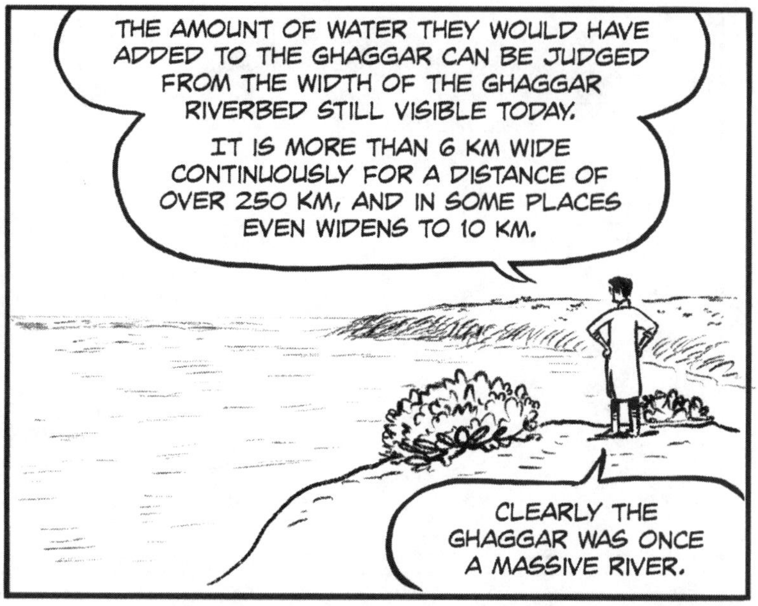
THE AMOUNT OF WATER THEY WOULD HAVE ADDED TO THE GHAGGAR CAN BE JUDGED FROM THE WIDTH OF THE GHAGGAR RIVERBED STILL VISIBLE TODAY.
IT IS MORE THAN 6 KM WIDE CONTINUOUSLY FOR A DISTANCE OF OVER 250 KM, AND IN SOME PLACES EVEN WIDENS TO 10 KM.
CLEARLY THE GHAGGAR WAS ONCE A MASSIVE RIVER.

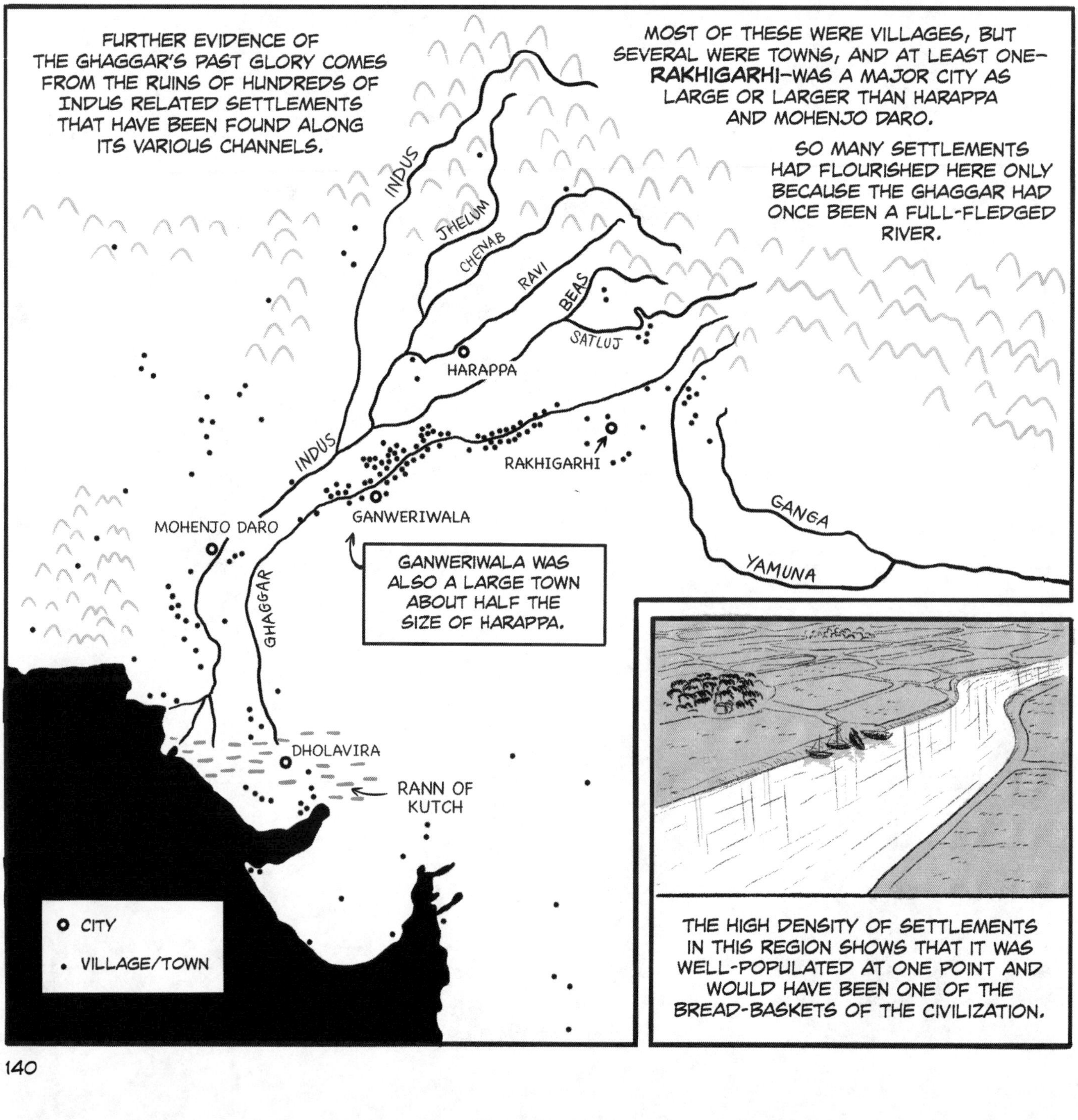
FURTHER EVIDENCE OF THE GHAGGAR'S PAST GLORY COMES FROM THE RUINS OF HUNDREDS OF INDUS RELATED SETTLEMENTS THAT HAVE BEEN FOUND ALONG ITS VARIOUS CHANNELS.
MOST OF THESE WERE VILLAGES, BUT SEVERAL WERE TOWNS, AND AT LEAST ONE—**RAKHIGARHI**—WAS A MAJOR CITY AS LARGE OR LARGER THAN HARAPPA AND MOHENJO DARO.
SO MANY SETTLEMENTS HAD FLOURISHED HERE ONLY BECAUSE THE GHAGGAR HAD ONCE BEEN A FULL-FLEDGED RIVER.
INDUS
JHELUM
CHENAB
RAVI
BEAS
SATLUJ
HARAPPA
INDUS
RAKHIGARHI
GANWERIWALA
MOHENJO DARO
GANGA
YAMUNA
GHAGGAR
GANWERIWALA WAS ALSO A LARGE TOWN ABOUT HALF THE SIZE OF HARAPPA.
DHOLAVIRA
RANN OF KUTCH
CITY
VILLAGE/TOWN
THE HIGH DENSITY OF SETTLEMENTS IN THIS REGION SHOWS THAT IT WAS WELL-POPULATED AT ONE POINT AND WOULD HAVE BEEN ONE OF THE BREAD-BASKETS OF THE CIVILIZATION.

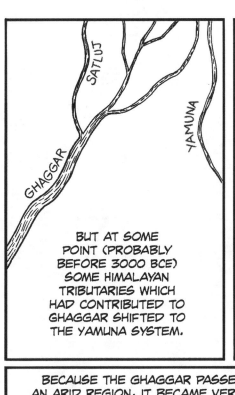

SATLUJ
YAMUNA
GHAGGAR
BUT AT SOME POINT (PROBABLY BEFORE 3000 BCE) SOME HIMALAYAN TRIBUTARIES WHICH HAD CONTRIBUTED TO GHAGGAR SHIFTED TO THE YAMUNA SYSTEM.
SATLUJ
YAMUNA
GHAGGAR
THEN, THE SATLUJ SYSTEM ALSO BEGAN TO SHIFT.
PARTIAL FLOWS FROM THE SATLUJ MAY HAVE CONTRIBUTED TO THE GHAGGAR DURING THE INDUS URBAN PERIOD, BUT EVENTUALLY IT TOO MOVED ENTIRELY TO JOIN BEAS, A TRIBUTARY OF THE INDUS.*
SATLUJ
YAMUNA
GHAGGAR
THE GHAGGAR THEN BECAME A SEASONAL, RAIN-FED RIVER.
* HIMALAYAN RIVERS ARE PRONE TO SHIFTING COURSES OFTEN DUE TO EARTHQUAKES (IN THE HILLS) AND SEDIMENTATION (IN THE PLAINS).
BECAUSE THE GHAGGAR PASSED THROUGH AN ARID REGION, IT BECAME VERY DEPLETED.
THIS WAS ONLY MADE WORSE BY THE THREE-HUNDRED-YEAR GLOBAL DROUGHT, SO MUCH SO THAT BEYOND A CERTAIN POINT, THE GHAGGAR STOPPED FLOWING COMPLETELY.
WITHOUT THE GHAGGAR'S NOURISHING WATERS, LARGE-SCALE AGRICULTURE BECAME IMPOSSIBLE.
THE HUNDREDS OF SETTLEMENTS ON ITS CHANGING CHANNELS COULD NO LONGER BE SUPPORTED.
SLOWLY THE DESERT ENCROACHED. TOWNS AND VILLAGES WERE ABANDONED. ONLY SOME PEOPLE CONTINUED TO LIVE HERE SEASONALLY WHEREVER THERE WAS SUFFICIENT RAINFALL AND WATER AVAILABILITY.
THE DRYING UP OF A BIG RIVER WAS HUGELY DISRUPTIVE. FOR ONE, THE WEALTH RESULTING FROM AGRICULTURE COULD NO LONGER BE SUSTAINED.
FURTHER, AS SETTLEMENTS WERE ABANDONED, TRADING NETWORKS ALSO STARTED TO FALL APART.

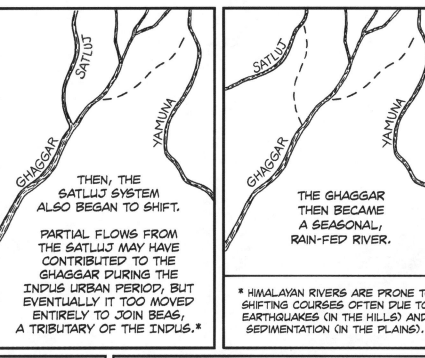

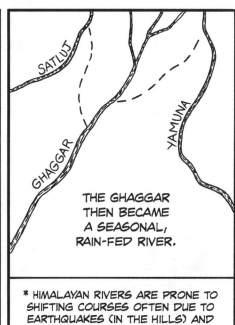

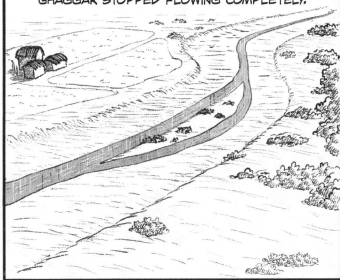

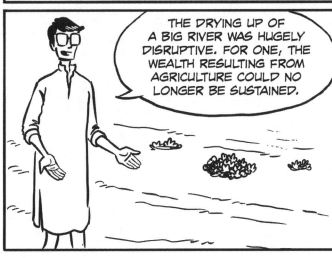

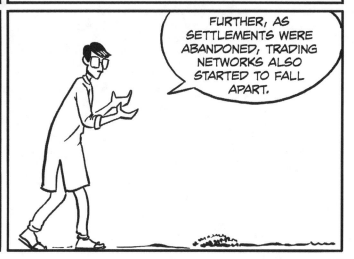

THE RANN OF KUTCH, ONCE THE ESTUARY OF THE GHAGGAR, NOW BECAME DEPRIVED OF WATER AND TURNED INTO A SWAMP.*

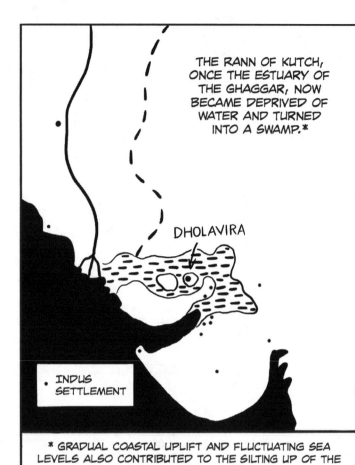

DHOLAVIRA

. INDUS SETTLEMENT

* GRADUAL COASTAL UPLIFT AND FLUCTUATING SEA LEVELS ALSO CONTRIBUTED TO THE SILTING UP OF THE RANN, RESULTING IN THE VAST SALT FLATS THAT ARE SEASONALLY PRESENT TODAY.

NAVIGATION THROUGH THE RANN BECAME IMPOSSIBLE AND DHOLAVIRA COULD NO LONGER FUNCTION AS A MAJOR PORT CITY.

THE INDUS, NOW CARRYING ALL THAT EXTRA WATER (FROM THE SATLUJ) SHIFTED EASTWARDS, FLOODING AND DESTROYING MANY OLD SITES ON ITS BANKS.
IT WOULD HAVE ALSO DISRUPTED THE AREAS SUITABLE FOR AGRICULTURE AND GRAZING.

ONE CAN ONLY IMAGINE THE UPHEAVAL THIS MUST HAVE CAUSED.

MANY ELITES AND MERCHANTS WHO BASED THEIR WEALTH ON AGRICULTURE WOULD HAVE BEEN UNABLE TO SUPPORT TRADE.

NOW, THESE CHANGES DID NOT OCCUR OVERNIGHT.

IT TOOK CENTURIES FOR THE LANDSCAPE TO BE SO DRAMATICALLY ALTERED.

BUT, UNDER THE GROWING ECONOMIC AND SOCIAL STRAIN, THE OLD ORDERS COULD NO LONGER HOLD UP.

THE INDUS URBAN SYSTEM BEGAN TO CHANGE.

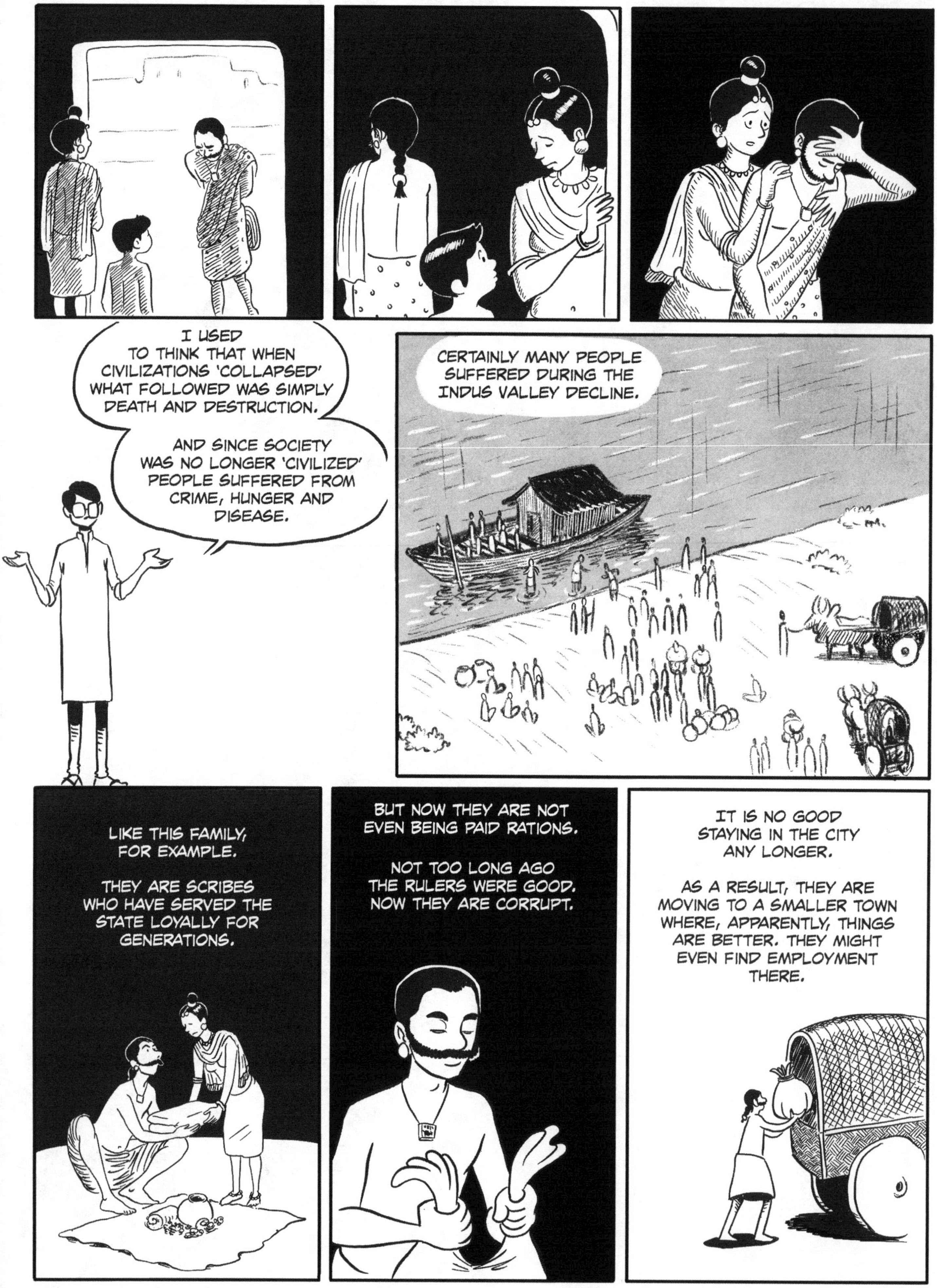
I USED TO THINK THAT WHEN CIVILIZATIONS 'COLLAPSED' WHAT FOLLOWED WAS SIMPLY DEATH AND DESTRUCTION.
AND SINCE SOCIETY WAS NO LONGER 'CIVILIZED' PEOPLE SUFFERED FROM CRIME, HUNGER AND DISEASE.
CERTAINLY MANY PEOPLE SUFFERED DURING THE INDUS VALLEY DECLINE.
LIKE THIS FAMILY, FOR EXAMPLE.
THEY ARE SCRIBES WHO HAVE SERVED THE STATE LOYALLY FOR GENERATIONS.
BUT NOW THEY ARE NOT EVEN BEING PAID RATIONS.
NOT TOO LONG AGO THE RULERS WERE GOOD. NOW THEY ARE CORRUPT.
IT IS NO GOOD STAYING IN THE CITY ANY LONGER.
AS A RESULT, THEY ARE MOVING TO A SMALLER TOWN WHERE, APPARENTLY, THINGS ARE BETTER. THEY MIGHT EVEN FIND EMPLOYMENT THERE.

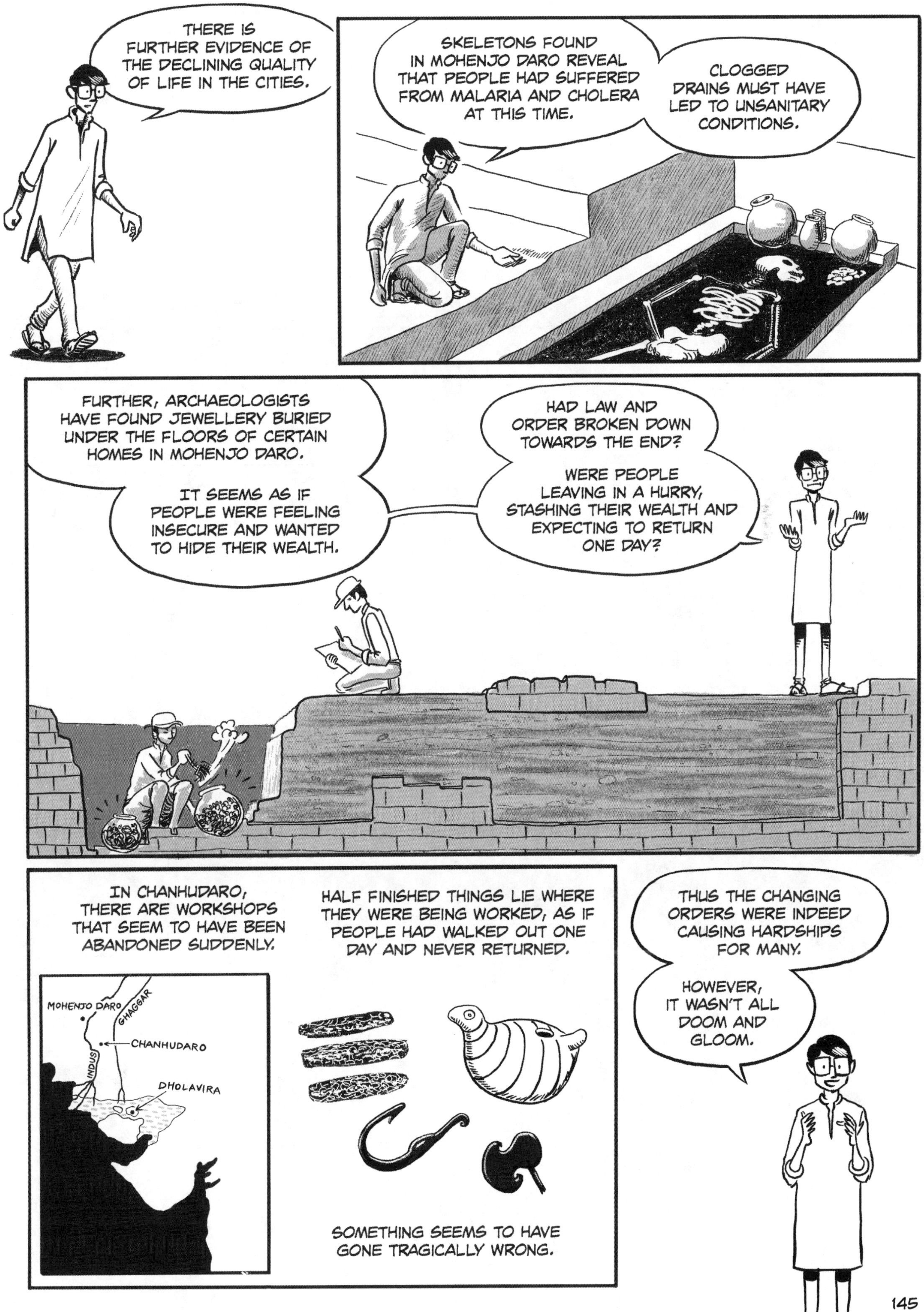
THERE IS FURTHER EVIDENCE OF THE DECLINING QUALITY OF LIFE IN THE CITIES.
SKELETONS FOUND IN MOHENJO DARO REVEAL THAT PEOPLE HAD SUFFERED FROM MALARIA AND CHOLERA AT THIS TIME.
CLOGGED DRAINS MUST HAVE LED TO UNSANITARY CONDITIONS.
FURTHER, ARCHAEOLOGISTS HAVE FOUND JEWELLERY BURIED UNDER THE FLOORS OF CERTAIN HOMES IN MOHENJO DARO.
IT SEEMS AS IF PEOPLE WERE FEELING INSECURE AND WANTED TO HIDE THEIR WEALTH.
HAD LAW AND ORDER BROKEN DOWN TOWARDS THE END?
WERE PEOPLE LEAVING IN A HURRY, STASHING THEIR WEALTH AND EXPECTING TO RETURN ONE DAY?
IN CHANHUDARO, THERE ARE WORKSHOPS THAT SEEM TO HAVE BEEN ABANDONED SUDDENLY.
HALF FINISHED THINGS LIE WHERE THEY WERE BEING WORKED, AS IF PEOPLE HAD WALKED OUT ONE DAY AND NEVER RETURNED.
MOHENJO DARO
GHAGGAR
CHANHUDARO
INDUS
DHOLAVIRA
SOMETHING SEEMS TO HAVE GONE TRAGICALLY WRONG.
THUS THE CHANGING ORDERS WERE INDEED CAUSING HARDSHIPS FOR MANY.
HOWEVER, IT WASN'T ALL DOOM AND GLOOM.

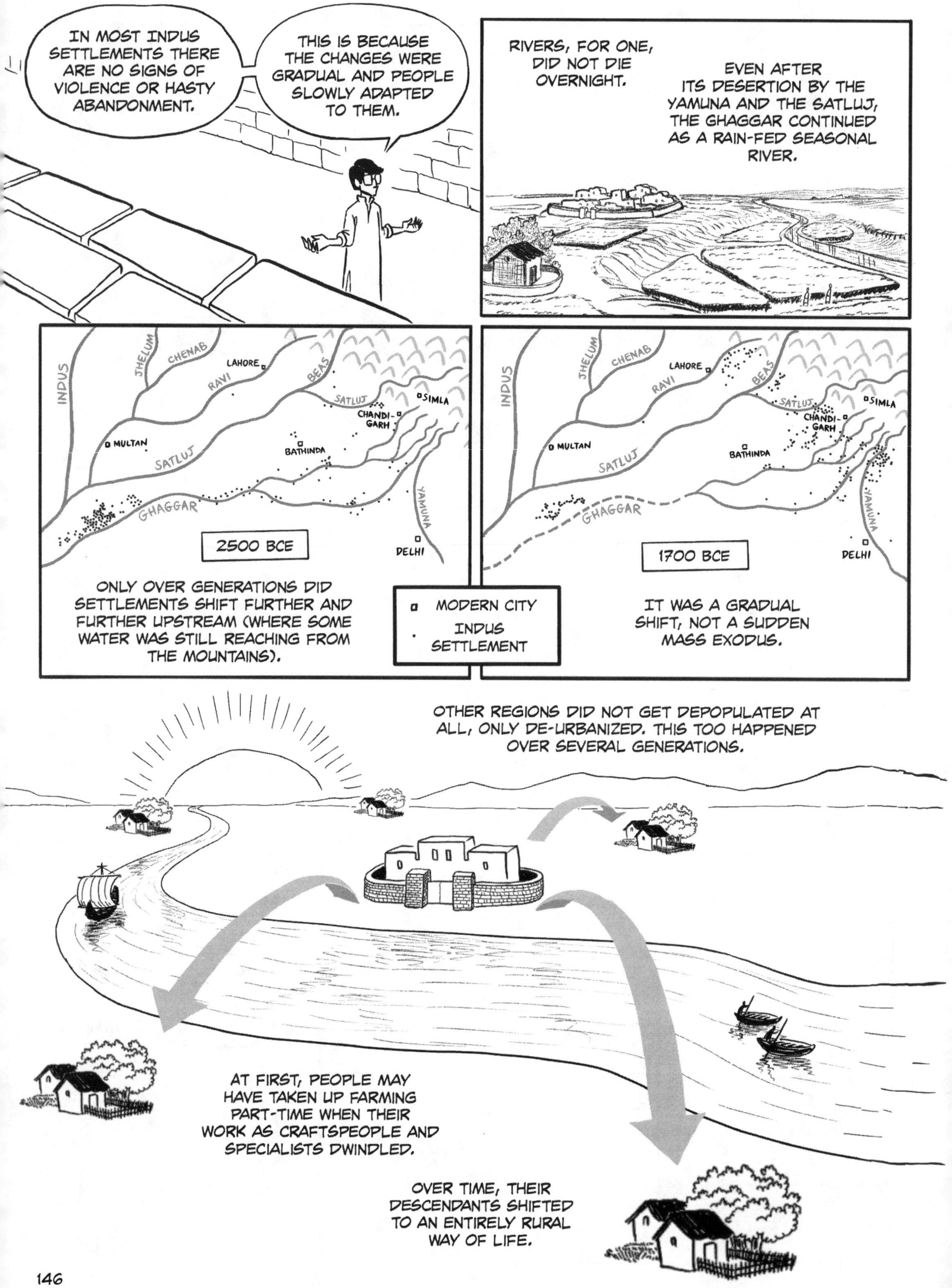
IN MOST INDUS SETTLEMENTS THERE ARE NO SIGNS OF VIOLENCE OR HASTY ABANDONMENT.
THIS IS BECAUSE THE CHANGES WERE GRADUAL AND PEOPLE SLOWLY ADAPTED TO THEM.
RIVERS, FOR ONE, DID NOT DIE OVERNIGHT.
EVEN AFTER ITS DESERTION BY THE YAMUNA AND THE SATLUJ, THE GHAGGAR CONTINUED AS A RAIN-FED SEASONAL RIVER.
INDUS
JHELUM
CHENAB
LAHORE
RAVI
BEAS
SATLUJ
SIMLA
CHANDI-GARH
MULTAN
BATHINDA
SATLUJ
GHAGGAR
YAMUNA
DELHI
2500 BCE
ONLY OVER GENERATIONS DID SETTLEMENTS SHIFT FURTHER AND FURTHER UPSTREAM (WHERE SOME WATER WAS STILL REACHING FROM THE MOUNTAINS).
MODERN CITY
INDUS SETTLEMENT
INDUS
JHELUM
CHENAB
LAHORE
RAVI
BEAS
SATLUJ
SIMLA
CHANDI-GARH
MULTAN
BATHINDA
SATLUJ
GHAGGAR
YAMUNA
DELHI
1700 BCE
IT WAS A GRADUAL SHIFT, NOT A SUDDEN MASS EXODUS.
OTHER REGIONS DID NOT GET DEPOPULATED AT ALL, ONLY DE-URBANIZED. THIS TOO HAPPENED OVER SEVERAL GENERATIONS.
AT FIRST, PEOPLE MAY HAVE TAKEN UP FARMING PART-TIME WHEN THEIR WORK AS CRAFTSPEOPLE AND SPECIALISTS DWINDLED.
OVER TIME, THEIR DESCENDANTS SHIFTED TO AN ENTIRELY RURAL WAY OF LIFE.

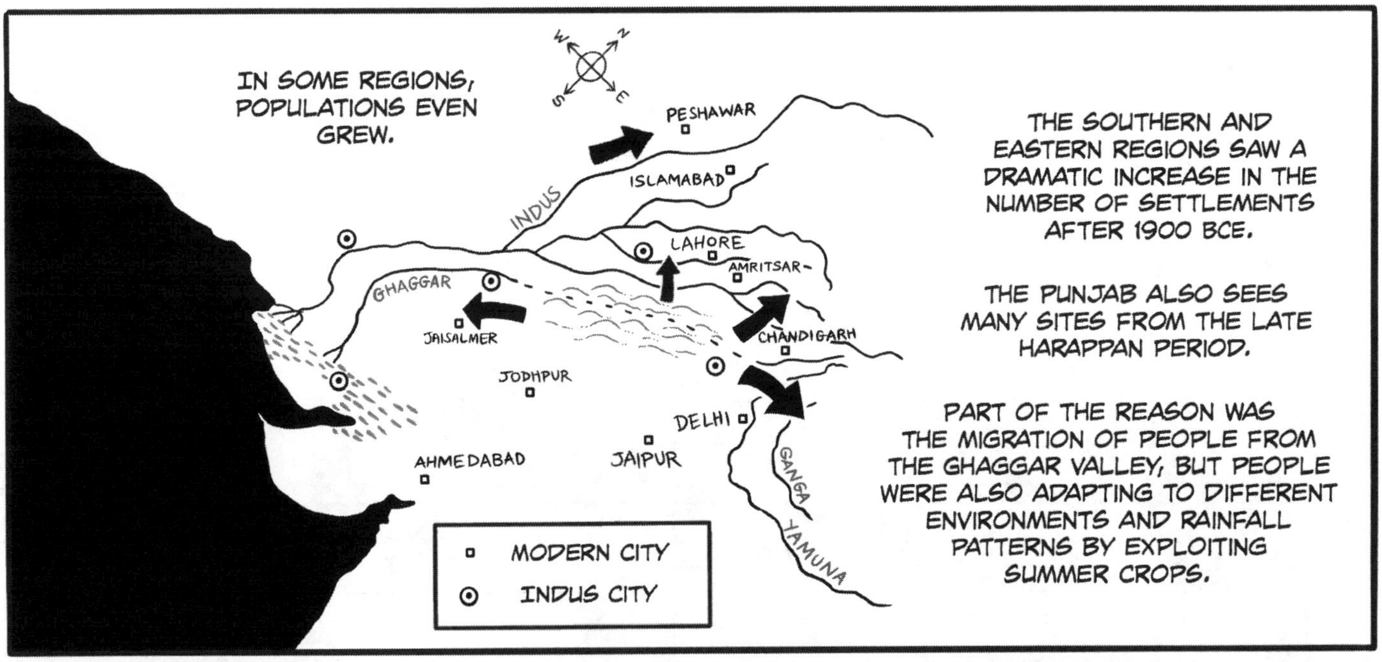
IN SOME REGIONS, POPULATIONS EVEN GREW.
W N S E
PESHAWAR
ISLAMABAD
INDUS
LAHORE
AMRITSAR
GHAGGAR
JAISALMER
CHANDIGARH
JODHPUR
DELHI
AHMEDABAD
JAIPUR
GANGA
YAMUNA
MODERN CITY
INDUS CITY
THE SOUTHERN AND EASTERN REGIONS SAW A DRAMATIC INCREASE IN THE NUMBER OF SETTLEMENTS AFTER 1900 BCE.
THE PUNJAB ALSO SEES MANY SITES FROM THE LATE HARAPPAN PERIOD.
PART OF THE REASON WAS THE MIGRATION OF PEOPLE FROM THE GHAGGAR VALLEY, BUT PEOPLE WERE ALSO ADAPTING TO DIFFERENT ENVIRONMENTS AND RAINFALL PATTERNS BY EXPLOITING SUMMER CROPS.

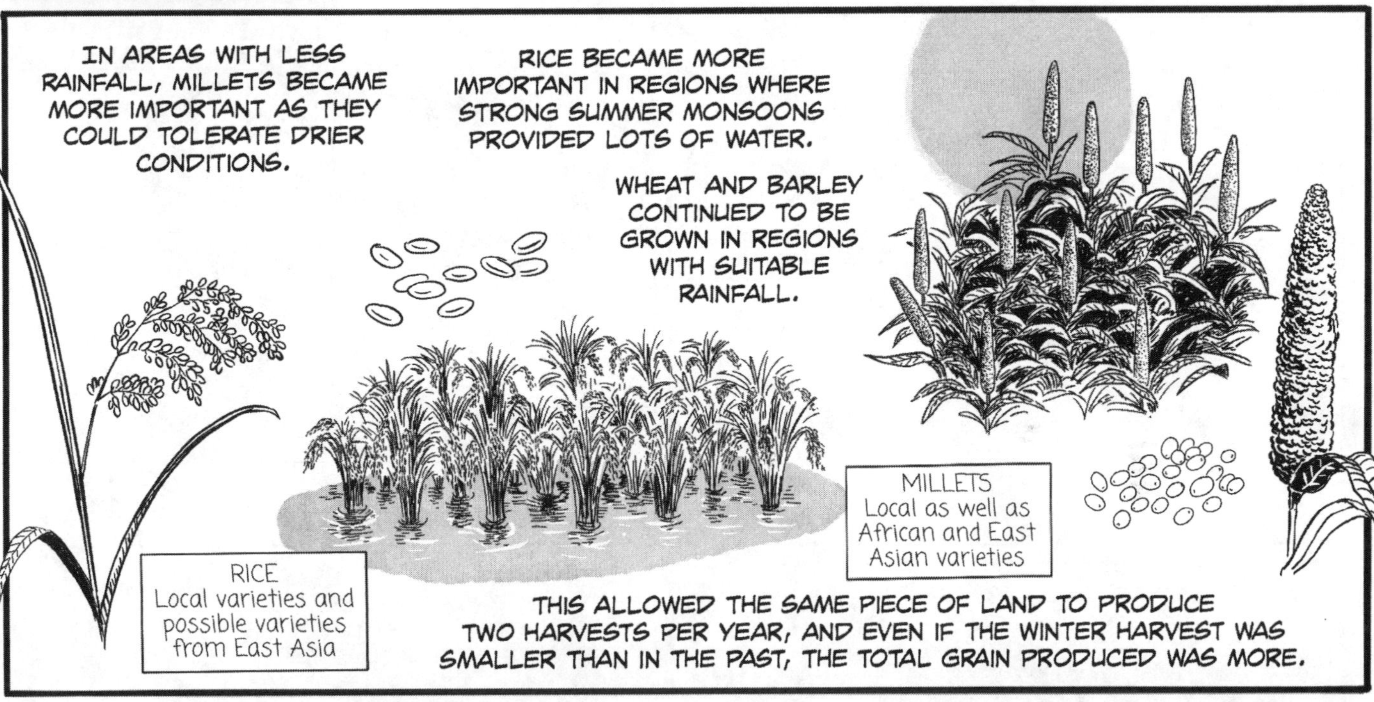
IN AREAS WITH LESS RAINFALL, MILLETS BECAME MORE IMPORTANT AS THEY COULD TOLERATE DRIER CONDITIONS.
RICE BECAME MORE IMPORTANT IN REGIONS WHERE STRONG SUMMER MONSOONS PROVIDED LOTS OF WATER.
WHEAT AND BARLEY CONTINUED TO BE GROWN IN REGIONS WITH SUITABLE RAINFALL.
RICE Local varieties and possible varieties from East Asia
MILLETS Local as well as African and East Asian varieties
THIS ALLOWED THE SAME PIECE OF LAND TO PRODUCE TWO HARVESTS PER YEAR, AND EVEN IF THE WINTER HARVEST WAS SMALLER THAN IN THE PAST, THE TOTAL GRAIN PRODUCED WAS MORE.

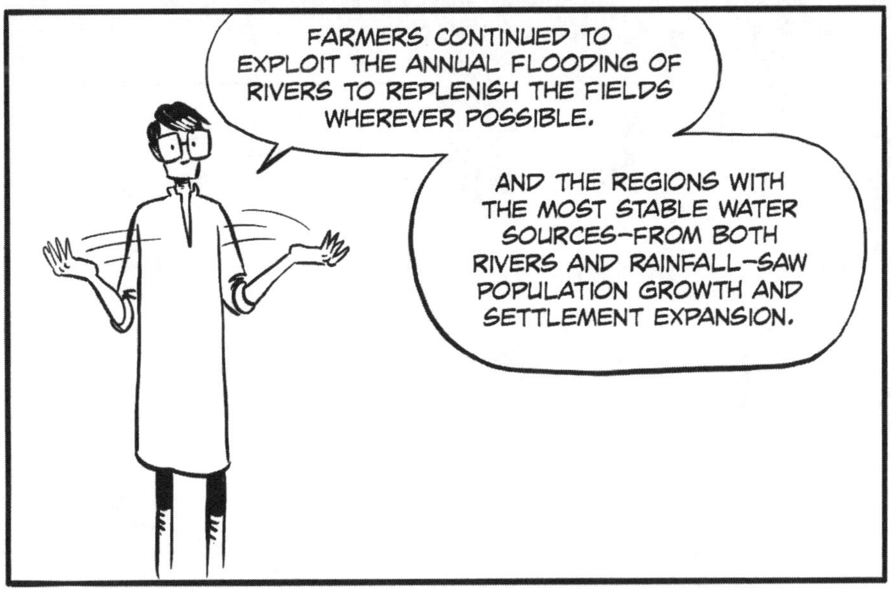
FARMERS CONTINUED TO EXPLOIT THE ANNUAL FLOODING OF RIVERS TO REPLENISH THE FIELDS WHEREVER POSSIBLE.
AND THE REGIONS WITH THE MOST STABLE WATER SOURCES—FROM BOTH RIVERS AND RAINFALL—SAW POPULATION GROWTH AND SETTLEMENT EXPANSION.

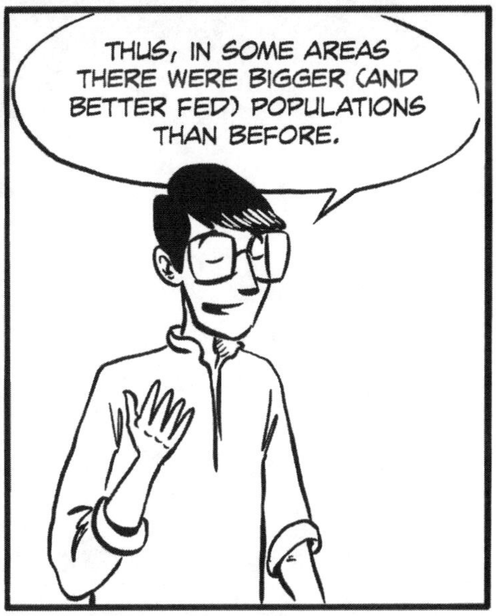
THUS, IN SOME AREAS THERE WERE BIGGER (AND BETTER FED) POPULATIONS THAN BEFORE.

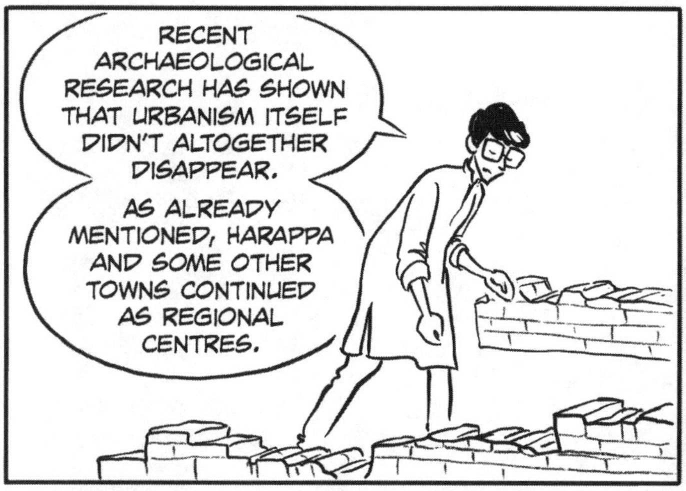
RECENT ARCHAEOLOGICAL RESEARCH HAS SHOWN THAT URBANISM ITSELF DIDN'T ALTOGETHER DISAPPEAR.
AS ALREADY MENTIONED, HARAPPA AND SOME OTHER TOWNS CONTINUED AS REGIONAL CENTRES.
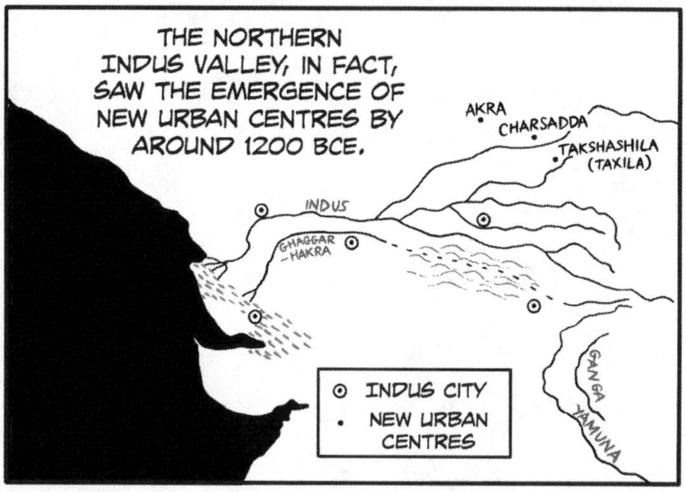
THE NORTHERN INDUS VALLEY, IN FACT, SAW THE EMERGENCE OF NEW URBAN CENTRES BY AROUND 1200 BCE.
AKRA
CHARSADDA
TAKSHASHILA (TAXILA)
INDUS
GHAGGAR –HAKRA
GANGA
YAMUNA
INDUS CITY
NEW URBAN CENTRES
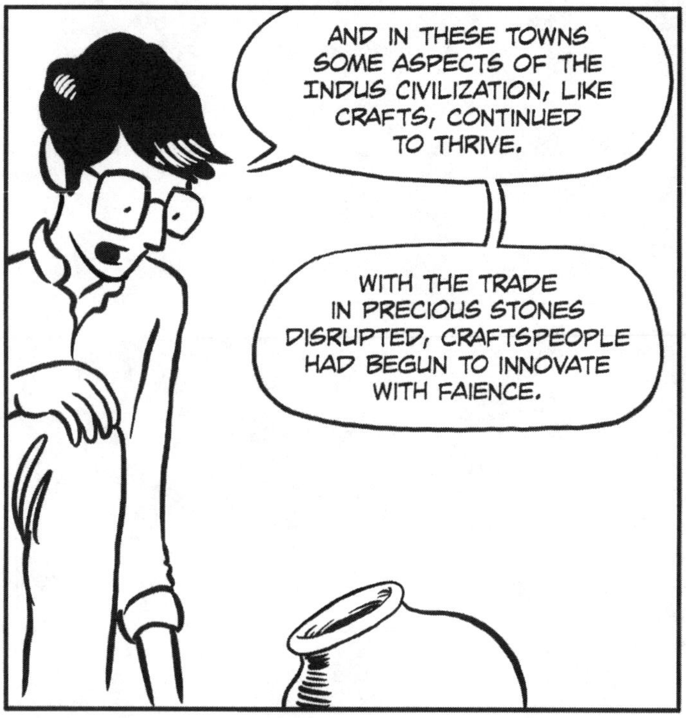
AND IN THESE TOWNS SOME ASPECTS OF THE INDUS CIVILIZATION, LIKE CRAFTS, CONTINUED TO THRIVE.
WITH THE TRADE IN PRECIOUS STONES DISRUPTED, CRAFTSPEOPLE HAD BEGUN TO INNOVATE WITH FAIENCE.
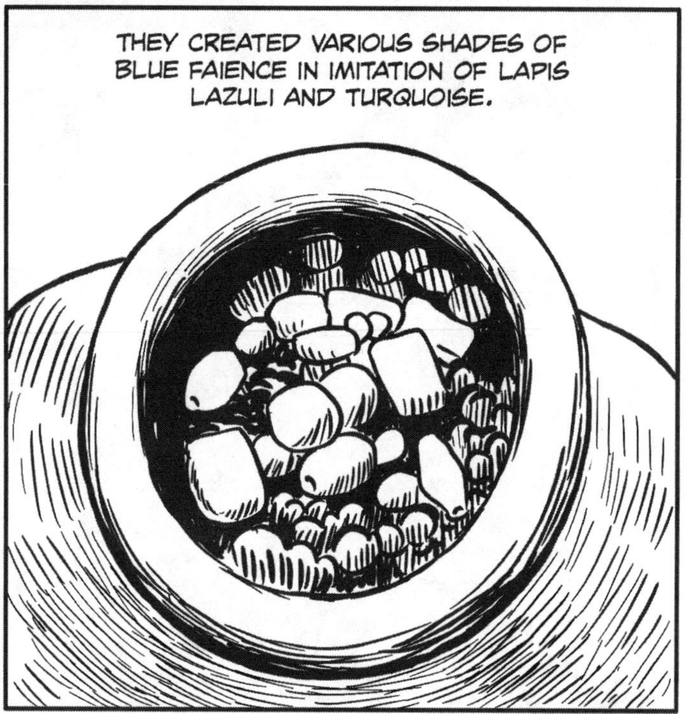
THEY CREATED VARIOUS SHADES OF BLUE FAIENCE IN IMITATION OF LAPIS LAZULI AND TURQUOISE.
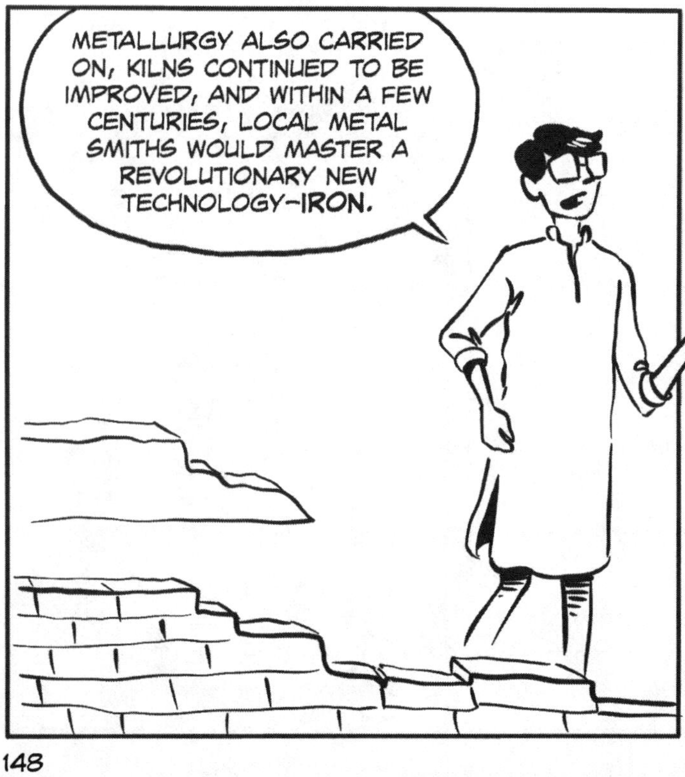
METALLURGY ALSO CARRIED ON, KILNS CONTINUED TO BE IMPROVED, AND WITHIN A FEW CENTURIES, LOCAL METAL SMITHS WOULD MASTER A REVOLUTIONARY NEW TECHNOLOGY–IRON.
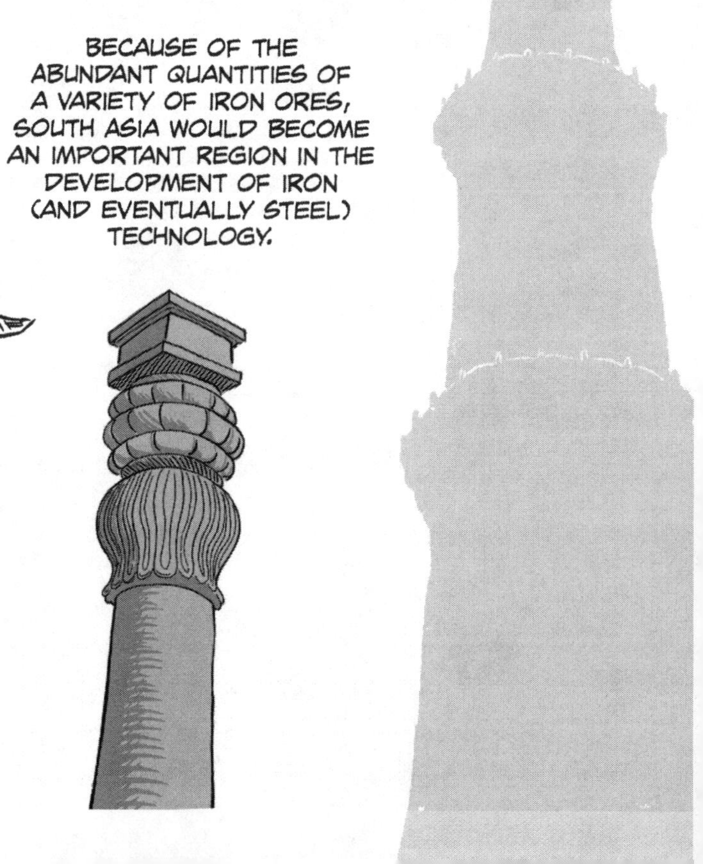
BECAUSE OF THE ABUNDANT QUANTITIES OF A VARIETY OF IRON ORES, SOUTH ASIA WOULD BECOME AN IMPORTANT REGION IN THE DEVELOPMENT OF IRON (AND EVENTUALLY STEEL) TECHNOLOGY.

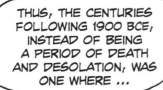

THUS, THE CENTURIES FOLLOWING 1900 BCE, INSTEAD OF BEING A PERIOD OF DEATH AND DESOLATION, WAS ONE WHERE ...

" A NEW SOCIAL ORDER " WAS BEING ESTABLISHED, AS NEW TECHNOLOGIES AND AGRICULTURAL PRACTICES SPREAD UP AND DOWN THE INDUS VALLEY.

– J. M. KENOYER[3]

THE NEW TECHNOLOGIES (IRON) AND AGRICULTURAL PRACTICES (TWO CROPS PER YEAR) WERE TRANSFORMING OLD CITIES WHILE SIMULTANEOUSLY LAYING THE FOUNDATIONS FOR NEW CITIES.

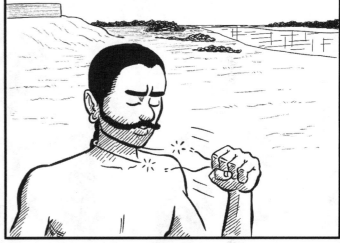

NEVERTHELESS, THE URBAN ORDERS THAT HAD SUSTAINED ON THE BANKS OF THE INDUS AND GHAGGAR RIVERS FOR SEVEN CENTURIES WERE COMING TO AN END.

THE INDUS PERIOD ...

... WAS OVER.

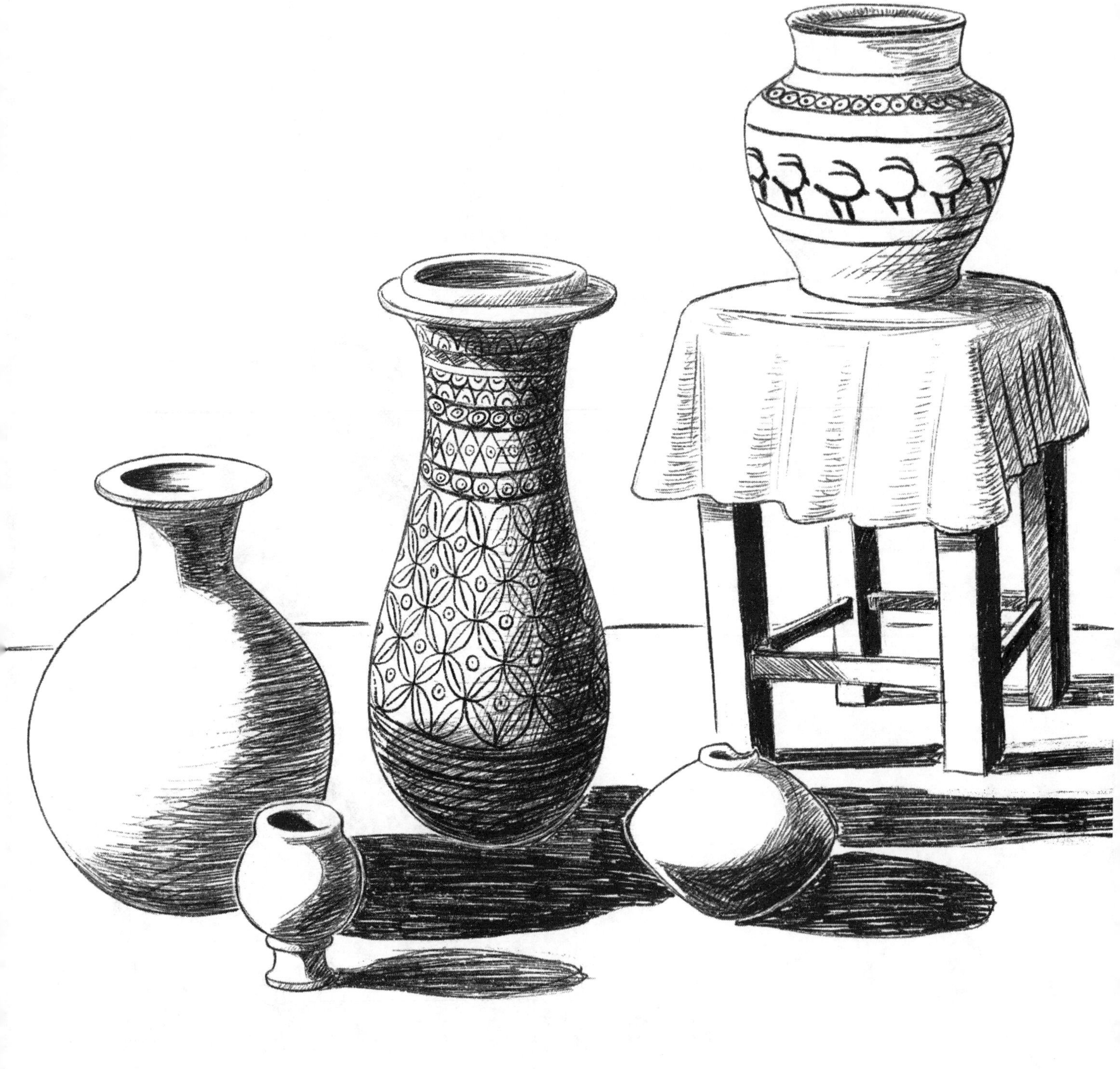

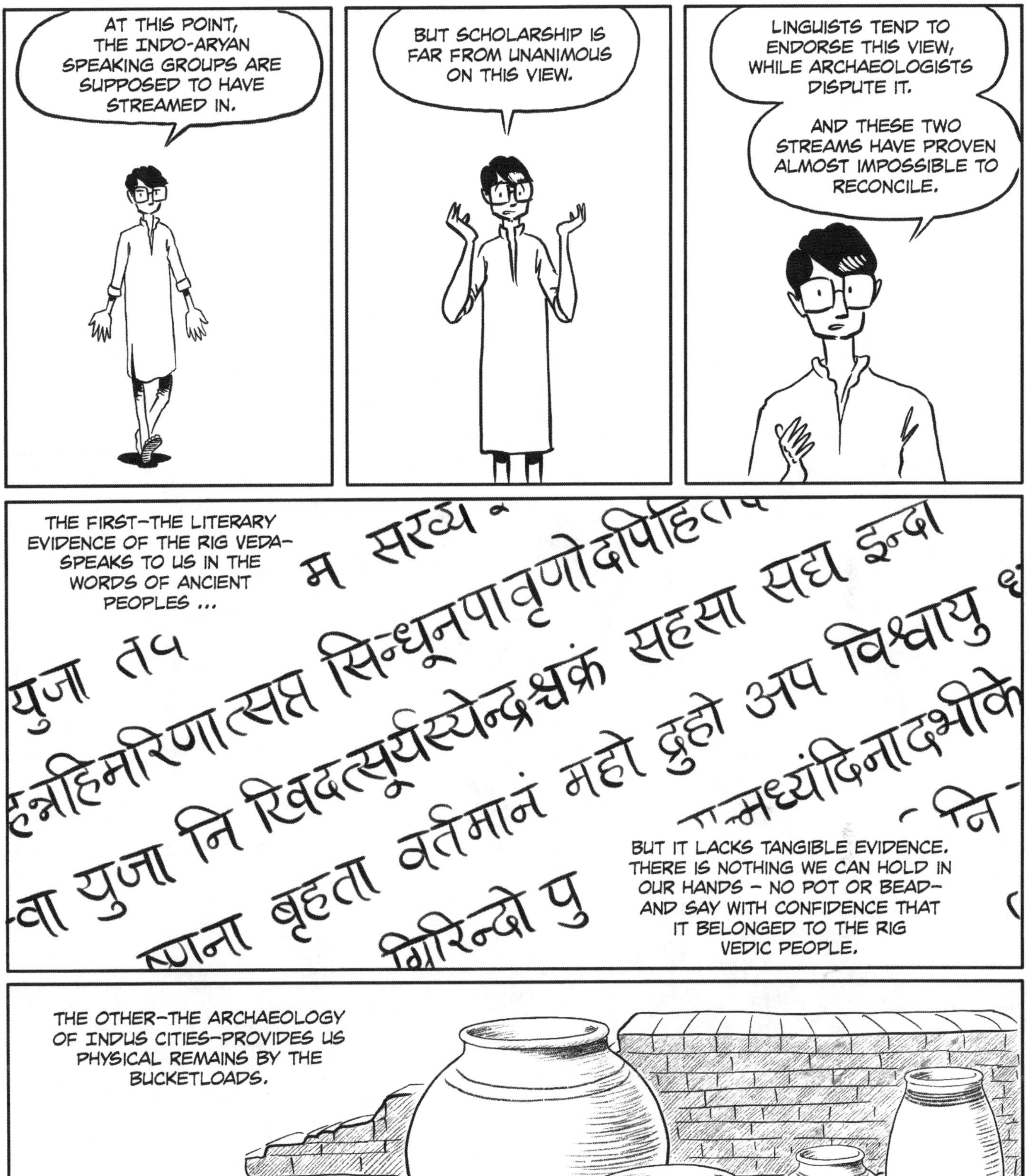
AT THIS POINT, THE INDO-ARYAN SPEAKING GROUPS ARE SUPPOSED TO HAVE STREAMED IN.
BUT SCHOLARSHIP IS FAR FROM UNANIMOUS ON THIS VIEW.
LINGUISTS TEND TO ENDORSE THIS VIEW, WHILE ARCHAEOLOGISTS DISPUTE IT.
AND THESE TWO STREAMS HAVE PROVEN ALMOST IMPOSSIBLE TO RECONCILE.
THE FIRST—THE LITERARY EVIDENCE OF THE RIG VEDA—SPEAKS TO US IN THE WORDS OF ANCIENT PEOPLES ...
BUT IT LACKS TANGIBLE EVIDENCE. THERE IS NOTHING WE CAN HOLD IN OUR HANDS – NO POT OR BEAD– AND SAY WITH CONFIDENCE THAT IT BELONGED TO THE RIG VEDIC PEOPLE.
THE OTHER—THE ARCHAEOLOGY OF INDUS CITIES—PROVIDES US PHYSICAL REMAINS BY THE BUCKETLOADS.
BUT IT IS ENTIRELY MUTE. IT TELLS US NOTHING CONCRETE ABOUT PEOPLE'S THOUGHTS, IDEAS OR BELIEFS, NOR THE LANGUAGES THEY SPOKE.

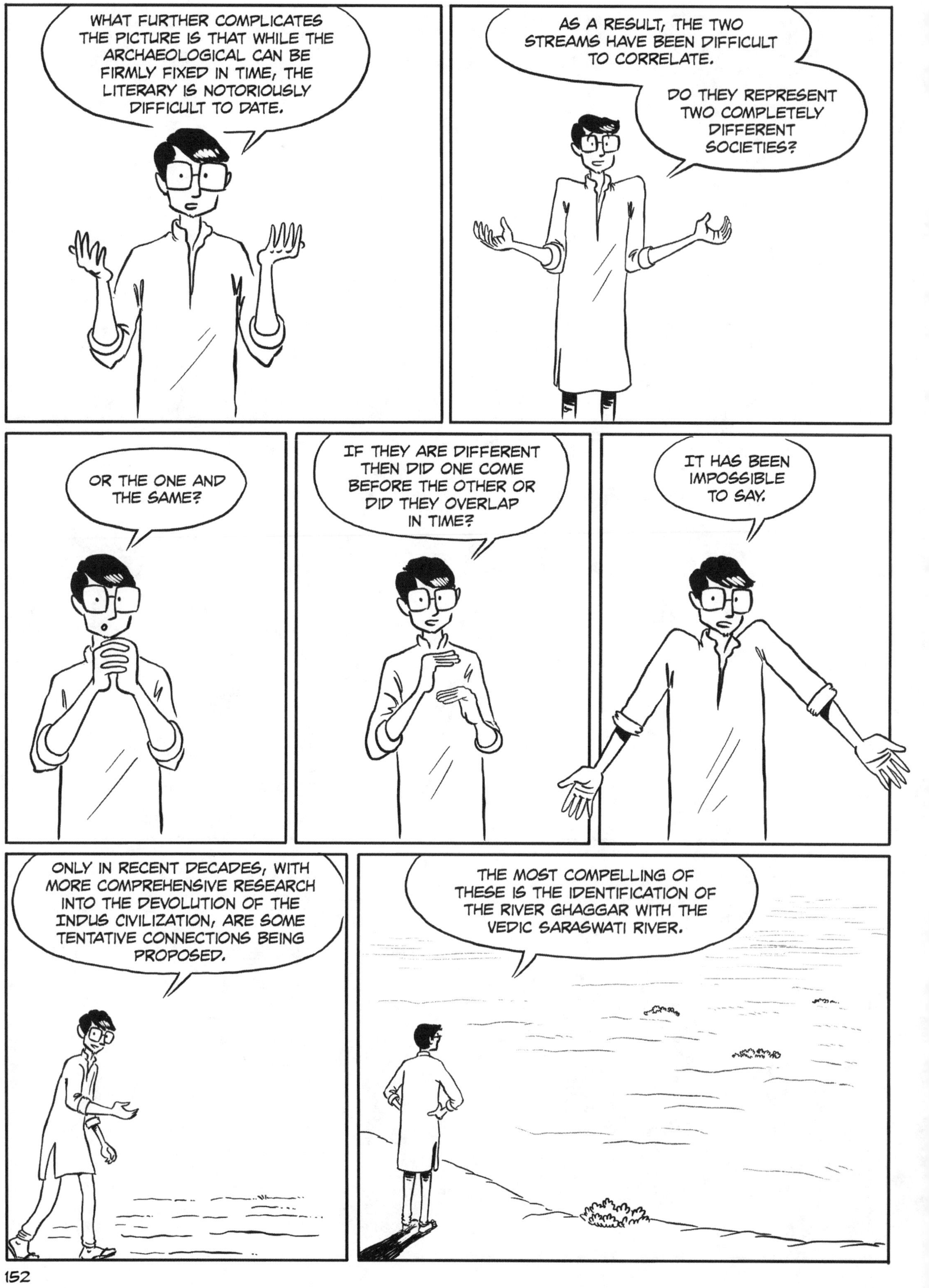
WHAT FURTHER COMPLICATES THE PICTURE IS THAT WHILE THE ARCHAEOLOGICAL CAN BE FIRMLY FIXED IN TIME, THE LITERARY IS NOTORIOUSLY DIFFICULT TO DATE.
AS A RESULT, THE TWO STREAMS HAVE BEEN DIFFICULT TO CORRELATE.
DO THEY REPRESENT TWO COMPLETELY DIFFERENT SOCIETIES?
OR THE ONE AND THE SAME?
IF THEY ARE DIFFERENT THEN DID ONE COME BEFORE THE OTHER OR DID THEY OVERLAP IN TIME?
IT HAS BEEN IMPOSSIBLE TO SAY.
ONLY IN RECENT DECADES, WITH MORE COMPREHENSIVE RESEARCH INTO THE DEVOLUTION OF THE INDUS CIVILIZATION, ARE SOME TENTATIVE CONNECTIONS BEING PROPOSED.
THE MOST COMPELLING OF THESE IS THE IDENTIFICATION OF THE RIVER GHAGGAR WITH THE VEDIC SARASWATI RIVER.

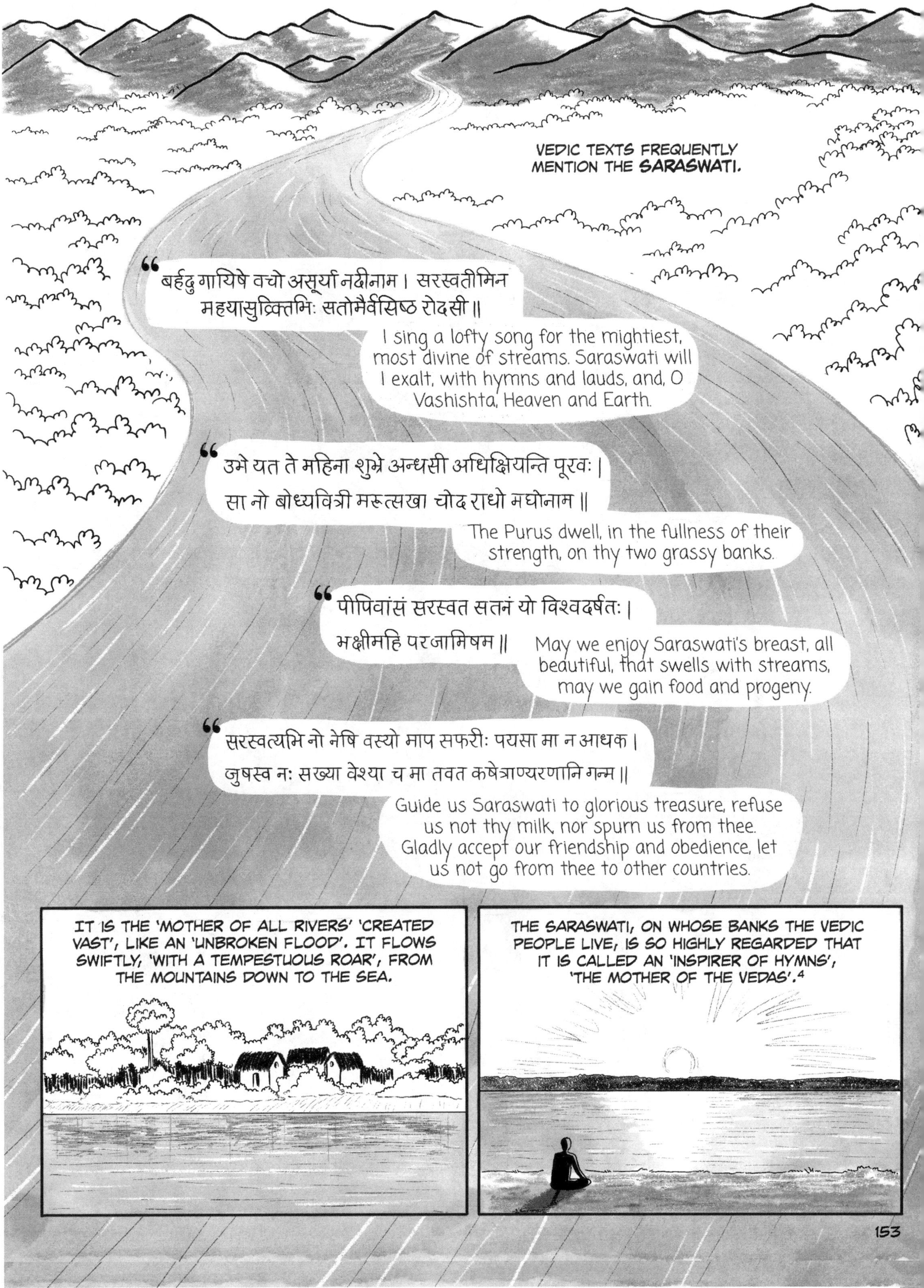
VEDIC TEXTS FREQUENTLY MENTION THE **SARASWATI.**
“बर्हदु गायिषे वचो असूर्या नदीनाम । सरस्वतीमिन महयासुव्क्तिभि: सतोमैर्वसिष्ठ रोदसी ॥
I sing a lofty song for the mightiest, most divine of streams. Saraswati will I exalt, with hymns and lauds, and, O Vashishta, Heaven and Earth.
“उभे यत ते महिना शुभ्रे अन्धसी अधिक्षियन्ति पूरवः ।
सा नो बोध्यवित्री मरूत्सखा चोद राधो मघोनाम ॥
The Purus dwell, in the fullness of their strength, on thy two grassy banks.
“पीपिवांसं सरस्वत सतनं यो विश्वदर्षतः ।
भक्षीमहि परजामिषम ॥
May we enjoy Saraswati's breast, all beautiful, that swells with streams, may we gain food and progeny.
“सरस्वत्यभि नो नेषि वस्यो माप सफरीः पयसा मा न आधक ।
जुषस्व नः सख्या वेश्या च मा तवत कषेत्राण्यरणानि गन्म ॥
Guide us Saraswati to glorious treasure, refuse us not thy milk, nor spurn us from thee. Gladly accept our friendship and obedience, let us not go from thee to other countries.
IT IS THE 'MOTHER OF ALL RIVERS' 'CREATED VAST', LIKE AN 'UNBROKEN FLOOD'. IT FLOWS SWIFTLY, 'WITH A TEMPESTUOUS ROAR', FROM THE MOUNTAINS DOWN TO THE SEA.
THE SARASWATI, ON WHOSE BANKS THE VEDIC PEOPLE LIVE, IS SO HIGHLY REGARDED THAT IT IS CALLED AN 'INSPIRER OF HYMNS', 'THE MOTHER OF THE VEDAS'.[4]

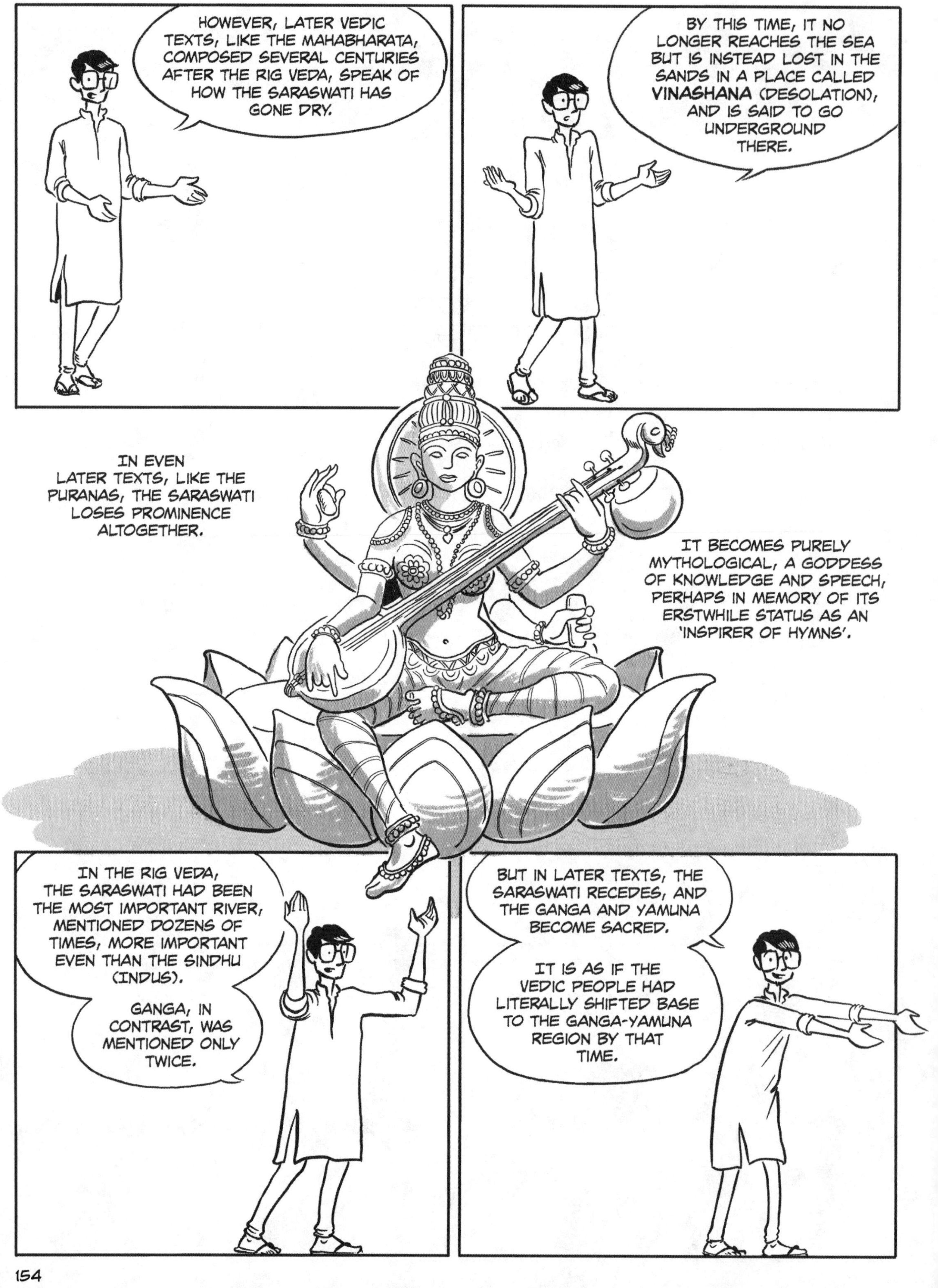
HOWEVER, LATER VEDIC TEXTS, LIKE THE MAHABHARATA, COMPOSED SEVERAL CENTURIES AFTER THE RIG VEDA, SPEAK OF HOW THE SARASWATI HAS GONE DRY.
BY THIS TIME, IT NO LONGER REACHES THE SEA BUT IS INSTEAD LOST IN THE SANDS IN A PLACE CALLED **VINASHANA** (DESOLATION), AND IS SAID TO GO UNDERGROUND THERE.
IN EVEN LATER TEXTS, LIKE THE PURANAS, THE SARASWATI LOSES PROMINENCE ALTOGETHER.
IT BECOMES PURELY MYTHOLOGICAL, A GODDESS OF KNOWLEDGE AND SPEECH, PERHAPS IN MEMORY OF ITS ERSTWHILE STATUS AS AN 'INSPIRER OF HYMNS'.
IN THE RIG VEDA, THE SARASWATI HAD BEEN THE MOST IMPORTANT RIVER, MENTIONED DOZENS OF TIMES, MORE IMPORTANT EVEN THAN THE SINDHU (INDUS).
GANGA, IN CONTRAST, WAS MENTIONED ONLY TWICE.
BUT IN LATER TEXTS, THE SARASWATI RECEDES, AND THE GANGA AND YAMUNA BECOME SACRED.
IT IS AS IF THE VEDIC PEOPLE HAD LITERALLY SHIFTED BASE TO THE GANGA-YAMUNA REGION BY THAT TIME.

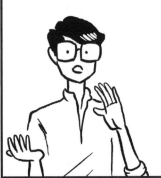

ARCHAEOLOGY TELLS US AN ALMOST IDENTICAL STORY FOR THE RIVER GHAGGAR.
IT TOO HAD ONCE BEEN A MASSIVE RIVER FLOWING FROM THE MOUNTAINS TO THE SEA.
IT TOO SUPPORTED HUNDREDS OF SETTLEMENTS.
AND IT TOO BECAME DEPLETED AT SOME POINT AND WAS LOST ... LITERALLY IN THE SANDS.
EVEN TODAY SATELLITE IMAGES SHOW THE DRY BED OF THE GHAGGAR ORIGINATING IN THE HIMALAYAS...
LAHORE
INDUS
CHOLISTAN
HARYANA
YAMUNA
DELHI
GANGA
KARACHI
JAIPUR
...UNTIL IT DISAPPEARS IN THE SANDS OF CHOLISTAN AND RAJASTHAN*...
AHMEDABAD
GUJARAT
...AND THEN RE-EMERGES ON THE OTHER SIDE.
SURAT
* A FEW VILLAGES SURVIVE IN THE REGION BY DIGGING WELLS ON THE DRY RIVER BED WHERE WATER IS STILL FOUND UNDERGROUND.
FURTHER, WHEN WE LOOK AT THE DISTRIBUTION OF ANCIENT SETTLEMENTS ALONG THIS RIVERBED ...
...WE FIND THAT THEY STEADILY SHIFT EASTWARDS OVER TIME.
JUST LIKE IN THE CASE OF THE SARASWATI.
INDUS
JHELUM
CHENAB
RAVI
BEAS
SATLUJ
GHAGGAR
YAMUNA
MODERN INTERNATIONAL BORDER
EARLY HARAPPAN
3200 – 2800 BCE
MATURE HARAPPAN
2600 – 1900 BCE
LATE HARAPPAN
1700 – 1300 BCE

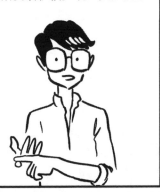

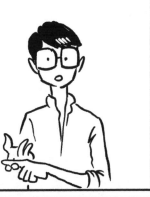

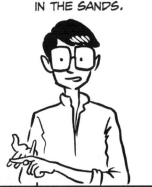

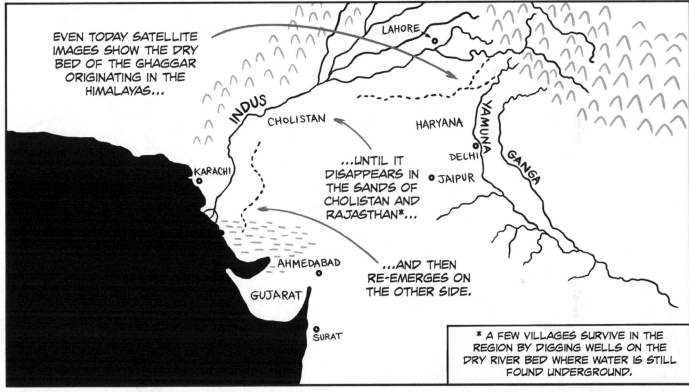

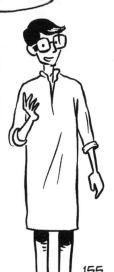

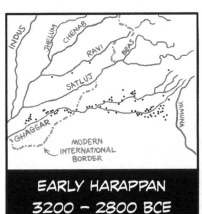

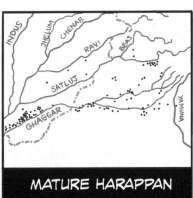

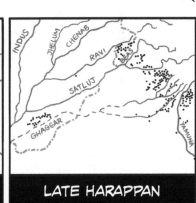

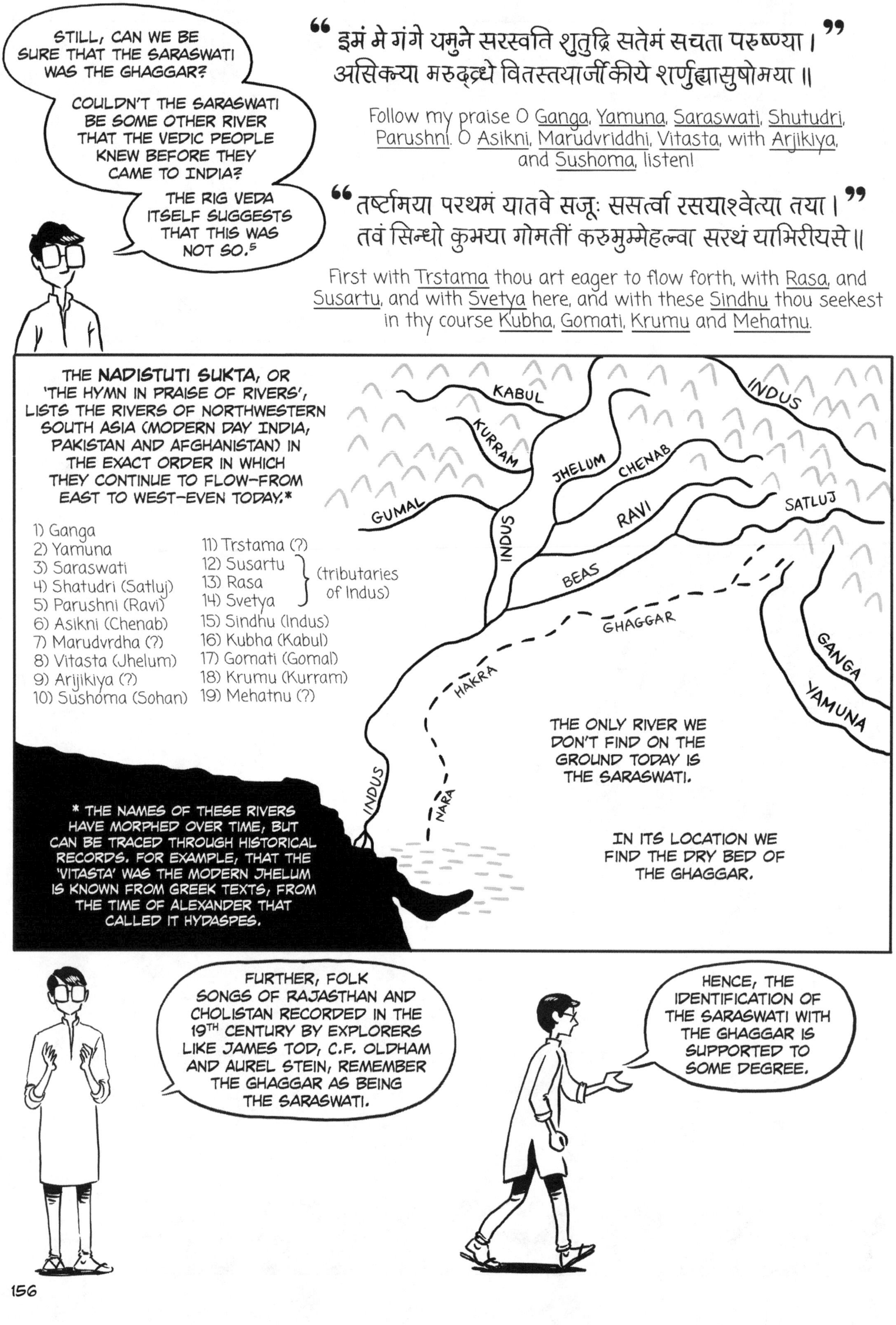
STILL, CAN WE BE SURE THAT THE SARASWATI WAS THE GHAGGAR?
COULDN'T THE SARASWATI BE SOME OTHER RIVER THAT THE VEDIC PEOPLE KNEW BEFORE THEY CAME TO INDIA?
THE RIG VEDA ITSELF SUGGESTS THAT THIS WAS NOT SO.[5]
"इमं मे गंगे यमुने सरस्वति शुतुद्रि सतेमं सचता परुष्ण्या ।
असिक्न्या मरुद्वृधे वितस्तयार्जीकीये शर्णुह्यासुषोमया ॥"
Follow my praise O Ganga, Yamuna, Saraswati, Shutudri, Parushni. O Asikni, Marudvriddhi, Vitasta, with Arjikiya, and Sushoma, listen!
"तर्ष्टामया परथमं यातवे सजूः ससर्त्वा रसयाश्वेत्या तया ।
तवं सिन्धो कुभया गोमतीं करुमुम्मेहत्न्वा सरथं याभिरीयसे ॥"
First with Trstama thou art eager to flow forth, with Rasa, and Susartu, and with Svetya here, and with these Sindhu thou seekest in thy course Kubha, Gomati, Krumu and Mehatnu.
THE NADISTUTI SUKTA, OR 'THE HYMN IN PRAISE OF RIVERS', LISTS THE RIVERS OF NORTHWESTERN SOUTH ASIA (MODERN DAY INDIA, PAKISTAN AND AFGHANISTAN) IN THE EXACT ORDER IN WHICH THEY CONTINUE TO FLOW—FROM EAST TO WEST—EVEN TODAY.*
1) Ganga
2) Yamuna
3) Saraswati
4) Shatudri (Satluj)
5) Parushni (Ravi)
6) Asikni (Chenab)
7) Marudvrdha (?)
8) Vitasta (Jhelum)
9) Arijikiya (?)
10) Sushoma (Sohan)
11) Trstama (?)
12) Susartu
13) Rasa
14) Svetya
(tributaries of Indus)
15) Sindhu (Indus)
16) Kubha (Kabul)
17) Gomati (Gomal)
18) Krumu (Kurram)
19) Mehatnu (?)
KABUL
KURRAM
INDUS
GUMAL
JHELUM
CHENAB
RAVI
SATLUJ
BEAS
GHAGGAR
HAKRA
NARA
GANGA
YAMUNA
THE ONLY RIVER WE DON'T FIND ON THE GROUND TODAY IS THE SARASWATI.
IN ITS LOCATION WE FIND THE DRY BED OF THE GHAGGAR.
* THE NAMES OF THESE RIVERS HAVE MORPHED OVER TIME, BUT CAN BE TRACED THROUGH HISTORICAL RECORDS. FOR EXAMPLE, THAT THE 'VITASTA' WAS THE MODERN JHELUM IS KNOWN FROM GREEK TEXTS, FROM THE TIME OF ALEXANDER THAT CALLED IT HYDASPES.
FURTHER, FOLK SONGS OF RAJASTHAN AND CHOLISTAN RECORDED IN THE 19TH CENTURY BY EXPLORERS LIKE JAMES TOD, C.F. OLDHAM AND AUREL STEIN, REMEMBER THE GHAGGAR AS BEING THE SARASWATI.
HENCE, THE IDENTIFICATION OF THE SARASWATI WITH THE GHAGGAR IS SUPPORTED TO SOME DEGREE.

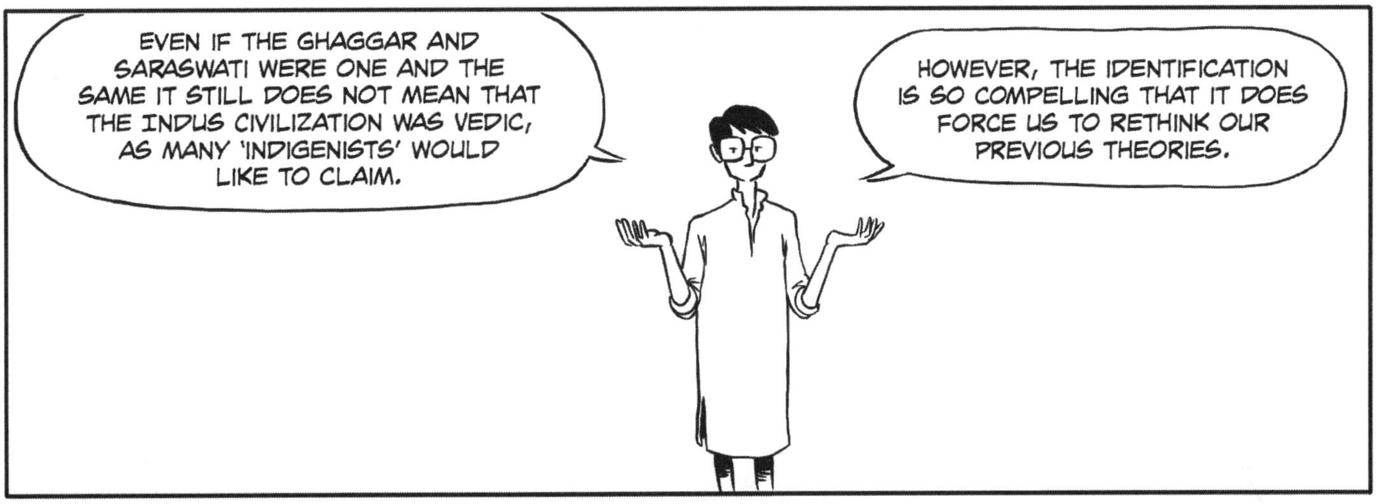
EVEN IF THE GHAGGAR AND SARASWATI WERE ONE AND THE SAME IT STILL DOES NOT MEAN THAT THE INDUS CIVILIZATION WAS VEDIC, AS MANY 'INDIGENISTS' WOULD LIKE TO CLAIM.
HOWEVER, THE IDENTIFICATION IS SO COMPELLING THAT IT DOES FORCE US TO RETHINK OUR PREVIOUS THEORIES.

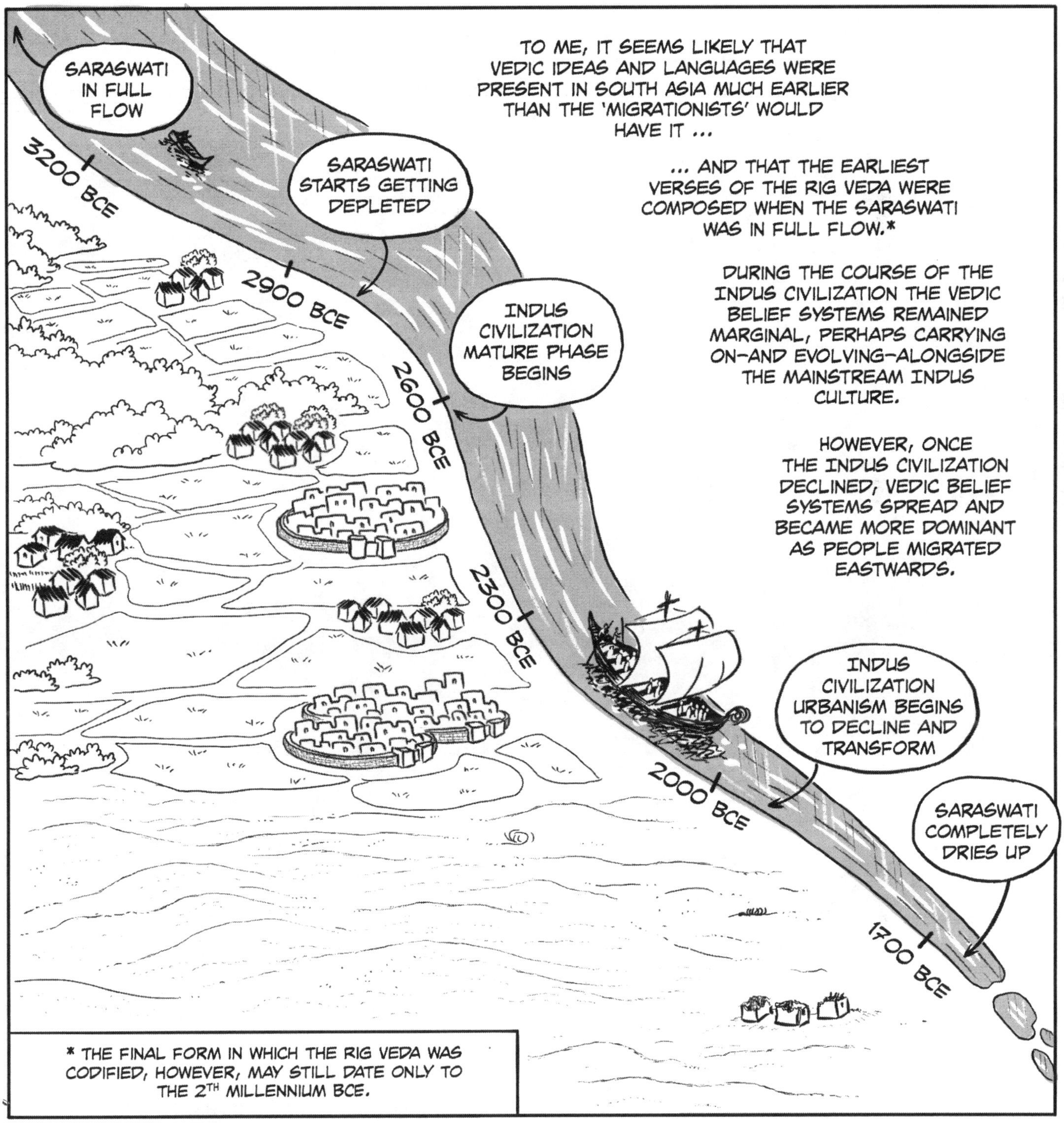
SARASWATI IN FULL FLOW
3200 BCE
SARASWATI STARTS GETTING DEPLETED
2900 BCE
INDUS CIVILIZATION MATURE PHASE BEGINS
2600 BCE
2300 BCE
INDUS CIVILIZATION URBANISM BEGINS TO DECLINE AND TRANSFORM
2000 BCE
SARASWATI COMPLETELY DRIES UP
1700 BCE
TO ME, IT SEEMS LIKELY THAT VEDIC IDEAS AND LANGUAGES WERE PRESENT IN SOUTH ASIA MUCH EARLIER THAN THE 'MIGRATIONISTS' WOULD HAVE IT ...
... AND THAT THE EARLIEST VERSES OF THE RIG VEDA WERE COMPOSED WHEN THE SARASWATI WAS IN FULL FLOW.*
DURING THE COURSE OF THE INDUS CIVILIZATION THE VEDIC BELIEF SYSTEMS REMAINED MARGINAL, PERHAPS CARRYING ON—AND EVOLVING—ALONGSIDE THE MAINSTREAM INDUS CULTURE.
HOWEVER, ONCE THE INDUS CIVILIZATION DECLINED, VEDIC BELIEF SYSTEMS SPREAD AND BECAME MORE DOMINANT AS PEOPLE MIGRATED EASTWARDS.
* THE FINAL FORM IN WHICH THE RIG VEDA WAS CODIFIED, HOWEVER, MAY STILL DATE ONLY TO THE 2TH MILLENNIUM BCE.

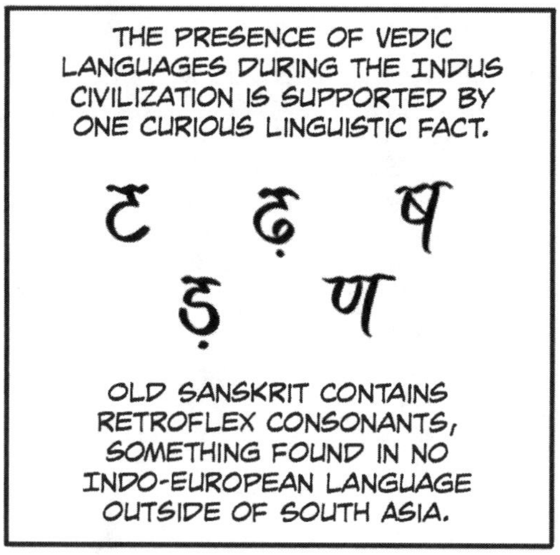
THE PRESENCE OF VEDIC LANGUAGES DURING THE INDUS CIVILIZATION IS SUPPORTED BY ONE CURIOUS LINGUISTIC FACT.
ट ढ़ ष
ड़ ण
OLD SANSKRIT CONTAINS RETROFLEX CONSONANTS, SOMETHING FOUND IN NO INDO-EUROPEAN LANGUAGE OUTSIDE OF SOUTH ASIA.

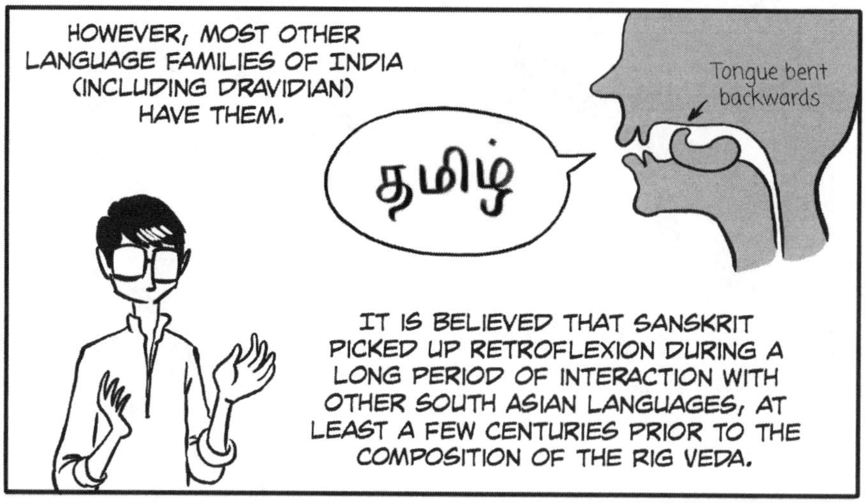
HOWEVER, MOST OTHER LANGUAGE FAMILIES OF INDIA (INCLUDING DRAVIDIAN) HAVE THEM.
தமிழ்
Tongue bent backwards
IT IS BELIEVED THAT SANSKRIT PICKED UP RETROFLEXION DURING A LONG PERIOD OF INTERACTION WITH OTHER SOUTH ASIAN LANGUAGES, AT LEAST A FEW CENTURIES PRIOR TO THE COMPOSITION OF THE RIG VEDA.

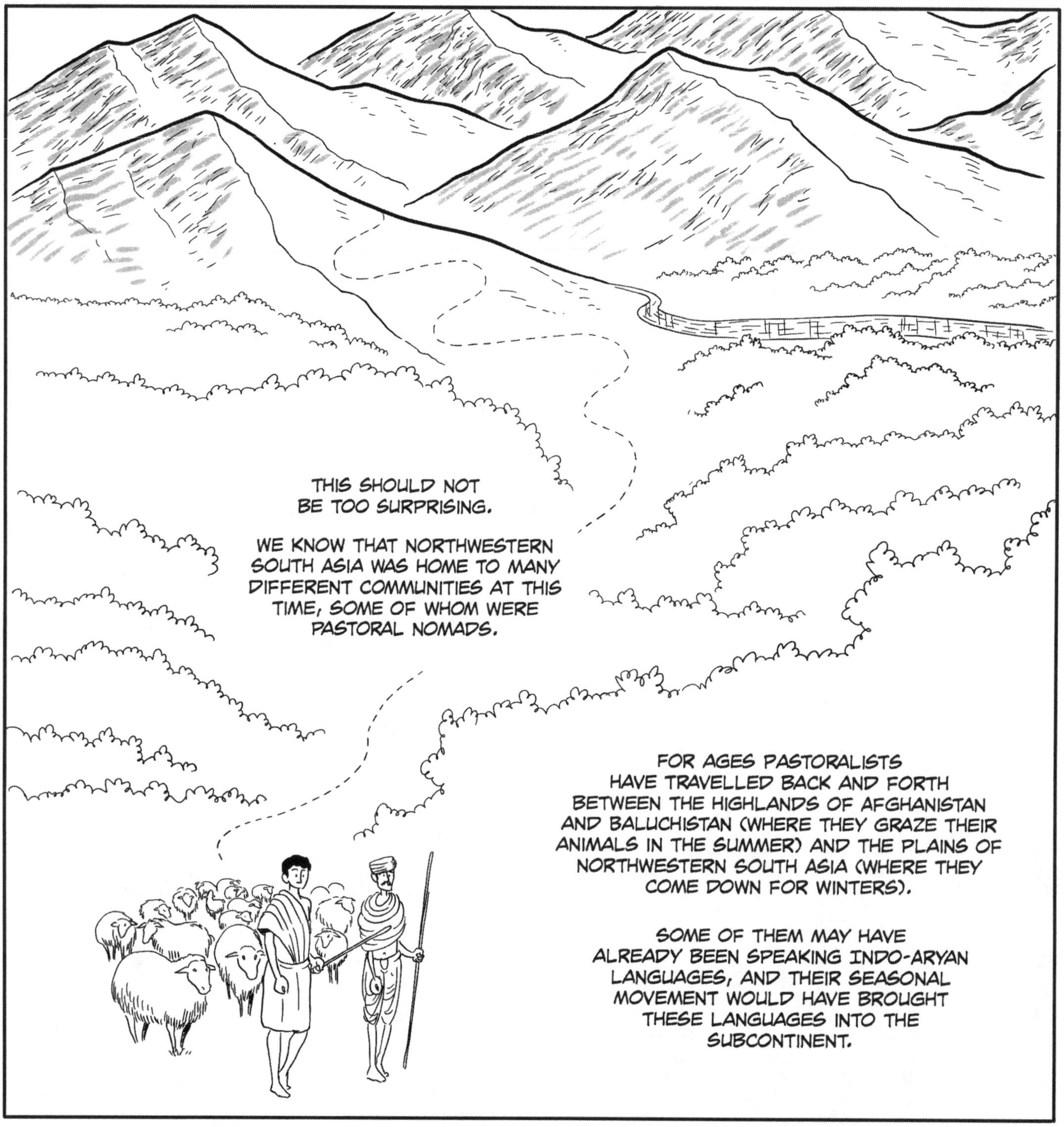
THIS SHOULD NOT BE TOO SURPRISING.
WE KNOW THAT NORTHWESTERN SOUTH ASIA WAS HOME TO MANY DIFFERENT COMMUNITIES AT THIS TIME, SOME OF WHOM WERE PASTORAL NOMADS.
FOR AGES PASTORALISTS HAVE TRAVELLED BACK AND FORTH BETWEEN THE HIGHLANDS OF AFGHANISTAN AND BALUCHISTAN (WHERE THEY GRAZE THEIR ANIMALS IN THE SUMMER) AND THE PLAINS OF NORTHWESTERN SOUTH ASIA (WHERE THEY COME DOWN FOR WINTERS).
SOME OF THEM MAY HAVE ALREADY BEEN SPEAKING INDO-ARYAN LANGUAGES, AND THEIR SEASONAL MOVEMENT WOULD HAVE BROUGHT THESE LANGUAGES INTO THE SUBCONTINENT.

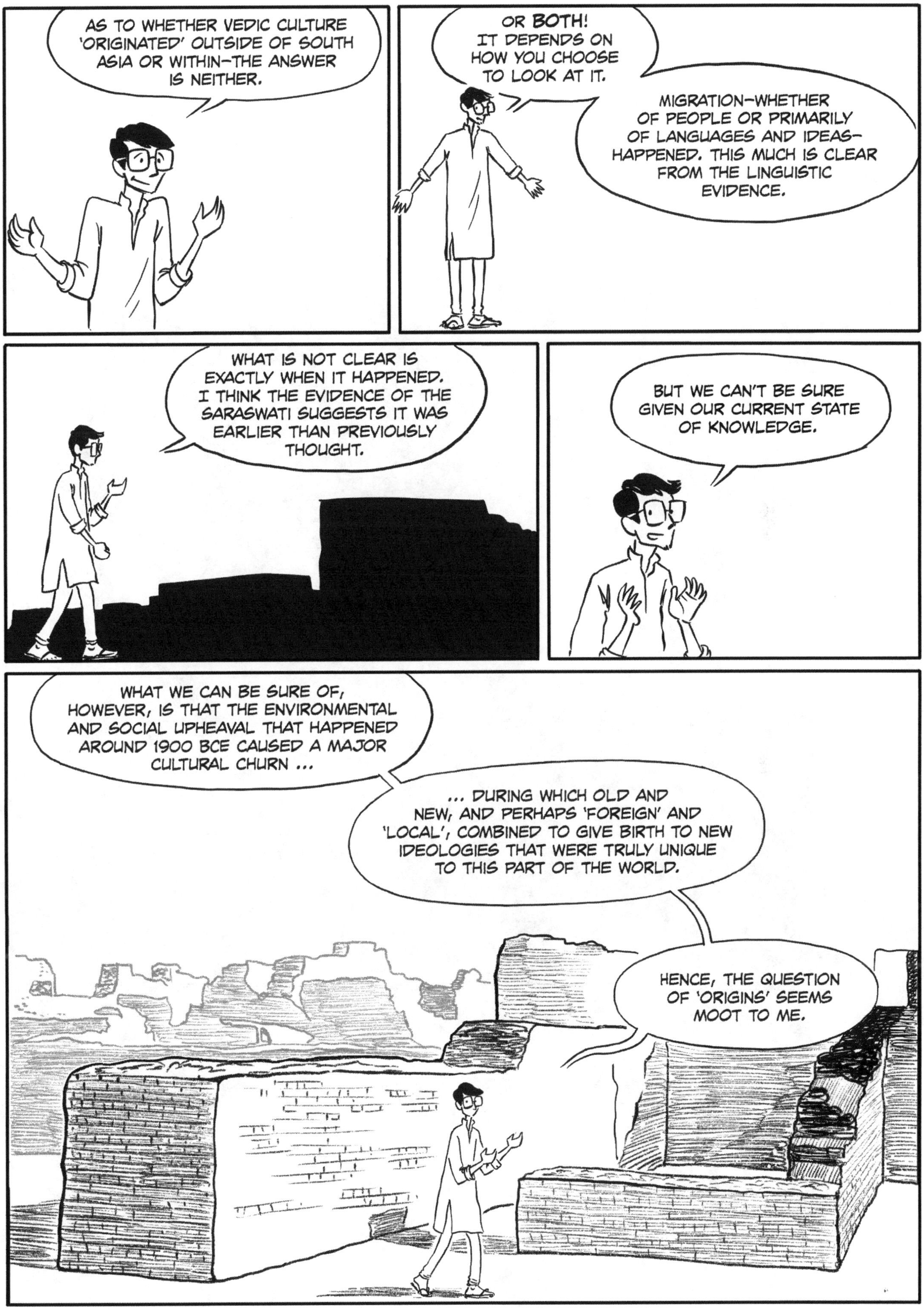
AS TO WHETHER VEDIC CULTURE 'ORIGINATED' OUTSIDE OF SOUTH ASIA OR WITHIN—THE ANSWER IS NEITHER.
OR BOTH! IT DEPENDS ON HOW YOU CHOOSE TO LOOK AT IT.
MIGRATION—WHETHER OF PEOPLE OR PRIMARILY OF LANGUAGES AND IDEAS—HAPPENED. THIS MUCH IS CLEAR FROM THE LINGUISTIC EVIDENCE.
WHAT IS NOT CLEAR IS EXACTLY WHEN IT HAPPENED. I THINK THE EVIDENCE OF THE SARASWATI SUGGESTS IT WAS EARLIER THAN PREVIOUSLY THOUGHT.
BUT WE CAN'T BE SURE GIVEN OUR CURRENT STATE OF KNOWLEDGE.
WHAT WE CAN BE SURE OF, HOWEVER, IS THAT THE ENVIRONMENTAL AND SOCIAL UPHEAVAL THAT HAPPENED AROUND 1900 BCE CAUSED A MAJOR CULTURAL CHURN ...
... DURING WHICH OLD AND NEW, AND PERHAPS 'FOREIGN' AND 'LOCAL', COMBINED TO GIVE BIRTH TO NEW IDEOLOGIES THAT WERE TRULY UNIQUE TO THIS PART OF THE WORLD.
HENCE, THE QUESTION OF 'ORIGINS' SEEMS MOOT TO ME.

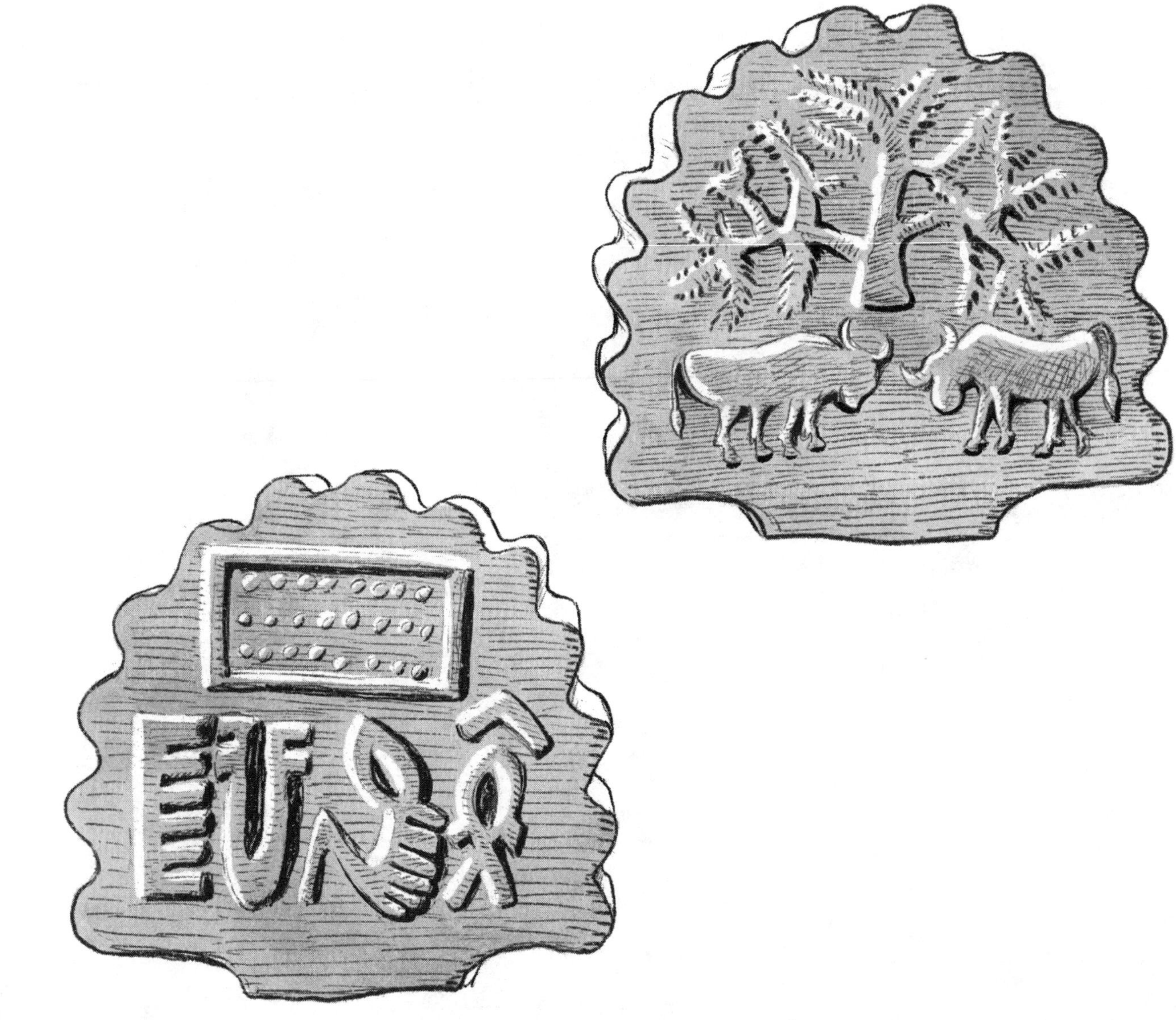
0
1
2
3cm

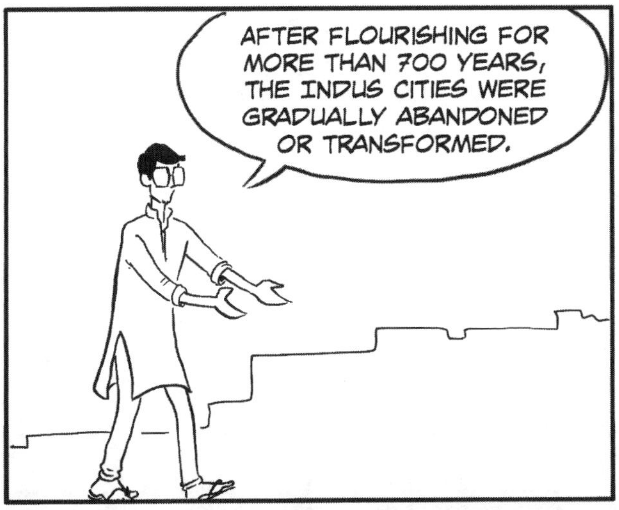
AFTER FLOURISHING FOR MORE THAN 700 YEARS, THE INDUS CITIES WERE GRADUALLY ABANDONED OR TRANSFORMED.

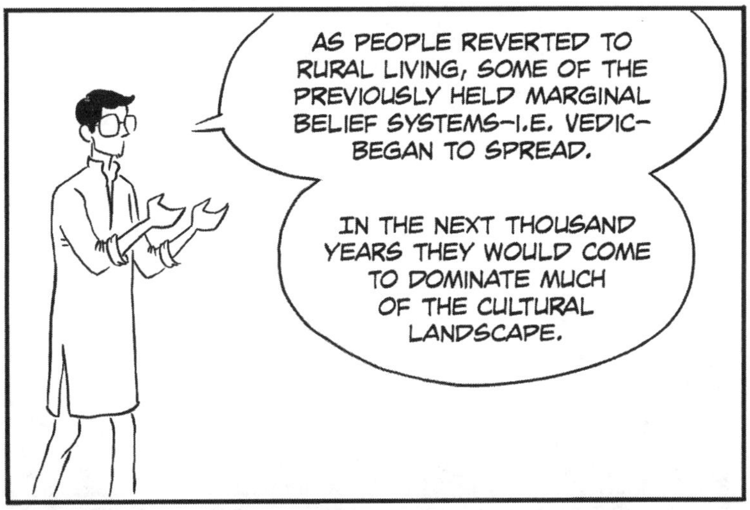
AS PEOPLE REVERTED TO RURAL LIVING, SOME OF THE PREVIOUSLY HELD MARGINAL BELIEF SYSTEMS—I.E. VEDIC—BEGAN TO SPREAD.
IN THE NEXT THOUSAND YEARS THEY WOULD COME TO DOMINATE MUCH OF THE CULTURAL LANDSCAPE.

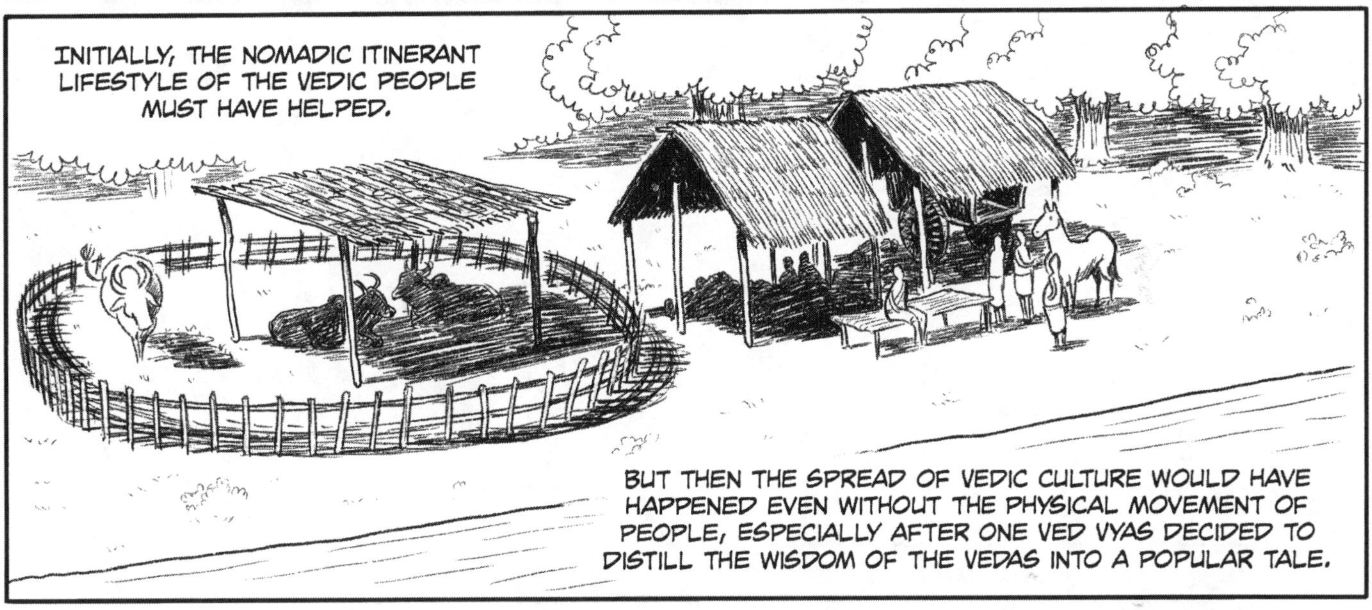
INITIALLY, THE NOMADIC ITINERANT LIFESTYLE OF THE VEDIC PEOPLE MUST HAVE HELPED.
BUT THEN THE SPREAD OF VEDIC CULTURE WOULD HAVE HAPPENED EVEN WITHOUT THE PHYSICAL MOVEMENT OF PEOPLE, ESPECIALLY AFTER ONE VED VYAS DECIDED TO DISTILL THE WISDOM OF THE VEDAS INTO A POPULAR TALE.

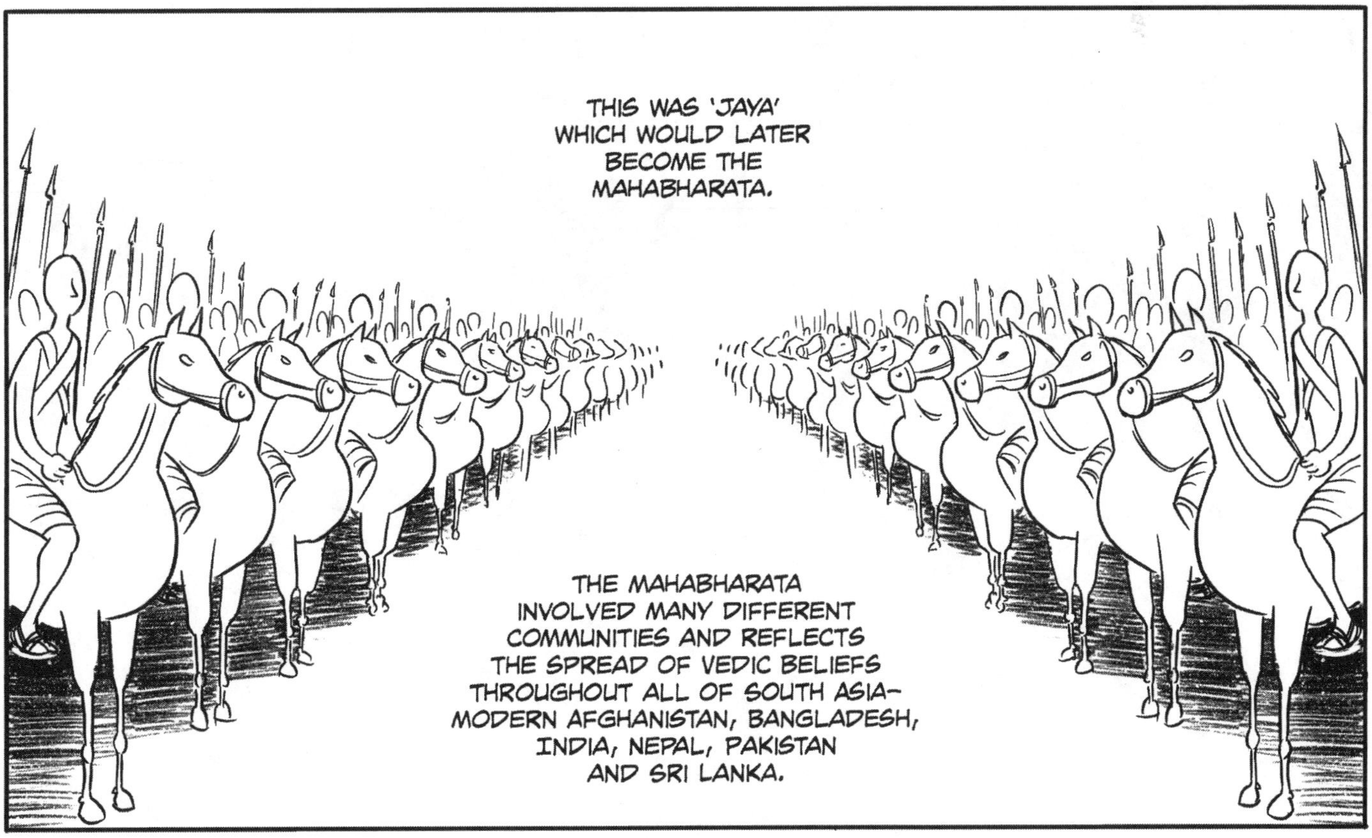
THIS WAS 'JAYA' WHICH WOULD LATER BECOME THE MAHABHARATA.
THE MAHABHARATA INVOLVED MANY DIFFERENT COMMUNITIES AND REFLECTS THE SPREAD OF VEDIC BELIEFS THROUGHOUT ALL OF SOUTH ASIA—MODERN AFGHANISTAN, BANGLADESH, INDIA, NEPAL, PAKISTAN AND SRI LANKA.

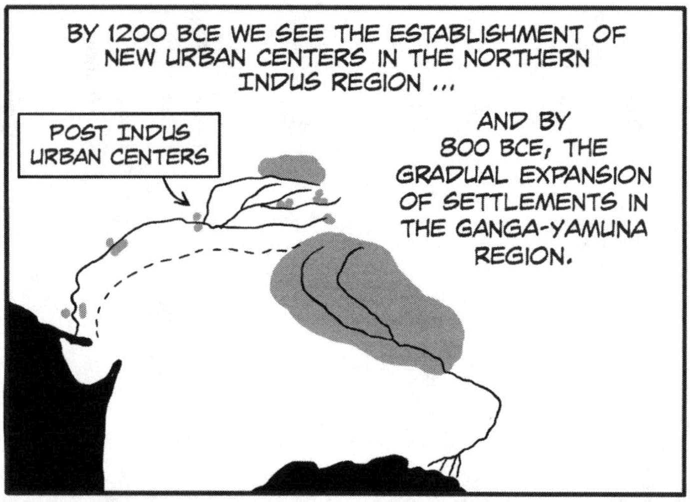
BY 1200 BCE WE SEE THE ESTABLISHMENT OF NEW URBAN CENTERS IN THE NORTHERN INDUS REGION ...
POST INDUS URBAN CENTERS
AND BY 800 BCE, THE GRADUAL EXPANSION OF SETTLEMENTS IN THE GANGA-YAMUNA REGION.

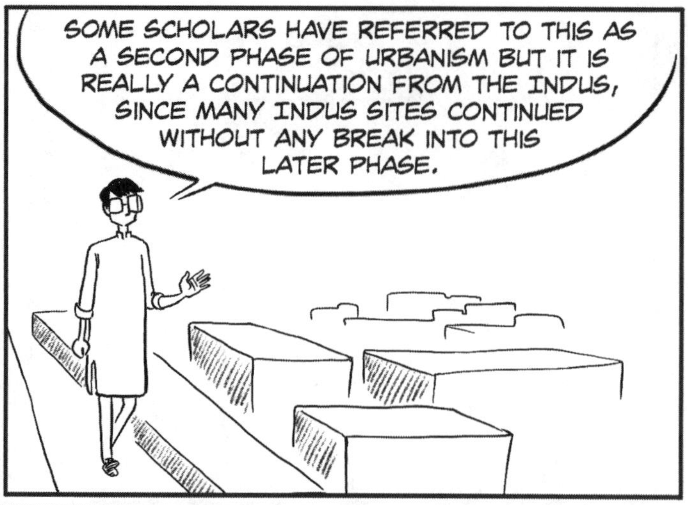
SOME SCHOLARS HAVE REFERRED TO THIS AS A SECOND PHASE OF URBANISM BUT IT IS REALLY A CONTINUATION FROM THE INDUS, SINCE MANY INDUS SITES CONTINUED WITHOUT ANY BREAK INTO THIS LATER PHASE.

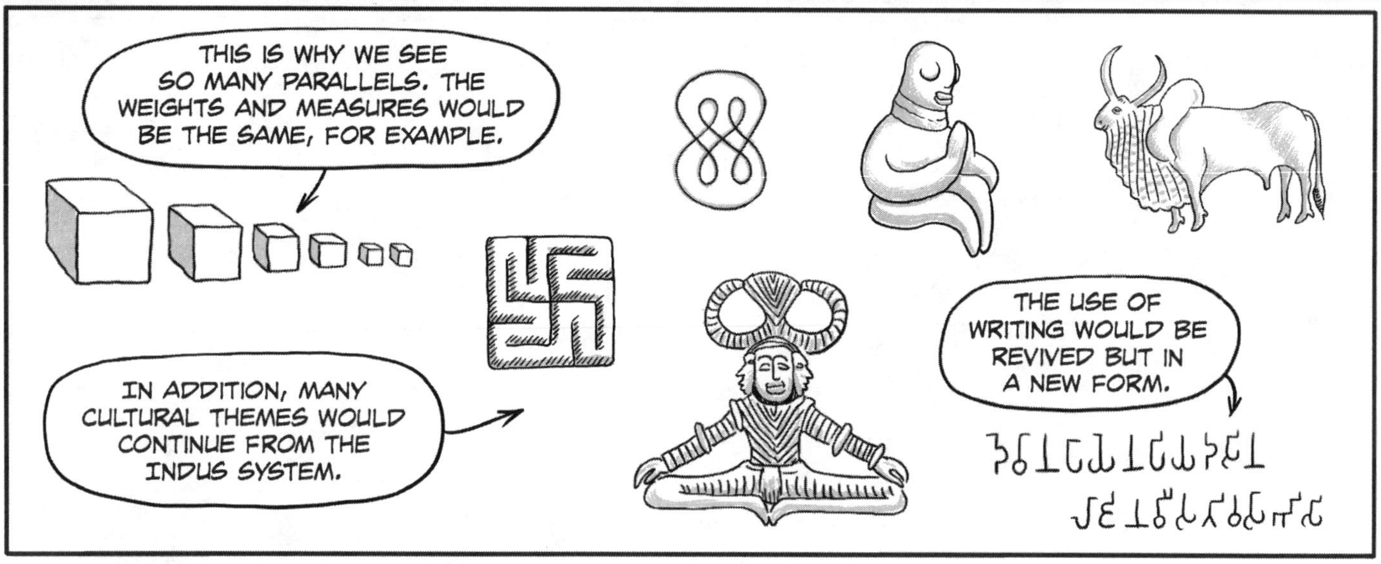
THIS IS WHY WE SEE SO MANY PARALLELS. THE WEIGHTS AND MEASURES WOULD BE THE SAME, FOR EXAMPLE.
IN ADDITION, MANY CULTURAL THEMES WOULD CONTINUE FROM THE INDUS SYSTEM.
THE USE OF WRITING WOULD BE REVIVED BUT IN A NEW FORM.

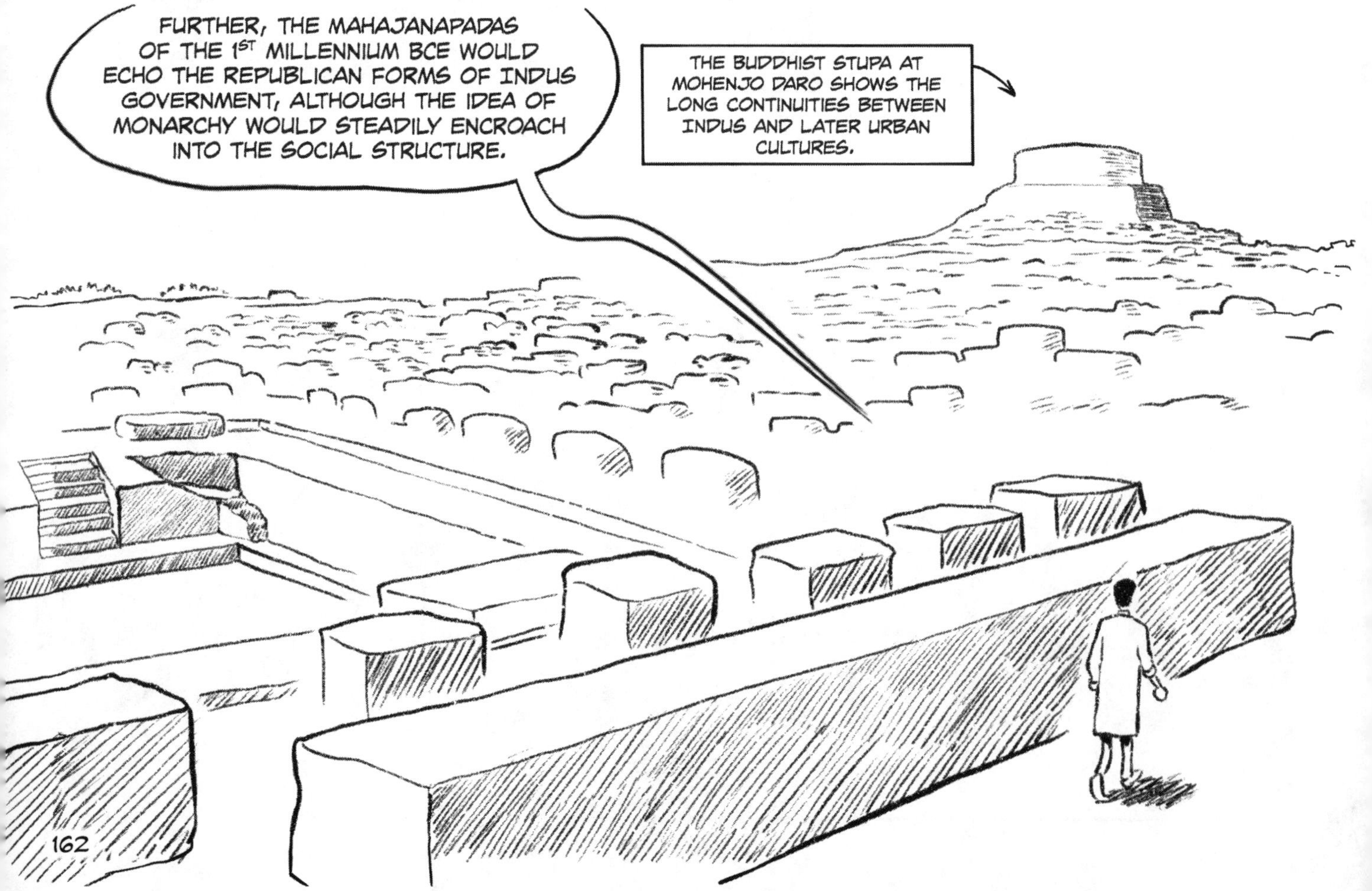
FURTHER, THE MAHAJANAPADAS OF THE 1ST MILLENNIUM BCE WOULD ECHO THE REPUBLICAN FORMS OF INDUS GOVERNMENT, ALTHOUGH THE IDEA OF MONARCHY WOULD STEADILY ENCROACH INTO THE SOCIAL STRUCTURE.
THE BUDDHIST STUPA AT MOHENJO DARO SHOWS THE LONG CONTINUITIES BETWEEN INDUS AND LATER URBAN CULTURES.

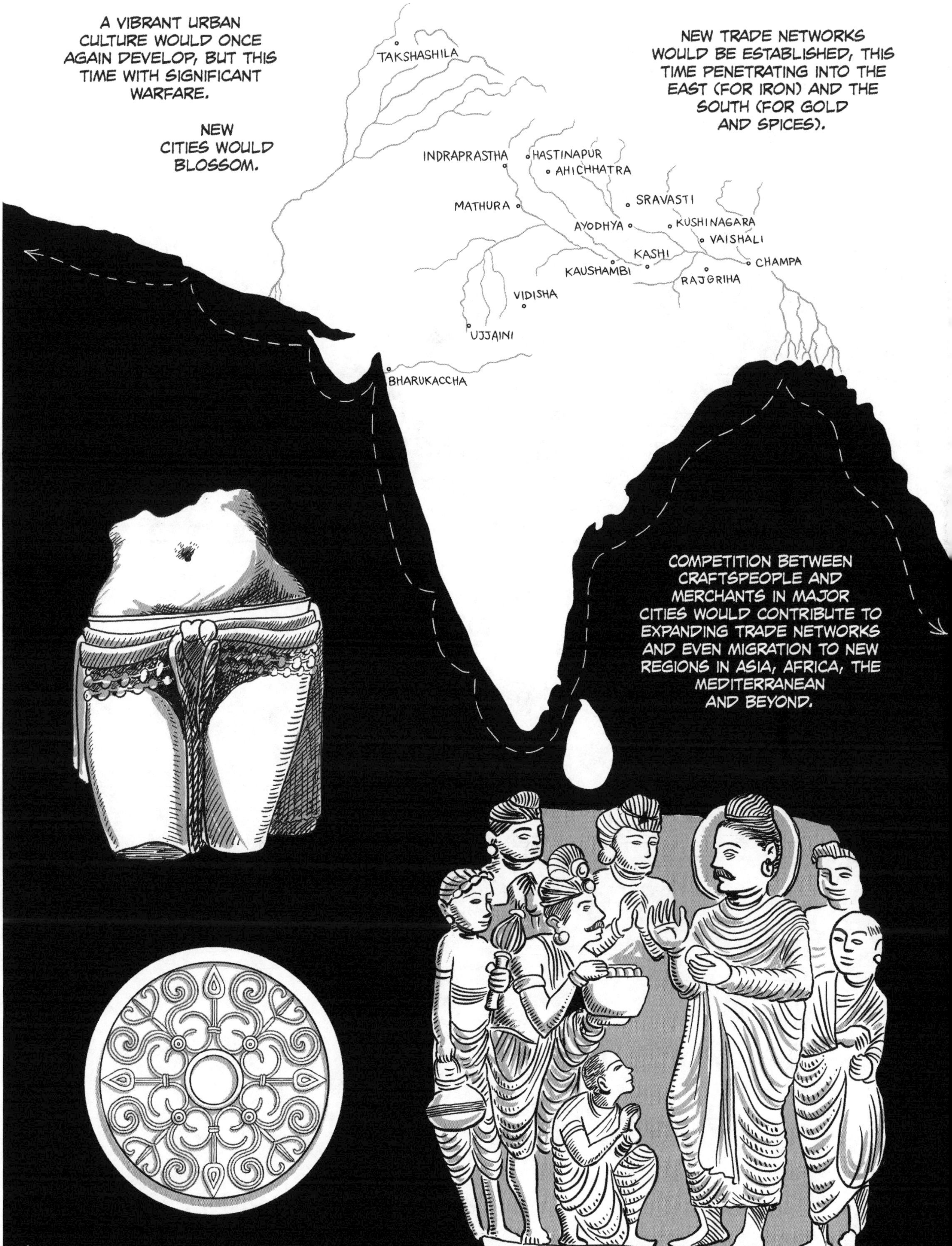
A VIBRANT URBAN CULTURE WOULD ONCE AGAIN DEVELOP, BUT THIS TIME WITH SIGNIFICANT WARFARE.
NEW CITIES WOULD BLOSSOM.
NEW TRADE NETWORKS WOULD BE ESTABLISHED, THIS TIME PENETRATING INTO THE EAST (FOR IRON) AND THE SOUTH (FOR GOLD AND SPICES).
TAKSHASHILA
INDRAPRASTHA
HASTINAPUR
AHICHHATRA
MATHURA
SRAVASTI
AYODHYA
KUSHINAGARA
VAISHALI
KASHI
KAUSHAMBI
CHAMPA
RAJGRIHA
VIDISHA
UJJAINI
BHARUKACCHA
COMPETITION BETWEEN CRAFTSPEOPLE AND MERCHANTS IN MAJOR CITIES WOULD CONTRIBUTE TO EXPANDING TRADE NETWORKS AND EVEN MIGRATION TO NEW REGIONS IN ASIA, AFRICA, THE MEDITERRANEAN AND BEYOND.

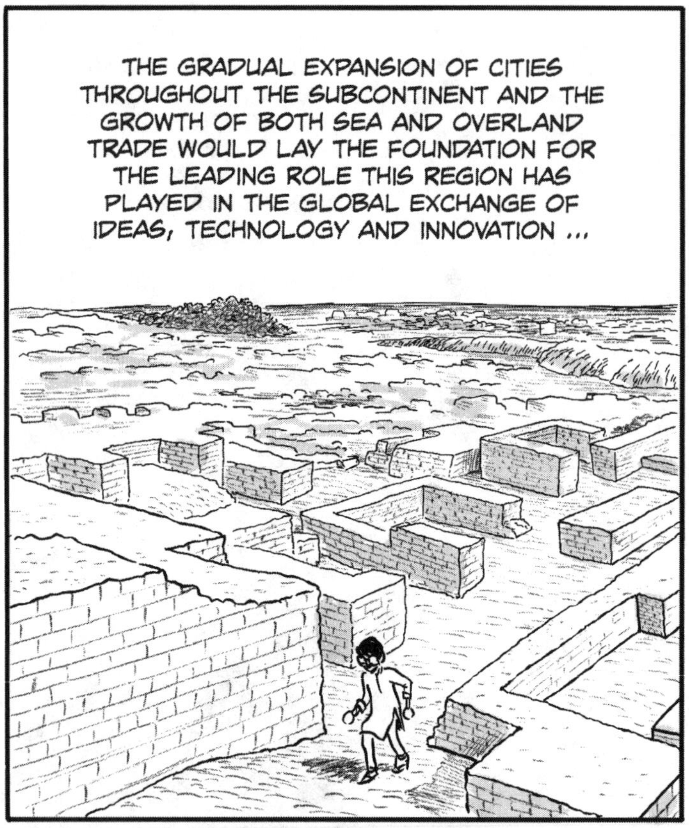
THE GRADUAL EXPANSION OF CITIES THROUGHOUT THE SUBCONTINENT AND THE GROWTH OF BOTH SEA AND OVERLAND TRADE WOULD LAY THE FOUNDATION FOR THE LEADING ROLE THIS REGION HAS PLAYED IN THE GLOBAL EXCHANGE OF IDEAS, TECHNOLOGY AND INNOVATION ...

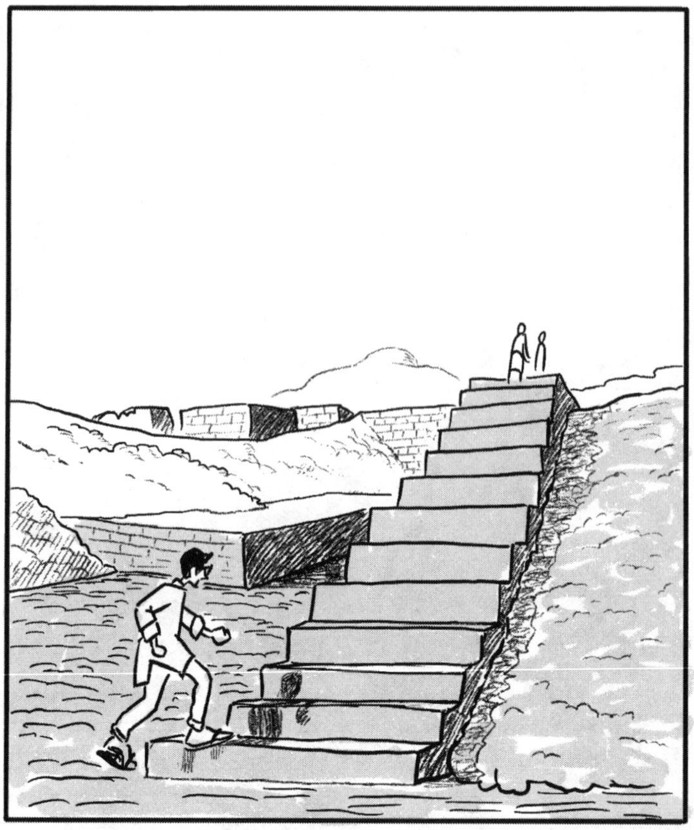

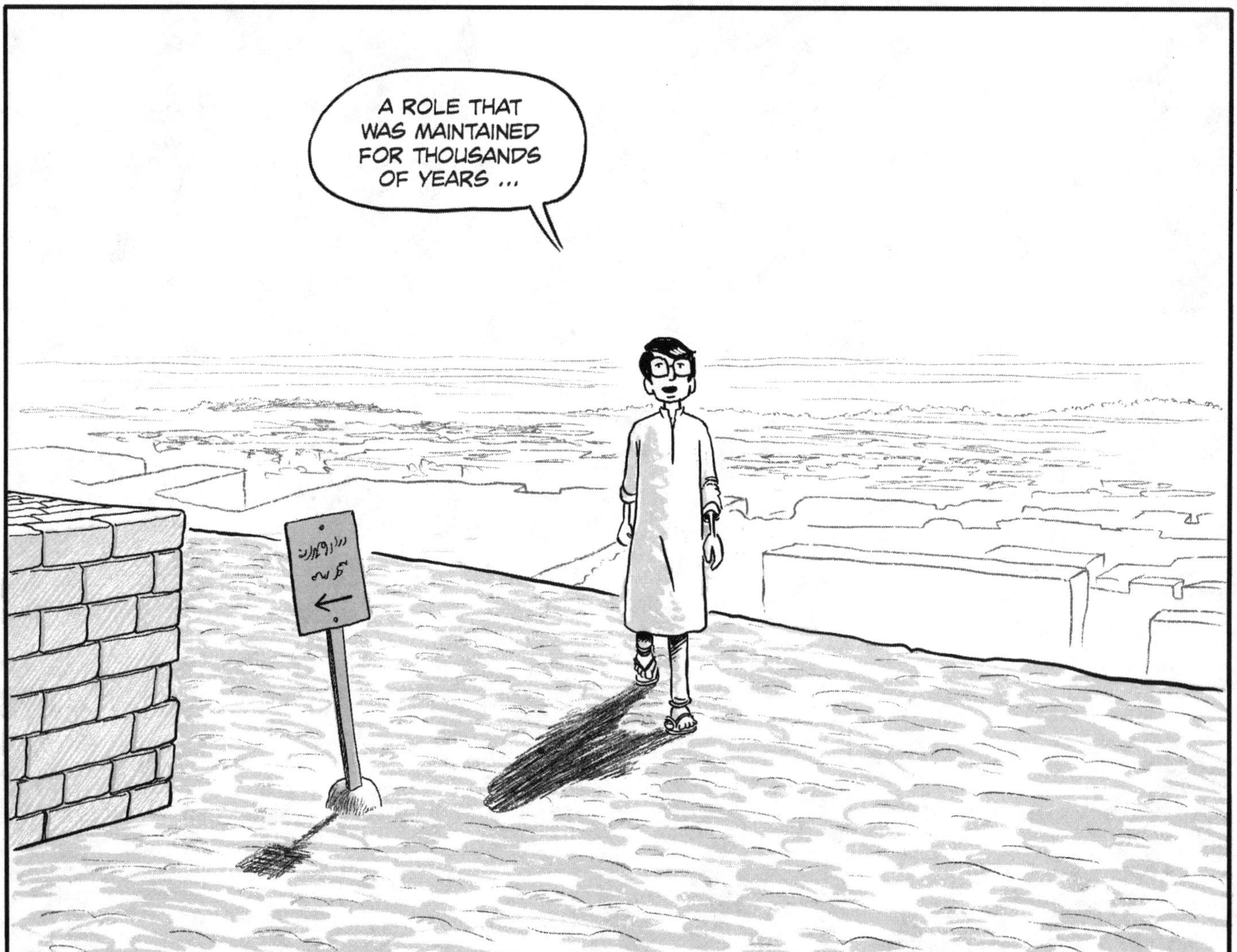
A ROLE THAT WAS MAINTAINED FOR THOUSANDS OF YEARS ...

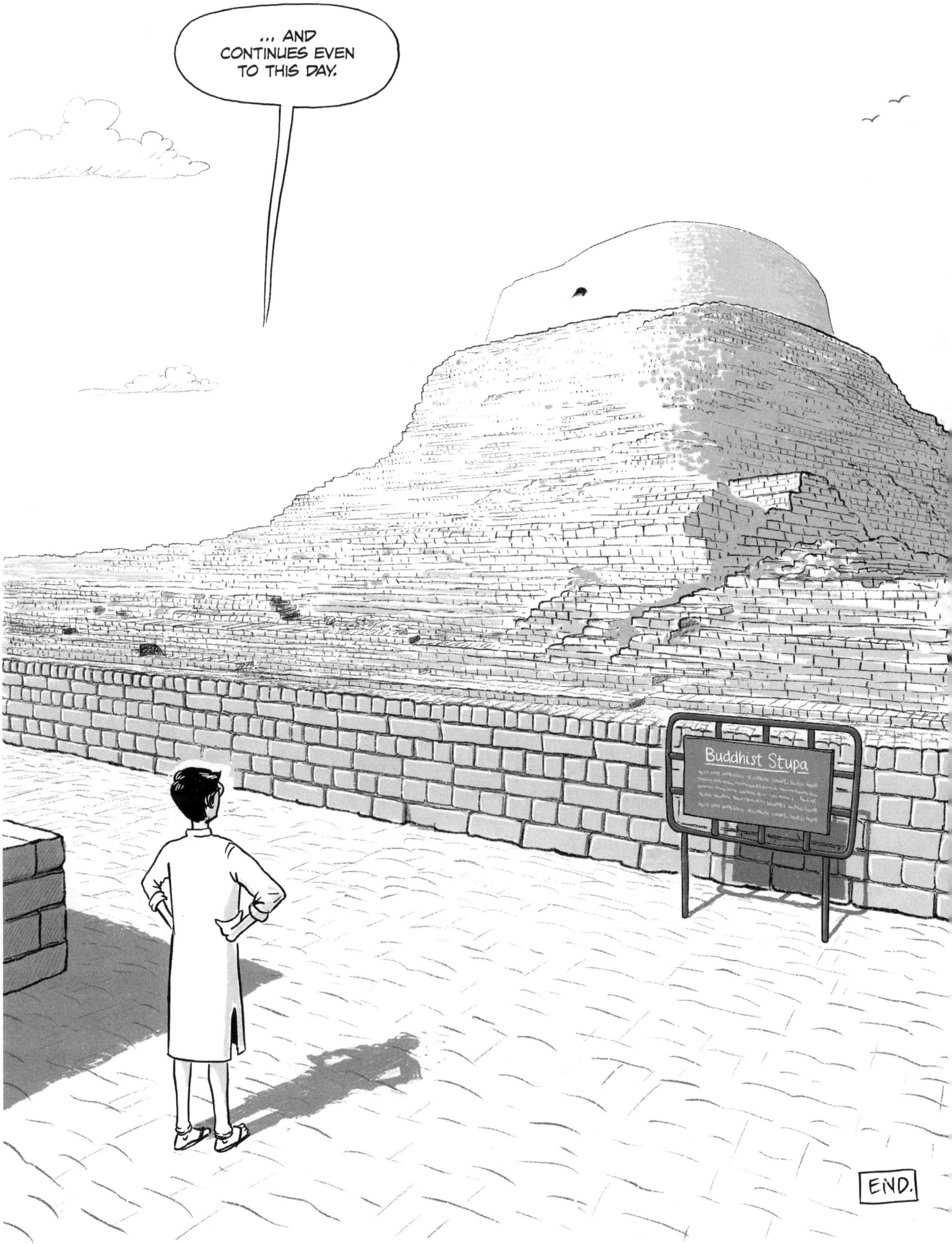
... AND CONTINUES EVEN TO THIS DAY.
Buddhist Stupa
END.

NOTES

Chapter 1: Mohenjo Daro 2600 BCE

1. Recreation of the Great Bath based on G.L. Possehl, *The Indus Civilization*, p. 189.
2. J. McIntosh, *Ancient Indus Valley*, p. 213.
3. *Oxford English Dictionary*, s.v. 'Civilization'.

Chapter 2: Why the Harappans Never Built Pyramids

1. Y.N. Harari, *Sapiens*, p. 115
2. J.M. Kenoyer, 'Early City-States in South Asia', pp. 55–58.
3. M. Wheeler, *The Indus Civilization*, p. 101.
4. Reconstruction of Dholavira based on 'The Indus Valley Civilization: Masters of the River', NHK Japan.
5. J.M. Kenoyer, 'Early City-States in South Asia', p. 62.
6. J. Marshall, *Mohenjo-Daro and the Indus Civilization*, Vol. 3, p. vi.
7. J.M. Kenoyer, 'Early City-States in South Asia', pp. 55–56.
8. G.L. Possehl, *The Indus Civilization*, p. 57.
9. As narrated by M. Wheeler in 'Buried Treasure', BBC, 5m 11s; S. Piggott quoted by J. McIntosh in *Ancient Indus Valley*, p. 34.

Chapter 3: Journey of a Bead

1. J. McIntosh, *Ancient Indus Valley*, p. 148 and p. 303.
2. J.M. Kenoyer, 'Early City-States in South Asia', p. 69.
3. As quoted by G.L. Possehl in *The Indus Civilization*, p. 89.
4. T. Vosmer, 'Early Bronze Age Navigation and Trade Routes', p. 314–16
5. M. Vidale, 'Growing in a Foreign World', p. 261.

Chapter 4: Writing Your Way to Civilization

1. D.T. Potts, *Mesopotamian Civilization*, p. 197.
2. Ibid., p. 191.
3. C. Woods, *Visible Language*, p. 77.
4. J. Aruz and R. Wallenfels, *Art of the First Cities*, p. 428.
5. This discussion is inspired by A. Parpola, 'Study of the Indus Script', p. 51.
6. J. McIntosh, *Ancient Indus Valley*, p. 371.
7. M. Witzel, 'Indocentrism', p. 341.
8. As quoted by B.B. Lal, 'Aryan Invasion of India', p. 50.
9. *Rig-Veda* verses 2.11.4.
10. As quoted by B.B. Lal, 'Aryan Invasion of India', p. 51.
11. J. Keay, *India*, p. 25.
12. M. Witzel, 'Indocentrism', p. 342.

Chapter 5: The End of the Beginning

1. J. McIntosh, *Ancient Indus Valley*, p. 396.
2. Ibid., p. 391.
3. J.M. Kenoyer, *Ancient Cities of the Indus Valley Civilization*, p. 174.
4. *Rig-Veda* verses 7.96.1, 7.96.6, 6.61.14 and 7.96.2. 6.61.8
5. Ibid., 10.75.6–7

BIBLIOGRAPHY

1. PUBLISHED BOOKS

Allen, James, et al., *Egyptian Art in the Age of the Pyramids*. New York: Metropolitan Museum of Art, 1999.

Aruz, Joan, and Ronald Wallenfels, eds. *Art of the First Cities: The Third Millennium B.C. from the Mediterranean to the Indus*. New York: Metropolitan Museum of Art, 2003.

Breasted, James Henry. *Ancient Times: A History of the Early World*. Boston: Ginn, 1916.

Danino, Michel. *The Lost River: On the Trail of the Saraswati*. New Delhi: Penguin Books India, 2010.

Frenez, Dennys. 'The Lothal Revisitation Project: A Fine Thread Connecting Ancient India to Contemporary Ravenna (via Oman)'. In *'My Life is Like the Summer Rose' Maurizio Tosi e l'Archeologia come modo di vivere: Papers in Honour of Maurizio Tosi for his 70th Birthday*, edited by C.C. Lamberg-Karlovsky and B. Genito. Oxford: British Archaeological Reports Publishing (BAR), 2014.

Harari, Yuval Noah. *Sapiens: A Brief History of Humankind*. London: Vintage Books, 2015.

Keay, John. *India a History: From the Earliest Civilisations to the Boom of the Twenty-First Century*. New Delhi: HarperCollins Publishers India, 2011.

Kenoyer, Jonathan Mark. 'Early City-States in South Asia: Comparing the Harappan Phase and Early Historic Period'. In *The Archaeology of City-States: Cross Cultural Approaches*, edited by D.L. Nichols and T.H. Charton. Washington: Smithsonian Institution Press, 1997.

——. *Ancient Cities of the Indus Valley Civilization*. Karachi: Oxford University Press, 1998.

Kenoyer, Jonathan Mark, and Richard H. Meadow. 'Inscribed Objects from Harappa Excavations 1986–2007'. In *Corpus of Indus Seals and Inscriptions, Memoirs of the Archaeological Survey of India No. 96., Vol. 3: New Material, Untraced Objects, and Collections Outside India and Pakistan*, edited by Asko Parpola, B.M.P Ande and Petteri Koskikallio. Helsinki: Suomalainen Tiedeakatemia, 2010.

Lahiri, Nayanjyot. *Finding Forgotten Cities: How the Indus Civilisation was Discovered*. New Delhi: Hachette India, 2011.

Lal, B.B. 'Aryan Invasion of India: Perpetuation of a Myth'. In *The Indo-Aryan Controversy: Evidence and Inference in Indian History*, edited by Edwin F. Bryant and Laurie L. Patton. London: Routledge, 2005.

Bibliography

Law, Randall. 'Moving Mountains: The Trade and Transport of Rocks and Minerals within the Greater Indus Valley Region'. In *Space and Spatial Analysis in Archaeology*, edited by Elizabeth C. Robertson, Jeffrey D. Seibert, Deepika C. Fernandez and Marc U. Zender. Calgary: University of Calgary Press, 2006.

Marshall, John. *Mohenjo-Daro and the Indus Civilization: Being an Official Account of Archaeological Excavations at Mohenjo-Daro Carried Out by the Government of India Between the Years 1922 and 1927*, vols. 1-3. New Delhi: Asian Educational Services, 1931.

Mcintosh, Jane R. *The Ancient Indus Valley: New Perspectives*. Santa Barbara, CA: ABC-CLIO, 2007.

Possehl, Gregory L. 'Lothal: A Gateway Settlement of the Harappan Civilization'. In *Ancient Cities of the Indus*, edited by Gregory L. Possehl. New Delhi: Vikas Publishing, 1979.

——. *The Indus Civilization: A Contemporary Perspective*. Walnut Creek, CA: AltaMira Press, 2002.

Potts, Daniel T. *Mesopotamian Civilization: The Material Foundations*. Ithaca: Cornell University Press, 1997.

Rao, S.R. 'Excavation at Rangpur and Other Explorations', *Ancient India*, nos. 18 and 19. New Delhi: Archaeological Survey of India, 1963.

——. *Lothal Vol. II: A Harappan Port Town (1955-62)*. New Delhi: Archaeological Survey of India, 1979.

Roaf, Michael. 'Palaces and Temples in Ancient Mesopotamia'. In *Civilizations of the Ancient Near East*, vol. 1. New York: Charles Scribner's Sons, 1995.

Vosmer, T. 'Early Bronze Age Navigation and Trade Routes', In *In the Shadow of the Ancestors: The Prehistoric Foundations of the Early Arabian Civilization in Oman*, 2nd ed., edited by S. Cleuziou and M. Tosi. Muscat: Ministry of Heritage and Culture of the Sultanate of Oman, 2018.

Wheeler, Mortimer. *The Indus Civilization: Supplementary Volume to the Cambridge History of India*, 3rd ed. London: Cambridge University Press, 1968.

Witzel, Michael. 'The Rgvedic Religious System and its Central Asian and Hindukush Antecedents'. In *The Vedas: Text, Language and Ritual*, edited by Arlo Griffiths and Jan E.M. Houben. Groningen, Netherlands: Egbert Forsten Publishing, 2004.

——. 'Indocentrism: Autochthonous Visions of Ancient India'. In *The Indo-Aryan Controversy: Evidence and Inference in Indian History*, edited by Edwin F. Bryant and Laurie L. Patton. London: Routledge, 2005.

Woods, Christopher, ed., with Emily Teeter and Geoff Emberling. *Visible Language: Inventions of Writing in the Ancient Middle East and Beyond* (Oriental Institute Museum Publications no. 32). Chicago: The Oriental Institute, 2015.

Woolley, Leonard. *Ur Excavations, Vol. 5: The Ziggurat and its Surroundings* (Publication of the Joint Expedition of the British Museum and the University Museum, University of Pennsylvania). Oxford: Oxford UP, 1939.

2. JOURNAL ARTICLES

Belcher, W.R. 'Marine Exploitation in the Third Millennium BC: The Eastern Coast of Pakistan'. *Paléorient* 31.1 (2005): 79–85.

Danino, Michel. 'New Insights into Harappan Town-Planning, Proportions and Units, with Special Reference to Dholavira'. *Man and Environment* 33.1 (2008): 66–79.

Dhyansky, Yan Y. 'The Indus Valley Origin of a Yoga Practice'. *Artibus Asiae* 48.1–2 (1987): 89–108.

Frenez, Dennys, et al. 'Bronze Age Salūt (STI) and the Indus Civilization: Recent Discoveries and New Insights on Regional Interaction'. *Proceedings of the Seminar for Arabian Studies* 46 (2016): 107–124.

Kenoyer, Jonathan Mark. 'Ornament Styles of the Indus Valley Tradition: Evidence from Recent Excavations at Harappa, Pakistan'. *Paléorient* 17.2 (1991): 79–98.

———. 'Changing Perspectives of the Indus Civilization: New Discoveries and Challenges'. *Purātattva* 41 (2011): 1–18.

Leshnik, Lawrence S., and K.H. Junghans. 'The Harappan "Port" at Lothal: Another View'. *American Anthropologist* 70.5 (1968): 911–922.

Mackay, Dorothy. 'Finds at Chanhu-daro'. *Asia: American Asiatic Association* July (1937): 500–504, accessed 18 April 2022, https://www.harappa.com/content/finds-chanhu-daro.

Meadow, Richard H., and Jonathan Mark Kenoyer. 'The Indus Valley Mystery: One of the World's First Civilizations is Still a Puzzle'. *Discovering Archaeology* April (2000): 38–43.

Parpola, Asko. 'Study of the Indus Script'. Paper presented at the 50th International Conference of Eastern Studies, Tokyo, Japan, 19 May 2005.

Possehl, Gregory L. 'The Harappan Civilization in Gujarat: The Sorath and Sindhi Harappans'. *The Eastern Anthropologist* 45.1–2 (1992): 117–154.

———. 'Shu-ilishu's Cylinder Seal'. *Expedition Magazine* Penn Museum 48.1 (2006): 42–43.

Rissman, Paul. 'Public Displays and Private Values: A Guide to Buried Wealth in Harappan Archaeology'. *World Archaeology* 20.2 (1988): 209–228.

Shaffer, J.G. and B.K. Thapar. 'Pre-Indus and Early Indus Cultures of Pakistan and India'. *UNESCO History of Civilizations of Central Asia* 1 (2003): 37—270, accessed 18 April 2022, https://en.unesco.org/silkroad/knowledge-bank/pre-indus-and-early indus-cultures-pakistan-and-india.

Vidale, Massimo. 'Growing in a Foreign World: For a History of the "Meluhha Villages" in Mesopotamia in the 3rd Millennium BC'. *Melammu Symposia* 4, proceedings of the fourth Annual Symposium of the Assyrian and Babylonian Intellectual Heritage Project, Ravenna, Italy, 13–17 October 2001: 261–80.

———. 'Aspects of Palace Life in Mohenjodaro'. *South Asian Studies* 26.1 March (2010): 59–76.

3. OTHER SOURCES

'Bead Technologies at Harappa 3300–1900 BC: A Comparative Summary'. By Jonathan Mark Kenoyer, *Harappa.com*, https://www.harappa.com/content/bead-technologies-harappa-3300-1900-bc-comparative-study.

'Buried Treasure: Mohenjodaro'. YouTube video, from a documentary produced by Paul Johnstone, televised by BBC on 23 December 1958, https://youtu.be/8iI1xbBIi_Y.

Griffith, Ralph T.H., trans. *The Rig Veda* (1896). Santa Cruz, CA: Evinity Publishing Inc, 2009, https://www.sacred-texts.com/hin/rigveda/index.htm.

'Harappa: The Ancient Indus Civilization'. *Harappa.com*, https://www.harappa.com.

'The Indus Valley Civilization: The Masters of the River'. YouTube video, from a documentary produced by NHK (Japan) and Canadian TV, posted by 'The Mysterious World' on 28 Feb 2015, https://youtu.be/p5bqAKixgYA.

Oxford English Dictionary, s.v. 'Civilization', accessed 23 January 2021, https://www.lexico.com/definition/civilization.

ACKNOWLEDGEMENTS

I have several people to thank without whom this book would not have been possible:

Dr Jonathan Mark Kenoyer, who, even though he came on board midway through the project, was instrumental in giving the book its final shape;

Ashwitha Jayakumar, for her encouragement and support of my work from day one;

My parents, Mohinder and Anita Gulati, for their faith in me and their help at every step;

Pragya Bhagat, for her open, honest, speak-it-like-it-is feedback, and for seeing me through the creation of most of this book;

Kush Dhebar, for his invaluable help in tracking down obscure journal articles and excavation reports, and for his infectious love for the topic;

Prof. Sunil Handa, who gave me the belief to get started on this journey; and

All the people I came in touch with through Penguin—my editor Yasmin Rahman, publisher Sohini Mitra, designer Samar Bansal, copy editor Prerna Chatterjee and Smit Zaveri of Pratham Books.

I would also like to thank Sarnath Banerjee, Devika Cariapa, Angshuman Chakraborty, Tony Joseph, Anirudh Kanisetti, Manu S. Pillai, V.N. Prabhakar, Sanjeev Sanyal, Orijit Sen and Romila Thapar for taking the time to review the manuscript and share their thoughts.